Understandin
Security

Mike Bourne

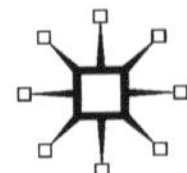

First published 2014 by
PALGRAVE MACMILLAN

Palgrave Macmillan in the UK is an imprint of Macmillan Publishers Limited, registered in England, company number 785998, of Houndmills, Basingstoke, Hampshire RG21 6XS.

Palgrave Macmillan in the US is a division of St Martin's Press LLC, 175 Fifth Avenue, New York, NY 10010.

Palgrave Macmillan is the global academic imprint of the above companies and has companies and representatives throughout the world.

Palgrave® and Macmillan® are registered trademarks in the United States, the United Kingdom, Europe and other countries.

ISBN 978-0-230-29123-2 hardback

ISBN 978-0-230-29124-9 ISBN 978-1-137-40210-3 (eBook)
DOI 10.1007/978-1-137-40210-3

A catalogue record for this book is available from the British Library.

A catalog record for this book is available from the Library of Congress.

Typeset by Aardvark Editorial Limited, Metfield, Suffolk

For Louise

Contents

Acknowledgements

I would like to acknowledge the extensive and enduring support given by Steven Kennedy, Stephen Wenham and all at Palgrave Macmillan. From this book's inception in a conversation with Steven to the final stages, several years later, they have been unerringly supportive, frequently insightful, and continually patient and accommodating. I would also like to thank the anonymous reviewers who provided detailed and constructive comments at various stages in the writing of the book, which have been essential in making it what it is. My gratitude also goes to my friends and colleagues in the School of Politics, International Studies and Philosophy at Queen's University Belfast for their encouragement and support. Finally, my deepest thanks go to Louise, to whom this book is dedicated and without whom it would have neither materialized nor been worthwhile. For her enduring support, for putting up with all the demands the process of writing this book placed on us both, and always for her love, I can only be amazed and grateful.

Introduction

What is Security?

Security is ultimately about life and death and therefore the things that ensure our continued existence. But as social animals, our security is not the same as that of animals and plants: basic biological functioning is not all we need to live and so not all it takes to be secure. Rather, security relates to the continuation of life and the protection and production of ways of life. To present our ways of life as merely a struggle for survival, in which all forms of social, political and economic organization are oriented to the prevention of death and the prolonging of life, would be to miss most of the experiences we have of living and seeking security. Security debates represent different views of what it is about life that is to be secured, how some deaths are to be avoided and other deaths deemed necessary or inevitable, and how the pursuit of life and prevention of death establish the ways in which both are organized.

The term 'security' has meant different things in different contexts and at different times (Rothschild, 1995). In common usage, 'security' relates to survival, to the protection from threats to existence, and being relatively free from harm inflicted by others. In academic usage, it generally relates to the protection of something that is valued, which may be physical life, the organization of political life in a particular nation-state, democracy, identity, language, property, territory and so on. Thus, for Arnold Wolfers (1952: 484), security means 'some degree of protection of values previously acquired'. This separates security from power and wealth, since wealth is a measure of material possessions and power is the 'ability to control the actions of others'. In contrast, security is characterized by other measures: 'security in an objective sense measures the absence of threats to acquired values, in a subjective sense, the absence of fear that such values will be attacked' (Wolfers, 1952: 485). Precise measurements of security are therefore impossible; clearly, we can have more security or less security. Perfect, complete security is unattainable.

The word 'security' derives from the Latin *securitas,* which comes from *sine cura* – *sine* (without), *cura/curio* (troubling). Thus, 'security' originally implied a condition of being without care, trouble or anxiety. This is not purely subjective. *Cura* relates to a state of mind and responsibilities – to be free from worries, but also from responsibilities – so that security is neither wholly positive (feeling secure in oneself) or negative (negligent, reckless) (Dillon, 1996). While etymology is important for understanding how the meaning of security came to be and came to change, it does not present us with a simple origin, a true meaning of security that we can return to. This is partly because it is always entwined with politics. Indeed, security is a foundational concept of the sovereign state and underlies what we conceive of as the political and how it works. Most understandings of security have not questioned security, but sought to explore how the state provides protection (to us and to itself), particularly in relations with other states; so security is often considered in terms of 'national security'. But while the invocation of security gives an issue the air of precision, distinguishing it from other issues, it remains, without further specification, an ambiguous term (Wolfers, 1952). Simply put, there is nothing within the term 'security' that sets the limits of that specification. For Barry Buzan (1991: 7), security issues 'encompass a whole domain, rather than just a fixed point, and for this reason cannot be defined in any general sense'. This domain used to be focused on the 'threat, use and control of military force' (Walt, 1991), but has expanded to include economic, societal and environmental issues, as well as political and military concerns. It has also moved beyond an exclusive focus on states as the 'referent object' to be secured to include the security of individuals, communities, regions or even the whole globe (see Chapter 1).

Understanding security is not a matter of definition but of understanding a concept in its living usage. There is little prospect of distilling the essence of security, since security is always related to other concepts. Security is better approached conceptually by asking questions: Security for whom? Security for which values? How much security can be expected or produced? From what threats? At what cost? In what time period? (Baldwin, 1997). These questions are linked, but they are not equivalent. Disagreement on such questions about security should not be viewed negatively (as a barrier to definition) but as the practice of debate that produces the concept. Some scholars refer to security as an 'essentially contested concept' (Buzan, 1991; Smith, 2005), indicating that not only are there many definitions of security, but that the differences between them contain an ideological element, which means that empirical analysis will never be sufficient to produce agreement. Similarly, Booth (1997) argues that security is a 'derivative concept', in that one's view of what security is derives from a philosophical and political perspective, complicated by the fact that security means nothing on its own. It is a term that is always used in (sometimes implied) conjunction with a threat or risk, an object to be made secure, and often in some balance or tension with other things, such as liberty, privacy, freedom of movement and so on. Without these relationships, definitions of security, such as freedom from threat, reveal very little about security's nature, scope, practice, ethics, dilemmas, purpose or possibilities.

Since security has no inherent meaning outside its relations with other concepts, there is no one 'security' but multiple securities. Perhaps the easiest way to begin to understand this is to look at the multiple meanings a single word, such as love, freedom and security, can have, depending on their usage as a noun, verb, adjective and so on. As such, security is a condition, a value and an indicator of the importance of other values; and a process through which that condition is achieved. Further, security, as a relational concept, always involves some concept of insecurity, such as threat, enemy, vulnerability and risk, that makes it understandable.

Security as a condition

The condition of security is being without threats to existence or something valued. While some say 'security is about survival' (Buzan et al., 1998: 21), others argue that it is about 'survival plus': 'the "plus" being some freedom from life-determining threats, and therefore [having] some life choices' (Booth, 2007: 104). While survival is an absolute, one either survives or perishes, security is a relative condition. The rich person, with security guards, alarms, fences, insurance policies, food, heat, water and luxurious accommodation, and the poor person, with meagre food and no protection from the elements or the violence of others, are both surviving but do not enjoy the same security.

As a condition, security may be viewed negatively, as the absence of threats, or positively, as the presence of something valued, which involves other concepts: order and stability, which render a given way of life relatively predictable and temporarily free from many cares, but do not eliminate all threats, and peace, which may denote an absence of war and violence, or the presence of justice, human dignity and emancipation (see Chapters 3 and 9).

As Wolfers (1952) argued, the condition of security is objective (actually being secure) and subjective (feeling or perceiving oneself to be secure). Clearly, one does not imply the other, as one might feel safe when one is in danger, or be afraid when there is no reason to be. However, these dual meanings of security are closely related: subjective security is integral to objective security, since perceptions of insecurity cause states to act in ways that may enhance or reduce their actual security. This relates to the limits of certainty in international relations: there are limits to knowing with certainty whether another actor intends to attack and, for some theorists, this lies at the heart of fear as a driving force of security politics (see Chapter 5). Indeed, in many understandings, the production of security is predicated on the elimination not of threats but uncertainties and the production not of safety but certainty and control (Der Derian, 1995; Dillon, 1996). This accords with the colloquial use of the term 'security' – to be secure in oneself is to be secure in the knowledge that the world is a particular way and can be understood, analysed, broken down, and optimal solutions and strategies identified. This condition is sometimes called 'ontological security' (Giddens, 1991). So, both security and understanding security are often a quest for certainty or at least for strategies of living with uncertainty.

Security as a value

Security is also a value. For many realists, it is the primary thing that states hold dear and seek in their interactions. It is also an indicator of the amount of value given to something else: to speak of 'state security' is to value the state, while to speak of the 'security of one's identity' is to attach a strong importance to particular characteristics and practices, such as language and social norms. Security, then, is one means of claiming something as particularly important, so central, in fact, that without securing that thing, many other valued things could not occur. While security is more than mere survival, not every value is something to be secured. For example, to value my right to drink Coke rather than Pepsi as a matter of security would be ludicrous, but to value my access to safe drinking water might not.

Security is a value among others (such as wealth) and the practice and analysis of security policy establishes the importance of that value. The classic 'guns or butter' debate, for example, poses two values, security and economic wellbeing, in competition with each other. When governments spend more money on military forces than health and education, as many do, they are implicitly valuing military security over developmental and welfare issues. But this relies on an understanding of security that is deeply questionable. Is not the economic wellbeing of people facing starvation or death from preventable diseases also a security issue for them? Security does not just compete with other values in the allocation of finite resources. Actions taken to ensure security may, in effect, conflict with other values. Notably, within Western societies, there is often a debate around the balance of security and liberty. The surveillance powers a government has to gather information on criminal groups or suspected terrorists may conflict with the right to privacy, the right to fair legal process, freedom of movement and so on. Here, Wolfers' claim that security relates to the protection of previously acquired values is somewhat problematic. To imply that values are acquired first and then made secure limits the questions that are asked about security. It does not ask how values are acquired (until critical approaches began to speak of intersubjective production of norms and values) or how the process of securing them affects what is valued and how. In other words, it separates the production of values from their protection in ways that have become deeply questioned.

Security as a good/commodity and a process

Security is also viewed as a public good – something that is provided for people on a relatively equal basis. This may be understood as founded on an imagined social contract with a higher authority and power, such as the sovereign state or even some international organization, to which states and peoples give authority to provide security. Increasingly, however, security is also seen as a commodity, a private good exchanged and distributed through a market. In practice, the status of security as a public or private good is becoming ever more complex.

Security also denotes the actions taken to achieve, distribute and protect the condition of security. It is thus a type of politics and practice. For many critical theorists, security gives a sense of urgency and importance to an issue (Buzan et al., 1998; Neocleous, 2008). This may mean that security is a realm in which the rules of 'normal', democratic politics are suspended and an 'exceptional' politics of secrecy, urgency and possible violence give interactions a different character (see Chapter 3). Thus, for many realist scholars, national security denotes a valuing of political institutions and territory and characterizes international relations about national security as inherently about power competition and modes of behaviour that exclude compromise (Morgenthau, 2006). In contrast, some critical scholars explore how invocations of security produce rather than just describe particular orders of relations. Security does not merely serve to protect but to create 'a particular way of organizing forms of life' (Huysmans, 1998: 231). This is most commonly understood as distinguishing different locations of security and politics; people group together in communities to protect themselves from others, and may invest security powers in a sovereign state. This splits the world into those to be feared (outsiders) and those to be trusted (insiders). So, security creates the foundational assumption of international relations: relations among peoples within a state are of a different character to the relations among states (Walker, 1993).

Insecurity: threat, enemies, vulnerabilities and risks

While security may be a condition, a value and a process, it is always such in relation to some sense of insecurity, which may be viewed through several concepts – threats, enemies, dangers, vulnerabilities and risks.

What is a threat? How are real threats distinguished from misperceived ones? Threats require an enemy, thus insecurity relates to the anticipation and actualization of harm inflicted by another. The understanding of who an enemy is, and why they may inflict harm, is integral to understanding security. For some, this limits what counts as a security issue: some things that can harm us, like natural disasters or accidents, are important but cannot be considered through the concept of security, as they lack the calculation of other actors' intentions and capabilities and cannot be responded to by deterring or persuading other actors not to engage in deliberately harmful behaviour (see Chapter 13). However, the issue is much deeper than that. For Schmitt (1996), the separating of friends from enemies is what constitutes the political. Political communities identify themselves by distinguishing between the self and the other on the basis of some particular characteristic (history, ethnicity, religion, language and so on). This is not just about asserting a difference, but establishing a relationship of threat between them so that the self and the other become the friend and the enemy. Enemies are not just different but dangerous. This Schmittian concept can mean that security is the defining feature of politics, which rather limits what politics can be (Aradau, 2006).

Danger is subjective, not merely a recognition of objective reality of someone who wishes to harm us. During the Cold War (1946–89), Western, and particularly US, national security practice was defined in terms of a struggle against communism, a difference in ideology that was deemed threatening to Western values and thus identity (Campbell, 1998a). In the post-Cold War era, similar arguments have been made about drug traffickers and terrorists. Threats to international order and stability are often explained on the basis of claims that power is the primary motive of states, or at least that power is the route to security that motivates states. Since states have unequal power, there is often a possibility that a state might seek to change its relative power position. Even if this does not threaten war, the physical destruction of a state's political infrastructure or the capture of its territory, it threatens the state in its valued international relations. For example, there are concerns among Western commentators that the growing economic and military power of China might challenge the position of the USA as the sole remaining superpower, and that its ongoing pursuit of greater influence in the global political sphere may threaten Western interests.

Two related concepts are vulnerability and risk. Threat relates to the actions, intentions and capabilities of other actors; vulnerability relates to those of the state being secured, particularly its capability to deter or defend itself against threats (Buzan, 1991). This is the second dimension of the condition of security: the absence of threats and thus particular relations with potential enemies, and the ability to defend against threats, which if inadequate are characterized as vulnerabilities. Importantly, vulnerabilities do not require a specific enemy, merely an anticipation of a future event that one is not sufficiently prepared for. For instance, a nation may be vulnerable because of inadequate military forces to counter those of an enemy, gaps in the security systems of computer networks, or poorly integrated emergency services unable to cope with natural disasters or terrorist attacks. A group of people may be vulnerable because their government persecutes them, or because they are poor and unable to prevent or respond to natural disasters or to ensure they have sustainable access to food and water. In the latter sense, vulnerability is now increasingly linked not just to threats but to risks. While threats are measured by calculating the intentions and capabilities of specific potential enemies, risks are found in the nature of general phenomena and are measured by the probability of these phenomena multiplied by their potential for harm. For example, there is much concern about the prospect of nuclear terrorism. While the probability of this is very low, the harm it could create would be very high, therefore it is seen as an important risk. In risk, vulnerability means the damage that might occur in a catastrophic event, so it relates to 'resilience', the ability to minimize the damage of an earthquake or terrorist attack and to ensure minimal disruption of daily life, rather than merely security as protection, which prevents the event in the first place (see Chapter 5).

Understanding security: logics and limits

How do we understand security amid all these differences and relationships? One useful device is to think about the logic and limits of security behaviours, that is, what sets in motion and what stops. These are interrelated: a car is set in motion by a combination of the driver's foot, an engine, petrol and internal combustion processes; what stops or limits that movement may be brakes, reaching a destination, or a wall. Both may result from the driver's intentions and capabilities, or from things external to the driver and the car, such as laws, road conditions or fuel shortages.

'Logic' means the dynamics and patterns of action, the driving forces of security behaviour. Some logics of behaviour developed in international relations scholarship also apply in security, which posits different logics:

- *the logic of consequences:* in which actions derive from assumed cost–benefit calculations made by states on the basis of anticipated consequences and prior preferences
- *the logic of appropriateness:* in which action derives from norms, values and identities
- *the logic of arguing:* where action comes from and within communication about norms and values
- *the logic of practicality:* more recently asserted, where the forms and habits of security practices establish the dynamics of security (March and Olsen, 1998; Risse, 2000; Pouliot, 2008).

These are, however, rather broad. More specifically, some theories articulate differing logics of power, such as realism, that views the pursuit of power as establishing the direction and form of action and the outcomes of interactions. This may follow a further logic of competition that is counterpoised with a logic of cooperation. Both may arise from anticipated consequences but posit different patterns (as seen in the diversity of rationalist thought in Chapter 2). If, for instance, the primary logic of security is one of competition for power in a world full of power-hungry, selfish and violent actors, the condition of security is scarce. If, however, the logics of political life are set by evolving patterns of rule and order between states and within them, then cooperative logics may predominate in how and how much security is produced. In more fine-grained accounts, we find other forces – fear, violence, uncertainty, hatred, greed, ambiguity, a desire for control and so on.

'Limits' means what constrains or stops. What limits the amount of security that can be achieved, or for whom it can be realized? What restricts the degree to which states are able to cooperate with each other? As Walker claims (1995: 307), theories of international relations are a 'primary expression of the limits of modern politics'. The limits of security may relate to limits on violence imposed by laws, limits on the scope of political communities imposed by geography, anarchy or human nature and so on. A focus on limits alone is problematic: we do not understand something merely by its boundaries but by its content. Thus, we must speak of logics and limits together. Booth and Wheeler (2008) posit 'fatalist', 'mitigator' and 'transcender' logics, which relate to whether the conditions of anarchy and uncertainty that produce insecurity in the global order can merely be lived within (fatalist), whether their effects can be mitigated, and if real progress can be made that transcends them.

About this book

Security is not just a condition of freedom from objective threat or subjective fear, it is a mode of thinking and acting in the world. As such, much of what is discussed in the book goes beyond simple logics and limits, or even their complex relations. Given that security is multifaceted, can we really speak of one single logic and set of limits to security? No. But how this is the case will require the rest of this book to explore. This book seeks to understand security by exploring different approaches to security and how they play out in the multifarious agendas and practices that constitute contemporary security. It brings diverse theories, concepts and claims into conversation with each other and shows how security has been understood when those understandings encounter complex political issues and relationships.

Chapters 1–3 focus on the different theoretical perspectives in the study of security. Chapter 1 discusses the building blocks of understanding security. It looks at the debates on the scope of the field of security studies, and outlines the various components that are put together in particular understandings of security. Chapter 2 examines 'traditional' or 'rationalist' theories that posit various logics of consequences. Chapter 3 explores various critical approaches, including forms of constructivism, critical theory, feminism, poststructuralism and peace studies, and their concepts, such as securitization and emancipation, which offer a wider range of logics and limits to security.

Since a distinction between security in domestic affairs and international relations is foundational to the study of security, Chapter 4 examines the state, state formation and internal security practices, such as policing and surveillance. Chapter 5 explores the conditions of uncertainty and how this establishes different logics and limits to the strategies of action in security, internationally and domestically.

The book then moves into more in-depth coverage of states and their security practices. Chapter 6 looks at how states come together in different groupings to seek security, from alliances to regimes and security communities. It also explores how geographical factors establish different logics and limits of security relationships by looking at hopes for global collective security and regional security practices. Chapter 7 addresses the logics and limits of killing, particularly in war, its causes and its contemporary transformations and limitations. Chapter 8 discusses the logics and limits of cooperation on issues of weapons and military technology by an examination of the arms trade, proliferation, arms control and disarmament.

The remaining chapters are concerned with security issues and practices that, to some degree, move beyond the state as the central object to be made secure and the main actor that provides security. They address common themes of whether and how the significance of private/non-state actors and the transnational threaten and disrupt the international and national frames of reference for security and what implications this has for security politics, policy, practice and analysis. Chapter 9 focuses on human security as an attempt to define and practise security without centring on the state. Chapter 10 looks at how human security and state security have become integrated into discussions of the phenomenon of 'failed states' and the extent to which the range of practices of conflict intervention seek to reassert security as being for states, by states, and located within an interstate framework. Chapter 11 engages with the phenomena of terrorism and counterterrorism that pervade contemporary security logics. Chapter 12 addresses other transnational security issues that relate to particular global flows, including migration and transnational crime, and the strengthening of international policing, border controls and surveillance. Chapter 13 considers understandings of security practices related to the environment, such as conflict over resources, climate change, energy security, and the security of the basic needs for food and water. Chapter 14 concludes the book with some reflections on how understandings of security combine all these issues, and how these might develop.

Chapter 1

Understanding and Theorizing Security

Understanding the logics and limits of security requires that we first understand the logics and limits of theorizing about security. For issues as complex and multifaceted as security, innumerable 'facts' arise from the real world – for example the end of the Cold War (1989), the al-Qaeda attacks of 11 September 2001, or the 2003 US-led invasion of Iraq – which do not speak unambiguously to us but require interpretation. Different understandings of security are not simply opposing evaluations of real-world security problems, leaving the student of security with the task of judging which theory best fits the facts of security. Rather, they contain widely varying underlying assumptions about the scope of security, the purpose and practice of developing theories, and the building blocks of those theories – deeper questions of what the social and political world is made of (ontology), and how we know, understand and produce knowledge (epistemology). These assumptions are formative of the way the academic field of 'security studies' has produced different understandings of security. This field initially arose as a subset of the wider discipline of international relations (IR), itself part of the study of politics. It has therefore been concerned with the international politics of security. However, it has increasingly focused on wider sets of relations, including domestic and transnational relations, and has frequently engaged with or drawn on concepts from other disciplines, most notably economics, sociology, history, geography and psychology. Security studies is now a hybrid field, whose foundational assumptions, and the challenges to them, often derive from wider theoretical and practical endeavours. It has also undergone periods of great theoretical innovation, and periods of a narrowing of debate onto empirical questions. As it has done so, the scope of its concern has changed (Walt, 1991; Booth, 1994; Baldwin, 1997; Prins, 1998; Buzan and Hansen, 2009).

The scope of security (studies)?

As understandings of security have developed since the Second World War (1939–45), the scope and distinctiveness of the field of security studies has evolved, intimately linked to the changing global landscape of security threats. In the first postwar decade, security theorizing was vibrant and diverse, but indistinct from IR (Baldwin, 1997). From the mid-1950s to the mid-1960s, a more distinct field of 'strategic studies' emerged and underwent a 'golden age' as the growing threat of nuclear confrontation produced a focus on matters of military force, such as how nuclear weapons could be made useful and how nuclear stability could be achieved through deterrence. This early development of strategic thought occurred particularly in government-linked think tanks (Walt, 1991). From the late 1960s, the US–Soviet detente made the prospect of a superpower war seem more distant and the field declined in relative importance. This enabled more theoretical innovation through the introduction of psychological approaches and organizational theory, which drew attention to subjective aspects of security, misperception and decision making in crises (Nye and Lynn-Jones, 1988). By the late 1970s, a resurgence of scholarly concern with matters of war brought with it an expansion of the field of strategic studies (Walt, 1991; Baldwin, 1997). Here, there was some broadening of issues of concern as conventional military conflicts rose in importance as well as matters nuclear. It also became a more mature academic discipline rather than being concentrated in think tanks (Walt, 1991; Miller, 2010). As it matured, its name started to change from strategic studies to 'security studies'. While some view this as a nominal change, in which the focus and concepts of the field remain rooted in 'strategy', others view security studies as a wider set of concerns that incorporates but goes far beyond matters of war and strategy. The post-Cold War development of security studies can be characterized as two interrelated processes of broadening and deepening: first, the breadth of issues covered and the deepening of referent objects to be made secure; and second, a similar expansion of the theoretical engagements and foundations of the field.

Broadening and deepening: issues and objects

For much of the second half of the twentieth century, the study and practice of security were defined in terms of the 'national security' of states, and related to military threats from other states and the practice of planning, deploying, threatening, controlling and using military force. Indeed, defending this focus, Stephen Walt (1991: 212) claimed that:

> Security studies assumes that conflict between states is always a possibility and that the use of military force has far-reaching effects on states and societies ... Accordingly, security studies may be defined as the study of the threat, use, and control of military force ... It explores the conditions that make the use of force more likely, the ways that the use of force affects individuals, states, and societies, and the specific policies that states adopt in order to prepare for, prevent, or engage in war.

Here, limiting the scope of security studies to issues of military force between states is justified by the claim that the field has its own assumptions about the possibilities and consequences of war. Yet these are not neutral assumptions, they are a restatement of the basic tenets of realist theory that determines the parameters of security for everyone (see Chapter 3). Amid the decline and end of the Cold War, security practitioners expanded the scope of security agendas and scholars debated the parameters of what counts as a security issue.

In his well-known discussion of national security, Wolfers (1952: 484) claimed that the term 'covers a range of goals so wide that highly divergent policies can be interpreted as policies of security'. This has broadened further as economic, social, environmental and wider political issues have been added to the list of security issues. Early arguments for broadening the scope of security beyond military issues came from within realist thought, although most realists do not welcome such moves. Herz (1981) argued that realism should endorse a wider security politics that tackled issues such as the depletion of energy resources, food scarcity and environmental harm. Ullman (1983: 129) claimed that 'defining national security merely (or even primarily) in military terms conveys a profoundly false image of reality' and that doing so 'causes states to concentrate on military threats and to ignore other and perhaps even more harmful dangers. Thus it reduces their total security.' The most common way of broadening security was provided by Buzan (1991), who attempted to systematize the types of issues that may now be considered part of security. Buzan (1991: 19–20) outlined five 'sectors' of security:

- *Military security:* remains conceived in fairly traditional terms as the 'interplay of the armed offensive and defensive capabilities of states and states' perceptions of each other's intentions'.
- *Political security:* relates largely to stability in the way states are organized and governed and the ideologies from which they draw legitimacy.
- *Economic security:* sustaining populations' levels of welfare and the power of the state in relation to their access to resources, finance and foreign markets.
- *Societal security:* the sustainability (and some evolution) of national identity and customs, and the culture, language and religious identity of social groups.
- *Environmental security:* reflecting the rising global interest in environmental issues from the 1980s onwards, this relates to the maintenance of the biosphere, locally and globally, as it is 'the essential support system on which all other human enterprise depends'.

Many of these issues had previously been part of security only inasmuch as they affected military power. Now, issues such as poverty, migration, terrorism and some aspects of environmental security are prominent security concerns in their own right (see Chapters 9, 11, 12 and 13).

The deepening of security relates to changes in the 'referent object' of security – that which is to be made secure. The primary, and largely exclusive, referent object of approaches to security has been the state: 'security' has meant 'national security'. For realists like Hans Morgenthau (2006: 561), 'national security must be defined as integrity of the national territory and of its institutions'. This integrity is threatened particularly in times of war and the use of military force between states, or the potential for such use to occur, has made up much of the business of security policy and security studies. However, the position of the state as the sole referent object of security has been challenged. As noted in the Introduction, attaching primacy to the security of some 'referent object' is an ethical statement of what should be valued and protected. Focusing on the state has meant that it has been assumed that the survival and wellbeing of human beings within a community are assured by the state, such that to secure the state is to secure people. Yet many states engage in widespread human rights abuses, or even genocide against their own populations. So, if it is not possible to assume that the security of citizens can be taken for granted within a state, perhaps the study and practice of security should emphasize 'human security' rather than state security (see Chapter 9). However, individuals are not made secure on an individual basis but as part of social groups. Thus, one might deepen security beyond the state but prefer to speak of 'societal' security (Buzan et al., 1998). Also, much security practice is above the level of the state. Increasingly, for instance, security practices are tied to regional groupings of states, and practised through regional organizations as well as states (see Chapter 6). Further, for some, the key to human security and state security lies not just at those levels, but in the nature of the global system. Thus, it may be desirable to theorize not just national security or even international security but to think about 'world security' (Booth, 2007).

The broadening and deepening of security is not always an ethically, politically or analytically desirable move. Critics of broadening reverse Ullman's critique and argue that expanding security distracts attention from the still urgent problems of military force. Some claim that this broader range of issues could cause security academics and practitioners to lose the hard-won coherence of the field (Walt, 1991; Morgan, 1992). However, broadening security has not necessarily entailed significant adjustment in what constitutes security. For Buzan, 'security' in each sector still relates to protection, to ensuring the existence and sustainability of something valued, or of something foundational to other values, be that forms of political life, social life, or economic welfare. While some welcomed the broadening of security as enabling thinking and doing security differently (Kolodziej, 1999), others argue that attaching the word 'security' to an issue often simply extends the militarized and competitive logics of military security to other fields. If this occurs, it is potentially problematic, such as when it is applied to migration or poverty reduction (see Chapters 9 and 12). Similarly, if all that changes is the referent object, then we risk militarizing human rights or climate change in ways that are not conducive to tackling these problems appropriately (see Chapters 9 and 13).

Broadening and deepening: theoretical underpinnings

The broadening of security issues and the deepening of referent objects can be accommodated within some extension of the basic theoretical paradigms of security developed during the Cold War. However, approaches to security have diversified and undergone their own broadening and deepening. Security studies today is characterized by many more different theories and concepts than it used to be. Some of this broadening has occurred with the developments of new forms of traditional theories like realism and liberalism, and took place throughout the Cold War (see Chapter 3). Other 'critical' approaches, encompassing constructivism, critical theory, feminism, poststructuralism and others, have developed more recently and differ fundamentally from traditional theories (see Chapter 3). This broadening is related to another form of deepening: the deepening of engagement with the political and social theory that underlies security theory. Indeed, for Kenneth Booth (2007: 155), the deepening of security relates primarily to this theoretical 'drilling down' into the origins of understanding security in political thought. This deepening of engagement has been seen in how security itself has become a contested concept (Buzan, 1991; Rothschild, 1995; Baldwin, 1997; Huysmans, 1998). This exposing of the political theoretical foundations of understanding security poses understanding in much more creative and open terms. Understandings of security are not just axiomatic statements that seek to simplify the complex empirical picture, but a set of beliefs and assumptions that shape how and why we seek to understand security and what understandings can result. Much like the broadening of issues and deepening of referent objects, the broadening and deepening of theorization is sometimes criticized for producing overly philosophical debates disconnected from the real world.

Approaches to security differ on what the purpose of theorizing is. For some, theory is a tool; like a hammer or a car, it is the means to a greater end of 'explanation'. For others, theories, the ideas we have about the world, are part of that world: they are 'constitutive', in the sense that they don't just describe the world but make it (Zalewski, 1996). This leads us to three possibilities: pure explanation, pure constitution, and a combination of the two.

Explanatory approaches see theory as a tool that allows us to grasp why events, such as wars, occur and how they can be avoided, mitigated, or won, and to deduce what the drivers and limits of security are. They treat the world of security as part of nature and attempt to explain what happens through discovering laws (like the law of gravity) – invariable truths – and causal relations (X action leads to Y result) in order to make predictions and thereby add to the sum of our knowledge of how the world works (Hollis and Smith,

1990). In explanatory views, theorists merely respond to the real world, to events like the end of the Cold War or the rise of transnational terrorism, and seek to find useful explanations. This is sometimes called a separation of the 'subject' (the theorist) and the 'object' (the nature of security policy and so on). This separation is defended by many realists and liberals as an extension of the modern Enlightenment project of gaining mastery over the world through rationalism (Zalewski, 1996). Claiming to produce value-free scientific knowledge of how security works, such security theorists are 'children of the Enlightenment', who 'seek knowledge in order to improve the quality of human action' (Haftendorn, 1991: 3). As Walt (1991: 212) claimed, security studies have tended to 'address phenomena that can be controlled by national leaders' and 'concentrate on manipulable variables, on relationships that can be altered by deliberate acts of policy'. Thus, explanatory approaches also tend to view the purpose of theory as producing knowledge that is useful for the strategic actions of states that seek to manipulate their environment to make themselves secure. In practice, this has also given security studies a short-term focus and an often unreflective tendency to make recommendations on what particular decision should be taken and how it should be done (Nye and Lynn-Jones, 1988).

In contrast, those who see theory as a tool and as constitutive see the purpose of theorizing as one of critique. Some critical approaches to security see the world of the theorist and the 'real world' of security politics as deeply entwined. Theory is still a tool, but not a neutral one, it is also constitutive of the real world. Seeing theory as constitutive means that our ideas about the real world are part of the real world, they shape what happens in it. For example, realist theory assumes that war is an inevitable part of international politics. Thinking this means accepting that war is always a possibility and the task of theorizing is to explain why and when it occurs, and how it can be won or avoided, but not eradicated. For some critical theorists, for example, the character of the world is not naturally given, but has been produced through particular historical processes that could have been different. If theorizing is constitutive not just explanatory, the point of theorizing may be not only to explain the existing rules of the game of security and to do better within them, but also to see how these rules emerged and how they may be changed in better directions (see Chapter 3). Here, theorizing does not necessarily portray itself as seeking to give advice only to state leaders but also to human rights campaigners, local groups, environmental groups and so on (Eriksson, 1999; Booth, 2007). Further, since theories are constitutive, theorizing is not merely the means through which advice for future action is produced, it is a political action itself.

A final type of theorizing goes beyond theory as a tool, a noun, and takes the constitutive nature of theory further. Theory, for poststructuralists, some feminists and others, is theorizing, a verb, the practice of giving meaning to the world and ourselves (see Chapter 3). This is something we all do, academics and policy makers alike, and is not confined to grand ideas about theorizing as a means of discerning the single truth of nature but to all sorts of daily practices; that is, the intersubjective ways we give meaning to the world are what constitute the practices of security and its omissions and silences. The real world is not separate from the world of the theorist, but constituted by theorists (of all types). Such constitutive approaches often conflict with instrumental notions of producing predictive knowledge for policy makers since they do not seek to identify manipulable variables. For explanatory theorists, like Walt (1991: 223), this makes them a 'self-indulgent discourse that is divorced from the real world'.

Are we to view this theoretical deepening and broadening as potentially liberating, giving us a wider range of tools to look at the world, which enable us to grasp different bits of the truth of security? Or should we despair at the loss of unity in focus that arises, which draws our attention to abstract metatheoretical questions rather than the security issues that affect people's daily lives and the survival of our way of life? Certainly, it would be a mistake to take a fully relativist stance that all theories are complementary. For instance, realist Colin Gray (1999: 165) claimed that 'poor – which is to say impractical – theories are at best an irrelevance, and at worst can help get people killed'. Yet how do we know which is the better theory? One might claim, as many have done, that the best theory is that which provides the most compelling explanation for security practices, that which fits the greatest amount of evidence. This may seem obvious, but actually it reflects different (explanatory) understandings of the purposes of theory. Importantly, however, the deepening of theory is not just a broadening of interpretations of what theorizing is, but a stronger engagement with the building blocks of theory – metatheoretical perspectives on ontology and epistemology.

The building blocks of understanding security

Understandings of security, and the role of theorizing, are built on assumptions about what the world is made of, how it works and how we understand it. In other words, they combine some basic building blocks that relate to ontology (what the world is made of and how it is organized) and epistemology (how we know, how understanding develops). These issues have also been important in shaping debates in IR (Lapid, 1989; Smith, 1996; Keohane, 1998). Indeed, much of the debate between different understandings of security reflects deeper divisions on these questions rather than just differing interpretations of evidence.

Ontology

Ontology, like metaphysics of which it is part, is a theory of what exists, what is real. The main ontological division is between those who assume that there is a 'real' world outside our ideas about it (ontological realism), and those who see the real world as constituted by our ideas about it (ontological idealism). In understandings of security, *ontological realism* is sometimes associated with naturalism, in which the character of security relations is given in nature, such as in human nature or the nature of the anarchic international system. Here, the real world is characterized by regularities that imply causal laws that need to be uncovered and understood. In contrast, *ontological idealism* draws attention to the historical processes or social interactions that create the world of security relations in a particular way. From these assumptions, understandings of security derive their specific ontologies of what the nature, units and content of security relations are. For instance:

- the *realist* view of the world as an anarchic system composed of states as units and their relations consisting largely of power competition
- a *liberal* view of a world comprising states, international institutions and non-state actors comprising competitive and cooperative relationships
- a *constructivist* or *poststructuralist* world of norms, identities and meanings, of discourses formed intersubjectively among states and powerful actors
- a *critical theorist* world of historical processes constructing the present, of competition, cooperation and ethics among social groups including states.

These more specific differences in the ontological building blocks of understandings of security point to a more complex array of distinctions. In security studies, as in the social sciences broadly, ontological questions are often understood through parsing up the world into different dualisms: subject-object, fact-value, material-ideational, structure-agency, system-unit, domestic-foreign. The first three are basic distinctions that are foundational to metatheoretical claims and debates, while the latter three are more derivative assumptions and distinctions that have prompted more explicit debate within approaches to security. For each distinction, four broad arguments are made: one is more important than (and determines) the other, or vice versa; third, some form of mutually constitutive relationship often conceived as a dialectic; and fourth, a denial of the distinction itself.

Basic distinctions

Basic distinctions of subject and object and fact and value relate to the nature of theorizing. The existence and nature of the distinctions between subject (person, theorist) and object (the object of study, security politics) are debated. Explanatory approaches rely on a clear separation of subject and object that interpretive and normative approaches deny. This is further reflected in the distinction between fact and value. Values are seen as belonging to the realm of the subject. If there is a clear subject–object distinction, then values are excluded from the realm of the object. Values are personal to the theorist and have no place in the study of the object: to do so would be to introduce bias and confuse one's own values with descriptions of the facts about the real world. If, however, values are seen as part of the object of study, we may have a constructivist view of the world made of two types of facts: 'brute' or 'material' facts that derive from the nature of the object itself, and 'social facts' that become facts through agreement rather than residing inherently in the nature of the thing.

The third distinction, between material and ideational factors, relates to the nature of theorizing and the things that are studied. A prior ontological commitment to materialism and idealism sets particular theories on a path to explaining security in terms of one set of factors. What matters most in explaining war? Is it material things, the amount of weapons and soldiers a country has, as many realists claim, or is it ideational things, norms and values and the identities of friends and enemies, or even socially constructed assumptions that tell us that war is an inevitable feature of the world, as constructivists argue? This is not a simple either/or choice. Some theories are almost wholly materialist, some are predominantly idealist, while others view security behaviour as a product of a combination of both (see Chapters 2 and 3).

Structure vs agency

What shapes behaviours and their outcomes, such as starting a war, negotiating a peace, forming an alliance, engaging in terrorism, trafficking drugs and so on? Is security politics a world of pure agency, of choices made freely, or is it a world in which something in the nature of the international system, or the collective implications of values and choices affect future decisions? Answers to these questions articulate arguments about structure and agency (Doty, 1997; Bieler and Morton, 2001; Wight, 2006). Broadly speaking, structure is something external to actors that shapes their behaviour. Agency relates to what actors (individuals or collectives, states or groups of states) do when they act. One metaphor used in IR theory is the billiard table. What shapes the movement and interaction of the balls on the table? Is it what the balls (state actors) do or what the table's cushioned edges (structure) do? Perhaps a better metaphor is to ask: What affects the course of a river? The properties of water, the shape of the river beds and banks, the gradient of hills, the presence of dams and boulders, or the interactions of all these things? While these metaphors imply material structures, it is important to note that social and ideational structures also matter. We drive on one side of the road not because cars and roads only permit that, but because socially and legally produced rules shape behaviour. They are not natural structures (some countries drive on the right, some on the left), nevertheless they affect drivers.

Structures may shape behaviours and outcomes. In social thought, from Emile Durkheim's sociology to Kenneth Waltz's structural realist security studies, structures explain behaviours and outcomes. The classic notion of structure in security studies is that of anarchy (the absence of hierarchical government) in the international system. For many realists, this structure imposes limits on how much security can be achieved and creates a competitive logic to states' security interactions. If structures are largely unchanging, then change and variation in security relate to some change in or among actors within the confines of pre-existing structural forces: in realism, this is changes in the distribution of material power among states (see Chapter 2). If structures are historically or socially produced, then change is more possible and both change and regularity need explaining, but still actors cannot simply decide to act differently and easily produce a new structure: those existing structures still shape their choices. This is the classic dialectic, as Marx (2001: 7) put it: 'Men make their own history, but they do not make it just as they please ... but under circumstances directly encountered, given and transmitted from the past.'

Agency relates to the extent and capacities of actors to act within a structure. How much choice do they really have? How could things have been different? There are two key elements to the dominant view of agency – power and rationality. Agency in much security theory is the 'faculty or state of acting or exerting power' (Buzan et al., 1993: 103). Power is defined in different ways by different theories of security. Some realists define it primarily in terms of material military capabilities (force levels, weapons), others view it in terms of the ability to persuade others, or to set the rules of the game. But agency also relates to the manner in which power is used. Many theories also assume that action is rational. Rationality is the assumption that actors act in accordance with particular interests they seek to maximize. This is really two assumptions. First, actors have a particular set of interests and are able to calculate which are more important (territory or trade for instance) and, for the purpose of theorizing, most actors of a given type (states) have similar basic interests (power, survival and so on). Second, having and knowing these interests, actors seek to pursue them through a rational (meaning calculating rather than sensible or wise) process of cost–benefit analysis. In deciding whether to go to war, for instance, a state will calculate whether war is the best approach to seeking its interests, what the costs of war would be, whether they would win and so on. However, this is an oversimplification. Many understandings of security do not posit pure rationality in which actors have perfect information and seek to make optimal choices, but a limited 'bounded' rationality, in which actors are constrained by imperfect information and may come under pressure to seek the easiest satisfactory strategy (known as 'satisficing behaviour') rather than the objectively optimal one. Further, some critical approaches to security emphasize that the interests states pursue are not pregiven but socially constructed, and so the subsequent cost–benefit analyses are shaped by different values, interests and identities.

The relationships between structure and agency can be viewed in four main ways: structuralism, in which structures determine outcomes; agency-centred approaches, in which the choices of individual actors matter more; some combination of structure and agency shapes behaviour and outcomes, for example Wendt's constructivism combines structure and agency in the concept of 'structuration' (see Chapter 3); or a questioning of the importance of the distinction – found in some poststructuralism. Beyond these foundational views, questions of structure and agency raise questions of where and what structures matter.

Levels of analysis: system, unit or more

Assumptions of structure and agency permeate questions of levels of analysis. Early in the development of IR, Singer (1961) posed the challenge of accounting for behaviour in terms of the units (states) or the nature of the system. This framed the structure and agency problem as one of a difficult choice between macro- and micro-levels. Waltz (1959) discerned three 'images' where the explanation of war was located. Is war explained by human nature (first image), as in classical realism; in the nature of the state (second image), as in bureaucratic politics models (Allison, 1971) and liberal claims that democratic states are less prone to war than nondemocratic states; or in the structure of the international system (third image), conceived particularly as anarchy for Waltz and many later theorists? While dividing up enquiry or explanation into distinct levels is useful for clarifying differences in explanations of war – as was Waltz's intent – one is not necessarily faced with an either/or choice and many approaches seek to combine second and third image explanations.

Questions of agency and level of analysis combine in the status given to states as the main security actors. Can we conceive of states as simple individual units, known as 'methodological individualism', where they are like people (or even are people) (Wendt, 1999; Wight, 2006)? States are complex entities made up of various government departments, private interest groups and so on. When a state acts, does this complexity matter? For some theorists, agency is only a property of individual human beings, and so when a state seems to act, it is really the actions of leaders or powerful people. Further, do we conceive of actors as having interests before they interact with each other? Waltz's structural realism assumes we do, but for others, states and their interests and calculations are formed in their relationships with each other. For instance, human beings exist physically before they interact socially (even if only in the womb), but what it means to be human, what interests an individual, has to emerge through interactions. If what it means to be a state is constituted through interactions being set beforehand, then the state has a different ontological status.

Domestic/foreign: political ontology and spatiality

Moving from social ontology – the nature of actors and their relations – to political ontology – the make-up of politics within that social universe – a further foundational distinction is that between domestic and international security relations. Spatial metaphors are common in security studies. Levels of analysis present a vertical differentiation from the small (individual) to the big (system); Buzan's security sectors present a metaphor of dividing issues into zones. The distinction between international and domestic politics and security is stronger than these, as it is less a metaphorical schema for clarifying different theories within the study of security and more a foundational assumption that legitimates the wider discipline of IR. As noted in the Introduction, this distinction pertains particularly to the limits of politics and security. Within states, supposedly, politics functions through the presence of a government that allows politics to pursue moral goals, justice, freedom and the rule of law because security is assured. Outside, or among, states, the possibilities of politics and security are seen as different when the organizing principle of international relations is commonly assumed to be anarchy rather than hierarchy (government). Here, security is not assured and politics itself is much weaker, baser and more limited (Walker, 1993). While much Cold War security studies adopted a strong inside-outside distinction, the emergence of transnational security issues and behaviours such as transnational crime, migration and terrorism have been argued to reduce the salience of this divide (see Chapters 11 and 12). Transnational simply means processes and interactions that occur across national boundaries. They usually involve at least one non-state actor, and so challenge the primacy of the state and the derivative spatial imagination of clear inside-outside division or easily identifiable levels of analysis (Risse-Kappen, 1995; Overbeek, 2000).

Building on the inside-outside distinction, many understandings of security have fallen into what Agnew called the 'territorial trap'. This combines three related assumptions: states are units within which territory and peoples are governed by a sovereign; the boundary between the domestic and the foreign is the boundary that defines political and economic interaction; and territorial states are prior to and containers of social orders, such that no other form or shape of social interaction can be imagined (Agnew and Corbridge, 1995). Together, these mean that conceptions of security are trapped into modes of thought with the state at the centre. This closes down permissible ontological claims about the universe of actors and their relations that can be made when articulating approaches to security. In particular, it encourages students of security to place themselves in the position of a state and think about security from that perspective (Morgenthau, 2006). This makes defining and understanding security beyond a state-centric paradigm difficult, and attempts to do this in relation to human security or transnational threats often end up falling back onto asserting that the state is the most important provider of security and container of insecurity. That is, the state may be challenged in its ability or willingness to provide security but it remains the defining point of the spatiality of security.

Epistemology

Epistemologies are theories of knowledge that underlie understandings of security. Understanding how we know relates to the status we give to the knowledge presented by theories of security and how they are built. While there are numerous approaches to this question, a central distinction has been drawn between 'positivist' and 'postpositivist' approaches. The dominant epistemology in security studies is most commonly referred to as 'positivism', although some criticize this label and argue that in IR and security, the term is erroneously used to describe 'empiricism' (Smith, 1996). In the philosophy of science, positivism, especially logical positivism, asserts that all phenomena are observable (Hollis and Smith, 1990). This is a pure empiricism, in which the only things that exist (ontology) are observable, and if something is not observable, it cannot be granted 'real' ontological status. However, it is not this pure empiricism that we find in much IR or security theory (Nicholson, 1996). Many theories labelled 'positivist' offer a wider empiricist view that allows for phenomena that are not directly observable but are asserted on the basis of what they appear to do; for instance, anarchy or the international system are observable only through their effects. These are, however, given the status of organizing ideas rather than real-world entities, although the distinction is all too often lost in the practice of theorizing. This means two things. First, seeing is believing: we know the world through our senses. Second, it has a correspondence theory of truth: a claim is 'true' when it corresponds to the evidence we see in the real world.

Pure empiricism can be contrasted with rationalism and pragmatism. Rationalism argues that good knowledge is derived from reasoned thought about the world, not merely the evidence one finds: simply put, all knowledge derives through reasoned thought, the facts do not simply speak for themselves. In IR, for instance, Morgenthau (2006: 4) claimed that 'theory consists in ascertaining facts and giving them meaning through reason'. However, this can be criticized for assuming a single 'reason' that is at odds with what we know from psychology. Both empiricism and rationalism presuppose a 'real' world separate from our knowledge of it and therefore rely on a clear distinction between subject and object, in which the subject is prior to what they encounter in the real world. Pragmatism defines good knowledge in somewhat different terms: good knowledge is that which is practically useful. In practice, while empiricism is dominant, many empiricist security scholars, such as Waltz, also claim the validity of their knowledge on pragmatic grounds.

Empiricism is not the same as valuing empirical evidence. Theorists of all kinds use empirical evidence (examples from the practice of security politics) and validate their claims on this basis. Rather, empiricists hold that we gain knowledge through particular processes of hypothesis formation and empirical testing. There is further diversity here. In the social sciences, behaviouralism has a particularly 'austere' view of what is testable (Hollis and Smith, 1990, 12), while others are more open in their ontology and methods and emphasize that it is only by the rigorous application of hypothesis formation and empirical testing that theoretical knowledge can be tested against its correspondence with an external 'reality'.

In understanding security, and wider social sciences, 'positivism' is more than a pure empiricism. It also combines assumptions of scientism, naturalism and value neutrality. Scientism is the assumption that the natural sciences represent the strongest form of knowledge and should be emulated. This is underpinned by ontological realism, and often a naturalism: the world, including political and social relations, is naturally a certain way (as opposed to being constructed) and is characterized by regularities that allow the discernment of fixed law-like relationships. This means that 'human beings and societies belong to a single natural order, which yields its secrets to a single scientific method' (Hollis, 1996: 304). Explanatory approaches to theorizing emphasize this by seeking to uncover such regularities underneath the seemingly endless variation in political reality. Value neutrality means that the process of producing knowledge should be free of one's own personal perspective and values. This has been emphasized since the political theorist Max Weber, who influenced the founders of IR such as Morgenthau (Barkawi, 1998), claimed that 'whenever the man of science introduces his personal value judgement, a full understanding of the facts ceases' (cited in Smith, 2004: 500). Conjoining the distinctions between subject and object and between facts and values gives empirical evidence a particular status – as the legible face the real world presents to us. Values are from another realm and should not be included. On the basis of an empiricist epistemology, this makes some sense; since moral claims cannot be proved correct (or incorrect) through observation of empirical evidence, a value-free science is essential.

These basic assumptions are criticized by a range of 'postpositivist' views, held particularly by critical approaches to security (see Chapter 3). They argue that the apparent value neutrality of positivism is not achieved by those who claim it, and for some critics, it is not achievable at all. Rather, knowledge is not a neutral set of facts separate from values, but is 'situated knowledge'. Critical IR theorist Robert Cox (1981: 128) thus claimed that 'all theory is for someone and for some purpose': there is no such thing as value-neutral theoretical observation, as all observers are situated within a particular historical and geographical context that they cannot simply leave at the door when theorizing. Many values and assumptions are seen as natural, or are held subconsciously, and cannot be stripped away. This means that no social scientist is unbiased or neutral in their pursuit of knowledge, and thereby all knowledge is not neutral in the way positivists have claimed. If knowledge is not the correspondence of theories with facts but is socially (and/or historically) produced and situated, then knowledge claims are located within the realm of the subject and intersubjective relations rather than in a relationship between the subject and the object. For some critical approaches, the resultant focus has been on language or discourse: the way we discuss the world through language, visual representations and so on is not only a description of separate reality but also affects the way we see things (see Chapter 3). This means that the knowledge we have is not just about power, but is itself related to power – the power to say what is 'true'. Thus, some constructivists, feminists and critical security scholars seek alternative foundations for producing and judging knowledge that can never be neutral but can be better when justified on pragmatic and ethical lines: the seeking of a more cosmopolitan knowledge, reflective not of one culture's specific ways of thinking but one that could be agreed by a wider range of peoples. Others, like poststructuralists, deny the possibility of such foundations against which we can judge the 'truth' of something. For them, there is no single 'Archimedean' point, no 'view from nowhere' from which we can discern truth from falsehood. This is sometimes mistaken for a denial of the existence of the real world (an ontological claim) rather than a more nuanced claim that our knowledge of the world does not and cannot attain an indisputable truth about the real world. Truth is always defined in relation to other potential truths, not discerned by discovering an objective truth. Here, the basis of truth is acceptance not correspondence to independent reality, and so truth and power are inseparable. Indeed, for poststructuralists, claims of an eternal and supposedly objective truth are associated with power and violence.

Some non-positivist approaches retain a stronger subject-object distinction, in which the two are mutually constitutive. Drawing on recent philosophy of science, especially the work of Bhaskar, 'critical realist' perspectives maintain that there is a reality independent of our knowledge of it, but that does not mean that our knowledge is or can be politically neutral (Patomaki, 2002; Wight, 2006). This view licenses an eclectic position in which relations between the subject and object, the material and the ideational are not to be decided on a priori but must be chosen to fit with the multiple and complex realities of security on a case-by-case, empirical basis (Patomaki and Wight, 2000; Kurki and Wight, 2007).

How does understanding develop? Methodology and progress

Numerous methods are used to produce security knowledge. Data may be gathered from official documents, archives, or other historical accounts, by interviewing key people or using questionnaires and so on. Different methods arise in part from differing ontological and epistemological warrants, which license particular methods as the most appropriate for generating 'good' knowledge. Many approaches use qualitative analyses, such as case studies or wider historical methods. Some, particularly rationalist, approaches may use quantitative methods by using statistics to find correlations between variables or developing formal mathematical models that elaborate particular logics of behaviour often without testing them against empirical evidence. Different views on rationality shape methodological differences among traditional approaches. For some, the rationality assumption is so strong that behaviour can be modelled on the basis of fixed and pregiven interests and calculations, and so use forms of analysis based on formal mathematical modelling, statistical analysis or game theory. For others, a softer rationality assumption guides theorizing but does not require or allow the reductive and parsimonious methods of game theory (Walt, 1999; Smith, 2004).

Critical and postpositivist approaches are diverse in their methods but tend not to use quantitative methods or formal modelling, as these are often features of positivist enquiry (Salter and Mutlu, 2013). Instead, they may use genealogical methods (historical philosophical accounts of how truths come into being), immanent critique (historical analysis of how a current state of affairs was produced and how it could have been different), deconstruction (a poststructuralist method of showing how seemingly natural or logical assumptions are actually particular combinations of sets of assumptions that may be internally contradictory) and forms of discourse analysis and ethnography.

Epistemological questions also relate to how understandings of security change. For instance, Robert Keohane's (1988) criticism that postpositivist approaches fail to articulate a coherent research programme assumes that knowledge progresses by proving or disproving particular propositions and moving towards some stronger truth. A broadly positivist view is that knowledge progresses through the collective efforts of 'scientists' making propositions about the world that are tested empirically and on that basis become accepted as true. Another influential view, even among those who adopt broadly positivist approaches, is that advocated by Popper, who argued that science advanced not through propositions being proved true but by being proved false (or at least incomplete and unsatisfactory). A process of 'falsification' implies that final and complete knowledge is never attained but progress occurs through refining ideas by proving earlier ones insufficient in some way. Assuming that understanding progresses in these ways underlies the dismay and dismissal expressed by some critics of the deepening and broadening of security.

In contrast, some theorists adopt a different view associated with Kuhn's philosophy of science. Kuhn speaks of paradigms, in which general theories cannot be contrasted with each other in a way designed to prove or disprove them. Paradigms establish different grounds for the truth of their theories: they have different types of units and basic concepts and different questions, different languages and different criteria for evidence. As such, they do not compete on the same playing field, they are 'incommensurable'. Not all theories differ paradigmatically: neorealism and neoliberalism share many of the same units, questions and understandings of what constitutes a research programme and good evidence (see Chapter 2). A Kuhnian perspective implies that the discovery of new facts, the falsification of key concepts, often has little effect on the ways in which security is understood. Rather, understandings of security change through paradigm shifts. It is arguable that the development of postpositivist approaches to security constitute such a shift, at least in respect of the development of some critical approaches (see Chapter 3), but these have not supplanted prior paradigms based on positivism. Importantly, while Kuhnian perspectives emphasize internal developments within disciplines, Buzan and Hansen's (2009) 'post-Kuhnian' history of the evolution of security studies shows how understanding security has also developed in relation to wider political and technological developments and changes in other disciplines, such as the philosophy of science, sociology and geography.

Conclusion

The study of security has a complex history of disciplinary development, interdisciplinary engagements (and disengagements) and multiple divisions on the theoretical building blocks of perspectives on security. Amid this complexity, one might question whether different approaches to the study of security are really constitutive of a single field of 'security studies'. While the changing scope of security certainly diversifies the field, it is the combination of ontological and epistemological assumptions that have divided the field most profoundly. In particular, distinctions between positivist and postpositivist approaches (and their ontological foundations) demarcate two fields of security studies: an empiricist and rationalist mainstream of realism and liberalism found in the mainstream academic discipline in the USA, and the largely postpositivist field of security studies practised in Western Europe (and Canada and Australasia) (Waever, 2004). Many conversations on security occur within rather than across this geographical division (Shah, 2010; Miller, 2010). Beyond this, it is also notable that much of security studies has been strongly 'Western centric'; even when talking about non-Western states, the basic assumptions and questions have their origins in the West (Bilgin, 2010).

It is impossible to know how security is understood by adopting only one set of building blocks. Rather, from debates on the scope of security to debates on the foundations of understanding, theories of security assemble these elements in particular ways. This chapter has explored the various distinctions and differences, and the underlying dualistic assumptions (subject-object, fact-value, material-ideational, structure-agency, inside-outside), that have shaped understandings of security. Chapters 2 and 3 explore how these multifarious differences coalesce into (more or less) coherent theoretical perspectives.

Chapter 2

Traditional Rationalist Approaches to Security

Understanding security has traditionally operated on the basis of rationalist approaches. These understand security behaviours as deriving from the rationality of actors who pursue their interests by making cost–benefit calculations attuned to their circumstances. The two main rationalist approaches to understanding security are realism and liberalism. These are diverse traditions but most rationalist approaches have an emphasis on the rational actions of self-interested actors, a focus on states as the primary or exclusive security actors, and a narrow conception of security as pertaining to the issues of war and military competition. Considerable diversity of thought can arise from rationalist, state-centric assumptions. Realism has been the dominant theoretical tradition in security studies, even more than in IR, although liberalism is also a well-established set of perspectives. In the story of security studies, the dominance of realism is continually affirmed and critiqued, and realism becomes the appropriator and defender of state-centrism and power politics. However, realism's tragic view of the logics and limits of security is not inherent in all rationalism or state-centrism. This chapter discusses the basic concepts of rationalist approaches and explores their evolution. It begins with the central principles of realism and the evolution of realist thought. It then draws out the logics and limits of security posited by realism by discussing its key concepts and orientations related to power (particularly the notion of the balance of power), rationality, and the potential for change. Finally, it explores liberal approaches and draws out the differences and similarities in the logics and limits of security they claim.

Realism

The central principles of realism can be stated simply: anarchy and self-help, states and power. First, the international system is anarchic. Unlike domestic politics where governments provide security and channel and regulate competition among people, in international relations there is no higher power to do the same for states, which must therefore provide security for themselves. Second, reinforcing this view, while other approaches also give some independent importance to international organizations and non-state actors, realists view security as comprising (almost) entirely relations among states. Third, the logic of relations among these self-interested and self-reliant states is competition for power. Power, and particularly military power, is seen either as something that states want as a goal in itself (for classical realists), or as a means to the end of survival and security (for structural realists). Since states seek power and, realists assume, there is not an infinite supply of power (or security), the interests of states are always potentially in competition. While liberals assert a degree of harmony of interests among states that can often best be served through cooperation, realists see limited potential for cooperation. In combination, these assumptions mean that security is a scarce condition that means 'a somewhat less dangerous and less violent world, rather than a safe, just or peaceful one' (Donnelly, 2000: 10). In realism, the logic of security is power competition and the limits of security derive in general from international anarchy or human nature, and specifically from the distribution of military power among states.

Realism before realists

Realist theories of security have a relatively recent history, arising particularly in the aftermath of the Second World War and developing through the Cold War. Thus, they have developed largely in relation to global-level conflict and division. However, realism is not limited to explaining the late 20th century and periods of potential military confrontation. Rather, realism's core principles draw on a longer tradition of thought through the 16th- and 17th-century political thinkers of Western Europe but stretching back to Ancient Greece.

The dominating logic of power in realism owes much to the ancient Greek historian Thucydides (431 BCE), whose history of the war between Athens and Sparta inspired early realists such as Morgenthau (2006) and Wight (1978). Thucydides argued that the growing power of Athens provoked fear in Sparta and led to war between them. He recounts a dialogue between the Athenians and the Melians, a weak Spartan ally, in which the Melians attempted to persuade the Athenians not to conquer them by appealing to ethics, the gods and reputation, and claiming that the Spartans would come to their aid. The Athenian response was simple realism, as all appeals were dismissed or ignored and trumped by pure power politics: 'The strong do what they will, the weak suffer what they must.'

Anarchy in realism derives from Thomas Hobbes (1993: 93), the 17th-century philosopher, scientist and translator of Thucydides, whose account of persistent insecurity and violence in human relations in the hypothetical 'state of nature' populated by naturally power-hungry people is paradigmatic for states in anarchy:

> in the nature of man, we find three principal causes of quarrel. First, competition; secondly, diffidence; thirdly, glory. The first, maketh man invade for gain; the second for safety; and the third, for reputation ... Hereby it is manifest, that during the time men live without a common

> power to them all in awe, they are in that condition which is called war; and such a war, as is of every man, against every man.

In anarchy, self-help is not merely an unfortunate situation but also a value to be protected. The early 16th-century political philosopher Niccolo Machiavelli (1532/1985) highlighted the importance of being self-interested in a world where one assumes all others are self-interested. This means retaining autonomy of action, since any loss of autonomy, any reliance on another for one's survival, limits the ability of a state to provide its own security: 'princes ought to avoid as much as possible being at the discretion of any one'.

Classical realism

Realist theorizing of security began in the 1930s with E.H. Carr (1946) and Reinhold Niebuhr (1932), but became a paradigmatic statement of IR theory in the postwar era with Hans Morgenthau (1948), John Herz (1950) and scholar-practitioners like George Kennan and Henry Kissinger. Herz (1950: 158) once described realists as the 'children of darkness', and working in the shadow of the Second World War and the emerging Cold War, many early realists posed themselves against interwar idealists in IR theory and practice who had too much faith in the potential for human reason, the driving force behind Enlightenment science and progress, to mitigate or eliminate war. They had diverse backgrounds but shared a pessimistic account of human nature as the source of explanation for war and violence. Basic biological and psychological drives shared by all human beings are 'to live, to propagate and to dominate' (Morgenthau, 1948: 16–17); and Morgenthau (1962: 7) argued that 'the social world [is] but a projection of human nature onto the collective plane'. Niebuhr, a theologian, emphasized the limits of moral action by collectives of human beings, such as states, that derived from the sinful drives of human nature. While human nature also contains the capacity for good and moral action, the prospects for such action in international politics were limited.

Carr (1946), a historian with Marxist influences, contrasted realism with 'utopianism'. While he found both lacking, 'utopians' had a mistaken belief that the incidence of war could be reduced through a triumph of reason, and that the wisdom of avoiding war could be built into world politics through international cooperation and institutions like the League of Nations. Echoing Marx's claim that dominant political ideals serve the interests of the powerful, Carr (2001: 65) argued that such hopes were not the product of universal and absolute moral principles but were 'historically conditioned, being both products of circumstance and interests and weapons framed for the furtherance of interests'. This was not a novel argument in itself. Machiavelli had oriented his work with a similar criticism of Plato,

Aristotle and St Thomas Aquinas, who he claimed talked about how the world ought to be, whereas his aim was to 'tell you how it is' (Morgenthau and Lang, 2004: 49). For early realists, it is the play of power not the rule of law or ethics that shapes international behaviour and its outcomes. Beyond this lies diversity, with Carr arguing that the competitive logics of security derive not from the sinful and aggressive tendencies of human nature, but the scarcity of material resources. Nevertheless, Carr's early realist ontological materialism and rejection of idealism, and other classical realist's extrapolations from negative human nature, reaffirmed the centrality of power in security relations (see Chapter 1).

Realism took its now familiar form of the centrality of states and the characterization of their relations as a struggle for power with Morgenthau's (1946) six principles of political realism:

(1) Politics, and society in general, is governed by *objective laws* that have their root in *human nature.*
(2) The confusing and complex landscape of international politics can be understood through the concept of *national interest defined in terms of power*, which is a theoretical device for simplifying complexity and an assumption backed up by the weight of historical evidence.
(3) *Interest defined as power* is an objective category.
(4) While political action has moral significance, states act in terms of interests not moral goals and there is an 'ineluctable tension between moral command and the *requirements of successful political action*' (2006: 12).
(5) This tension can be navigated by the concept of interest defined in terms of power, since this saves the policy maker from the political folly of moral excess.
(6) Politics is a separate and autonomous sphere from ethics, economics and law, and the logics of political action are different from the logics of these other spheres (Morgenthau, 2006: 4–13).

While later realism downplays some of Morgenthau's thought, such as the similarities he identified between international and domestic politics, the role of a community of states, and more open (and rather vague) notions of power, these principles of self-interest, power and a tension between politics and ethics are common markers of realism.

Herz (1950: 158) declared that 'realist thought is determined by an insight into the overpowering impact of the security factor'. Security is seldom defined in classical realism, but is approached via the national interest and power-seeking behaviour. Power is seen as both ends and means; power is what is valued, power is what states use to gain more power, and when threatened, power must be countered with power. Security is viewed as national security, which Morgenthau claimed is the principal national interest and pertains to the integrity of territory and political institutions. In all realist approaches, security relates to issues of war. Realism neither condemns nor celebrates war but views it merely as an instrument for pursuing power and security (see Chapter 7). The pursuit of national security has a harsher, more amplified, competitive logic than other forms of power competition: 'National security, then, is the irreducible minimum that diplomacy must defend with adequate power without compromise' (Morgenthau, 2006: 382). Since security is irreducible, Morgenthau claims that security politics pertains to questions of 'adequate power'. While compromise may be wise in other areas of political life, security is to be pursued 'without compromise'.

In early realism, power and security had objective and subjective dimensions. Power was viewed in material and social and ideational terms and, for Morgenthau (1946: 9), comprised 'anything that establishes and maintains the control of man over man. Thus power covers all social relationships that may serve that end, from physical violence to the most subtle psychological ties by which one mind controls another.' Likewise, security was an objective condition and a subjective perception (Lott, 2004), and Morgenthau (1972: 404) claimed that 'the generally professed and most frequent actual motive for armaments is fear of attack; that is a feeling of insecurity'.

For Morgenthau, the task of producing security involves diplomacy and the threat of military action, both to reassure an opponent and to deter them. This becomes a complex issue in much realism through the concept of the 'security dilemma' (Herz, 1950). Rooted in anarchy rather than human nature, this concept emphasizes that there are severe constraints on the amount of security that can be achieved, since actions intended to make oneself secure may have negative impacts by producing fear in others and thereby inviting aggression (see Chapter 5).

Structural realism

In the 1970s, easing global tensions led to a resurgence of liberal approaches that identified greater cooperation than realism anticipated. Realism diverged, and in the UK, a softer form of realism, known as the 'English School', grew in prominence and combined liberal and realist principles in its understandings of international society. This soft realism, founded by Martin Wight, Herbert Butterfield, Stanley Hoffman and Hedley Bull, has been inherited by current security scholars like Barry Buzan and Richard Little. In contrast, the US mainstream of realism became harder, more rigid and deterministic. Realism was redefined as 'structural realism' (sometimes called 'neorealism'), with the publication of Kenneth Waltz's *Theory of International Politics* (1979).

Structural realism retains the hallmarks of realist thought in its pessimistic account of security politics derived from the centrality of power competition.

While all realist views are state-centric, Waltz and later structural realists like Mearsheimer reinforced this with an assumption that states were unitary (one can treat them as individuals rather than as sets of decision-making institutions) and rational (calculating) actors. While earlier realists located interstate competition as an expression of human nature (within conditions of anarchy), Waltz shifted the primary location of explanation to the structure of the system, to anarchy itself. He strengthened the significance of anarchy by claiming that there are only two organizational principles of social and political life: hierarchy (characteristic of political life within states) and anarchy (characterizing international political life). Although subsequently criticized for assuming that only two possibilities exist, this provides a simple distinction that gives explanatory value to his theory. A further distinction arises from these two distinct organizing principles: that of functional differentiation. Within a hierarchy, like a state, different actors have different roles; the legislative branches of government are separate from the executive and judiciary, and ministries of trade seek different ends than ministries of defence. Within anarchy, however, Waltz (1979: 107) claimed that there can be no such functional differentiation among states that all seek the same ends. This reinforced the primacy of security in states' relations: 'in a self-help system, considerations of security subordinate economic gain to political interest'. While these changes re-emphasize and rigidify already present elements of realism, perhaps the biggest difference between structural and classical realism is that the latter views power as a means to the end of security rather than an end in itself. Further, power and security were shifted to a more material and objective footing, with power increasingly defined in narrower material and military terms, and security reunderstood by downplaying subjective dimensions in favour of a predominantly objective conceptualization. Indeed, Waltz (1979: 99) developed his theory by seeking to 'abstract from every attribute of states except their capabilities'.

States act differently at different times. Sometimes there is war, and sometimes a basic peace. How does one explain peace if all human behaviour, including that of states, is driven by a 'will to power'? Human nature is, by definition, invariant and unchanging so cannot explain differences. For Waltz, the explanation of this difference cannot lie in human nature, or in the character of the state (democratic or authoritarian). However, anarchy is also invariant and so difference must be explained by something else. For Waltz, differences can be observed in the distribution of power (material capabilities) that explain different actions, thus, states act according to the distribution of power within the anarchic system.

So what types of behaviour do states exhibit? One distinction is that between cooperating and competing. For realists, and especially neorealists, there is a 'dominating logic of security competition, which no amount of cooperation can eliminate' (Mearsheimer, 1994/95: 9). Since security is obtained by gaining power and pursued without compromise, the potential for cooperation is limited and when it does exist, it is short-lived and largely a mask for selfish behaviour. This is reinforced by realists' emphasis on the autonomy of states. In searching for more scientific study, Waltz (1979: 106) elevated the Machiavellian wisdom of seeking to maintain autonomy to a law of states' actual behaviour, claiming that 'states seek to control what they depend on or to lessen the extent of their dependency'.

Since realists reject cooperation as a major mode of security seeking, they discern different categories of behaviour. In order to make rational self-interested calculations in seeking security through power, states must, as Morgenthau advised, look at the world from the perspective of the distribution of power and form a strategy for action. Two broad strategies present themselves: balancing or bandwagoning. Simply put, balancing means positioning oneself to counterbalance a more powerful state or group of states by forming alliances or building up one's own military forces. Bandwagoning, in contrast, means joining up with the more powerful state. Consider familiar playground politics. To make oneself secure when faced with an overgrown bully, do you balance by forming your own gang, or bandwagon by making friends with the bully? For structural realists, these are not equally valid choices made on a case-by-case basis. Rather, one of Waltz's major conclusions was that states tend to balance rather than bandwagon. Bandwagoning always carries risks of being dominated or betrayed, so while it may work in law-based hierarchic orders, where the risks of siding with the bully are mitigated by the rule of the teacher, in self-help anarchy these risks are unrestrained. The tendency to balance relates particularly to more powerful states, since weaker powers have less choice and may have few options for balancing. However, some realists argue that bandwagoning may be more rational in particular circumstances, such as when there is a strong rising power intent on altering their position in the world, as some see China today (Schweller, 1994).

Even if one assumes balancing to be more common, the imperative of anarchy does not clearly indicate who will balance with (or against) whom (see Chapter 6). This depends on the distribution of power, and particularly on the number of concentrations of power in the world, known as 'polarity'. Categories of world order are often distinguished as unipolar (only one superpower), bipolar (two predominant concentrations of power as in the Cold War) and multipolar (many centres, and thus many choices). Unipolar orders are not seen as particularly stable or enduring; balancing behaviour will probably lead to the rise of rival great powers. However, when unipolarity is strong, in the sense that the single power has far more power than others combined, a situation of 'hegemony' exists that may provide some stability. The stability of bipolar and multipolar orders is more widely debated. Bipolar orders are rare and only four have existed over the past 2,500 years (Copeland, 1996). Some realists argue that bipolarity is more stable, because when seeking security in a bipolar order, a state only has to consider the interests, intentions and capabilities of one major potential adversary. In a world of limited resources for intelligence gathering and military preparations, this is seen as more practical and predictable. Multipolar orders, in contrast, may make establishing security strategies more complex as they are inherently more unpredictable. Yet, Waltz claims they are more stable, because multipolarity encourages more prudence, taking into consideration the perspectives of many more states. Regardless of varying perspectives on the relative stability of different polar orders, realism views systemic stability as central to security, although it is much criticized for focusing on the security of only the most powerful states.

Diversity in realist security logics and limits

Realism is a diverse tradition that understands security through differing propositions about the combination of power and rationality under the general conditions of anarchy or human nature, and the specific conditions of the distribution of power. Understanding realist approaches to security requires engagement with the development of the concept of the 'balance of power', and the different rationality assumptions of various realisms. Further, seeing how strongly fixed the logics and limits of security are in realism requires engaging with the challenge of change in the international system and the prospects for progressive change through ethics.

Balance of power and threat

Realists conceive security as the national security of states in their relations with each other. International security is characterized as the stability of a given order. Wars occur when an order is destabilized. Instability is, however, only a periodic feature of international orders. For realists, this is due largely to the balance of power. The concept of the 'balance of power' arose in the 17th century, but realists use millennia of history to prove its importance (Sheehan, 1996). Waltz (1979: 117) claimed that 'if there is any distinctively political theory of international politics, balance of power theory is it'. It is, however, a loose concept with diverse and contested meanings (Haas, 1953). Like security, 'balance of power' denotes a condition (an equilibrium of power internationally, such that there is approximate equality among major blocs and no preponderance of power), a practice and a value (of seeking, building and maintaining that equilibrium, although this goes beyond the choice of balancing or bandwagoning behaviour) (Sheehan, 1996). While it is not purely a realist concept, realists use the balance of power as a characterization of the limits and logics of security politics, while liberals and others see it as an ideology whose pursuit led to the First World War.

In the balance of power, as in realism broadly, power is conceived largely in military and material terms, although this has developed gradually

(Schmidt, 2007). Carr (1946: 109) asserted the centrality of military power when he claimed that 'every act of the state in its power aspect, is directed to war, not as a desirable weapon, but as a weapon which it may require in the last resort to use'. However, Morgenthau (1946) defined power in broad terms, because although interest defined as power is an objective category, given in the world, he recognized that it was historically changeable. The potential for different interests and concepts of power to shape security in different eras was lost as neorealism adopted a predominantly material concept of power, and further restricted that to an emphasis on military materials. Thus, realism gradually narrowed the balance of power concept from its wider 17th-century forms, and emphasized only balances that result from competitive adversarial practices rather than the associative social practices emphasized by liberal approaches (Little, 2007). Beyond this narrowing, realism remained diverse on questions of how balances form and how much power states will seek.

Realists generally claim that states do not seek to create a balance that is of benefit to all states, they merely seek their own power. Balances emerge by all states doing this, such that the quest for predominance of one state cancels out that of another and equilibrium results. Whether this is a sufficient explanation for the formation of balances is more debated. For classical realists like Morgenthau (2006), the nature of the system tends towards a balance of power, but this is a precarious form of stability that needs to be re-established by some states enacting policies that seek to preserve the balance, even though this is in tension with his rigid grounding of states' behaviour in acquisitive and competitive human nature. For structural realists, especially Waltz, the emergence and maintenance of a balance of power is merely the result of systemic pressures – they emerge with or without the intentions and actions of states to produce or maintain them.

Realists also disagree on how much power states will seek. They often distinguish 'revisionist' states, which actively seek to change the distribution of power, and 'status-quo' states, which seek to maintain it and their position in it. While in classical realism, this distinction is important in the character and choices of states, structural realism views such choices as determined by states' positions in the distribution of power. For structural realists, there are two drives at play in states' power-seeking behaviour: survival and domination. The latter brings structural realism closer to the original conception of classical realism's will to power, but still locates explanation in the pressures of anarchic structure rather than innate human drives. Facing structural pressures, states may seek enough power to survive or to become dominant. Those who view anarchy as compelling states to seek 'appropriate' amounts of power for survival are referred to as 'defensive' structural realists (Waltz, 1979; Walt, 1987; Glaser, 1997; van Evera, 1999), while those who argue that anarchy leads and permits states to pursue maximum possible power, dominance and even hegemony are known as 'offensive' structural realists (Mearsheimer, 2001). This distinction is not one between state strategies, to build defensive capabilities and act only in self-defence, or to engage in offensive military action whenever possible. Rather, it is a distinction between what types of behaviour the structural pressures of anarchy encourage or punish. It articulates distinct views on how scarce security is in international life. Offensive neorealists view security as extremely scarce, while defensive neorealists view it as potentially less scarce, with its achievement shaped by a wider range of political and technological factors (see Chapter 5).

Importantly, these differences do not affect realism's basic premise that states seek relative not absolute gains: they do not want simply more and more power, just more than other states. If states seek absolute gains, as in liberalism, a different logic of behaviour is implied, one that may include much greater cooperation. The classic example used to explain this is Rousseau's stag hunt scenario: if several hungry men want to eat, they will hunt. Their chances of gaining more meat are greater if they band together and hunt a stag. But this requires trust that realists see as unlikely. What if, when hunting a stag, a rabbit crosses their path? Realists claim that self-help means that an individual will break from the group to catch the rabbit. The rabbit will feed the individual for a short time, but the others will lose the stag. If rational men (states) want more meat (absolute gains), they will cooperate and get a quarter of a stag; if, however, they are only interested in survival (or having more meat than others), they will pursue the rabbit and ignore the plight of the rest. Seeking relative gains is reinforced by the military-centric notions of power of structural realism. Military power is certainly relative to that of others and has no value in its own terms, but economic wealth, for instance, may be better pursued by groups rather than individually (hence companies and large corporations), although relative power still matters.

While consistently emphasizing relative gains, structural realism nevertheless provides only a partial explanation for balances of power. In describing the pressures of anarchy, Waltz (1996: 54) is content to assert that states all have 'a single motive – the wish to survive', although he acknowledges that some states may seek other goals, for example wealth or territory, and value them more highly than survival (Waltz, 1979). Donnelly (2000) argues that this limits the explanatory and predictive power of Waltz's model, which only describes the pressures states are subject to but cannot predict their behaviour. Even for Waltz (1979: 71), prediction would require some 'knowledge of their internal dispositions'. Thus, Waltz admits diverse motives but fails to distinguish their implications systematically, even though history is replete with wars beginning not for mere survival but for expansion (Donnelly, 2000). There have been several attempts to modify structural realism in this regard. One is Snyder's (1996) use of 'process variables': things that arise not only from structure or units but specific processes that vary more widely. The other is to ask the question: Do states merely respond to the power of others? If this were so, then why have Britain and America not gone to war for 200 years? Is the fact that the USA has viewed Cuba as more of a threat than Canada explicable only on the basis of their military power? Clearly not, as Canada has often had more soldiers and weapons than Cuba. Thus, for some realists, power alone is insufficient to explain behaviour; rather, states respond to perceived and anticipated threats. Thus, Walt (1987: x) reconceived the balance of power as the 'balance of threat', in which states' behaviour 'is determined by the threats they perceive and the power of others is merely one element in their calculations'.

Further revisions to the balance of power theory seek to account for an apparent lack of balancing in the contemporary era. Since it is clear that states do not only expend their resources in building up military power, some realists view the balance of power in relation to both military power and wealth (Gilpin, 1981). Others have broadened the concept by expanding beyond the predominantly adversarial practices emphasized by other realists. Paul (2004) distinguishes between 'hard balancing' as the formation of strong alliances and building up military capabilities (the main focus of realist accounts of balance of power), and other forms that are a more common feature of contemporary great power politics, such as 'soft balancing' (made up of short-term forms of cooperation) and 'asymmetric balancing' (balancing indirectly against non-state actors such as terrorists). In recapturing the broader view of balance of power found in the concept's longer history, such revisions in the light of evidence may mean that the concept has lost its distinctively realist foundations, as realists have taken on arguments with a decidedly liberal or constructivist flavour (Vasquez, 1997). It is also notable that while the metaphor of a balance may be useful, it may also be a habit of thought rather than a reflection of real behaviours. Notions of balance are pervasive in the security literature: from a balance between values (such as security and liberty) to a balance of power, balance metaphors pose security relations in a particular light that obscures all else. It thus presents a limited view of the prospects and form not just of how international security politics operates, but of whether and how that may change.

Rationality

Realism is a broadly rationalist tradition. However, realists differ on the form and implications of the assumption that security actions take place on a foundation of rationality. In particular, they differ on questions of wisdom, the universality of rational calculation, and the implications this has for the location, logics and limits of security. For Morgenthau (1952), the pursuit and exercise of power is the action of state leaders. However, state leaders can be wise or unwise and the task of theorizing is to support wisdom in state policies. Wise leadership mitigates the potential for war but does not attempt to eliminate war from global politics. Wise political action should, in the first instance, be through diplomacy and peaceful means, but includes the preparation for national defence. Morgenthau argued that defining the national interest 'restrictively and rationally' in terms of power enables leaders to act wisely. However, he held open the possibility that not all states would act rationally. The national interest has to be defended against those of other nations 'which may or may not be thus defined'. If faced with another nation that has not defined their interest restrictively and rationally, politics is to take the form of 'armed diplomacy' to convince other leaders that their interests have nothing to fear and that their 'illegitimate interests have nothing to gain in the face of armed might rationally employed' (Morgenthau, 1952: 978).

Waltz utilized a narrower view of rationality derived from microeconomics, which asserts not that wise state leaders should seek to act rationally, as Morgenthau did, but that states are inherently rational. Structural realism's materialist and objectivist view of states and power, and thus of security, reduces rational calculation to material cost–benefit analysis. Such a narrow rationalism had come to dominate strategic thought in the 'golden age' of strategic studies but was amplified by structural realism's emphasis on a third image (structural) explanation (see Chapter 1). It is rationality that intervenes between structural pressure and political action: the rational calculation of relative power is 'a reliable but invisible transmission belt connecting objective [material] change to adaptive behaviour' (Friedberg, 1988, cited in Rose, 1998: 158). Holding rationality as constant rather than variable is what permits structural realism to argue that variations in states' behaviour derive only from variations in the distribution of material capabilities (Keohane, 1986). In doing so, however, the politics of international security is diminished since behaviour and outcomes stem not from wise choices but from more or less automatic responses (Ashley, 1984). This has prompted even other realists, like Gray (1999: 164), to characterize structural realism as 'reductionist nonsense'. Indeed, a further characteristic of the distinction between classical realism and structural realism is that the former emphasizes praxis, while the latter focuses more on the limits of political and security action.

Structural realists differ on how simply this rationality can be construed. For offensive realists, the pressures of seeking security in anarchy are unambiguous to the degree that similarly situated states will always behave in a like manner. Defensive realists tend not only to view the pressures of anarchy in different terms, with less scarcity of security, but also to combine structural pressures with some domestic variables in explaining action and thus identify more varied security behaviours and possibilities. This makes defensive realism difficult to distinguish from 'neoclassical' realist perspectives, in which the main parameters of states' foreign policies are determined by relative material capabilities in the international system, but these impact only indirectly on actual policy since they are 'translated through intervening variables at the unit level' rather than there being a simple and direct 'transmission belt' between material capabilities and policy (Rose, 1998: 146). In this view, international anarchy is difficult to read and domestic political factors shape the manner in which calculations of capabilities are developed into more detailed and widely varying policies (Schweller, 1994). This reintroduces subjective perceptions of leaders who make wise or unwise decisions rather than security actions being a simple and direct effect of material capabilities.

Realist views of rationality are diverse at a theoretical level and in the conclusions different realists draw on the scarcity and variability of security in international life. The centrality of rationalism in realist thought, however, does not imply an optimistic view of reason, especially not of the possibility of progress through human reason as emphasized by early liberal approaches.

Change and ethics

Realism was criticized for failing to anticipate the ending of the Cold War without significant bloodshed. This failure reflects a deeper tendency to see little change in the basic patterns and drivers of interstate security behaviours since, for realists, 'the fundamental nature of international relations has not changed over the millennia' (Gilpin, 1981: 7). While states have choices in their security behaviours, they cannot reshape the world as they wish. With one of two unchanging foundations (anarchy or human nature), the driving force of security is seen as given in the nature of something, as therefore unchangeable.

Realists view change as limited and criticize those who emphasize it for expressing naive utopian hopes for a different security. Realists emphasize that power politics is tragedy (Mearsheimer, 2001; Schmidt, 2004). For Carr (1946: 93), 'the tragedy of all political life [is that] politics are made up of two elements – utopia and reality – belonging to two different planes which can never meet'. However, early realists saw some potential for change, for peace, even on the foundations of sinful human nature, and were critical of unrestrained realpolitick (Scheuerman, 2007). Carr wished to retain an element of utopianism, Herz claimed to espouse a realist liberalism, and Morgenthau even argued for a future world government. Change, however, must go with the flow and force of the law-like regularities of interstate action and reaction.

Structural realism is even less able to explain significant change (Wohlforth, 1994/95), and its primary response to apparent change is to deny its significance. Structural realism anticipates change, on an almost continual basis, but only changes within the distribution of power. While changes within a system are important, they are not the same as changes of the system. Waltz (2000: 5) viewed specific events and longer historical processes that many liberals see as progress in this light: 'big changes in the means of transportation, communication, and war fighting, for example, strongly affect how states and other agents interact' but 'such changes occur at the unit level'. They change the capabilities of states, but the logics and limits of politics and security remain intact. This, of course, is questionable: How are the interests and interactions of states unaffected by the multiplicity of communication channels? Why must such changes only be confined to the unit level? The answer, it seems, is that such changes are often technological, and since technology serves the purposes of its masters, it does not alter the first order structure of anarchy, only the second order structure of the distribution of material capabilities. Similarly, contemporary classical realist Gray (1999: 161) argues that 'the future is the past – with GPS'. In addition to technological change, liberals posited changes in the nature of security relations on the basis of trends towards democratization, great interdependence of states and stronger potential for international institutions. Waltz (2000) responded to each of these by reasserting the primacy of self-help in anarchy and the centrality of power competition and balancing. Democracy is merely a unit-level change, interdependence (as opposed to complete independence) is a mask for selfish behaviour, and institutions are formed and persist only through the interests and efforts of powerful states (see Chapter 6).

The limits of security relate not just to the limits of change, but also to the constraints on ethical action. Realists tend to echo Machiavelli's (1532/1985: 61) claim that: 'For a man who wants to make a profession of good in all regards must come to ruin among so many who are not good.' Many realists view moral statements as a useful rhetorical device for justifying self-interested political actions but not as principles that guide progressive or successful political action. Thus, human security, conflict intervention and other seemingly ethical projects in security are viewed largely as a mask for the play of power (see Chapters 9 and 10). In spite of appearances, early realists did not dismiss ethics. Carr and Cox (2001: 65) viewed ethics as historically situated rather than universal truths, and saw the task and achievement of realism as revealing 'not merely the determinist aspects of the historical process, but the relative and pragmatic character of thought itself'. Similarly, Morgenthau's (2006: 12) rejection of ethical principles as a guide to politics is not an amoral position but a critique of moralizing (rather than morality). It espoused a different ethics of political life among power-seeking states: 'while the individual has the moral right to sacrifice himself in defense of a moral principle, the state has no right to let its moral disapprobation ... get in the way of successful political action, itself inspired by the moral principle of national survival'. The place of ethics in security was diminished by early realism, and later realists and neorealists have had little to say on the matter. This does not mean that their claims are ethically neutral. Many critical approaches raise ethical critiques of realism that emphasize how the diminution of ethics and change in classical realism make it complicit in producing an insecure world, and the determinism of structural realism imposes as well as describes rigid limits on security through a dramatic rationalization of political possibilities (see Chapters 3 and 14).

Liberalism

A static, tragic and pessimistic view is not as inherent to rationalist and state-centric approaches to security as realists and its critics often hold. Liberal theories of security are also characterized by rationalism and often by state-centrism but produce a different view of the logics and limits of security. In political theory, the Enlightenment tradition of liberalism emphasizes order based not on raw power but on law, justice and, more recently, human rights. Liberals thus share a common optimism that contrasts with the tragic pessimism of realism. They envision the potential for progress in interstate relations through generating common interests and forms of cooperation. While security is about stability in realism, more peaceful and just orders are possible in liberalism. Beyond this, liberalism offers several theories of security: some espousing economic liberalism as a path to peace, some emphasizing democratic governance, and others rule-based international institutions.

Contemporary liberalism remains largely state-centric, but this differs from realism in important ways. First, individual human beings are the ultimate valued object of politics and security, and liberalism has strong affinities with human security (see Chapter 9), but security politics is still largely analysed through the state as the most important actors in securing individuals. Second, other actors, like international organizations and nongovernmental organizations, are given independent importance rather than being viewed as mere masks for power-seeking agendas or arenas for interstate competition. Third, states are institutions that work as transmission belts for the interests and preferences of social groups and individuals rather than just being unitary actors with structurally determined fixed interests. Thus, conceptions of security are not fixed and homogeneous but changeable and multiple. This means that liberals emphasize the importance of preferences, where realists assert power. The global configuration of different interests shapes states' behaviour, but these interests are not defined only in terms of universal conceptions of power and survival but as constellations of preferences (it is therefore not a purely second image explanation since global interactions shape preferences and behaviours). States still act on the basis of rational cost–benefit calculations but may do so sometimes through cooperation and at other times through competition. Liberals differ on the sources of preferences, with some highlighting ideational factors related to identity, ideology and legitimacy, some focusing on material factors (particularly defined in economic rather than military terms), and others emphasizing the characteristics of state polities, particularly republican or democratic governance, as shaping preferences and behaviours (Moravscik, 1997).

Wider liberal political theory has a long history, with foundational ideas traceable to Locke, Kant and Bentham, who placed a great deal of faith in human reason to deliver progress. While realism views war as a natural and inevitable part of international relations, liberal thinkers believe that war is not natural (whether peace is natural varies more widely) and can therefore be abolished or at least significantly reduced. For Kant (2005), the way to build this perpetual peace was a combination of republican (not necessarily democratic) government domestically and a confederation internationally in which states agreed to abolish war. Likewise, Bentham argued that states often went to war because they misperceived their interests as in conflict, but that in reality 'between the interests of nations there is nowhere any real conflict' (cited in McGrew, 2002: 270).

While realists argued that liberals took the world as they would want it to be, liberals deny this and argue that the real world contains change, and human reason produces possibilities for a different politics. For Bentham, the experience of the German Diet, the Swiss League and the American Confederation showed that previously separate and conflicting states could come together in a federal system (Luard, 1992). Likewise, during and after the slaughter of the First World War, the first consolidated attempts to develop theories of international relations proceeded along liberal lines, in which domestic democratic governance and international institutions were emphasized as a path to peace. In interwar idealism, associated with Woodrow Wilson and the League of Nations, liberals sought to produce a different security politics from the balance of power politics that preceded it through the formation of a general association of nations. Security was conceived not only as national security but also 'collective security' based on the principle that the security of one is the concern of all and that security threats will be met with collective responses (see Chapter 6). Clearly, this failed, and the realist critique that these projects of peace paid too little attention to power politics is a compelling one, but extending this failure to a general distinction between a naive 'utopianism' and a grounded true realism is perhaps unfair, although obviously useful as a heuristic for early realists in establishing the dominance of their views.

While eclipsed by realism in security studies, post-Second World War liberal thought continued in two major strands. First, integration theories explored how states become integrated into cooperative arrangements, particularly in the context of increasing European cooperation. In the 1950s, Deutsch developed a liberal/constructivist theory of security that emphasized increasing transnational links that tied some states together into 'security communities', where war between some states became unthinkable and security relations are marked by extensive cooperation (Chapter 6). Similarly, functionalist integration theories, associated with Mitrany, argued that that cooperation in one area, such as trade, would lead to a range of collaborations in others, including security. Second, liberal pluralist theories emphasized a wider range of actors and argued that states should be seen as composed of competing individuals, government departments, bureaucracies and interest groups rather than simple unitary actors. Rosenau (1980: 1) claimed that 'international relations conducted by governments have been supplemented by relations among private individuals, groups, and societies that can and do have important consequences for the course of events'. While these give a different view of the international system than the realist anarchic realm inhabited exclusively by power-seeking or security-seeking states, dominant forms of liberalism in later decades accepted much of this content of realist thought, but not the conclusions realists assert.

Neoliberalism

Neoliberalism arose in the 1970s and 80s as a response to neorealism. It accepted neorealism's core premises of the need for a scientific approach to theorizing and basic concepts of international anarchy, the primacy of states, and even the nature of politics as power politics. However, it maintained the classical liberal emphasis on the possibility of progress through the independent and progressive role of international institutions, and the significance of democracy. It produced two major neoliberal approaches: interdependence liberalism, which evolved into neoliberal institutionalism, and democratic peace theories.

Interdependence and institutions

Interdependence neoliberalism, developed by Robert Keohane and Joseph Nye, built on integration theories and pluralism and argued that, by the 1970s, the world had become more pluralistic, with international institutions, multinational companies and transnational social movements, among others, shaping international politics as well as states. Within this plurality, proliferating channels of interaction and communication across national borders made actors more dependent on each other, such that national interests were served by mutual interests rather than competition. This constituted a different world to that predicted and valued by realists' emphasis on state autonomy, a world better described as a situation of 'complex interdependence', in which 'actors other than states participate directly in world politics, in which a clear hierarchy of issues does not exist, and in which force is an ineffective instrument of policy' (Keohane and Nye, 1977: 24). In this world, security does not necessarily dominate politics and violent means of pursuing security are counterproductive. However, this pluralistic view was soon simplified when neoliberals accepted that, for the purposes of theorizing, states can be seen as the main actors that rationally pursue their national interest. For neoliberals, those interests are not reducible to survival and security, and international rules and institutions, and transnational actors, shape these interests and the rational decisions of states.

While states seek power in neoliberalism as in realism, power is defined differently in an interdependent world. By emphasizing military forms of power, realists are bound to see the world as inherently violent and conflictual, and states as primarily driven by these motives. The old adage that 'if all you have is a hammer, everything looks like a nail' is apt: neoliberals identify a great deal of cooperation and peace in the world that realism ignores because of its military focus. Importantly, power is not fungible, meaning the most militarily powerful state does not set the rules for economic politics, or vice versa. Power is not purely a material capability but relates to '*organizationally dependent capabilities*, such as voting power, ability to form coalitions, and control of elite networks: that is, by capabilities that are affected by norms, networks and institutions associated with international organization' (Keohane and Nye, 1977: 55).

The emphasis on mutual interests, interdependencies and organizationally dependent views of power underlies the principal neoliberal alternative to the balance of power: international institutions. Pursuing more modest goals than interwar idealists, forms of collective and cooperative security practice are not viewed as emerging naturally from shared interests, but as immanent and realizable through the construction of international institutions. Two important types of institutions exist: organizations, which may be global like the United Nations (UN), regional like the European Union (EU), or specific issue-based organizations; and regimes, which are social institutions based on rules, norms (understandings and values) and procedures for decision making (see Chapter 6). For neoliberals, institutions exert causal force on states' relations by shaping their preferences and locking them into cooperative agreements. Cooperation in neoliberalism does not require altruism or philanthropic intent by states. Rather, like realists, states are viewed as 'rational egoists' (selfish and calculating actors), and thus under conditions of anarchy, in which agreements cannot be hierarchically enforced, neoliberals expect cooperation only when there are significant common interests (Keohane and Martin, 1995).

For neoliberals, cooperation is possible and desirable but not inevitable. International institutions assist cooperation in practical ways: they provide for information flow among actors, give opportunities to negotiate, often include monitoring of compliance with agreements, and sometimes have limited enforcement powers – they firm up expectations of behaviour and provide for some reciprocity. Importantly, however, institutions only mitigate the effects of anarchy and do not approach conditions of hierarchical governing (see Chapter 6). They enable but do not necessarily lead to fairer or better outcomes.

Neoliberal institutionalists argue that stable international order was maintained in the post-1945 world not because of deterrence and power balancing but because the postwar international institutions 'embedded' liberalism into the international system. When building liberal principles into organizations like the UN, the International Monetary Fund and the World Bank, the USA forsook short-term gains in return for a durable settlement that benefited all states – something that realism would not predict (Ruggie, 1982). Liberals also claim that institutions are durable in spite of changes in the distribution of power, a point that some neorealists concede but explain in different ways (see Chapter 6). While some structural realists come close to liberals in this respect, arguing that cooperation may, at times, be the best strategy for pursuing their interests (Glaser 1994/95), most see institutions as having no independent importance, thus presenting a 'false promise' of security (Mearshemier, 1994/95).

The difference between the logics and limits of security in neoliberalism and neorealism can be clarified by exposing the underlying assumptions of each on institutions in security. Mearsheimer's realist dismissal of institutions argues that they can have no effect on states' security behaviour because of three major points: states are selfish, short-term power maximizers; cooperation on security cannot eliminate power competition; and institutions are formed by self-interested states so there is always a fear of betrayal in military affairs. This argument, however, misconstrues the liberal view it is articulated against. To say that states are selfish does not reveal what gains they seek. For realists, states seek relative gains ('winning'), while for neoliberals, states may seek absolute gains ('doing well') (Snidal, 1991: 701). Further, while in realism states always seek relative gains, in neoliberalism the gains sought are variable and states sometimes seek relative gains and sometimes absolute gains, so the competitive logic of security is not fixed and universal. The question is under what conditions they will seek absolute or relative gains, and neoliberals argue that institutions shape these conditions (Keohane, 1993; Keohane and Martin, 1995). Directly contradicting Mearsheimer, the liberal view of states is of long-term utility maximizers not short-term gains seekers, so the first criticism is founded on a different view of what it means to say that states are instrumentally rational, calculating and self-interested (Donnelly, 2000). While realists claim that states will cheat on cooperation when an opportunity arises, liberals argue that cheating now invites being cheated on in the future, and institutions can help to 'lengthen the shadow of the future' (Axelrod and Keohane, 1985).

The claim that cooperation cannot eliminate power competition also misreads liberal arguments: the point of cooperation, and institutions, is not to completely eliminate competition, but to pursue goals that lead to greater (not complete) peace and stability (Donnelly, 2000). This aspect of Mearsheimer's dismissal relies on and reinforces the separation of domestic and international orders: domestic governing institutions clearly have some effect on stability, but the fact that they do not prevent all unrest and crime cannot be read as implying they have no effect. Further, Mearsheimer misses the point by claiming that because institutions are formed by self-interested states, they can have no effect. Donnelly (2000: 135) responds by saying: 'To use the currently popular phrase, "Duhhhhh!" If states don't want to cooperate, of course they won't form cooperative institutions.' Underlying Mearsheimer's point is the idea that anarchy means states will cheat, particularly in security politics. Yet, a wealth of empirical evidence suggests that cooperative security arrangements and institutions, while often imperfect, are not always cheated on (see Chapter 6). For neoliberals, states will invest in institutions where they see mutual benefits and greater opportunities for their international interests. Thus, most states see benefits in an open trade system, and are willing to support trade rules that support that against protectionism. In contrast, in areas where states perceive less mutual gain, they will be less likely to cooperate, or will cooperate to a lesser degree. Cooperation in security, then, may be more difficult to achieve, but neoliberal institutionalists reject the idea that political economy and security are separate worlds, with cooperation possible in one and impossible in the other (Axelrod and Keohane, 1985). Institutions hold more potential to produce rule-based order and cooperation in security than realists can countenance. They may be imperfect, but that does not imply they have no effect (see Chapter 6).

Democratic peace

While institutions may not hold the prospect of perfect peace, Kant's 1795 proposal for the creation of a perpetual peace has been influential in liberal security studies. This suggested three foundations for peace: states should be founded on republican (not necessarily democratic) constitutions; the law of nations to be founded on a federation of states – not a world government but more like a global peace treaty; and a law of world citizenship – not citizenship of a world government, but a limited citizenship based on universal hospitality under which people have the right to be greeted and treated as guests – think of the laws on asylum and refugee status. Current liberal security thought emphasizes the first of these, with much less to say on the others.

Kant (2005) suggested that certain conditions need to be met before these foundations could be established. These include:

(1) When states agree a peace treaty, they should not hold on to the possibility of future war.
(2) States, whether large or small, should not come under the domination of another by becoming property donated, inherited or otherwise.
(3) States should not get into debt when pursuing war.
(4) All standing armies should be abolished 'in time'.
(5) There should be a principle of not interfering by force in the internal affairs of another state.
(6) Practices in war that reduce trust in a future peace, such as espionage, incitement to treason, the use of poison and assassination, should be outlawed.

The second and fifth of these resemble the principle of sovereignty and noninterference in other states in international law that creates much debate today on issues such as humanitarian intervention and human security. The sixth can be found in some aspects of current international law (on chemical and biological weapons and assassination, but not espionage and treason). Perhaps the most jarring thought of all is the abolition of standing armies. While this may sound naive, the reasons for it are familiar within the concepts of the security dilemma and balance of power (see Chapter 5). Kant (2005: 4) claimed that standing forces 'are always threatening other states with war by appearing to be in constant readiness to fight. They incite the various states to outrival one another in the number of their soldiers, and to this number no limit can be set.'

Democratic peace theory is the main inheritor of the Kantian perspective. This begins with the empirical observation that democratic countries do not (or very rarely) go to war with other democracies. Some even claim that the 'absence of war between democracies is as close as anything we have to an empirical law in international relations' (Levy, 1988: 662). Democracies are not necessarily inherently more peaceful and they go to war as often as any other country, but this tends to be with nondemocracies rather than each other. There are three major elements to liberal explanations for the democratic peace. First, democratic governments tend to avoid war due to institutional constraints. Democracies are controlled by their citizens, who will not support wars as they will bear the costs and risks. Democracies also have complicated bureaucracies for approving war and these make a decision to go to war more difficult. Thus, democracy leads to better decisions about war and restrains the impulse to go to war (Russett, 1993). In other words, democracy causes caution. Second, democracies have shared values. Domestically, democratic states use peaceful means to resolve disputes and value human rights. The democratic peace is partly explained by states extending these values to their relations with other democratic states, and valuing peace more strongly than nondemocratic states. Because democratic states have a free press, transparency in decision making, an opposition party to outline alternatives and so on, they can more easily judge each other's intentions and thus can build relationships of trust that are not possible with nondemocratic countries (see Chapter 5). Third, democracies tend to be more interdependent economically and so there are 'crosscutting transnational ties that serve as lobbies for mutual accommodation' (Doyle, 1986: 1161). Conversely, mistrust with nondemocratic states can lead to a narrowing of contacts with them, creating less impetus for accommodation, fewer opportunities for it, and greater potential for minor conflict to begin a cycle of retaliation. Doyle claimed that through these three elements, liberal states have created a separate peace for themselves that has lasted three centuries and has expanded as democracy has spread. These explanations do not fully address why wars occur with nondemocratic states. This is explained by two further observations: liberal democracies are more 'imprudent' in their relations with nondemocratic states because the conditions that allow democratic peace are absent; and many of these wars have been defensive (the undemocratic states started it).

There are numerous criticisms of democratic peace theory. The empirical correlation between democracy and peace may not imply the liberal interpretation of causation. Simply put, this is a logical fallacy. There are more fire engines at big fires, more people die in big fires, but fire engines don't cause people to burn to death. Global consumption of opiate drugs also increased in a similar trend to the increase of democracies, yet nobody would claim that narcotics make the world more peaceful. Rather, reflecting their wider theories, realists reply that the balance of power explains the observed peace among democracies (Layne, 1994). Additionally, some accuse liberals of selecting evidence to fit their theory. Exceptions to the rule have been ignored, such as the USA sponsoring the overthrow of the democratically elected socialist government in Chile in 1973 and replacing it with a brutal military dictatorship under Augusto Pinochet (Ray, 1995), or several near misses when democratic powers came close to war (Layne, 1994). Further, the correlation depends on flexible definitions of democracy and war, such that some states at peace are counted as democracies when only 30 per cent of adults had the vote, and exceptions to the rule are ignored, such as imperial Germany in the First World War, or the 1812 conflict between England and the USA, by arguing that these cases were not democracies at that point, or that hostilities did not reach the level of war (Doyle, 1983; Ray, 1995). However, these technicalities produce relatively minor exceptions to the rule, and while it may not be a full 'law' of international relations, the proposition that democracies *very* rarely go to war with each other remains robust (Lynn-Jones, 1998). Indeed, some exceptions seem to prove the rule: countries undergoing transitions to democratic rule have demonstrated a greater propensity to go to war, but as they develop their institutional constraints and links with other democracies, their relations become more peaceful (Mansfield and Snyder, 1995). Overall, the democratic peace is neither proven by liberals, nor disproven by realists but simply demonstrates that widely differing accounts of causation in security relations can be applied to the same evidence.

If democracy, shared values and economic interdependence create secure, peaceful relations, then how can the world be made more peaceful? The prescriptive implications of the liberal explanation of the democratic peace are simple: spread liberalism around the world. This has been seen in numerous forms, from promoting democracy and free trade in international institutions to forms of liberal imperialism, in which powerful states engage in regime change through military intervention or impose liberal systems on weak states in the aftermath of conflict – known as the 'liberal peace' (see Chapter 10).

Conclusion

Traditional approaches to understanding security share a state-centric view, in which states are instrumentally rational calculating actors acting in their own self-interest. What those interests are and what patterns of behaviour are expected are more diverse and result in differing views of the scarcity or opportunities for security. The world of power-seeking and security-seeking states competing within conditions of anarchy has become the archetypal 'realism'. Encountered this simply, realism posits either sin or structure as the driving forces of insecurity that constrain cooperation and encourage competition. In abstract terms, these are reductionist accounts in which great variation in behaviour is attributed primarily to one source. In practice, most realists are not this reductionist, and do not view states merely as puppets whose actions are wholly determined by disembodied forces of anarchy and self-help. Most allow for some other factors to play some role, just not as strong a role as these basic characterizations. Evolving differences between realists on the strength of the power logics of security and the limits of security politics reflect deeper differences on rationality, the location and limits of political action, and the extent of change and the role of ethics. In this evolution, security itself has changed, shifting from being an objective condition and a subjective perception to become a purely objective condition in neorealism as the rationality assumption took central position, and objectivism further reduced security to strategizing on the basis of objective realities of the distribution of material military power.

In all rationalist approaches, security is primarily associated with stability. In realism, this may be produced by judicious power balancing to cancel out the effects but not the dynamics of military competition. For liberals, it is developed by building better institutions internationally or by democratization domestically, both of which enable more security behaviours to demonstrate cooperative logics that break the rigid limits to durable security and peace that realists purport to be universal and eternal. While liberal approaches often seek to explain and produce progress through reason, they have moved far from the utopian visions of collective security of interwar 'idealists' or Kantian hopes for perpetual peace. They have accepted the elementary facets of realist rationalism but emphasize different conclusions, in which the logics of security can include cooperation and mutual benefit not just competition, autonomy and eternal prospects of war. However, liberals are not all (or even primarily) pacifists and many see war as a tool for expanding the global reach of liberal values and systems. Holding a common basic rationality assumption, a focus on states, and an acceptance of international anarchy can still lead to widely divergent accounts of security. In Chapter 3, however, other alternative foundational assumptions reveal similar diversity among 'critical' approaches.

Chapter 3

Critical Approaches and New Frameworks

Chapter 2 explored the traditional theories of security found in various strands of realism and liberalism. While these are diverse, a range of new approaches to understanding security have emerged that have different foundations and pose different questions. These approaches are critical of the underlying rationalist assumptions of realism and liberalism. Some also criticize the traditional focus on military security and engage more with the broader range of security issues and deeper range of security referents discussed. They have tended to be more explicitly theoretical and have produced a deeper and more direct engagement with social and political theory (see Chapter 1). Much of the critique of traditional theory has targeted realism and neorealism, but is also critical of the assumptions shared with liberalism and the practices of liberal security that dominate many Western states' security politics. These new theories of security have evolved through disagreements with each other. For instance, in contrast to realism, almost all these approaches emphasize the importance of ideas as well as material factors in understanding security, but they differ on which ideas matter and how. Critical approaches not only give different answers to the questions posed by traditional approaches, but also ask different questions that they failed to ask and could not answer: they therefore differ on where security is to be found, produced and studied, ranging from the construction of national identity and international norms, through the discourses of security of political leaders, to the daily practices of security professionals or the daily insecurities of the poor. They also differ profoundly on the purposes of theorizing: from telling better stories about how security politics works, to telling the neglected stories of insecurity and security practice, to articulating alternative ways security politics could, and should, work. This chapter moves broadly from the first to the last of these projects. It will introduce and explore their key concepts and emphases as they are encountered throughout this book. It is increasingly common to refer to some of these perspectives as 'schools' of thought in which – by coincidence and design – particular universities or research centres became focal points for scholars with similar aims and assumptions. This chapter introduces constructivism, the Copenhagen School, the Paris School, poststructuralism, feminism, peace studies and critical security studies.

Constructivism and the Copenhagen School

Constructivism arose in IR theory in the 1980s, and was initially oriented towards a critique of the foundational assumptions of neorealism. Constructivism begins with the premise that all major concepts and categories of international relations are socially constructed. This means that human actors, and states, are not simply rational actors viewing the world objectively and calculating a utility maximizing strategy on that basis, but they interpret the world through a range of social values, norms and identities. These values, norms and identities are not naturally given, but are constructed in 'intersubjective' relations between people or states. When Alexander Wendt (1992) said that 'anarchy is what states make of it', his claim, against neorealism, was that anarchy is not an immutable force producing competitive behaviour among pregiven power-seeking or security-seeking states. To understand how and why states seek security, it is not sufficient to assume that states observe each other as a physicist observes atoms, but rather their interpretation of the capabilities and intentions of others are mediated by other factors – an actor's own identity and set of values always intervene in the process of viewing and acting in the world. The central constructivist argument is that states act on the basis of how they see themselves and others, and what types of behaviour they see as natural or desirable. While this is the main point of difference between constructivism and traditional security theories, there are many different forms of constructivism.

Some constructivists emphasize norms – sets of shared expectations and beliefs and assumptions that in turn guide states' behaviour – and identity as factors in international relations, but also accept much of the research programme of traditional theories, with a notable focus on states and a military-centric definition of security. Such constructivists seek to provide a richer and more compelling explanation for observed interstate security behaviour. Thus, Katzenstein's (1996) book *The Culture of National Security* used constructivist insights to show how different norms and identities shape how a state conducts its security practice. Likewise, Wendt (1999), Adler and Barnett (1998a) and others explored how states view each other on the basis of their relationships and identities rather than the comparatively simple calculations of intentions and capabilities. Building on preconstructivist work with similar claims (Deutsch, 1957), Adler and Barnett argue that states can become tied into 'security communities' where war between them becomes unthinkable (see Chapter 6). For constructivists, this offers a better explanation of the limitation of war than liberal democratic peace ideas. Since the norms, values and identities that states have are formed through changing social relationships, security relations are not eternal (as in much realism) but can change. While neorealism saw the distribution of material power as forming the structure within which rational calculating actors determine how to pursue their interests, constructivism sees the ideas, values and identities of actors as producing the structure within which they act and the interests they seek to pursue. Change in security, then, is not only about the distribution of military capabilities but also about the social foundations of action. For example, in relation to nuclear weapons, Tannenwald (2007) argues that a taboo against the use of nuclear weapons has developed, which explains why they haven't been used since 1945 much better than simple assertions of deterrence.

Other constructivists take the insights of social construction further to engage in productive critique by questioning IR and security assumptions more deeply – particularly the focus on states and military security. They disagree with Wendtian constructivists' largely successful attempts to insert themselves as a middle way between 'rationalists' and 'reflectivists'. Much of the focus of scholars, such as Onuf (1989) and Kratochwil (1989) in IR theory and Weldes et al. (1999) and Fierke (1998) in security studies, is on the constitutive role of language and how particular understandings of security, and particular assumptions of the importance of states and military security, become dominant.

Copenhagen School and securitization

Perhaps the most sustained and influential constructivist attempt to analyse how the language of security has real-world effects is found in the so-called 'Copenhagen School' and its central concept of 'securitization'. The key Copenhagen School scholars are Barry Buzan, whose influential framework of the five 'sectors' of security was discussed in Chapter 1, Ole Waever, who developed the concept of securitization, and Jaap de Wilde. While some critical approaches to security have normative intentions in retheorizing security, the Copenhagen School sought the more attenuated goal of developing a new framework for analysis (Buzan et al., 1998). This framework analyses how issues become 'security' issues and the implications this has for politics. Thus, Copenhagen School authors tend to eschew lengthy discussion of what *should* be a security issue, and how security *should* be practised, in favour of analysing *how* security issues are made. The concept of 'securitization' was initially developed by Waever (1995: 54) to criticize the apparent ease with which many security theorists engaged in debates about broadening and deepening the meaning of security by simply adding the word 'security' to more issues and referent objects. For him, this did not help in understanding what 'security' meant. His question was, simply: 'What really makes something a security problem?' His answer was that it is not something about the issue or actor that meant it was or was not a security issue. Rather, issues are made into security issues (or not). 'Securitization', then, is the process of making something a security issue.

Just as Buzan conceived of security sectors in spatial terms, Waever's securitization can be seen in this way. The act of securitization is about moving something between two realms: normal politics and security politics. Indeed, the Copenhagen School envisioned a spectrum on which different issues could be located. This ranged from nonpoliticized issues, through 'politicized' issues, 'meaning the issue is part of public policy, requiring government decision and resource allocations', to 'securitized' issues, 'meaning the issue is presented as an existential threat, requiring emergency measures and justifying actions outside the normal bounds of political procedure' (Buzan et al., 1998: 23–4). Here, security is not a positive value, a state of being secure or safe, nor is it the absence of threats nor the presence of sufficient power to deter them; it is a different type of politics – a different game with different rules and different players than we find in normal politics. In a clear division between normal and security politics, normal politics is characterized by relatively open decision making, long-term planning, consensual decision making, and the protection of civil liberties. Security is much nastier: in 1995, Waever likened the move to the Clausewitzean concept of war (see Chapter 7). Once war is begun, or security politics entered, politics functions by different logics. 'Security' sees the issues in its field as 'existential threats'– threats to the existence of something valued. These issues are viewed as high priority, urgent and demanding high resources, but also as requiring secretive decision making, aiming at short-term solutions within which the suspension or breaking of human rights and civil liberties and the use of violence become a possible (but not inevitable) feature. This echoes the political thought of Schmitt (1996), who theorized that it is through determining the exception to the rule (of open decision making and nonviolence, for instance) that sovereignty operates. 'Security' politics is an exceptional politics.

If securitization means moving an issue from one field to another, then it is important to look at how this is done, who can do it, and under what conditions. This is the main focus of the Copenhagen School framework. Here, Waever used Austin's (1962) language theory to characterize securitization as a 'speech act'. This means that when the word 'security' is spoken (or written), it is not merely a sign, a description of something; it is an action that does something. Just as making a bet or a promise is more than just a description, so too is the 'securitizing move' of calling something a 'security' issue. Thus, moving an issue into the field of security is achieved through an action consisting of speech. However, not everyone can successfully securitize an issue. For the Copenhagen School, the 'securitizing move' is an *attempt* to securitize. To be successful, the attempted securitization needs to be accepted by an audience. This is where certain conditions for success arise. Notably, none of these have anything to do with whether an issue really is what it is presented to be. Rather, it is that successful securitizing speech acts tend to portray something as an existential threat and thus tap into already existing themes in what we recognize as security issues. Further, those making the speech act have some recognized authority to do so, and so most Copenhagen School analyses focus on elite declarations and view securitization as a means by which state elites gain control over an issue.

Securitization, then, is a relatively simple concept prompting a clear set of questions about how issues become securitized. It is a productive concept for analysing the practice of broadening and deepening security and its limits. Thus, Buzan and Waever (2003) have used the framework to analyse how and why different issues and sectors are securitized in different regions of the world (see Chapter 6). The applications of Copenhagen School concepts in empirical analysis and the criticisms of them are too numerous to fully detail here, although they will be encountered at many points throughout this book. However, it is important to note the broader conceptual critiques of the framework. Broadly speaking, these argue that, in various ways, the framework fails to live up to the opening out of security that it begins. Security is seen as socially constructed, but the process by which this takes place, who participates in the processes, and what that process does are portrayed as much less open to the possibilities for change than the simple statement of social construction implies.

Debating securitization

One important aspect of securitization is the warning it implies about the dangers of treating issues through security politics. Those broadening and deepening definitions of security tended to see the securitization of new actors and issues as a positive move, one in which greater importance could be attached to previously neglected issues (see Chapter 1). For Buzan and Waever, though, moving these issues into security politics could be dangerous because the rules of the new game do not necessarily mean that better, longer term consensual decisions were made about them. For instance, poverty and environmental issues may be important but it is debatable whether they should be securitized (see Chapters 9 and 13). Waever has also claimed that while states may gain control over an issue by securitizing it, he had a normative preference for desecuritization: 'Security should be seen as negative, as a failure to deal with issues as normal politics' (Buzan et al., 1998: 29), and thus desecuritization for would be better for many issues. However, the process and possibilities for desecuritization are undertheorized (Aradau, 2004).

Others criticize the clear and rigid distinction between normal politics and security politics that both securitization and desecuritization rely on (Abrahamsen, 2005; Acharya, 2006). Clearly, not all securitized issues are dealt with the same way. Why this is, if one takes constructivism seriously, is as likely to be as socially constructed, not naturally given, as the initial question of why some issues are or are not securitized. Abrahamsen (2005), for example, claims that it may be more useful to conceive of a more nuanced 'sliding scale' of issues than a simple binary. For some, this is a broadly sympathetic critique leading to a need for greater nuance in the securitization framework. For others, there is more to it than the ability to tell ever more nuanced stories about security. Booth (2007) argues that the framework is flawed because while particular issues may be securitized or desecuritized, the naturalization of the distinction means that the security has an essence (as exceptional politics) and thus the nature of security politics is taken as given, unconstructed and unchangeable. It therefore does not allow significant theorization of how the nature of security politics might be changed. While recent securitization studies have added more sophistication to the clear division of normal and exceptional politics, and noted that exceptional politics works differently in different places (Roe, 2012), some critics of the Copenhagen School argue that the concept remains wedded to a process of security, in which security is achievable only at the expense of others, and through the instantiation of relationships premised on the Schmittian distinction of friend and enemy (Aradau, 2004). The question, then, is whether one needs to escape 'security' (Aradau, 2004), or whether it can be rethought and reworked in positive ways not premised on exclusionary 'us' and 'them' distinctions (Booth, 2007) (see below).

Further conservatism is evident in the Copenhagen School's empirical and theoretical emphasis on state elites. While any actor can, in principle, securitize an issue, it is state elites that are the focus of most analysis of securitizing moves, and also the main actors in the reified security politics. This is not to say that the Copenhagen School falls into the statist values (a preference for the state) of neorealist security studies. The framework it proposes integrates Buzan's five sectors (see Chapter 1); and while Waever (1995) notes that the referent object in these sectors often ends up being the state, he argued in favour of a 'duality of security', in which the main referent objects are the state (whose ultimate criterion is sovereignty) and societal security (whose ultimate criterion is identity). This has been criticized for reifying identity: treating identity as if it were relatively fixed. In contrast, McSweeney (1996) claims that identity has no referent other than the process of its formation, and the Copenhagen School misses out much of that formation.

The combination of theoretical paradigms evident in the Copenhagen School is also a cause of some tension. The framework is seen as a problematic joining of concepts, with Buzan's concepts having roots in realism (or at least the realist strand of the English School) and Waever's in constructivism and poststructuralism. This means that there are underlying contradictions in the framework, or at least that the sets of concepts it combines are uneasily married together. This is most clearly revealed in the ontological ambiguities that arise from combining such different underlying metatheoretical perspectives. For instance, are the sectors socially constructed or do they reflect some natural pregiven distinctions? Certainly, one important critique of Buzan's sectors is that while they enable discussion of the constructed character of security issues, they fail to recognize the constructed character of the sectors (Eriksson, 1999; Waever, 1999). It is common in social and political thought to use spatial metaphors like sectors to manage complex pictures of the world by distinguishing between different types of issues. However, in wider security thought, sectoral divisions do not just reflect different issue areas, but assert differing logics of behaviour. For Morgenthau (2006), for example, political man was different from economic man in that he (invariably he rather than she) operated on the basis of different *logic*. Further, the five sectors are relatively poor containers of issues, with many issues combining political, economic and social aspects that are securitized. For instance, many types of transnational security issues are securitized on the basis of multiple overlapping claims of threats to several sectors (see Chapter 12), which serves to amplify the portrayal of threat but may merely be the effect of counting one issue in several sectors. Overall, the theoretical status of sectors has been rather ambiguous. For the initial framework, the sectors were an analytic device rather than holding particular ontological status as functionally different realms in which actors and behaviours follow different logics. However, this initial view is in tension with the claim that securitization works differently in different sectors. Albert and Buzan (2011) have revisited this question and argue that the process of functional differentiation characteristic of modern social life, and the ways in which sectors (parts) relate to each other and the social whole, holds great potential for the future development of securitization studies, in which the strengthening of differentiation in contemporary life is a focus. This does not replicate Morgenthau's appeal to politics as an autonomous sphere into which other issues should not intrude, but nor has it (yet) displaced the differentiation of security politics and normal politics as essentially different and distinct realms.

Some critics have also claimed that the reliance on speech acts potentially limits the framework. It neglects other ways in which security is presented that may have securitizing effects, such as visual representations in the media (Williams, 2003), the claims made or implied by security experts and practitioners in their everyday practice (Bigo, 2002), and even violent physical practices (such as so-called 'honour killings'), in situations where security need not be spoken to be justified (Hansen, 2000). Others question the applicability of the framework outside Europe and Western models of 'normal' democratic politics, although the framework is applicable to nondemocratic contexts where the relevant audience may be different but the process may be similar (Wilkinson, 2007).

The concept of securitization has continued to evolve and prompt debate (Balzacq, 2011). Indeed, both Waever's securitization and Buzan's sectors have moved beyond their origins and become integral to much security studies discourse, especially in Europe. Both concepts have a life beyond their uneasy marriage in the Copenhagen School framework. The term 'securitization' is widely used in the security literature, although often in the most literal sense (of something or some actor becoming defined as a security issue) without necessarily bringing with it all the Schmittian politics, sectoral distinctions and speech act theory that it initially combined. Recent developments in securitization theory include empirical applications and amendments via studies of HIV/AIDS, environmental security, rogue states, religion and regional security. Theoretically, many of the limitations of securitization theory have become fruitful arenas of debate and development. Some now argue that the idea can be used to develop normative approaches to security (in spite of the avoidance of such issues in the initial framework) (Floyd, 2011). Many others have gone beyond the initial speech act theory. Balzacq (2005) argues that successful securitization depends on speaking in ways that resonate with audience experience (a more audience-centred approach) and that successful securitization is more context dependent and power-laden than the initial theory recognized. Such expanded securitization theory has produced a greater exploration of the relationship between fear and securitization and an argument that fear may resist not just enable securitization (Williams, 2011), and has also opened up theoretical debate on what it means to 'act' (Huysmans, 2011) and to 'cause' (Guzzini, 2011). This has done much to mitigate the early essentialism of the framework and clearly takes securitization beyond the realm of a key concept within a framework for analysis into a powerful and expanding research agenda.

Poststructuralism and the Paris School

'Poststructuralism' emphasizes some similar themes to constructivism such as identity formation, and an emphasis on language, or more widely on discourse, is a stronger theme in poststructural work than constructivism. However, poststructuralism has tended to call into question the basic categories and concepts of security studies in a much deeper way than most constructivism. Indeed, for some critics of poststructuralism, this is all 'they' do.

There is often little common ground among 'poststructuralist' work, and those to whom the label is applied often reject it almost as vehemently as they reject the common alternative 'postmodernist'. While many draw on continental social and political theorists and philosophers, such as Foucault, Derrida, Bourdieu and Deleuze, this body of work does not provide a simple framework to be straightforwardly applied to the study of security. However, Campbell's seminal *Writing Security* (1998a: 4–5) locates itself in a ground of dissent that much poststructuralist work could be seen to share:

> My argument is part of an emerging dissident literature in international relations that draws sustenance from a series of modern thinkers who have focused on historically specific modes of discourse rather than the supposedly independent realms of subjects and objects. Starting from the position that social and political life comprises a set of practices in which things are constituted in the process of dealing with them, this dissent does not (and does not desire to) constitute a discrete methodological school claiming to magically illuminate the previously dark recesses of global politics.

For Campbell (1998a: 5), this form of dissent does not speak from a position of knowing where all other theories have gone wrong, but rather it 'celebrates difference'. It is not, as many approaches' engagements with each other seem to be, 'concerned to seek a better fit between thought and the world, language and matter, proposition and fact'. Rather, it 'questions the very way our problems have been posed in these terms and the constraints within which they have been considered, focusing instead on the way the world has been made historically possible'.

Campbell analysed US security discourse to argue that the formation of national identity is bound up with identifying threats, or rather identifying others as dangerous. Following a broadly Derridean argument, he showed that an identity is produced in discourse, rather than given. In this production, identity is always defined in opposition to something different. This does not rest on objectively identifying facets of similarity and difference between the self and other, between 'us' and 'them', but the assertion of total difference of radical, dangerous and threatening 'others'. Thus, national identity is formed by seeing enemies. This construction of national interest and security differs profoundly from the assumptions of rationalist theories, in which states view others with suspicion because of international anarchy and power competition. Campbell's detailed analysis of foreign policy texts showed that US identity was produced and continually reproduced by demonizing the USSR in the Cold War, and later a range of other post-Cold War threats. This produced strong boundaries between the self and other and the domestic and the international.

This production of difference is found in rationalist theories of security as well as security practice. Klein's (1994) poststructuralist analysis of realist strategic studies argued that it did not merely describe the world of security and strategy but was constitutive of it (see Chapter 1). Rationalist security approaches operate on the basis of dichotomies between 'us' and 'them' – domestic and foreign, peace and war, and order and anarchy. These are not objective and given but produced and reproduced in theoretical discourse (see also Ashley, 1988). Klein (1994: 5) argued that strategic studies provides 'a map for the negotiating of these dichotomies in such a way that Western society always winds up on the "good" ... side of the equation'. Importantly, it is the production of these dichotomies that sets the place of violence in security, rather than the eternal objective truths of anarchy and human nature (in realism), or the moving of issues into a potentially violent sphere of security politics (in the Copenhagen School). Violence is related to the constitutive role of strategic theory, in which theoretical and national distinctions are established and 'strategic violence is then called in to mediate the relationship, patrol the border, surveil the opponent and punish its aggression' (Klein, 1994: 6).

Practice and insecuritization

Recent poststructural work also looks at the Copenhagen School's question of securitization but takes a broader view of what this means and how it takes place. The so-called 'Paris School' has drawn on Foucault and particularly Bourdieu to produce an 'international political sociology' of security. The emphasis in this work is on *practice* rather than grand speech acts by elites. Didier Bigo, the most prominent of 'Paris School' scholars, has argued that 'insecuritization' (rather than securitization) takes place through the daily practices and assumptions of security practitioners in a world of bureaucratic decisions, surveillance techniques, and the web of competitive relations among security agencies, government officials and private companies. Beyond securitizing speech acts and audiences, the management of insecurity is framed and justified by these daily practices. Importantly, this insecuritization is not a declaration of an existential threat that is made, and accepted by a general audience under certain conditions, as in the Copenhagen School, but is the cultivation of a wider sense of 'unease' and worry in relation to the wider uncertainties of daily life (conceived as risks) (see Introduction and Chapter 4). It is this fear and unease that is managed by security professionals (Bigo, 2002). Here, it is not that security speech precedes security action, but that insecurity is enacted (not just spoken) and meaning follows action (Aradau and van Munster, 2012).

In their detailed empirical work, Bigo and others have shown that the production and reproduction of binary distinctions such as 'us' and 'them' and 'inside' and 'outside' are changing as they take place in this field of security professionals. The development of policing bodies beyond national borders, such as Europol, is said to be changing the distinction between inside and outside. Indeed, the (re-)production of the inside-outside distinction has been a major theme in poststructuralist work (Walker, 1993). Poststructuralists reveal that inside and outside are not separate hermetically sealed realms, but are connected and rely on each other in mutually constitutive ways (Bigo, 2001a) (see Chapter 12). Likewise, they emphasize that liberal states increasingly use and justify 'illiberal' (exceptional) practices in their management of insecurity, such that the supposed tensions between security and liberty are understood and practised in particular ways (Bigo and Tsoukala, 2008). Here, 'insecuritization' extends the already justified and routinized logics of previous practice. Thus, with its emphasis on daily practice and diverse forms of 'insecuritization', security and normal politics are not two distinct realms, and a focus on the speech acts of major actors misses much of what securitization does:

> The result of the (in)securitization process cannot be assessed from the will of an actor, even a dominant one. The actors never know the final results of the move they are doing, as the result depends on the field effect of many actors engaged in competitions for defining whose security is

important, and of different audiences liable to accept or not that definition. (Bigo and Tsoukala, 2008: 5)

The 'Paris School' is a prominent example of a wider 'practice turn' in international and security theorizing. Emphasizing both discursive and non-discursive practices, and blurring the already indistinct lines between constructivism and poststructuralism, practice theories have increasingly been used to explore security and insecurity. Classical realism is also a practice theory (Brown, 2012), but the 'Paris School' approach goes beyond wisdom in statecraft and looks at the daily practices of security professionals. This is not only a shift in the level of analysis, from state leaders and elites to workaday security actors, but also an elaboration of an analysis of the production of practices and how they themselves produce the logics and limits of security. Drawing particularly on Bourdieu's concepts of field, capital and habitus, such practice theories emphasize the theorization of how security is practised (Bigo, 2011; Brown, 2012). Bourdieu's concepts are complex but they can be summarized. Field is a fairly self-explanatory concept, pertaining to a relatively autonomous social space within which actions, interactions and transactions take place (a sports field is an appropriate metaphor). Within a particular field (not sectors), certain rules and logics of play hold. In a field, actors compete and cooperate and form hierarchies through material, symbolic and cultural resources ('capital'). Habitus is more complex but can be grasped (somewhat problematically) as habits: as dispositions, tendencies, inclinations to act in a certain way. These are often unspoken assumptions and expectations. In security studies, this approach has been developed by Williams (2007) and Adler and Pouliot (2011), among others. Pouliot's (2010) in-depth analysis of NATO–Russian diplomacy showed that what counts as practical knowledge, effective diplomacy, is related to how diplomats construct a field that also structures their actions through their habitus, and that through this, NATO (North Atlantic Treaty Organization) and Russian diplomats – former enemies – have constructed a common field. Importantly, for many such scholars, it is the 'logic of practicality' (Pouliot, 2008) that shapes security interactions rather than the abstract realist logics of power or constructivist logics of appropriateness. The logics and limits of security, then, are set and evolve in practice rather than being theoretical abstractions of universal human nature, global anarchic structures, or exceptional politics.

Poststructuralist practice

Security work that draws on major poststructuralist thinkers has looked at most major themes of security, from deterrence (Klein, 1994), proliferation (Mutimer, 2000), war and violence (Reid, 2003; Dillon and Neal, 2008), human trafficking (Aradau, 2008), the role of virtuality and the media (Der Derian, 2009) and many others. The focus on the practices of security has been used to analyse a range of other issues including insurance (Lobo-Guerrero, 2010) and migration (Bigo, 2002; Huysmans, 2006) (see Chapter 12). It has explored, usually in considerable detail, a wider range of sites and practices of security than other approaches. In spite of this, early criticisms of poststructural work remain pervasive: that it is a 'self-indulgent discourse that is divorced from the real world' (Walt, 1991: 223).

Perhaps the more biting critique of poststructuralist work is of its emphasis on deconstructing key concepts and binaries that have been formative in security theory and practice but its failure to articulate an alternative. However, Campbell's (1998b) work on the Bosnian War and many of the sociological works in recent poststructuralist security studies represent sustained and important attempts to show the silencing of alternatives in much security discourse and the possibilities that reveals. The logic of this deconstruction is further reflected in an antipathy to 'metanarratives' that would assert a superior view of security that can lead to abstractly articulated alternatives. This is the central response to criticisms that poststructuralist work leads to nihilism and is self-indulgent: the production of overarching alternatives would fall into the same traps poststructuralists criticize of producing knowledge claims that are deemed to be more stable than they can be, more real than they are. Thus, while deconstruction and other poststructuralist work share some goals with other critical approaches to security (reflexivity and the questioning of foundational concepts), they do not share in the same understanding of the projects of theorizing security as telling more accurate stories or articulating overarching alternatives.

Feminism

Feminists draw attention to how security theory and practice has tended to be blind to gender, but still shaped by it. Beyond that, however, feminist perspectives are diverse. Indeed, the term 'feminist' is often added to other designators of theoretical approaches, such that there are poststructuralist feminists (V. Spike Petersen), liberal feminists (Cynthia Enloe), standpoint feminists (J. Ann Tickner), critical/radical feminists, postcolonial feminists and so on. Of course, all security theories are a combination of influences and perspectives, but it is striking that this habit of using compound adjectives only applies to feminist work. However, feminism does more than draw out gender dimensions in combination with applying other theoretical frames to security.

Enloe (1989) was one of the first to highlight the hidden gender dimensions of military security practice. She showed how women's work as teachers included roles inculcating nationalism, and how their roles in unpaid work on military bases supported both their husbands' military careers and the relations of US military bases with local communities. More broadly, she showed how the international domain relies on a gendered division of labour, and military relations that were seen as the preserve of men are supported by the work of women. Other feminists, however, criticize this for simply adding women and gender into broadly realist understandings of international politics (Steans, 2009).

Feminist scholars have gone further than this, and examined not just the role of women but the construction of gender. Both critical and poststructural feminists have shown that among the formative dichotomies of security theory and practice is the socially constructed distinction between masculinity and femininity. For Tickner (1992), security relations are portrayed in terms usually seen as masculine (competitive and security related to strength, aggressiveness and violence), while domestic politics is defined in terms seen as more 'feminine' and peaceful. Thus, realism, in particular, has relied on gendered discourse but failed to recognize it. It has also failed to recognize that gender distinctions on the qualities associated with men and women are social constructions not inherent in biological sex. Poststructuralist feminist work goes further and claims that even biological sex, on which we often superimpose gender distinctions, is also constructed – in the sense that it is a contingent assembling of factors such as appearance, psychology, gonads and chromosomes that often but not always produce easily identifiable 'male' and 'female' (Butler, 1990; Petersen, 1992). For Judith Butler and Petersen, gender is reproduced or 'performed' in daily practices that also reproduce power relations that are often violent (in terms of structural violence – see below).

Whether seeking to raise the profile of women and gender, or going further to question and explore the construction of gendered categories and power, feminist security scholars have increasingly engaged in wider empirical research as well as continued theoretical critique. Recent feminist contributions include work on the experiences of women in war in ways that complement and extend practice theories. Indeed, standpoint feminism is primarily concerned with empirical analysis of the experiences of women. While much feminist work in IR has steered away from the central questions of war, recent scholarship argues that feminist perspectives on war conceive it not as the interplay of states, military institutions and weapons, or even strategic relations, but as a set of social relations of experience. Feminist experiential accounts focus not only on the causes of war between rational egoist states but on the conduct and effects of war. This draws attention to the effects of war on bodies and the role of emotions neglected by rationalism. Feminist perspectives foreground the body as an agent and target in war. Such bodies are not the material home of the reductionist strategic rational egoists of realism and neoliberalism, but experience and act on rationalities inseparable from emotion. Rationalist approaches to war abstract much of the corporeal and emotional content of war for men and women, boys and girls (Sylvester, 2012). Feminists also draw attention to the conduct of violence. The identification of women as victims, while often empirically accurate, has not necessarily challenged the processes of gender construction even as international security politics has engaged in supposedly gender-sensitive forms of political action on their behalf. Laura

Shepherd (2008a, 2008b) examined UN Security Council Resolution 1325, which argues for sensitivity to gendered dimensions of violence and inequalities in armed conflict and conflict interventions, but does so in a discourse that reproduces women as a category viewed as a homogeneous group of 'peacemaker/victim', thus neglecting the diversity of 'women' and their roles in violence as well as peace, and perpetuating the equating of gender issues with the status of women as neglected victims of violence. Indeed, many representations of women in security discourses portray women in this way, and particularly rely on motherhood as a device for representing them (Shepherd, 2008a; Åhäll, 2012). In this way, the gender-blindness of security theory has practical effects: killing by women in war is relatively neglected, and thus post-conflict measures designed to reintegrate soldiers into peaceful life tend to ignore this experience (MacKenzie, 2009). Likewise, the role of women as terrorists and terrorist recruiters has been neglected in spite of empirical evidence that women constitute 25 per cent of suicide bombers and half of terrorist operatives in some countries (Bloom, 2011).

The achievements of feminism have prompted greater attention to wider issues, including the experiences of men and boys, not just women and girls, such as in the conduct or observation of rape in wars in the Democratic Republic of the Congo (Baaz and Stern, 2009) and Bosnia (Hansen, 2001). Indeed, Sylvester (2012: 498) argues that war requires the perpetrators of violence to engage in gendered behaviours and experiences that, following Enloe (2010), she calls 'militarised masculinity'. Studies of armed violence increasingly highlight how young men and boys are the primary victims of armed violence, including but not limited to gang-related criminal violence and violence within civil wars, in which some forms of sexual violence, forced conscription and sex-selective massacre are gender specific towards men and boys (Carpenter, 2006). Indeed, while often discussed together, 'women' and 'children' have different experiences of vulnerability, oppression and physical violence. Age, however, remains a neglected dimension of security theory, with the exception of studies of child soldiers (Singer, 2006; Gates and Reich, 2009). Likewise, gender is implicated in other categories of political and social life that are important in the study of war and security, such as the production of race, class, nationality and ethnicity (Handrahan, 2004; Hudson, 2005).

Feminist scholars have also added much to the broadening of security. Early feminist work identified a limitation in traditional security perspectives, in which the insecurity of women experienced in war and in wider systemic oppression was 'not taken seriously' (Petersen, 1992: 49). The broadening of security into more humanitarian concerns and issues of the daily insecurity experienced by people rather than states has not improved this neglect as much as might be assumed. Thus, the concepts and practices of human security (see Chapter 9) often neglect gendered differences in referring to a homogeneous concept of the human, but feminist scholars argue that grounded gendered approaches offer a means through the tension between universalism and cultural relativism that besets human security debates by strengthening the articulation of security from the bottom up (Hudson, 2005; Hoogensen and Stuvøy, 2006). Nevertheless, feminist engagement with broader security has continued to challenge foundational assumptions and aporias. For instance, feminist work on human trafficking for purposes of sexual exploitation highlights the experience of victims rather than the border-centred security approach to trafficking of much policy and practice in this area (Lobasz, 2009).

Feminists have contributed theoretical resources that go beyond the production or neglect of gender dimensions to question the nature of rationality, the relationships of power that are relevant to security, the nature of the state, and the possibilities for less militarized security politics. They pose a continuum of violence and power, where traditional security studies sees a clear distinction between war and peace. Further, grounded in experiences and a wider range of power structures, feminist security studies has a different view of the logics and limits of security from traditional approaches. As Blanchard (2003: 1290) claims, 'feminists contest the possibility of a perfectly controlled, coherent security policy that could handle every international contingency', and focus instead on how security is 'always partial ... elusive and mundane' (Sylvester, 1994: 183).

If the practice and theory of security rely on silenced gender distinctions and hierarchies, the question remains of what is to be done about it? For liberal feminists, drawing out the role of women and perhaps increasing the role of women in decision making is sufficient. For poststructural feminists, it is impossible to speak for all 'women' as if they had particular perspectives and interests to bring to bear on security practice, and thus the political practice needed is the continual deconstructive process of critique and questioning that they engage in. For Tickner (1992), however, theorizing security is a normative activity, which may necessitate some arbitrary speaking for 'women' to avoid yielding the ground to those security theories that speak only from a masculine perspective. However, this is no easy task. As Carol Cohn (1987) showed in relation to traditional security paradigms and their 'technostrategic' discourse, it is difficult to be heard when speaking a different language in conversations dominated by 'militarised masculinity'. Thus, most traditional, and much critical, security studies has been limited in its engagement with feminist thought (Sjoberg, 2009). Yet, for Tickner and Cohn, the reconstructive aspect of critique is as essential as it is difficult.

Normative security theories

Many critical approaches to security articulate normative concerns that seek not only to incorporate the ethical into existing theoretical frameworks but also to construct alternative securities. As noted, much feminist scholarship holds strong normative commitments integrated with wider theoretical critique and reconstruction. However, much normative security theorizing has alternative foundations in other fields or in wider normative critical political theory.

Peace research

Thinking about security in alternative and explicitly normative ways has a long history beyond security studies. Peace research/peace studies is best conceived as a parallel discipline to security studies rather than a school within it, although it is often noted as a productive field for much critical theorizing about security (Booth, 2007; Buzan and Hansen, 2009). Peace studies has largely developed in empirical rather than theoretical works, and these are often unabashedly positivist in their method and epistemology. However, since its origins in the 1950s, it has always been explicitly normative and transformative in its intent. Many of its key concepts are borrowed by critical schools of security. For example, Galtung (1969) drew a distinction between direct violence and structural violence. Direct violence includes war, but also other forms of interpersonal violence. Structural violence is the violent effects that are built into social structures and manifest as unequal power and the resulting unequal life chances that accompany economic, race, gender and other forms of discrimination. This has clear parallels with much critical security studies, and has been taken on by feminist scholars like Tickner. Peace studies has also striven for building both 'negative peace' (the absence of direct violence) and positive peace (the presence of social justice and the absence of structural violence), largely with an emphasis on using only nonviolent means. The fact that critical security studies has entered much of the ground once explored and developed by peace studies should not blind us to the fact that there is a long, if often problematic history of thinking about security and peace beyond the orientation of 'new' theories of security that articulate themselves against realism and each other.

Critical security studies

Perhaps the most prominent explicitly normative theoretical perspective is the so-called 'Welsh School' of critical security studies (CSS). This approach aims to produce a different form of security politics and practice. The most well known scholars in this school are Ken Booth and Richard Wyn Jones. Over the past 20 years, these scholars and their colleagues have drawn on Frankfurt School critical theory (particularly Adorno, Horkheimer and the more recent work of Habermas), as well as other post-Marxist work, especially Gramsci, to develop a critique of traditional and other theories of security and to reconstruct an alternative view. While Wyn Jones (1999) developed the first and most substantial exploration of the relationship between Frankfurt School critical theory and the project of CSS, it is most often Booth's 20-year project that provides the most sustained attempt to develop a wide-ranging school of thought.

A key point of departure for CSS and many other critical approaches was Robert Cox's claim (1981: 128), drawing on Gramsci and Frankfurt School thinkers, that there is no such thing as a value-neutral international relations theory. He claimed that 'theory is always *for* someone and *for* some purpose'. All theories have a perspective and neorealism's claims to be scientific and value neutral did not hold true in their practice even if its values were masked by those claims. Following Horkheimer's distinction between traditional and critical theory, Cox distinguished between 'problem-solving' theories and 'critical' theories. Problem-solving theories claim to be neutral representations of the world and therefore assume that much of the world politics they see is natural and unchangeable. They task themselves with managing problems to ensure the smooth running of the international system. Critical theories are those that attempt to stand outside (in a non-value-neutral way) prevailing structures and seek to change them. They too see a lot of problems in the world and seek to solve them, but they see the problems as arising from the way the world has been made to work and thus focus on deeper problems that the problem-solving theories take as natural. CSS views security as a derivative concept: definitions of security – in terms of the actors and issues included or excluded, and what is hoped for when speaking about security – derive from particular social and theoretical positions. It is not a simple reflection of an external reality, but a reading of a reality it was implicated in producing. Realism, then, is an ideology: 'a theory of the powerful, by the powerful, for the powerful' (Booth, 2005a: 5–6).

Booth (1997) has referred to himself as a 'fallen realist' and has developed a wide-ranging and emphatic critique of realism that is worth outlining at length, not least because the development of CSS has significantly relied on it. Booth (2005a: 5–6) claims that realism is 'not realistic' (it doesn't present an accurate picture) and is 'a misnomer' (it is an ideology that has 'appropriated the cloak of objectivity and practicality'). Further, it is static, it describes an inevitable and unchanging world of conflict that, by definition, is presented as 'the best of all possible worlds' (Booth, 2005a: 6). As a result, it is methodologically unsophisticated, being based on a 'crude positivism' with a lack of theoretical reflection, has failed 'the test of practice' by producing a world with much insecurity and suffering, and has regressive, unspoken assumptions – privileging the victims of politics (war) over the victims of economics, human rights abuses and the neglect of gender and race. Importantly, its approach to security has too narrow an agenda, and as a result, its ethics are 'hostile to the human interest' – by being state-centric and portraying the international as a world without ethical choices, and their theory as unconcerned with ethical matters. Further, it will probably remain so because all questions and challenges are dismissed due to realism being 'intellectually rigid' (Booth, 2005a: 6–7). Booth's discussion of realism, then, is no sympathetic critique, no addition of norms to the material interests of states, no call to add women (or race, or the poor) to an existing framework. It is a vehement and complete rejection of all that realism held dear, held itself to be, and held to be 'real' and natural in the world (although, importantly, not of all the debates it had produced). However, Booth's point is not to ignore the 'real' world. In agreement with critical realists (in the epistemological sense) (see Chapter 1), he claimed that what is at stake in theoretical debates is 'not whether one should be a realist, but of what kind' (Booth, 2005a: 10)?

For realists adopting a positivist epistemology, we know the real world through sense experience. For postpositivists, discourse and intersubjectivity are real. For Booth and CSS, power is conceived in material and representational terms and thus both are real. Further, these contested and competing claims to the truth simply reflect that 'what is real in the social universe is created by the theory conceiving it. Truth is elusive and disputed, but it is essential for the functioning of human relations at all levels' (Booth, 2005a: 10). This means that there is no easy divide between theory and practice, as theory is constitutive of the social universe. If theory is constitutive (see Chapter 1), then realism and other ideas it helped legitimate had contributed to the production of:

> an imperfect present and a future tense with danger. Poverty, oppression, war, misery, death, and disease are the everyday realities of life across swathes of humanity; then add fear, and stir. Debilitating and determining insecurity seem to be in permanent season, and *you and I, him and her, and us and them* will never be what we might become as long as human society, globally, is imprisoned by the regressive ideas that sustain world insecurity. (Booth, 2007: 11–12)

In contrast, CSS articulates an alternative view of security that is 'conceived comprehensively, embracing theories and practices at multiple levels of society, from the individual to the whole human species' (Booth, 2005a: 15–16). It therefore embraces much of the broadening and deepening of security. In particular, it emphasizes the security of human beings, but not as essential individuals divorced from communities and the intersubjective relations that form identity. While deriving its normative intent from the security needs of individuals, CSS emphasizes that 'community is the site of security' (Booth, 2007: 278). This is a more open and flexible 'community' than found in Buzan's societal security, but less celebratory of all difference found in poststructuralist works. CSS seeks to support inclusionary and emancipatory forms of community against exclusionary ones that may combine, in overlapping ways, to produce 'the potential community of all communities – common humanity' (Booth, 2007: 31).

Emancipation

The central concept for rethinking security, and the central point of distinction between many other critical schools of security and CSS, is 'emancipation'. This is where CSS owes most to the Frankfurt School, as well as ideas drawn from peace research. In CSS, security is not to be juxtaposed with liberty or freedom. Rather, security is freedom from life-determining threats:

> Security means the absence of threats. Emancipation is the freeing of people from those physical and human constraints which stop them carrying out what they would freely choose to do ... Emancipation, not power or order, produces true security. (Booth, 1991: 319)

This is important in the normative work of CSS. Emancipation is not just the end point, a picture of a better world against which the realist-influenced world can be compared. Rather, it is both the end point and the means to achieve it. 'Ends are means' for Booth (2007: 112) and 'Emancipation is the philosophy, theory and politics of *inventing humanity*.'

This contrasts with the normative aspects of the Copenhagen School. Their preference for desecuritizing issues to remove them from the negative politics of security is seen as insufficient for several reasons: security would remain associated with survival – thus, when free from threats to physical existence, people would be 'secure' (Booth, 2007: 107) – and it would mean that the nature of security politics goes unchallenged. For CSS, desecuritization risks issues losing their political importance, while securitization subjects them to a potentially militarized and undemocratic politics. This is no solution; rather, the challenge is to politicize security, to change security politics (Booth, 2005a).

How, then, to do so? In the abstract, emancipation may seem as unquestionably virtuous as it is difficult to achieve. Thus, Booth's *Theory of World Security* (2007) articulated an 'emancipatory realism'. Two further concepts are useful to clarify how this is imagined. The first is the sense of hope that is needed to imagine emancipation: 'Hope, it must be stressed, is categorically different from optimism: it involves a refusal to rule out the possibility of a better future, but – unlike optimism – does not assume it' (Booth, 2007: 179). Such hope is absent in any view of the world that sees the world as unchanging, while optimism places faith in inevitable human progress (as found in liberalism). The possibility for hope is raised by not taking the world as it is to be given in its nature, but as historically produced. The point of historical (as well as social) construction is that other possibilities remain, there are always unfulfilled potentials for a better world (see Chapter 1). Thus, the key practical task of CSS is conceptualized in terms of practising immanent critique, which

> involves identifying those features within concrete situations (such as positive dynamics, agents, key struggles) that have emancipatory possibilities, and then working through the politics (tactics and strategies) to strengthen them. Emancipation is a politics of careful calculation as well as of hope. (Booth, 2007: 250)

Such careful practical and historical engagements with security from a broadly CSS perspective have included a substantial reconsideration of the security dilemma (Booth and Wheeler, 2008) (see Chapter 5); security in Southern Africa (Booth and Vale, 1997) and the Middle East (Bilgin, 2004), failed states (Bilgin and Morton, 2002), the potential for trust in nuclear arms control (Ruzicka and Wheeler, 2010), ballistic missile defence (Peoples, 2010), and providing a foundation for a critical terrorism studies with similar goals (Jackson et al., 2009a) (see Chapter 11).

Critics of CSS

Linking security and emancipation is one major contribution of CSS, but it is also the ground on which it is criticized. For many critics, 'emancipation' is a concept too closely associated with a particular Enlightenment project that tends towards its own hegemonic and disempowering metanarrative. Further, the linkage between security and emancipation, indeed their conflation, may mean that emancipation 'can no longer envisage social transformations outside of the logic of security' (Aradau, 2004: 397). This is a particularly concerning problem if one accepts the broader Copenhagen School assertions of the historical linkage between security and exceptional forms of politics. Indeed, the close links between security and emancipation may foreclose options for transformative change that it is intended to produce. Both Aradau (2004) and Peoples (2011) have pointed out that unifying security and emancipation has tended to mean that CSS paid little attention to the possibility of violence in emancipation, or the importance of resistance as well as emancipation in transformative change. Importantly, while the ethical force of CSS's case for transformative change may seem compelling, there are other grounds for 'hope' beyond Booth's. For some critics of CSS, the resources needed are to be found in other post-Marxist thinkers such as Ranciere and Badiou, or in the struggles of the Frankfurt School's own Herbert Marcuse in thinking about violence (Aradau, 2004; Peoples, 2011). Further, other approaches that offer hope for emancipation, such as human security, do so on alternative foundations and interpretations. Some, like Tickner's feminism, are utilized by Booth, but others, like human security, are dismissed (see Chapter 9). Simply put, one can share the goals and some of the values of CSS without accepting Booth's specific formulations.

Conclusion

Critical approaches developed over the past two decades have enriched the theoretical terrain of understanding security. While often arising at the same time as debates on broadening the scope of security and deepening its referent objects, these approaches do not all embrace that process, and have not primarily developed through participating in that debate. Rather, they have made understanding security deeper in its theoretical and normative reflections by drawing on a wider range of theoretical perspectives, traditions and techniques to produce a diverse set of theories and frameworks of security (see Chapter 1). They have raised new questions and given new answers to old ones. They differ in their theoretical building blocks, with many adopting some form of postpositivist approach and shifting the ontological foundations of understanding security towards an emphasis on processes of construction, ideas and identities. They have revealed and spoken for the neglected and silenced dimensions of security missed in the military, state and rationalism-centred approaches of traditional approaches. However, they differ on where security is made or found, with answers ranging from the mediating role of norms and identities to elite speech acts, bureaucratic techniques and discourse; from unseen work and hidden violence to exceptional politics or the daily lived insecurities of millions.

Critical approaches significantly challenge the universalism and naturalism of traditional approaches, pointing to differences (and their construction), change, and the importance of ideas, discourse, daily practices and the practical effects of security theorizing. This means that the logics and limits of security are different in critical approaches. While realism is dominated by the logics of power, self-help and anarchic structure, and liberalism by a logic of progress through reason via institutions and democracy, critical approaches assert varying logics, such as the logic of appropriateness in relation to norms and expectations, the logic of exceptionalism in securitization theory, the logic of practicality, the dynamics of discourse, or the potential paths towards security as emancipation. Similarly, while the central role of rationality assumptions in realism and liberalism hold in place the limits and potentials of security, different logics and theoretical insights move these limits. For realists, security is scarce and progress limited, and ethics are denied importance, thus setting strong limits on how much security is possible, how it can be sought, and how structural pressures can be mitigated. For liberals, the limits are less universal or intransigent, but evolve and are overcome on the basis of reason. For critical approaches, the limits of security are instantiated more by the habits of thought about security than by natural or semi-permanent conditions of international life. This does not make all critical approaches 'idealist' rather than realist, although their critics sometimes replay this old distinction. Instead, the limits of security derive from intersubjective relations that, while not easily manipulated, contain immanent and often neglected possibilities for transformation. Chapter 4 explores the logics and limits of security within states, and the role of the state as a security provider, since particular understandings of 'internal' security set much of the foundation by which the international is viewed differently as a less secure, more limited arena of the logics of power, fear and violence that traditional approaches assert and critical approaches mitigate or reject.

Chapter 4

The Sovereign State and Internal Security

The sovereign state is often viewed as the primary actor in security politics and the primary provider of security to its citizens. Indeed, the development of sovereign states is centrally related to issues of security and binds security in relationships between authority and legitimacy, territory, community and violence. In most understandings of security, the distinction between domestic and international security is produced and policed by the state. The logics and limits of security are posed in radically different terms, with internal security provided through the rule of law and the gradual professionalization of policing, and external security provided in interstate relations via the military and diplomatic organs of the state but governed by anarchy and self-help. This chapter examines understandings of the state and its internal security roles. First, it explores how security is related to concepts of the state and processes of state formation. It then discusses states' internal security practices through an exploration of the supposed pacification of domestic social relations, and the practices of policing and surveillance. Many of these go beyond the commonsense notions of security through control and domination found in understandings of security. It then explores contemporary transformations of the state and its security roles as these have come to cross and reconfigure the boundaries of internal and external security and public and private in how security is provided. These transformations are also increasingly entangled with moves towards homeland security that are reconfiguring the responsibility for and conduct of domestic security practices and politics in Western societies. Thus, the chapter explores how sovereign states provide security, how security itself is conceptualized in this practice (moving from physical protection to the protection of ways of life), and how the state is continually reproduced and evolving in this process.

Understanding the state

The sovereign state is the primary actor in many understandings of security. It is also a foundational concept of much political theory, sociology, criminology and geography. Indeed, the development of the social sciences and statistical methods has been shaped and driven by the state's need for knowledge. Given the centrality of the state in many theories of security, it is surprisingly under-theorized in security studies. However, there are several different concepts of the state (Hobson, 2000). The most common definition of the state comes from

Weber (1919/1991: 78), who claimed that 'a state is that human community which (successfully) lays claim to the monopoly of legitimate physical violence within a certain territory, this "territory" being another of the defining characteristics of the state'. While a common reference, Weber's concept of the state is something of a middle-ground theory. Narrower concepts of the state see it merely as the most (militarily) powerful actor in a territory that establishes control and authority on the basis of force. This is the essence of the state in Hobbesian terms, and the character of the state in a range of Marxist and realist views, and those of some historical sociologists such as Michael Mann and Charles Tilly. Wider conceptions speak of the state as an idea and an entity with responsibilities not just power. This is closer to the Weberian view but also includes liberal approaches that see the state not only as a powerful actor demanding allegiance, but also as an actor with responsibilities to the society it contains, governs and represents; and neo-Marxist Gramscian approaches that view the state not only as material power but also as an ideational hegemony.

The state combines ideas and material factors and techniques. Some see it as the outgrowth of the idea of the social contract, and the technical and material aspects of the state are put in place to deliver the contracted public goods (including security). Others see material aspects and governing techniques as preceding and producing the idea of the state, in more multifaceted and complex accounts, such as Mann (1993) and Tilly's (1975, 1985) emphasis on military technologies, Soja's (1971) emphasis on cartographic techniques as enabling the growth of the territorial state, or Anderson's (1991) claim that nations are 'imagined communities' of symbolic allegiance produced in part through the print media. Differing views of the state have implicitly shaped the definition, limits and logics of security. The traditional view of security as national security, in Morgenthau's (2006: 382) words, relates to the 'integrity of the national territory and of its institutions'. This captures much, but not all, of the essence of Weber's state: it is the territory and the institutions that govern it. In contrast, Buzan (1991: 65–6) goes beyond the narrow Weberian concept to claim that the state and its security comprise three elements: the 'physical base' comprising territory and population in a relatively unified form; the institutions of the state that govern the physical base; and the idea of the state 'which establishes its legitimacy in the minds of its people', conceived largely in terms of national identity, which defines much of the relationship between state and society. Indeed, this echoes many perspectives on the development of the nation-state as comprising, at minimum, a combination of sovereignty (including legitimacy and authority), community, territory and violence (Held, 1995; Pierson, 2004). Each of these elements have a central relationship with security.

Sovereignty

The state claims sovereignty: it claims to be the supreme legitimate ruling authority within a given territory. In most concepts, sovereignty is indivisible and absolute and no other actor can claim co-sovereignty within a territory nor any right to intervene in the territory and politics of a sovereign. Krasner (1999) argues that there are four meanings of sovereignty that have varied over time:

(1) *International legal sovereignty:* the principle that all states are equal under the law and they are legally recognized as independent.
(2) *Westphalian sovereignty:* the Westphalian state as a form of political organized based on the exclusion of other actors from holding political authority within a given territory.
(3) *Domestic sovereignty:* the formal organization of political authority and the ability of public authorities to exercise effective control.
(4) *Interdependence sovereignty:* control over the movement of information, ideas, people, goods, capital and so on across the borders of their state.

The first two relate to authority and legitimacy, but not necessarily to control. This is sometimes referred to as de jure (in law) sovereignty. This contrasts with the de facto (in fact) sovereignty characterizing the last two meanings, which relate more to effective control. That all four have become associated with the 'state' in a particular configuration of authority, territory and population (society, nation) is due to the long and continuing process of the formation of states and the state system. To the extent that these are legal rules by agreement, produced through interactions among states (and earlier entities) in long historical processes, sovereignty is socially constructed (Biersteker and Weber, 1996).

This implies that sovereignty is composed not only of power, but also authority. As the history of state formation progressed from absolutist and monarchical states in the 15th century to the modern nation-state traceable to the 1789 French Revolution, notions of legitimacy and authority have shifted. Rather than being embodied in a divinely authorized monarch, the notion of 'popular sovereignty' emerged, in which true authority lies with the people (who become citizens rather than subjects) and the state is representative of and responsible to them (Axtmann, 2004; Pierson, 2004). This built on earlier ideas, found in Hobbes, Locke and Rousseau, that the sovereign state is founded on a 'social contract', whereby members of a society create a sovereign, giving it the right to coercive means, in exchange for protection (of life or property). This mythic implied contract, perhaps given form in constitutional documents, establishes a particular relationship between sovereignty and community.

Community

Communities are (relatively large) groupings of people. The state is the dominant form of political community. In principle, communities could be based on any commonality: religious or ethnic identities being strong possibilities. However, in the modern sovereign state, it is the dual and related notions of nation and territory that have come to predominate. Nationality, and nationalism, relate to an invented identity of a community of persons sharing some cultural commonality among themselves and some difference with 'foreign' others. The notion of the nation-state as the (relatively) perfect overlaying of social and political identity does not often hold and the two are best seen as mutually constitutive human inventions. Security and insecurity are constitutive of states and nations as forms of political community. Echoing Schmitt's claim that the distinction between friend and enemy is the essence of politics, it can be claimed that the fear of death at the hands of an enemy is mediated by the protective role of the state (Huysmans, 1998). Further, the fear of enemies and the protection against them is central to the production and reproduction of a community such that states must constantly articulate a threat against which they promise security (Weldes et al., 1999). Thus, security is not just a category of political issues, nor even a basic function of the state, but an idea that is productive of the state. Further, war has often made communities: through wars of 'national liberation' national identities have been formed and reinforced. So, the state is an exclusionary political community (defined by what and who it excludes) as well as an exclusive (sovereign) arrangement of political authority. This, however, is not inevitable, and is challenged by critical theorists and liberal cosmopolitans who articulate the potential for other forms of political community based on universals such as human rights.

Territory

States are territorially defined exclusive political communities. As noted in Chapter 1, the conflation of territorial space and political authority has led much IR, and social science more broadly, into what Agnew refers to as the 'territorial trap': the set of assumptions about the territorial nature and boundaries of political and economic life that permit state-centrism in theoretical approaches (Agnew and Corbridge, 1995). What is now a familiar and settled form of international politics – the global system composed of sovereign states – was not achieved until the latter part of the 20th century, after several periods of decolonization removed formal empires and colonial powers and (non-sovereign) colonies from the political map. However, the origins of this system are usually understood through the myth of the Westphalian state. The Peace of Westphalia, the two treaties of Münster and Osnabrück that ended the Thirty Years' War in 1648, is presented as beginning the period in which political units were to be defined territorially rather than by any other commonality, and sovereignty was, in the first instance, over territory not people (as in tribal or other authority structures). According to this central myth of IR, prior to this point, political life took the form of numerous overlapping forms of authority and identity: the church, local lords and others all claimed authority, as well as sovereign kings and queens. However, there are some important problems with this account. First, the foundational assumptions of the Westphalian myth are highly questionable, such as the presentation of the Thirty Years' War as a struggle between those wedded to a modern concept of state sovereignty and those loyal to the pope and the Habsburgs seeking universalist government and control over religious affairs (Krasner, 1999; Osiander, 2001; de Carvalho et al., 2011). Further, the post-Westphalian territorialization of political authority was a thoroughly European development, and the range of developments and forms of political authority in other parts of the world do not conform to an easy linear development from overlapping identities and authorities towards a national sovereign, a secular politics, or the primacy of territorially defined political communities. Finally, the links between territory and authority are evolving, and the implications of 'globalization' for the territorialization of politics are hotly debated, as are the implications of transnational and seemingly deterritorialized threats of crime, terrorism, disease and environmental degradation (see Chapters 12 and 13). Nevertheless, territory remains a central defining point of statehood and political life.

Violence and war

The monopoly on the legitimate use of force is a major or even the primary defining feature of the state. Simply put, violence is something that states can do legitimately, and all others do illegitimately. Weber (1919/1991: 78) invoked Trotsky's claim that 'every state is founded on force' and argued that:

> If no social institutions existed which knew the use of violence, then the concept of 'state' would be eliminated ... Of course, force is certainly not the normal or the only means of the state – nobody says that – but force is a means specific to the state.

However, the relationship of state formation and the potential for violence is more complex than this. Indeed, historical sociologists argue that the state was produced through violence and continues to have a strong relationship with violence (Giddens, 1985; Tilly, 1985; Mann, 1993). As Tilly (1975: 42) famously said: 'War made the state and the state made war.' Rather than the liberal social contract, Tilly characterizes the state as a 'protection racket', in which the process of territorial consolidation, the centralization of sovereign power, the growth of large bureaucracies and the monopolization of violence occurred because of the building of effective military forces in order to fight wars against other states.

However, the creation of the state is also seen as separating violence from much political life. The central achievement of the Peace of Westphalia is seen as the secularization of political authority that established rationalism not religion as the basis for politics (Buzan and Hansen, 2009). What this meant, supposedly, was that war could no longer be fought for religious reasons (if one ever really had been), but rather a rationalism in which the legitimate grounds of conflict and causes of war could only be material not abstract ideas. For Williams (1998: 215), this restriction of the notion of threat to material terms not ideational ones placed 'the discourse of war and peace within the bounds of *physical* threat and the capacity for it was a pacifying move'. This distances violence from domestic politics in two important but problematic ways. First, it feeds the modern myth of religion as a cause of war and secular politics as somehow less violent and more enlightened, a view that now informs debates on religiously motivated terrorism (see Chapter 11). Second, it instantiates the inside-outside distinction in which domestic politics is not an arena of violence that is confined to international relations. This claim of pacifying internal security continually runs up against the plethora of civil wars and human security concerns of daily encounters with state-perpetrated violence.

State-building

The development of the modern nation-state and the states system can be said to have emerged gradually, falteringly and incompletely over the past five or six centuries (or more). That states have become the dominant form of political authority and action in international relations, and in security relations between states and within their territories, is due to what Linklater (1998) refers to as the 'totalising project of the state', in which the state gradually claimed to have a monopoly on the right to use force, the right to mediate disputes among citizens, the right to tax, the right to demand undivided allegiance from its citizens and to be the sole subject of rights and representation in international law.

The state and its predominance is not historically static and its totalizing project is not necessarily complete or permanent. Indeed, Booth (2007: 75) argues that:

> Grammar has achieved what history could not. It has produced a universal type out of historical entities that have come in all shapes and sizes ... The ideal model of this universal type is the textbook Western state.

This is not just a theoretical issue. Much international politics and security politics seek to attain and reinforce this ideal type as an existing phenomenon. New states continue to be formed, albeit relatively infrequently, usually as an aim or solution to violent conflict, and seek to establish exclusive territorial control and international recognition, as with the recognition of Timor-Leste in 2002, Montenegro in 2006 and South Sudan in 2011.

Likewise, the ongoing politics of possible Palestinian statehood and the incomplete international recognition of Kosovo as an independent state reflect the value of sovereign statehood. In addition to ongoing politics of de jure sovereignty and recognition, the politics of de facto sovereignty in so-called weak and failing states has grown over the past decade, such that the ability of governments in such countries to control territory and provide security have become major concerns in global security agendas and practices (see Chapter 10).

Security practices

There is no universal model of how states organize their security practices. While Western states have a strong division between policing and military organizations, with the military role confined to international roles rather than domestic law and order roles, this is not the case in many other states. For some observers, the different organization of coercive capabilities reflects the limited development of the state in some places, placing them further back in a linear history of state formation. Others argue that it is an artefact of imperial rule and the uneven and unequal conditions produced in the development of global capitalism. While in current security discourse, the notion of 'weak' and 'failing' states relates to their inability (or unwillingness) to provide security for their citizens (see Chapter 10), it is notable that this inability does not mirror the international power of the state. Indeed, most rationalist approaches to international security assume that states have strong abilities to determine and control domestic politics but differ widely on how much agency states have in their international interactions (Hobson, 2000).

Empirically, the ability of the state to provide physical protection (a narrow view of security) for its citizens is historically and geographically variable. Certainly, as states in Europe developed stronger bureaucracies and ever larger and more sophisticated policing and penal systems, from the 16th to the 18th century, everyday violence declined from high levels (Ruff, 2001). More specifically, homicide rates show a marked decline from the 16th to the early 20th century (Eisner, 2003). This can be explained partly in relation to the growing sophistication of law enforcement institutions and sanctions against violent behaviour and partly by the development of social norms against violence and their deeper internalization as norms of individual self-restraint, which Elias called the 'civilising process'. However, it is important to note that a decline in violence did not merely accompany the rise of the modern state. Indeed, the decline in homicide rates in the West was reversed in the second half of the 20th century even as states grew stronger (Eisner, 2008). There is also considerable variation that challenges such explanations. For example, US homicide rates have not shown this long-term decline, but saw growing and consistently high levels of homicide in spite of its wealth, education and democracy (Monkkonen, 2002). Indeed, the USA and Russia have homicide levels similar to many less developed countries (Geneva Declaration, 2008).

The provision of protection from violence that is seen as a central role of the state incorporates wider security issues and the relationship between protection, privacy and liberty. Two major areas of domestic security provision here relate to policing and surveillance as the central means by which states secure (or not) their citizens. Here, it can be seen that traditional theories adopt a view of the state as protector, while critical views argue that the state arises through protection and that protection (through policing and surveillance) becomes a mode of governing.

Policing and protection

Probably the dominant and commonsense understanding of security provision by the state is as the protector of populations and property through policing and penal systems. Here, an important distinction can be made between policing and the police. The former is an aspect of social control that seeks to preserve the security of a particular social order, particularly through 'the creation of systems of surveillance coupled with the threat of sanctions for discovered deviance' (Reiner, 2010: 5). While policing activity is generic to all societies in some form, the police, as formal state organizations, are more specific facets of the modern state. Policing, therefore, is not just what the police do, but a wider set of practices that are associated with the institutions of the state. The growth of what we now know as specialized and professional police accompanied not just the growth of the state but of more complex and stratified social orders of class (Reiner, 2010). Indeed, the police are a more recent invention than the state. The development of professional police forces began in the 18th century, particularly with the formation of the Bow Street Runners by author Henry Fielding in London in 1749. Over time, the police have taken on a great range of tasks, from directing traffic to protecting against terrorism, maintaining social order in situations of protest, unrest, and, in many places, forms of political repression. For Reiner (2010: 7), what unites these diverse functions is that they all 'arise in emergencies, usually with an element of at least potential social conflict'. While the police use various legal powers and other techniques, he argues that 'underlying all their tactics for peacekeeping is their bottom-line power to wield legal sanctions, ultimately the use of legitimate force'.

In many Western societies, particularly in the aftermath of the 9/11 al-Qaeda attacks on New York and Washington, security practices, ranging from powers of surveillance, legal frameworks for punishment and deportation, to the security systems at airports, ports and many public places, have changed. This is often seen as reconfiguring the balance between liberty and security – a central dimension of concepts of the social contract formative of the state. Critical scholars, however, see this notion of balance as deeply problematic. Bigo, and others, analysed attempts by the EU to promote itself as an 'Area of Freedom, Security and Justice', and argued that while previously the rule of law was seen as an absolute, and liberty and security were closely linked, the post-9/11 resurgence of a logic of balance poses liberty and security as competing values requiring differing strategies and a careful trade-off. In this equation, he claims, security becomes privileged over liberty: security trumps liberty (Bigo et al., 2007).

Beyond this notion of balancing liberty and security, a deeper distinction relates to whether policing practices are to be understood simply as protecting social order or also producing it. This is a deeply political question. Couched in terms of protection, the nature of society is pregiven and the job of the state is to identify breaches of law and order and punish offenders, although there are debates about whether the role of prisons should be to exact punishment, deter crime, or rehabilitate offenders. In this view, found in liberal understandings of the state and traditional criminology, the state is interposed between civil society and criminal (or terrorist) threats. In contrast, critical security scholars and criminologists emphasize that the identification of certain people and acts as criminal is part of constituting a community (and therefore the state). In critical IR theory, Linklater (1998) claims that while relations of difference, imbued with threat and danger, are constitutive of political communities, these are not just differences between the national and the foreign but also between the civilized and the criminal or the insane. More widely, the production and policing of this distinction is a central theme of much of the poststructuralist social and political theory of Foucault. Drawing on critical theory and/or Foucault, some criminologists and security scholars see crime and security as not just the object of governing, but policing as a technique of governing. For example, Neocleous (2000) claims that policing fabricates rather than just protects social order, and that liberalism narrowed the concept to one of social protection in ways that masked the expansive set of institutions (beyond the formal police) in which policing takes place. In his study of crime control in the USA, Simon (2007) argues that the USA has been increasingly characterized by 'governing through crime', in which the fear of crime and the logics of protection have spilled over from the 'war on crime' to dominate diverse aspects of daily life from schools, workplaces and even within the family.

Surveillance

Security relates to knowing about threats and risks, and knowing relates to information (see Chapter 5). In relation to policing and public order, knowing and protecting relate to surveillance and the detection and punishment of deviance. While surveillance, watching people, has been a feature of all governing, the centrality of surveillance in securing Western societies has grown substantially in recent years. It has not, however, grown merely in response to global terrorism, in which changes were so fast and substantial that political debate could raise the prospect of a balance of liberty and security, but through slowly evolving and expanding forms of information collection and analysis.

Debates on surveillance also oscillate around a balance between liberty and security, particularly framed as privacy vs security. This is a potentially dangerous framing as it poses a symbiotic relationship between being secure and the ability of the state to know about all kinds of aspects of our lives. Chesterman (2010), for instance, bases his criticism of this framing on a Rawlsian version of the social contract and claims that the choice between liberty and security overly polarizes the debate but that the social contract is being reformed through emerging surveillance practices. Others derive inspiration from Foucault's complex analyses of the techniques and logics of governing to argue that changing surveillance practices reflect and produce transforming modes of governing. Foucault famously drew on Bentham's design for a prison, the panopticon – a design in which guards in the centre of the prison can see all prisoners simultaneously, but the prisoners do not know when they are being watched and therefore act in an orderly fashion consistent with being watched. For Foucault, this captured a form of governing in Western societies where much of the work of producing and policing social order was achieved by making people (like Bentham's prisoners) discipline themselves. Social order, then, was produced not just by the central power of the state to punish, but by inculcating discipline into the population. Some recent analyses of surveillance claim that contemporary Western surveillance practices now go beyond this disciplinary mode and are much more decentralized and are built into the circuits of everyday life. Surveillance is practised by a range of actors, from the state to private companies and beyond. Here, individuals are not just monitored – as seen in the expansion of CCTV cameras in public spaces – but are also encountered not as unitary individuals but as a diverse set of data points, from fingerprints and biometrics at the airport to online transactions (Amoore and de Goede, 2005; Muller, 2010).

Interpreting these changes, Lyon (2001) claims that many Western societies are now 'surveillance societies' – societies dependent on information and communication for administrative and control processes, in which surveillance is pervasive, and power and surveillance are dispersed rather than centralized. In this diverse system, security is encountered as risks (relations of the probability and harm arising from an event, such as crime or terrorism) rather than threats (related to the intentions and capabilities of specified enemies). Indeed, many social theorists argue that contemporary governing increasingly operates through the management of risks, of complex and unpredictable safety and security problems created in part by the complexities of modernization (Beck, 1992) (see Chapter 5). Here, insecurity cannot be eliminated only managed. The logics of risk are related to the surveillance society, as surveillance seeks to reduce uncertainty and control outcomes by understanding and managing risk. For criminologist Richard Ericson (2007), the prevailing obsession with security across different spheres of life has been fostered by neoliberal governments and produced huge expenditures on risk assessment and management, which, ironically, increase uncertainty. This has also produced 'counter-law' (law against law), where the traditions of due process, the presumption of innocence and so on are increasingly replaced by suspicion and precautionary logics (Aradau and van Munster, 2007; Amoore and de Goede, 2008). This includes the expansion of surveillance systems such that there has been a criminalization of the merely suspicious and of security failures – the presence of vulnerability when those responsible for security fail in some way. For Ericson (2007), the result is that 'security trumps justice, and uncertainty proves itself'.

Should this be seen as the logics of security taking on such a dominating position that all aspects of daily life are submitted to its voracious appetite for surveillance and control? The answer is often a qualified no. Rather than simply replacing threat for risk, and liberty for security, what emerges in Western societies is perhaps better seen as what Rose (2000: 322) calls a:

> hesitant, incomplete, fragmentary, contradictory and contested metamorphosis, the abandonment of some old themes, the maintenance of others, the introduction of some new elements, a shift in the role and functioning of others because of their changed places and connections within the 'assemblage' of control.

Indeed, Garland (2001) has argued that just such an inchoate assemblage of new and old ideas, in often contradictory forms, characterizes the schizophrenic late modern 'culture of control' in US and UK penal practice. Certainly, most of these trends in surveillance are a peculiarly Western development. However, they raise wider themes of the dispersal of security practices across multiple places, and in relationships between the state and other actors, that can be seen more broadly as transforming the role and significance of the state in providing domestic security.

Transformations

The role and scope of state provision of security in various forms are changing. Processes of globalization and the rise of transnational threats and security practices mean that the traditional distinction of the internal and external functions and politics of security are being reconfigured. As security issues widen and states are reconfigured, the foundational state monopoly on security provision erodes and is supplemented by relations across another key distinction, that between the public and the private. Combining these trajectories of transformation, national and international security are increasingly interlinked and dispersed, as security is redefined as 'homeland security' and the objects of protection shift towards dispersed networks of physical and virtual critical infrastructure.

Globalization, transnationalization and the territorialization of security

Increasingly, the central place of the state, and the predominance of sovereignty, territory and state monopoly on violence, is changing and may even be unravelling. For some, this is the outgrowth of economic and social 'globalization' that undermines the coherence and centrality of the state. 'Globalization' is not a singular process, a move towards the global scale of political and economic interactions, but a set of increasing interconnections and flows that are uneven and fragmented. These include the flow of goods and trade, the migration of people, information flows and communications, and the transnational spread of cultural values. Two key facets and effects of globalization are the growing power and authority of private actors (Hall and Biersteker, 2002), and the declining power and authority of states (Strange, 1996). While globalization is seen predominantly in economic and social terms, both trends have been observed in relation to security; the former in relation to the rise of non-state sources of threat such as terrorist groups, insurgencies and organized crime, including the supposed migration of coercive (violent) power to non-state actors (Davis, 2009), and the latter in relation to the ability of weak and failing states to provide security or the ability of all states to tackle transnational threats (see Chapters 10, 11 and 12).

There are three major ways of interpreting such changes:

- as the breakdown of the Westphalian system, interpreted negatively as a source of threat and insecurity
- as the maturing of systems of governance above the state, potentially in more effective or more cosmopolitan directions (see Chapter 6)
- as a more complex set of contingent transformations, in which old and new forms of governance, security and insecurity reconfigure (rather than erode) familiar distinctions produced alongside the modern state.

The first perspective views globalization as signalling a return to the overlapping and contested forms of political authority (and thus the control and use of violence) seen before Westphalia, a form of neomedievalism (Cerny, 1998). This is often interpreted as inherently threatening and damaging to security, such as the dystopian vision of Kaplan (1994: 8), who pointed to a 'coming anarchy' of disorder and violence as the state became merely one of many levels and actors of order and security. Here, 'city states and the remaining nations' could be 'confused in places by shadowy tentacles, hovering overhead, indicating the power of drug cartels, mafias, and private security agencies'. While extremely hyperbolic, these transnational and non-state security issues and actors are now central to many states and international organizations security agendas. Hyperbole remains part of this discourse, however, as the US National Intelligence Council (2008: 108) predicts 'a "shadow" international system by 2025', as criminal organizations 'penetrate' governments in areas rich in energy resources (see Chapter 12). But globalization is a deeply ambiguous process, both in its character and extent and its implications. The second perspective sees the development of multiple layers of governance within, above and beyond the state, as potentially enhancing the governing and provision of security (cf. Krahmann, 2003; Wood and Dupont, 2006; Kaldor, 2007). Mabee (2009: 145) argues that the state is no longer at the centre of security concerns as it 'loses the ability to exclusively provide insurance against contingency', as security issues increasingly arise at the global and local levels and the state functions of governing and providing security are integrated with institutions at other levels. Indeed, much security practice and politics are practised not only at the local level but also within, among and by regional and other international organizations. The degree to which these sites of security politics engender different forms of security practice among states and the degree to which security can still be defined as a state-centric politics are hotly debated (see Chapter 6). The third perspective, which may or may not accompany the second, is that distinctions of inside-outside are being reconfigured such that the connections between the realms are more relevant than the distinction itself. For Mabee (2003, 2009), the change goes beyond the multiple layers of security governance and affects internal and external dimensions of security. The role of the 'security state' as provider of security internally and externally is a recent (postwar) construct, in which the security provision of the state domestically (through policing and wider social security such as healthcare) was linked to the growing integration of the state in the international political economy; thus, the security role of the state produces globalization and is reconfigured rather than eroded by it (Clark, 1999).

These changes are connected to changing relationships between territory and security. While the territorialization of political life has been profoundly important, the particular form of post-Westphalian territoriality does not have a universal or timeless quality (Murphy, 1996). Indeed, this particular territorialization of political community has become naturalized and has therefore limited notions of the political and simplified notions of security. In particular, it has meant that any other spatiality of politics, economics or security is conceived of as 'deterritorialization' – a loss of any relationship between territory and politics – a new development brought through globalization and in conflict with stability and security. Thus, globalization is seen as facilitating the rise of transnational threats to state security and the protection the state can provide. Echoing the dystopian interpretations of globalization noted earlier, threats from transnational crime and terrorism, in particular, are portrayed as freed from the confines of territory, as endlessly flexible and adaptable and posing deep challenges for states whose security practices remain bound by legal and territorial boundaries (see Chapters 11 and 12).

Critical forms of security studies and criminology emphasize not only the transnationalization of threats, but also the transnationalization of security practices. Here, changes in policing and protection are not just a feature of a self-contained national scene. Rather, there are extensive and expansive transnational dimensions to the production of crime control as a logic of governing. The growth of transnational policing and related regional and international institutions, articulating themselves against transnational criminal threats, are an increasing feature of the politics and practice of policing (Sheptycki, 2000). There is a growing international body of technocratic police experts through which particular concepts and practices of policing, like community policing, are being spread (Reiner, 2010).

More broadly, amid the globalization of flows of information, goods and people, governing and protecting people increasingly emphasize their flow and the monitoring of flows as well as the traditional territorial forms of state security provision. For Bigo (2006: 97), this means that 'territory is not homogenised and purified, but rather is delineated as trajectories of flows and a channelling of the population living in the same territory'. There are several changes here; the object of governance is population not territory, and policing occurs at a distance – distance meaning territorial but also temporal, a policing of the future. Bigo (2006) argues that this changes the meanings of protection. The traditional dual meanings of protection of the individual by providing a safe space and protection of national territory through defence have come under strain and a third meaning of protection has become more dominant, particularly in Europe: the monitoring of individuals and groups through the technologies of filtering, channelling and surveillance of individuals for their own protection. More broadly, this implies a reconfiguration of the inside-outside distinction, such that the two are not distinct spheres of security politics and practice, but increasingly intimately connected. Bigo (2001a) uses the image of the Möbius strip, seen in numerous M.C. Escher pictures, a single surface, like a loop of ribbon twisted into a figure of eight, so that the inside and outside cannot be easily distinguished: the outside is inside, and the inside is outside. Importantly, this is not just the response of states to transnational threats, where the production of internal-external connections lies with the threat to which states must respond, but with the daily practices of security professionals who themselves produce interconnections beyond the state borders, which used to be the administrative and political boundaries of security provision (Bigo, 2001a) (see Chapter 3).

The privatization of security or assemblages of security practices

The state's monopoly on the legitimate use of violence is commonly expressed through the police and the military, yet the role of private sector actors in the provision of policing and military services has increased significantly in recent years. This may be interpreted as an erosion of the state monopoly and a threat to security, which has been so associated with the state, or as a capacity enhancement to states' abilities to provide security in an increasingly complex security environment. Others argue that much gets lost in posing the relationship between public and private in exclusive and oppositional terms, and that the changes are best analysed as complex rearticulations of authority in security.

Private sector actors provide much of the daily security we experience in Western societies. Certainly, the police and rule of law are still important, but we do not rely solely on the state for all forms of protection: private insurance protects from the consequences of theft or fire; private health systems protect against the consequences of disease and lifestyle for health; and private companies provide software to protect against cyber-attacks on our computers. Yet, the private sector is also increasingly involved in those elements of protection that relate more directly to violence and the state's supposed monopoly on its legitimate threat, and use both internationally and domestically. Internationally, this can be seen in the growth of private military and security companies (PMSCs) (see Chapter 7). PMSCs challenge the control on the use of force exercised by states in the international system, but also enable some states to use force (supposedly more cheaply). Often neglected in international security studies, private companies have also increasingly taken on many domestic security roles. In many countries, private security guards outnumber the police – in the USA, the 2 million private security personnel outnumber police 3:1, while in the UK, the ratio is around 2:1. But this is not just a feature of rich Western countries: in Latin America, an estimated 1.6 million registered private security personnel outnumber the police, and there are a further 2 million working informally or illegally (some of whom are moonlighting police officers). Further, many such companies are also increasingly transnational: the largest, the British-based G4S, has over 100,000 personnel in 29 African countries (Abrahamsen and Williams, 2011). They do not just guard private businesses and residences, but often operate in formal public–private partnerships to police public spaces from Cape Town in South Africa to Canary Wharf in London.

While the debate on PMSCs centres on their implications for the Weberian monopoly of force, the encounter with domestic private security companies is less concerned with this. First, this is a stronger reflection of what Weber (1919/1991: 78) actually said about this monopoly:

> Specifically, at the present time, the right to use physical force is ascribed to other institutions or to individuals only to the extent to which the

> state permits it. The state is considered the sole source of the 'right' to use violence.

In other words, the state can authorize other actors to use force without its monopoly being eroded: it is the state's monopoly on legitimate authorization, not its conduct of the use of force, that matters most here. Further, the growth of private security companies, the use of privately run prisons and so on is posed more in neoliberal terms of partnership than opposition. Here, the question of who provides security is less important than questions of effectiveness, efficiency, cost and accountability. Such a framing significantly limits the space for debating the wider political question as to how security is produced and distributed. Crude notions of privatization imply a shift, in whole or part, from state control and governance to the market. The privatization of security, then, implies not only a shift in who provides security (from state actors to private companies), but also a change in the logics driving the distribution of security from public good to price and profit. Here, the notion of privatization is perhaps unhelpful. Certainly, in many places, security provision follows wealth, with security in many wealthy neighbourhoods being provided by private companies in 'gated communities'. The poor are excluded from such spaces and denied the benefits of security, relying instead on nominal state protection. One cannot assume, however, that the state always provides security on utilitarian terms, let alone on the basis of need. State security actors have often been oriented towards the protection of elites and the preservation of their position rather than as a public good. So, the distribution of security does not follow simply from the type of actor providing it, such that states provide only public goods and private actors only private goods in a market system. Instead, a hybrid of state and private actors provide security in more, or often less, coherent ways.

Yet, there is potentially far-reaching change involved in the growth of private sector security provision; notably the notion of security as a collective or 'public' good may be changed and with it the social contract. This relates not only to the actors providing security but also the basic principles and features of the production and distribution of security. A public good is made available to all persons, often on a 'non-excludable' basis; that is, the good itself cannot be distributed only to some and not to others (fresh air for example). The issue with the private sector is that security is increasingly provided as a commodity, as a 'private' good, something that can be provided only to those who pay for it. Krahmann (2008) claims that this move shifts the form of security. If security is only to be provided to those who pay for it, then it is provided as an excludable good, which means that forms of protection against threats (guards, fences and so on) dominate over security provision that seeks to reduce or eliminate threats. For Loader and Walker (2007), the notion of a public good of security is central not only to criticizing the failures of states, their role as threat, or the role of private actors, but is also crucial to rethinking security provision and the role of the state in less black and white terms and finding a way of 'civilizing security'.

This means that another foundational distinction of modern political life is being reconfigured. The distinction between public and private has been a central organizing principle of political theory and practice, including in the security field. Yet, as Owens (2008) points out, this is not a natural distinction but one produced historically and reproduced and reconfigured through these processes of transformation of the power relations of security. Further, the distinction is not just produced nationally but is affected by the transnational dimensions of the actors involved and the values and norms related to security provision and the role of the state. Thus, Abrahamsen and Williams (2011: 217) speak of 'security assemblages' as fields of security in which:

> security provision and governance take place within assemblages that are deterritorialized in terms of actors, technologies, norms and discourses and are embedded in a complex transnational architecture that defies the conventional distinctions of public-private and global-local.

In such assemblages, security practices are related to state and private actors in ways that reconstitute and reconfigure rather than erode the public-private distinction.

It is important, however, not to overstate the novelty of private security actors authorized and operating alongside the state. The state has not always been opposed to private companies using force and combating non-state actors: the British and Dutch East India Companies, for example, were private actors used by the state that used violence, as were the privateers (pirates on behalf of the state). Such actors had complex and evolving relationships with the state that reinforced rather than challenged the process of European state-building (Thomson, 1994). Nevertheless, historical parallels do not negate the central way in which these myths and distinctions organize political, economic and social life and the provision of security therein. For instance, the fact that debates over PMSCs are framed as eroding the monopoly on violence and private security providers internal security roles are framed as enhancing the state and security implies that the dominance of the domestic/international divide for framing the politics of security remains strong, even though they connect and reconfigure in practice. However, other changes in security provision do more than cross and reconfigure these foundational distinctions, they disperse and reconfigure the practice of security in deeper ways.

Securing the 'homeland'

Security, like charity, starts at home (and at work and play) – at least that is the view of Janet Napolitano, director of the US Department of Homeland Security, when she said 'homeland security starts with hometown security' (quoted in Petersen and Tjalve, 2013: 1). The growing notion of 'homeland security' in Western practices of security can be seen as significantly transforming security and the character of the state, while also depoliticizing both these things. By naming the homeland as the referent object of security, a range of new concepts of security come into play. While the boundaries and logics of national security traditionally emphasized national territory as a core of protection, homeland security shifts to a new set of logics that combines strengthened border security (see Chapter 12) with the protection of critical infrastructure and cyber-security among many other things. The creation of the US Department of Homeland Security in response to the 9/11 al-Qaeda attacks quickened a process already underway. The central aim was for 40 diverse government departments to be more effectively integrated, since a lack of coordination contributed to a failure to prevent the attacks and protect security. While other states have not created the integrated homeland security architecture seen in the USA, they have increasingly emphasized many of the same things, such as border control, contingency planning and civil protection capabilities, and greater governmental integration and cooperation.

Homeland security first and foremost seeks to secure not just survival but ways of life. For Duffield (2010: 65), the life and ways of life of many in developing states are uninsured, but in Europe, North America and East Asia private and social security systems are stronger. In these 'mass consumer societies', the bureaucracies and infrastructures of welfare, housing, health provision, education, employment, energy and economic activity that characterize 'developed-life' are characterized by 'chronic dependence upon ... bureaucracies and infrastructures; without them, life itself would be difficult if not impossible'. The security of ways of life is relevant to many transnational and international security issues too, such as the security of energy supplies, the challenges of climate change, and the security implications of migration (see Chapters 12 and 13).

In doing this, homeland security focuses on networks rather than (just) territory, and creates new spatialities of protection that extend across national borders. For instance, the US *National Strategy for Homeland Security* produces a notion of 'layered defence', in which security operations of the state are carried out beyond its borders, at airports and ports around the world (see Chapter 12) (Rees and Aldrich, 2005). However, perhaps the most pervasive dimension to homeland security (whether it is called that or not) is the growing emphasis on critical infrastructure protection (CIP) (Dunn Cavelty and Kristensen, 2008). Critical infrastructure tends to be rather widely defined, but in the USA and the EU, it officially covers the physical and virtual systems that are seen as of critical importance, such that their incapacitation, disruption or destruction would debilitate valued security referents and systems, including national and economic security and public health and safety. Such infrastructure may include some (but not all) energy installations and networks, communications systems, finance systems (banking, investments), healthcare, food security, water supplies, including dams, water storage and water treatment facilities, many types of transport infrastructure – airports, ports, railways, mass transit networks, traffic control systems – facilities involved in the production, storage and transport of dangerous chemicals, nuclear materials and biological agents, and critical government networks and facilities and even monuments. In 1997, the US President's Commission on Critical Infrastructure Protection (1997: 3) defined infrastructure as 'a network of independent, mostly privately-owned, man-made systems and processes that function collaboratively and synergistically to produce and distribute a continuous flow of essential goods and services'. Critical infrastructure is viewed an interrelated system, not just particular facilities; for example, healthcare systems are linked to energy supplies to hospitals and water purification systems that provide drinking water. If these break down, the strain on one part of the system may create crises in others. Thus, the logics of security and its referent objects shift from territory and political institutions, or law and order, to include many of the systems on which our daily activities depend. As with homeland security more broadly, CIP understands the protection of life and ways of life in terms of the protection of a network (Lewis, 2006; Coward, 2009a).

CIP understood as a network expands the sources of danger and the sites of protection of security. For instance, both the USA and the 2006 European Programme for Critical Infrastructure Protection (EPCIP) adopt an 'all-hazards' approach that is concerned not with the everyday failures and disruptions of small power cuts, transport delays or industrial accidents, but with an unpredictable catastrophe produced through random attacks, natural disasters and technological failures (Aradau, 2010). Thus, climate change is viewed as a threat to critical military and civilian infrastructures, such as naval bases, low-lying airfields and energy infrastructure (Busby, 2008; Dabelko, 2009; Paskal, 2010). Practices of protection also disperse the logics of security to new sites such as buildings, transport systems, power stations and so on as well as territorial borders.

Security is conceived differently in homeland security and CIP. The network view of physical and virtual systems means that the key security concepts at play in CIP relate not just to protection, but to vulnerabilities and 'resilience', specifically resilience against disruption (see Introduction). Resilience relates to the ability of systems to withstand and recover from crises, minimize disruption and return to 'normal' (Lundborg and Vaughan-Williams, 2011). It best fits with a risk logic that emphasizes probabilities and harm, in which security is viewed in terms of vulnerabilities and resilience rather than the direct countering and elimination of threats through power (see Chapter 5). Thus, while the USA may be militarily powerful, it can still be thought of as vulnerable (Flynn, 2002) and as a 'brittle nation', in need of building resilience to terrorism and natural disasters (Flynn, 2008: 3). This approach does not seek total security, but accepts a degree of risk, a view espoused in the 2007 US *National Strategy for Homeland Security*, which aims to produce 'resilience' and a 'culture of preparedness', even though 'we cannot envision or prepare for every potential threat, we must understand and accept a certain level of risk as a permanent condition' (US Department of Homeland Security, 2007: 25). In this view, total protection and total security are impossible. Some critics argue that these contemporary constructions of resilience produce a notion of security attuned to securing neoliberal priorities of transnational elites, capital circulation and trade rather than traditional models of security as a general public good provided within a bounded territory (Coaffee and Murakami Wood, 2006).

Critical infrastructure protection and wider homeland security cross the familiar boundaries that shape understandings and practices of security. They cross national boundaries; for example, a failure in energy systems in Germany in 2006 led to loss of power in Germany, Austria, France, Belgium, Italy, Spain and Portugal (Aradau, 2010). So, the EPCIP sets out principles for both European and national-level CIP. They also cross the boundaries between the public and private sectors and, as Kristensen (2008: 69) argues, 'moving security into society requires engagement with the civilian and private actors of society'. Approximately 85 per cent of US critical infrastructure is owned or operated by private sector actors (US Government Accountability Office, 2006).

This shifts the role of the state in security by seeing CIP as intertwined with the functioning of systems in other states, creating a shared vulnerability; so the role of the state in providing security moves from taking sole responsibility and monopolizing security to becoming a partner and facilitator of private actors securing themselves. Indeed, Petersen and Tjalve (2013) argue that this is true of homeland security more widely, as it recasts the relationship between state and society away from the delegation of responsibility to the state in exchange for control in a social contract towards a situation of shared responsibility, in which the state shapes and facilitates security rather than just providing it. Here, civil society is responsibilized for the security of the community, and techniques of protection and surveillance become dispersed throughout society as citizens are asked to ensure vigilance. This functions not only by neoliberal models of efficiency and marketization but also by older republican liberal notions of civic virtue and duty, in which the national/homeland interest is asserted but not debated and the state enables and facilitates others to provide security while evading ultimate responsibility for it.

This dispersal and reconfiguration of security roles and responsibilities is a further development of earlier security practices, rather than a complete break with the pre-9/11 past. The term 'infrastructure', for instance, arose largely in relation to the military equipment needed for military operations, and has expanded over time, through development programmes, to apply to water and roads (Aradau, 2010). Similarly, notions of 'resilience' began in relation to ecological security and sustainable development, and were then taken on in financial, urban and environmental planning (Coafee, 2006; Walker and Cooper, 2011). Further, the responsibilization of civil society and the private sector for protection and defence builds on the growth of Cold War civil defence practices, which shifted the focus of security to the vulnerability of urban and industrial centres to strategic bombings and nuclear attacks. In the latter, systems of civil preparedness (through drills in schools to the building of networks of fallout shelters) were created, which fed into concepts of the mapping of vulnerabilities and the distributed and pervasive practices of security (Collier and Lakoff, 2008; Boyd and Scouras, 2010).

In addition to reconfiguring the security roles and responsibilities of state and society, CIP challenges some of the metatheoretical assumptions of many understandings of security. While most theories of security view material things in terms of resources to be fought over or used in war, CIP's predominant concern with physical objects casts the material world as constitutive of social relations (Dunn Cavelty and Kristensen, 2008; Lundborg and Vaughan-Williams, 2011). Here, critical security scholarship is beginning to move away from a seemingly exclusive focus on ideas and identities towards engagement with forms of 'new materialism', which seek to collapse the traditional ontological distinctions between ideas and matter, the social and the technological, by exploring how non-human 'objects' are active in constituting complex relations (Coward, 2009a, 2012; Aradau, 2010; Lundborg and Vaughan-Williams, 2011; Adey and Anderson, 2012). In addition to reconfiguring the theoretical assumptions about the material, CIP raises issues of virtual as well as physical systems. Contemporary ways of life, and infrastructure systems, rely on virtual information systems and thus cyber-security (Deibert and Rohozinski, 2010). This has become a priority for many states, and while most cyber-attacks consist of mundane, familiar things (worms, viruses, denial of service attacks), fears of state or terrorist cyber-attack raise the spectre of the virtual disruption or undermining of national and homeland security (see Chapter 11). Indeed, some constructivists argue that cyber-security has become a new sector of security, in which two referent objects of security, the network and the individual, are interlinked. This not only securitizes cyber-infrastructure but also shifts security from the political to the technical, since cyber-security practices are entwined with the technical knowledge of experts in the private sector and the development of new technologies (Nissenbaum, 2005; Hansen and Nissenbaum, 2009).

Conclusion

Understanding security within sovereign states requires thinking beyond the confines of the discipline of security studies that has focused largely on inter-state relations. Critical approaches to security have moved away from this exclusive focus, and the foundational assumption that the logics and limits of security can be described differently in two distinct realms: the inside and the outside. Combining security studies with historical sociology of state formation and various forms of sociological and criminological thought on the nature of security within states and their contemporary transformations yields a richer picture of the relationships between states and security. It understands the state as a process of monopolization of violence and protection in specific forms characterized by sovereign authority, delimited territorialization, the growth of exclusive national political communities, and the control and authorization of violence and protection. While the state is often marked as a modern institution beginning with the Peace of Westphalia, the process of state formation in the developed and developing world can be seen as ongoing and incomplete. Whether the state is viewed as merely a coercively powerful protection racket, or the outgrowth of a social contract in which security is provided in exchange for certain rights and duties, security lies at the heart of the state. Here, security may be conceived narrowly as physical protection against the violence of others, or more widely as the rule of law and the securing of liberty and particular ways of life. While states vary considerably in the organization of security provision and the authorization of violence, contemporary internal security relates particularly to myths and logics of the pacification of social relations within a sovereign state's territory, the rationalization of violence as a political but not religious or social instrument, and the development and continued evolution of the practices of policing, punishment and surveillance.

While the state may be understood in relation to security via notions of protection domestically and internationally, security practices are undergoing considerable transformations that are redefining the responsibilities, territories and sites of security provision across domestic-international and public-private divides. In some places, the security of the homeland and the protection of the infrastructures of ways of life are rearticulating the state and security in more dispersed and amorphous relationships. These changes reconceive the logics of security in terms of risk, resilience and shared responsibility, and disperse security provision. This articulates novel limits to security beyond what the state can do *for* society to what the state can do *with* society. Whether security is framed in terms of simple protection or the production of resilience, it is also clear that security requires knowledge. Knowing the nature of threats and risks is integral to the ability of states and societies to form strategies for producing security. Indeed, the practices of surveillance, the development of bureaucratic forms of government, and their contemporary transformations are closely related to different forms of knowing and understanding security. In all fields, then, security relates to the limits to which decision makers can be certain about threats and what strategy will work. Security, therefore, is bound up in the conditions of uncertainty that limit knowledge and establish some of the logics of security. It is this that Chapter 5 explores.

Chapter 5

Acting under Uncertainty: The Security Dilemma, Strategy and Risk

The previous chapters explored how we know about security and how states provide it within their borders. This chapter shifts the focus to how security actors (states and others) know about security and addresses the perennial questions of security action and interaction: How, what and how much do security actors know? How does that knowledge affect how they act? In much theorizing, the logics of security set its limits: the logics of anarchy and power set limits on cooperation and shape the scarcity of security, which limit how and how much security can be achieved. This chapter explores the reverse relationship: How do the limits of certainty in practical security knowledge set the logics of security action? Even if one assumes that states are rational calculating actors, it cannot be assumed that states have reliable information on which to form their calculations. Thus, the conditions under which security is sought are characterized by a degree of uncertainty about the dangers actors face and therefore what the most effective actions will be. This chapter explores the challenges of action under conditions of uncertainty and how understandings of uncertainty shape the possibilities, scope and form of security action. First, it discusses the central concept of the security dilemma that relates primarily to interstate relations. Here, anarchy amplifies uncertainty and produces the logics and limits of action that policy makers must navigate. It then explores the practical implications of uncertainty and differing interpretations of it in forming and implementing a strategy for security. Finally, moving beyond the traditional notions of the security dilemma that emphasize threats from other states, it examines contemporary reinterpretations of security not as the mitigation of threats but as the management of risk. Here, too, notions of uncertainty set the character of security action, but are understood in different ways.

Uncertainty and the security dilemma

States are afraid of the dark – they fear what they do not know. Fear of the unknown sets much of the logic and limits of security practice, but theories of security differ widely on the character and implications of uncertainty. The concept of the 'security dilemma' captures the importance of uncertainty. Coining this term in 1950, Herz (1950: 157) claimed that:

> the self-help attempts of states to look after their security needs, tend, regardless of intention, to lead to rising insecurity for others as each interprets its own measures as defensive and the measures of others as potentially threatening.

Similarly, Butterfield (1951: 20) argued that this was an 'irreducible dilemma' in security that caught states in a 'Hobbesian fear'. Both viewed the problem of interpreting the intentions and capabilities of others as tending inevitably towards power competition and the paradoxical situation that actions taken to make oneself more secure may make others and thence oneself less secure. For Herz, this derives not from the power-acquisitive human nature emphasized by his contemporary 'classical' realists, but from the condition of anarchy and the fact that since all humans have the capacity to hurt or kill each other, there is perennial mutual suspicion and a dilemma of 'kill or perish'. The choice of kill or perish may seem easy, if abhorrent. However, it is made difficult by the fact that people (and states) depend on each other for material and social goods: 'social co-operation and social struggle seem to go hand in hand, and to be equally necessary' (Herz, 1951: 3). Killing may therefore lead to perishing and so the choice is not easy: it is a dilemma. Posed in this way, the obvious choice may be not to kill but to be prepared to kill (build military capabilities, form alliances) in case the need arises. But this is not a safe middle ground between killing and perishing. Paradoxically, it 'renders the others more insecure and compels them to prepare for the worst. Since none can ever feel entirely secure in such a world of competing units, power competition ensues, and the vicious circle of security and power accumulation is on' (Herz, 1950: 157).

The security dilemma sees security as the driving force of international power competition. The paradoxical situation that 'many of the means by which a state tries to increase its security decrease the security of others' (Jervis, 1978: 169) is sometimes used to define the security dilemma. However, Booth and Wheeler's (2008) recent re-engagement with the concept avoids conflating the paradox with the conditions that cause it by unpacking two dilemmas and a paradox. Since a dilemma is a proposition that can be assumed to be valid, a dilemma is a difficult choice between two equally valid alternatives. The security dilemma first comprises a 'dilemma of interpretation', which places decision makers in the unenviable position of having to make a choice under conditions of 'unresolvable uncertainty' about whether or not a possible rival state intends to attack or has the capability to do so. The second dilemma follows once this has been settled and comprises the 'dilemma of response': to communicate to other states through words and actions that they will respond in kind to a threat (deterrence) or to signal reassurance. This second dilemma risks producing the unintended security paradox that actions seeking to produce security may actually reduce it.

Uncertainty lies at the heart of the security dilemma. States cannot know with certainty what another state intends to do. This is sometimes referred to as the 'problem of other minds': we cannot see inside each other's heads, therefore we cannot satisfy our (apparent) need for certainty about another's intentions. This establishes a logic of fear between two actors: one may have only peaceful intentions, but the other cannot be certain of this. The security dilemma entails the operation of this uncertainty and the forgetting of it, since each actor is uncertain of the other but cannot understand that the other is also uncertain and afraid. Thus, Butterfield (1951: 21) argued that:

> You yourself may vividly feel the terrible fear that you have of the other party, but you cannot enter into the other man's counter fear, or even understand why he should be particularly nervous. For you know that you yourself mean him no harm, and that you want nothing from him save guarantees for your own safety; and it is never possible for you to realise or remember properly that since he cannot see the inside of your mind, he can never have the same assurance of your intentions that you have.

The problem of other minds is exacerbated by the uncertainty of the future. We may never be 100% certain of others' current intentions, but we may, through conversation, reputation and surveillance, gather information that gives some knowledge of them. In other words, we may not 100% certain, but we need not be 100% uncertain. However, things change. Mearsheimer (2001: 31) asserts that 'intentions are impossible to divine with 100 percent certainty' and 'intentions can change quickly, so a state's intentions can be benign one day and hostile the next'.

Discerning current and future intentions is made even harder by incomplete and potentially unreliable information. One might gain information on intentions by listening to what other states say, but, for many theorists, words are cheap and states may lie. An alternative is to look at capabilities as an indicator of intentions and a component of threat. This may enhance the predictability of the future, since the means by which states prepare for defence or offence involve building or buying weapons and building and training military forces, all of which take considerable time and expense. Certainly, states assess others' military capabilities in judging their intentions and capacity for aggression. However, reliably interpreting intentions from capabilities requires being able to distinguish offensive and defensive military capabilities. This is inherently difficult because the sources and forms of military power include diverse things from the number of soldiers, the number and types of weapons systems, to intangible and unmeasurable things like the quality of military training and military culture. Even the material dimensions of military power, weapons systems, are 'ambiguous symbols' (Booth and Wheeler, 2008: 42). Are weapons inherently defensive or offensive? Some types of weapons, such as antiballistic missiles (missiles that can shoot down ballistic missiles that may be used to deliver nuclear warheads), seem largely defensive. But a shield is as much a part of preparation for an offensive action (to defend against counterattack) as it is preparation for defence. Further, the meaning attributed to weapons is not just about the intrinsic destructive or defensive capabilities they embody but is influenced by context (see also Chapter 8). The USA does not view British nuclear weapons as a threat, but does view North Korea's smaller arsenal as threatening. Uncertainty about military capabilities is impossible to eliminate, and their significance will always be interpreted through wider issues of trust, fear and perception.

Given these forms of uncertainty, must states err on the side of caution and build their military capacities? In some circumstances, it may seem wise to build up military power, as when faced with an aggressive enemy intent on invasion. In others, however, it may be counterproductive by producing fear and unintended consequences among states previously holding peaceful intentions. Jervis (1976) characterized these two basic scenarios as the deterrence model and the spiral model. In the deterrence model, a state (usually seen as a 'status-quo' power or the 'security seekers' posited by defensive structural realism) is faced with a threat from a 'revisionist' or 'greedy' state (Glaser, 1997). Here, the task of policy makers is to secure their state by producing effective deterrent strategies to convince the aggressor that the costs of war would outweigh the benefits. In the spiral model, an almost automatic cycle of action and reaction takes hold as states respond to each other's acquisitions of arms by increasing their own military capacities, as seen in arms races. Similar to Butterfield's Hobbesian fear, parties without aggressive intentions may misperceive each other's intentions, particularly by focusing on the destructive potential of weapons, and thus act according to their worst fears (Booth and Wheeler, 2008). Spirals are dangerous because they increase mistrust, making war more likely and also raising the level of destructive capacities, thus making war more destructive if it occurs. Jervis added a psychological dimension to the security dilemma in the spiral model, arguing that the psychological dynamics of individual leaders and groups affect the interpretation of information and produce the misperception of hostile intent that initiates and sustains the spiral. While misperceptions exacerbate the security dilemma and may make 'spiral' processes more acute, Jervis (1976) emphasized that they still retain a rational foundation. In part, this relates to what Butterfield described as a failure to enter into the other side's 'counter-fear', or to exercise what Booth and Wheeler (2008) call the 'security dilemma sensibility': the spiral of mutual fear and arming could be mitigated or broken by states realizing that their actions are causing that which they most fear.

There are two major differences between the models. First, in the deterrence model the incompatibility between states is 'real', and in the spiral model it is 'imagined' (or the result of 'misperception'). Second, in the deterrence model, the risk of war stems from 'greedy' states with malign intentions, and in the spiral model from the anarchic structure of international relations producing uncertainty and enabling misperception (A. Collins, 2004). There are some problems with this. First, it poses only two possible worlds: a world in which perceptions are correct and aggression is recognized and deterred, and a world in which misperceptions occur and tragedy dominates such that peaceful intentions may lead to war. This limits strategic action to a choice of deterrence or reassurance, when, in fact, many more choices exist and combine. Second, it rests on a distinction between 'security seekers' and 'greedy' states, since some security seekers may deliberately decrease the security of others to make themselves secure but not to be greedy (A. Collins, 2004). Finally, since both examine what leads to war rather than peace, they offer a limited explanation of the logics of insecurity.

Uncertainty and war

Is the security dilemma a feature of all security politics? Early theorists of the security dilemma saw it as inherent in all levels of human social interaction from the individual to interstate relations; thus, Butterfield (quoted in Jervis, 1976: 66) saw it as 'the basic pattern for all narratives of human conflict, whatever other patterns may be superimposed upon it later'. Yet, while a degree of uncertainty may always be present, there is disagreement on whether all wars can be explained in terms of the security paradox that may result. The First World War inspired Herz's conceptualization of the security dilemma, and while some realists reject the view of 'inadvertent war' arising from the security dilemma (Trachtenberg, 1991; Lieber, 2007), many defensive neorealists argue that this was a clear spiral situation. They argue that prewar decision makers were seduced by a 'cult of the offensive', believing that offensive strategies were militarily superior, which yielded an arms build-up that increased mutual fear and the 'lure of conquest' that eventually led to war (Snyder, 1984; van Evera, 1999; Snyder and Lieber, 2008). Indeed, Lord Grey, the prewar British foreign minister, argued that the arms build-up created suspicion and 'evil imaginings of all sorts, till each Government feels it would be criminal and a betrayal of its own country not to take every precaution, while every Government regards every precaution of every other Government as evidence of hostile intent' (cited in Jervis, 1976: 65). The Second World War, in contrast, is often portrayed as a case of an aggressive and 'greedy' Germany seeking expansion. Indeed, the dangers of mistaking a deterrence situation for a spiral are clearly illustrated with the failure of appeasement, which sought reassurance rather than deterrence. Yet, the appeasement attempt to 'enter into the counter-fear' of German policy makers may have been too little too late, as there is debate over whether the development and acceptance of Hitler's aggressive intentions resulted from a German belief that Britain and France were preparing to attack (Taylor, 1964; Booth and Wheeler, 2008).

It is also questionable whether the security dilemma provides a complete explanation for conflict. The Cold War certainly included many periods in which cycles of action and reaction were found in a nuclear arms race that took both sides close to war. However, understanding this in terms of the security dilemma is too limited, since it presents conflict as driven by threat perceptions derived from and measured by military capabilities, but the Cold War was also driven by ideological factors, the identities of the major protagonists, and a resultant belief in the incommensurability of ways of life (Ralph, 2001; Jervis, 2001; Booth and Wheeler, 2008). Some scholars have also applied the concept to conflicts within as well as between states. Amid rising incidences of civil wars in the 1990s (see Chapter 7), some argue that the conditions of anarchy that give rise to uncertainty and fear were 'domesticized' in weak and collapsing states in Africa and the Balkans (Sørensen, 2011: 118; see also Job, 1992; Posen, 1993; Roe, 2005). Ethnic groups acted in the same way states do and feared each other's intentions. However, these accounts emphasize only the spiral of escalation and the potential for actions to have unintended consequences rather than the foundational issues of uncertainty (Roe, 2000: Booth and Wheeler, 2008). Critics argue that such accounts ignore the fact that much of the mobilization of armed groups related not to the defensive needs of communities but to the 'predatory' ambitions of political leaders (Sambanis, 2000). Importantly, there are ethical dimensions to using security dilemma concepts. First, Jervis (2001: 38) objects to its use for the Cold War, since it implies a 'no-fault' argument, in which conflict is blamed on the tragedy of circumstances not the actions or intentions of state leaders and so a lot of bad ideas and bad actions are let off the ethical hook. Security dilemma accounts of civil wars also conflict with attempts to build peace through power-sharing agreements and the restoration of multiethnic states, and instead support solutions based on the partition of communities into ethnically homogeneous geographical enclaves and states, which end up advocating forced partition and widespread displacement of people from their homes (Mearsheimer and van Evera, 1995; Kaufmann, 1996).

Uncertainty and the logics of security

In the concept of the security dilemma, conditions of anarchy and uncertainty combine to establish fear as the driving logic of security behaviour. However, there are diverse views on the relationship between uncertainty and fear that generate different interpretations of this logic. Booth and Wheeler (2008) categorize these as 'fatalist', 'mitigator' and 'transcender' perspectives. Fatalist logics see insecurity as inescapable in international politics, mitigator logics suggest that insecurity can be reduced at times, but not eliminated, and transcender logics hold greater hope for escaping insecurity on a longer term and global basis.

'Fatalism' is found in the determinism of offensive structural realism, which sees 'a consistently more competitive and dangerous world' than other approaches (Glaser, 1997: 172). Mearsheimer (2001: 43) posits anarchy and uncertainty about intentions as constants of international life, which 'create an irreducible level of fear' that leads to power-maximizing behaviour. While a basic level of fear is constant, its intensity varies in relation to polarity and the distribution of power: 'The more power a state possesses, the more fear it generates among its rivals.' This reductionist account is founded on the questionable assumption that states will treat a lack of 100 per cent certainty as a condition of absolute uncertainty and fear. It is also a highly deterministic view, in which insecurity is certain and interpretations of intentions will always be pessimistic. There is, therefore, no dilemma, no difficult choice of interpretation and so no dilemma about action: states must always seek more power and never be satisfied with the status quo (Glaser, 1997; Snyder, 2002; Booth and Wheeler, 2008). Other offensive structural realists adopt a less fatalistic position. Posen (2003: 33) views the security dilemma as always present, but not always intense. He argues that while military organizations may favour offensive doctrines for their own reasons, and civilian leaders may sometimes agree, states are not 'newborn children' and they learn from their own and others' histories that attempts to become hegemons are rare and seldom successful; thus, most states are generally 'status-quo' powers. Similar to offensive realists, Schweller (1996: 104) posits a world full of war and aggression, but says that 'the resulting insecurity cannot be attributed to the security dilemma. States acquire more arms not because they misperceive the security efforts of other benign states but because aggressive states truly wish to harm them.'

Mitigator perspectives are more common among defensive neorealists, neoliberals and others. Herz held little hope for eradicating the security dilemma, but did argue that judicious power-balancing strategies offered some mitigation of war. More recent mitigator perspectives derive inspiration from the diversity of experiences of the security dilemma rather than asserting a permanent base level of uncertainty and fear. Defensive neorealists envision many possible worlds in which variation in the intensity of fear derives not simply from the distribution of material capabilities but from the 'offence-defence balance' (Lynn-Jones, 1995). At any given point in history, the character of military technology favours either offence or defence: for example, if a state has to invest \$3 billion in offence to counter the effects of a \$1 billion investment in defence, then the balance is a 3:1 ratio. Jervis (1978) moved away from a fatalist perspective by arguing that the offence-defence balance shapes the intensity of the security dilemma and the limits and opportunities for its mitigation. He argued that there are differing levels of acuteness of the security dilemma depending on whether defensive and offensive weapons and behaviours looked similar or different and whether military capabilities give the advantage to offence or defence. Depending on these circumstances, it may be possible for states to prepare for defence without affecting other states' security. Thus, there are varying degrees to which states may avoid the security paradox. If states cannot distinguish between offensive and defensive behaviour, the security dilemma is intense. Here, there will be more aggression if offensive technologies have the advantage, but if defensive technologies have the advantage, there are possibilities to build up military capabilities without endangering others. If offensive and defensive action can be distinguished, the security dilemma is less intense. Here, if the offence-defence balance favours offence, aggression will still arise, but if it favours defence, the environment is 'doubly safe' (Jervis, 1978). Some periods of the Cold War demonstrated a mitigator logic (Collins, 1997). In 1985, Soviet leader Gorbachev indicated a desire to wind down bipolar confrontation. While US President Reagan and UK Prime Minister Thatcher could have viewed this with suspicion, they chose to explore the possibility that it was a serious intention. The conditions for this were partly established by earlier NATO attempts to pursue 'non-provocative defence', in which it sought to signal reassurance: a policy that reflected a belief in the possibility of distinguishing between offensive and defensive capabilities. While it was difficult for Gorbachev to gain domestic acceptance for this policy, it also illustrates that dilemmas pose positive choices, not just two equally negative ones. Much depends on the choices of political leaders, not just the structural conditions of power distribution or even the offence-defence balance (Ralph, 1999; Booth and Wheeler, 2008).

Transcender logics are more diverse, and range from early realism to contemporary critical security studies. Muted and distant prospects for transforming anarchy and transcending insecurity were present in the work of early classical realists (see Chapter 2). While structural realists are more pessimistic, some constructivist and critical scholars inherit the view of early realists that anarchy is made by the interactions of states and can be changed. Wendt (1995: 76) argues that 'war and security dilemmas are the exception rather than the rule', and that even when wars occur or power politics is pursued, 'realism does not have a monopoly on the ugly and brutal side of international life. Even if we agree on a realpolitik description, we can reject a realist explanation.' Many liberal theories from Kant to democratic peace theorists posit transcender logics, in which uncertainties are replaced with certainties of peaceful intentions of democracies reinforced by open political systems or economic linkages that allow democracies to view each other's minds. Likewise, the constructivist concept of 'security communities' shows the prospect of transcending war, when numerous social links and transactions among nations establish expectations for peaceful change and make war unthinkable (Deutsch, 1957; Adler and Barnett, 1998a, 1998b) (see Chapter 6). Welsh School CSS also identifies strong prospects for transforming the security practices of states and the structures that shape them. While much security dilemma theorizing assumes that the response to uncertainty (not knowing) is fear, the opposite of fear is trust, not certainty. For them, while uncertainty is likely to remain 'the existential condition' of all human relations, trust can be built even on issues as difficult as nuclear weapons (Booth and Wheeler, 2008: 1; Ruzicka and Wheeler, 2010).

If uncertainty cannot be eradicated, are the only options to accept it and reduce its effects through power (the fatalist view), through exploring its variety to identify the opportunities it still permits (the mitigator view), or to transcend its effects through trust? There is a fourth option: to abandon the quest for certainty or the control of contingency through power and live as the world is, uncertain, contingent and ambiguous. Poststructuralists criticize the dominance of a Hobbesian view in which security pertains to the reduction of doubt, ambiguity and unpredictability and insecurity pertains to uncontrollability (Der Derian, 1993). These merely reflect a particular modern conception of politics, science and philosophy as a 'quest for certainty' (Toulmin, 1990). They demand the impossible as they seek but can never attain a politics based on certain and objective foundations (Dillon, 1996). In contrast, poststructuralists seek wider political imaginations that embrace contingency and complexity and do not seek to eradicate ambiguity. Thus, Der Derian (1993: 104) claims: 'The security of the sovereign, rational self and State comes at the cost of ambiguity, uncertainty, paradox – all that makes life worthwhile.' This critique does not pose a singular alternative view but seeks to question the assumption that security requires certainty and certainty requires control. This quest for control through certainty produces particular logics and limits to strategic action to achieve security.

Strategy: decision and action

If uncertainty can never be eradicated and it limits the possibilities for security, what implications does this have for the decisions states will make? Most understandings of security accept that decisions are difficult. Indeed, Machiavelli's (1532/1985: 91) advice to the prince was that:

> Nor should any state ever believe that it can always adopt safe courses; on the contrary, it should think it has to take them all as doubtful. For in the order of things it is found that one never seeks to avoid one inconvenience without running into another; but prudence consists in knowing how to recognize the qualities of inconveniences, and in picking the less bad as good.

Under uncertainty, then, wisdom lies in prudence. But what is a prudent course of action? How do states decide this? Rationalist theories assume that states are instrumentally rational and seek optimal strategies on the basis of information about others' intentions and capabilities. In contrast, constructivist and critical approaches do not assume that all states calculate in the same way, or that states share the same values and identities that inform those calculations. This has important implications for the dilemmas of deciding and acting in conditions of uncertainty.

Security decisions

States face a dilemma of interpreting intentions and capabilities. Making a decision therefore relies on three related things: information, communication, and interpretation.

States do not settle for abstract certainties of uncertainty, but collect information through their communications with each other and through intelligence. They expend great effort to ensure the secrecy of some information, and may deliberately mislead each other or seek to maintain ambiguity about their military capabilities. However, they have also developed formal confidence and security-building measures (CSBMs) and other transparency measures through which they report relevant information on arms transfers, military expenditures and force deployments. While this information is often incomplete or possibly deliberately inaccurate, and reporting may be sporadic, such measures enhance the information flow between states and are argued to produce a norm of transparency in some aspects of military capabilities (Holtom, 2010). Although formally exchanged information may be misleading and thus mistrusted, states also use intelligence techniques, including monitoring communications (signals intelligence), informers, spies and government officials (human intelligence), and open source intelligence from the media and government. The problems of intelligence often relate not to limited information but to the opposite problem of drawing clear conclusions from vast quantities of information. There are also inherent limits in intelligence that mean it cannot eliminate uncertainty. Betts (2007) argues that intelligence is inevitably imperfect due to the physiological limits of human cognition and memory and the tensions inherent in the process of intelligence, such as that between accuracy and timeliness, and the need to share information and the need for secrecy.

States also seek to communicate with each other. The issue here is whether and how states can communicate appropriate information to each other in ways that enable the correct (or desired) interpretation of intentions. For fatalists, this is simply impossible: states cannot 'signal type' (signal either offensive or defensive intentions), since 'words are cheap' and offensive and defensive capabilities are indistinguishable. Even if it were possible, states would still pursue offensive capabilities in case of future changes (Mearsheimer, 2006). Defensive neorealists argue that some signalling of intentions is possible through developing non-offensive capabilities and postures. For them, actions speak louder than words, and peaceful intentions can be signalled by tailoring military capabilities to defensive intentions and engaging in forms of reassurance. However, even the language of 'signalling' implies a limited and impoverished form of communication – like semaphore or smoke signals – in which some basic information is shared but greater detail and important contextual information that affects interpretation is not. By assuming that states must communicate in this limited fashion, and that mistrust must always accompany states' words, realists significantly narrow the range of relevant communications that feed into security relations. In contrast, constructivist theories of security communities were initially based on communication theory and argued that social and economic transactions between societies enhance communication and share contextual information that improves interpretation and produces shared expectations of peaceful behaviour (Deutsch, 1957) (see Chapter 6). Thus, states can improve their communications beyond mere signalling.

How do decision makers interpret information and communications correctly? At its purest, the rationalist belief that states are rational egoists implies that they seek optimal strategies on the basis of accurate information. This abstract rationality is present in some formal game theoretic and rational choice approaches. Most understandings of security, however, argue that states operate on the basis of 'bounded rationality' limited by imperfect and incomplete information. Further, insights from psychology (Jervis, 1976), organizational theory and bureaucratic politics approaches (Allison, 1971) indicate that complex decision-making structures, bureaucratic competition and time pressures mean that decision makers may engage in 'satisficing' behaviour, in which they choose the first adequate solution rather than evaluating all evidence and options to pursue the best. These limits, however, retain a foundational assumption of common and natural rationality. In addition, interpretation is shaped by the communication and use of information. For instance, the failure to predict and prevent the 9/11 terrorist attacks on the USA was partly due to the organizational structures and cultures of US intelligence agencies, which meant pertinent information was not shared between the FBI and the CIA (9-11 Commission, 2004), and that these agencies had also failed to adapt to the transnational character of terrorist threats (Zagart, 2009) (see Chapter 11). Intelligence failures may also generate 'false positives' when analysts are pressurized to draw the conclusions that policy makers want, as in the litany of errors and misinterpretations that produced an erroneous certainty about Iraqi weapons of mass destruction that fed into US and UK decisions to invade Iraq in 2003.

Many theorists emphasize cultural variations in strategic decision making. Classically inspired realists like Snyder (1977) and Gray (1986) argue that states have different 'strategic cultures' that produce different national styles of strategizing. They claimed that Soviet military culture exhibited a preference for offensive and pre-emptive use of force that derived not from universal rationality but a specific history of authoritarian rule. Constructivists take differences in strategic and bureaucratic cultures further to argue that states decide on the basis of expectations, norms and identities formed through intersubjective processes and experiences. Thus, Wendt (1995: 77) argues that the realist view that security decisions and behaviours derive from anarchy is the wrong way around: anarchy arises from behaviours. Thus, 'security dilemmas are not acts of God: they are effects of practice. This does not mean that once created they can necessarily be escaped (they are, after all, "dilemmas"), but it puts the causal locus in the right place.'

Interpretation also involves understanding oneself as well as the potential enemy. Booth and Wheeler (2008: 7) argue that a reflexive 'security dilemma sensibility' is needed to understand the fear felt by others (Butterfield's 'counter-fear'). Cold War decision makers often failed in this regard, viewing their own actions positively and others' responses negatively. For instance, US policy makers in the early 1980s believed that the USSR had no reason to fear their nuclear modernization programme since they 'knew perfectly well' that the USA would not launch a first strike; yet evidence suggests that the Politburo knew no such thing. In November 1983, NATO's 10-day exercise named 'Able Archer 83' tested nuclear release procedures, a simple test that the USSR interpreted as a possible attack and so placed its own forces on alert, thus coming closer to an unintended nuclear war than at any other time since the Cuban missile crisis in 1962.

Strategy and the dilemma of action

After deciding the interpretation of others' intentions and capabilities, decision makers must form a strategy. Strategy is the judicious selection of means to achieve a desired end, and generally relates to the use of political and military power. The first and foremost strategy for security has been war. Indeed, the dominant understanding of war is as a tool to achieve political aims (see Chapter 7). However, in the nuclear age, this arguably shifted, and Brodie (1978) claimed that the purpose of military institutions changed from winning wars to averting them. This resonates in Jervis's two models that posit two major strategies – deterrence and reassurance – which also demonstrate the effects of uncertainty on the conduct as well as aims of strategic action. Such strategies are underpinned by rationality assumptions and operate by altering some aspect of the cost–benefit calculations of rational adversaries.

Deterrence

Deterrence attempts to prevent an action (including but not only military attack, invasion or nuclear strike) by persuading a rational adversary that the costs of the action would be greater than its advantages. This assumes that adversaries engage in cost–benefit analysis and largely entails creating a credible threat of retaliation (punishing the action and increasing the costs) or prospects of defence (making the action unlikely to succeed and decreasing the benefits). The former was particularly important in theories of nuclear deterrence, while Mearsheimer (1983) and Pape (1996) argued that conventional deterrence rests on the latter. Deterrence strategies may be 'general', in which capabilities, reputation and other factors ensure a generalized deterrence, or 'immediate', focused on a particular adversary in a time of crisis which may involve issuing more explicit threats (Morgan, 2003). In the Cold War, deterrence shifted from being a tactic to a pre-eminent, overarching strategy that was seen as sufficient on its own and appropriate for all circumstances (Morgan, 2003).

Deterrence has a simple and familiar logic, and early understandings were based on the well-known game of 'chicken' (Kahn, 1962; Schelling, 1966; Jervis, 1979; Zagare, 1987; Nicholson, 1989). Early rational deterrence models simplified security politics by ignoring many of the complexities of decision making discussed earlier and reducing strategy to highly abstract notions of rationality – often expressed in algebraic formulae that gave them a rather spurious 'air of authority' (Green, 1966). Indeed, they were criticized for being based on 'nonexistent decision makers operating in nonexistent environments' (Lebow and Stein, 1989: 223). Later deterrence theories attempted to account for greater complexity. Rational deterrence theory assumes actors have common processes of cost–benefit analysis, but others criticize this abstraction and argue that strategic culture and the different ideological and cultural systems in the USA and the USSR affected decision making in the functioning of deterrence (Rapoport, 1964; Jervis, 1982/83; Gray, 1986).

Deterrence relies on a particular understanding of information, communication and interpretation. These relate to what Freedman (2003: 92) called the 'magic ingredient' of deterrence: credibility. The adversary must believe that if it attacks, the deterring state is able and willing to respond in the way it claims, such as by using nuclear weapons. This credibility is undertheorized and often simply assumed to exist (Zagare and Kilgour, 2000). The operation of the security dilemma underpins deterrence here, since it implies that states are predisposed to interpret a possible threat as credible. But this precautionary logic provides only a minimal level of credibility that may not be sufficient. Rather, Jervis (1976) claimed that deterrence requires adopting a posture that shows no sign of weakness, no attempt at conciliation and no concessions, since any sign of weakness cannot be taken back in future stronger posturing. Thus, deterrence may be necessary if reassurance cannot be signalled, but still requires signalling 'resolve' and 'saving face' (Morgan, 1985). Likewise, while deterrence is based on negative incentives, it requires some signalling of reassurance (Knopf, 2009). For deterrence to work, it must be credible in its threat of retaliation and its assurance that retaliatory action will not be undertaken if the target state does not attack. While the security dilemma obviously militates against communicating assurances, 'pairing a threat with certain positive messages or inducements' is still essential to its functioning (Kydd, 2005).

Deterrence is a risky game and has some counterintuitive and unethical implications. Most notably, the stability of deterrence relies not on enhancing one's own security but on ensuring one's own vulnerability. For example, when mutually assured destruction became the official US strategic doctrine in the 1960s, Secretary of Defense Robert McNamara welcomed Soviet attempts to develop nuclear capabilities that meant that either side, if it launched a nuclear attack, would face retaliation capable of destroying 50 per cent of its population and industry (Lebow and Stein, 1995). Further, deterrence does not stabilize itself, but requires managing and ensuring vulnerability. For instance, because the development of missile defences could diminish vulnerability and produce incentives for attack, the superpowers negotiated the 1972 Anti-Ballistic Missile Treaty to stop their development. This framework collapsed in 2001, as the proposed deployment of US missile defences in Poland and Hungary prompted severe Russian concerns.

Rational deterrence theories are challenged by the empirical record of the Cold War – for which most theories were developed – and other conflicts. While it is common to argue that deterrence preserved the stability of the Cold War, which Gaddis (1987) termed the 'long peace', deterrence theories do not explain why nuclear war did not occur before the USSR reached nuclear parity with the USA in the 1970s, and why the USSR continued to expand its nuclear capabilities beyond parity thereafter. Rational deterrence logic cannot explain why most major power wars occur in situations of parity rather than asymmetry, and why power imbalances are poor predictors of war (Zagare and Kilgour, 2000). In addition, the focus on deterrence strategy in security theory and practice during the Cold War had some important implications. Deterrence theory generally assumed that nuclear war was abhorrent, irrational and avoidable. Some realists argued, however, that nuclear war was not unavoidable, deterrence could fail, and sought to counteract the focus on deterrence by arguing that nuclear weapons might be useful in war and a nuclear war might be winnable (Gray and Payne, 1980). In contrast, critical approaches, from peace research to contemporary CSS, argue that focusing on deterrence legitimated the nuclear standoff and the development of ever higher levels of nuclear armaments, and its place as the commonsense framework of the Cold War closed off avenues for the creation of peaceful order through disarmament (see Chapter 8). More broadly, deterrence theorizing embodied attempts to develop rational and objective strategic theories that produced a wider legitimation of strategic violence, which also tended to pose Western society as the 'good' side (Klein, 1994) and purported to merely explain the strategic world that it helped to constitute (Booth, 1997).

Reassurance

Reassurance is a process of building a degree of trust. It may be an alternative to deterrence, or a means to stabilize it (Stein, 1991). Osgood (1962) argued that deterrence theory was a 'neanderthal mentality', and that reassurance was preferable and achievable through graduated reciprocation in tension reduction (GRIT). GRIT involves making unilateral (rather than negotiated) gestures of cooperation in ways that do not significantly diminish one side's security but increase the security of the other side and thus gradually increase trust. Critics claim that there is little reason to expect that an adversary will be reassured by measures that are not costly to the reassuring party, especially when 'ordinary communication does not work' (Kydd, 2005). Rather, 'costly signalling' is required, whereby policy makers seek to undertake actions that would only be enacted by a state without hostile intent – such as the removal of some conventional military deployments by Gorbachev in the late 1980s. This is a delicate balancing act:

> The signals cannot be too cheap, or untrustworthy types will send them too in an effort to lull the other side. They cannot be made too costly, or the trustworthy types will be afraid to send them lest the other side turn out to be untrustworthy. Balancing these two considerations is the key to achieving reassurance. (Kydd 2005: 188)

Fearon (1994) suggests that since democracies are able to generate costs from domestic political audiences, they are more able to signal their intentions credibly and clearly and thus ameliorate the security dilemma. However, while deterrence may posit a game of chicken, reassurance is caught in a chicken and egg paradox: a state is only likely to undertake costly unilateral measures when it already believes that the other side does not have hostile intent. This severely limits the possibilities for engaging in costly signalling and explains its limited success when attempted (Montgomery, 2006; Tang and Montgomery, 2007). However, costly unilateral measures need not be the sole foundation of reassurance. Trust-building and the hope of reciprocation can take place in more socialized relationships, through regimes, international institutions or security communities, which enable stronger reciprocity than the hope of stimulating it through unilateral force reductions or changes in posture. As discussed in Chapter 6, however, socialized relationships require theorizing to move significantly beyond simple rationality assumptions or emphasis on the primacy of uncertainty in determining security logics.

Other strategies

In practice, there are many more options than deterrence or reassurance. States may choose 'compellence' or 'coercive diplomacy', which seeks the opposite goal to deterrence: it seeks to compel another state to do something that is desired rather than not to do something that is not. These strategies also rest on the credibility of threats and assurances communicated through words and actions, which cannot be understood solely on the basis of an assumption of pure rationality and perfect information (George, 2004). Unlike deterrence, compellence has not become an overarching strategic framework but a strategy used in particular relations. In addition to preventing an undesired action by deterrence, military force can be used in a strategy of pre-emption – attacking first before a rival state can gain sufficient capabilities to attack or otherwise harm the state's interests. This is sometimes suggested as a means of preventing nuclear proliferation (see Chapter 8), and characterized the 2003 Iraq War, when a strategy of containment shifted to a doctrine of pre-emption. This also shifted traditional understandings of pre-emption as relating to immanent attack towards a longer term preventive agenda. Finally, a major aspect of Cold War strategy was containment, which seeks to limit the possibilities of a rival to expand their power and influence. This was largely defined in terms of the geographical spheres of influence and major powers and superpowers. However, in recent years, a similar strategy of containment has characterized attempts to tackle the transnational threats of crime and terrorism by strengthening weak and failing states (see Chapters 10–12).

These diverse strategies are often combined in practice, as containment and deterrence in the Cold War, or compellence and pre-emptive military action in counter-proliferation. Indeed, while deterrence was a preoccupation of Cold War strategic thought, it lacks universal purchase on contemporary security issues, in which the dominant assumption is that 'rogue' states and terrorists cannot be deterred because they lack rationality – or at least the forms of rationality predicted and promised by various forms of deterrence theory (Christensen, 2002). Rather, such threats see a resurgence of containment and compellence strategies (see Chapter 10).

Risk and security

Much contemporary security practice and politics are not framed in terms of the security dilemma, but the 'risk' of some damaging or catastrophic event – crime, terrorism, natural disaster, disease and so on. Risk is a different calculus of danger. In notions of threat under anarchy, particularly the security dilemma, danger = intentions + capabilities. In risk, danger = probability x harm. Risk also focuses on uncertainty, but views security issues through the formula of likelihood multiplied by the impact of general phenomena, rather than the intentions and capabilities of specific potential enemies. While common in broader security agendas, risk has become a focus of contemporary studies of war, which emphasize that Western powers use war as a means of risk management (Shaw, 2005; Rasmussen, 2006;

Coker, 2009), and that their conduct of war seeks to transfer the risk of death from their troops to enemies (and even civilians) (Shaw, 2005) (see Chapter 7).

Understanding risk

The distinction between threat and risk is not clear-cut. Deterrence theories also sought to model future scenarios to predict and prevent catastrophic events. However, the recent rise of risk-based understandings shifts the understanding of the logics and limits of security away from models of rational calculative action, but retains an emphasis on uncertainty and the logics of action it produces. There are various approaches to risk in understandings of security. Some follow Beck (1992) and argue that there has been a transition to a 'risk society', in which the processes of modernization have produced the major dangers Western societies now face. Others point not to an epochal change, but draw on poststructuralism to view risk as social technology, in which uncertain futures and dangerous possibilities are rendered knowable and actionable in a mode of governance that extends neoliberal ideology. Importantly, while threats are viewed in a negative light, risks present dangers and opportunities (think of economic risks and the opportunities for profit) (Petersen, 2012).

While the security dilemma operates on threats arising through the intentions and capabilities of specified enemies in conditions of anarchy, risks are viewed in general and unspecified terms, such as the risks of climate change, crime and disease. These tend to have some formal order rather than anarchy, from natural climate systems to disease patterns, criminal behaviour, or economic relations. In earlier times, this correlated with the inside-outside distinction, such that security issues within the state's territory could be characterized in terms of risks, and security issues outside, in terms of threats (see Chapter 4). Now, risk-based security concerns the issues and responses that blur the boundary between domestic and international political life, such as transnational crime, terrorism and disease (see Chapter 12). Further, contemporary risks are less predictable than older risks. Giddens (2002: 26) argues that societies used to face 'external risks' that derived from 'the fixities of tradition or nature'. These natural or traditional systems were familiar and offered opportunities for mastery by understanding their patterns and dynamics. In contrast, contemporary 'manufactured risks' arise from the process of modernization (of seeking mastery over nature), and are 'created by the very impact of our developing knowledge upon the world' (Giddens, 2002: 26). These risks are less predictable, because unlike previous risks, we have no experience of them (think of climate change, nuclear terrorism and so on), and they arise partly as the unintended consequences of human action. The political projects of providing security, predicting the future and protecting humankind from modernization's worst effects are challenged when there is no fixed natural system to provide an anchorage of dependable expectations for strategic political action.

While the security dilemma is concerned with uncertainty about specified others' intentions now and in the future, risk primarily emphasizes the uncertainty of the future. As Beck (1999: 52) notes, in risk society: 'future events that have not yet occurred become the object of current action'. Risk-based political action relates to what Giddens (1991: 119) calls the 'colonisation of the future'. The future is rendered predictable not through intelligence and communication but on the basis of past experiences. While the future is the object of current action, the past is the source of data that creates the view of the future by revealing the character of the problem. On this basis, risk does not need to prove the existence of a threat in the present, but merely asserts a continued pattern where manifestation of threat is possible but not precisely predictable. Since risks are seen as persistent, inevitable and having fixed characteristics, they produce 'a sense of comprehensive and ever-present insecurity' (Hagmann and Cavelty, 2012: 89).

Risk also has different notions of causation that limit the achievability of security. While threats arise from the intentions of other specified actors, risks arise from general phenomena. These phenomena are more complex than specified enemies and rather than the linear causation (action and reaction, threat and response) beloved of many positivist approaches, risks are viewed more in terms of complexity and interconnected issues in which small causes have big effects, and prediction is difficult if not impossible (Dillon, 2005; Kavalski, 2008; Coker, 2009). As noted by Rasmussen (2006: 2), this means that:

> From a risk perspective a danger is much less computable than from a threat perspective. A risk is a scenario followed by a policy proposal for how to prevent this scenario from becoming real. However, such a policy proposal does not aim to achieve perfect security: from a risk perspective the best one can hope for is to manage or pre-empt a risk; one can never achieve perfect security because new risks will arise as a 'boomerang effect' of defeating the original risk.

Risk approaches accept a degree of uncertainty, but also are founded on the premise that risks can be classified, quantified and predicted to some degree (Aradau et al., 2008). Rather than posing a choice between fatalism, mitigation or transcendence, risk is concerned with the management of a future that is amenable to intervention. For instance, in relation to the risk of death from disease, Rose (2001: 7) argued that the politics of public health and the systems of hygiene that emerged in the 19th century sought to act on factors of mortality and morbidity through the collection and tabulation of numerical information and the calculation of probabilities to identify and modify risk factors. It is here that risk encompasses a view of the future as 'calculable, predictable, and as dependent upon identifiable factors some of which were manageable'.

Interpreting risk

As with the security dilemma, in risk, the response to uncertainty is to seek certainty, but the arrangements and forms of information, communication and interpretation differ. Certainty is sought in terms of probabilities rather than an assessment of the intentions and capabilities of other actors. Risk calculation requires information and the time and systems needed to process and act on it. While risk analysis accepts a degree of incalculability of dangers and futures, the key task remains to better know the future by establishing ever more accurate predictive models. The types of knowledge and the means of seeking it are different in risk. For traditional military threats, forms of communication and intelligence gathering are prioritized. Risk's emphasis on probabilities means that forms of actuarial knowledge and complex mathematical algorithms are the primary means of risk assessment. The need for knowledge about populations and risk factors dramatically expands the amount of information required, so the growth of risk concerns has led to an expansion and dispersal of surveillance practices and a reliance on technology (Ceyhan, 2008).

Interpreting risk tends to mean that the demand for certainty increases and expands into all spheres of life. Security practices, such as critical infrastructure protection, the control of transnational flows, border controls, biometrics, terrorism prevention, homeland security and so on, extend risk-based security rationalities into daily business transactions, banking, travel, communications and other areas of daily life (see Chapters 4, 11, 12 and 13). Indeed, for Ericson and Haggerty (1997: 426–7): 'Institutionalized risk communication systems form the foundation of contemporary society and provide the governing basis of social life.' The prevalence of 'manufactured' risks has important implications for the possibilities for interpretation. While Machiavelli (1532/1985) claimed that political action lies in a realm governed half by *fortuna* (fate) and half by human action, for Giddens (1991: 111–12), risk cannot accept the random forces of fate and 'fate has disappeared'. Rather than accepting the unpredictability of risk or fate, then, risk societies assume that some broad assessment of risks is possible for all activities and their outcomes. In doing so, they enable the intrusion of abstract systems into day-to-day life, such 'that awareness of risk seeps into the actions of almost everyone' (Giddens, 1991: 111–12). As risk logics expand into daily life, governing through risk moves security practice beyond the exclusive role of the state. Partnerships between the public and private sector are particularly evident in risk issues, such as critical infrastructure protection (Chapter 4) and countering terrorist financing (Chapter

11), but also in crime prevention and many other areas. Indeed, risk has tended to expand relationships of 'responsibilization', in which states, businesses, communities, families, churches, universities, other actors and institutions take on roles in surveillance, risk assessment, reporting and risk analysis, as well as actions to prevent and protect against risk events.

Acting on risk

In risk, the condition of security that is aimed for does not consist of the absence or elimination of threats but the management of risk and the production of a condition of resilience and a reduction in vulnerability (see Introduction and Chapter 4). Resilience seeks to minimize the harm that results from a particular event when it occurs rather than just the prevention of that event. This can be interpreted, as it is by poststructuralists, as part of a shift towards 'biopolitical' governance, in which the referent of governing shifts from territory towards populations, characterized by a move from the right to kill to 'making life live' (Dillon, 2008). Resilience underlies many human security practices that seek to empower the vulnerable (Chandler, 2012), such as disaster management (Comfort, 2005) and the growing importance of homeland security, energy security and cyber-security to secure ways of life (see Chapters 9, 11 and 13). A further shift occurs in relation to contemporary vulnerabilities, since rather than the national autonomy of future political action that motivates realist security practice, vulnerabilities are often shared by several states. Rather than security being achieved at the expense of others, in a risk-based system a different logic holds: 'when populations are organized in the form of "risk pools", they instantiate a political economy of profit and protection rather than an ethos of danger' (Aradau et al., 2008: 151). Importantly, some critics argue that by subjecting risks to supposedly neutral scientific processes that render the world knowable and predictable through probabilities and costs of events, the production of risks and the character of response are depoliticized and often technocratic (Hagmann and Cavelty, 2012).

Managerial responses to risk also reflect the complexity of risk calculations in which the consequences of actions are unpredictable and so strategic actions of the type licensed by traditional understandings of threat are difficult to achieve. Traditional strategies seek to alter some aspect of another actor's cost–benefit calculation. In risk, while this may be part of some strategies, for example the risk of crime and use of deterrence, it is not the sole or primary intervention. Further, rather than a clear relationship between means and ends found in most strategic thought (Weber's means–ends rationality); in risk, means and ends interact in complex ways and the limits of predictability mean that 'governments no longer master ends, only means' (Rasmussen, 2006: 37). Risk management does not establish grand strategies but a series of small but pervasive interventions, whereby incremental, technocratic changes rather than wholesale reform are the order of the day. Indeed, climate change and other potentially catastrophic changes are largely approached in technocratic and managerial ways rather than far-reaching reform and transformation (see Chapter 13). In many cases, this juxtaposition of catastrophic imaginations of the future with managerial responses in the present can be seen as combining the logics of securitization and risk management, of threat-based security and risk (Aradau and van Munster, 2007; Methmann and Rothe, 2012).

The significance of risk and the strategies of managerialism, responsibilization and prediction are most clearly illustrated in the archetypal risk-based security practice: insurance. Global spending on insurance is over three times defence expenditure and represents one of the largest economic sectors, with an industry worth $18.5 trillion, or 11% of global financial assets. Yet insurance, like military power, is concentrated in relatively few countries, with around 70% of policies bought in 2007 purchased within the G7 countries, and 88% in OECD countries (Lobo-Guerrero, 2008). In insurance, security is not conceived as a public good provided by the state, but a good provided by the market (see Chapter 4). Lobo-Guerrero's (2010) genealogy of insurance shows that it is a risk technology through which uncertainty is tamed, commodified and traded. Insurance not only provides protection of something valued against the contingencies of life, but establishes systems in which life and lifestyles are given a value in terms of revenue. This promotes and protects particular neoliberal entrepreneurial ways of life predicated on circulation, connection and certain forms of risk taking and produces the values it also seeks to protect.

There is, however, a deeper logic to much action on risk, that of precaution (Amoore and de Goede, 2008). This is particularly the case when the limits of prediction are reached with manufactured risks. While insurance seeks actuarial knowledge to clearly specify probabilities and distribute costs accordingly, the logic of precaution takes over when risk is not calculable. This comes close to the fatalist logic in the security dilemma: if we cannot know with certainty, the prudent thing to do is to prepare for the worst. Thus, Aradau and van Munster (2007) argue that the 'war on terror' introduced a new precautionary logic to security encouraged by the limits of calculability and prediction for terrorist events. Precautionary logics have fed into violent action justified on the basis of prevention. Indeed, some argue that the same logic of attempting to manage uncertainty can lead to pre-emptive action (de Goede and Randalls, 2009). Danger still inhabits the unknown in this precautionary logic, but the foundation of securitization is different. While for some the challenge is to develop better calculations of risk, for others the fact that there is no experience of the catastrophes imagined by contemporary security practices means that precautionary logics celebrate the unknown, and securitize on the basis of 'simple suspicions' (Ewald, 2002) and a threat that 'cannot be specified' (Massumi, 2007).

Conclusion

The limits of certainty in practical security knowledge shape the logics of security action. While total certainty is impossible, much security theory and practice sees the production of a degree of certainty as foundational to security. The security dilemma emphasizes the limits of certainty that can be achieved about other states' intentions and capabilities under conditions of anarchy. Difficult decisions between doubtful courses of action, the choosing of the lesser evil, rely on the dilemma of interpreting ambiguous and possibly misleading information in a context of imperfect communication and limited trust. The resultant paradox that actions to ensure security may have negative effects is common to all approaches. In the security dilemma, this paradox operates through the production of fear. The extent to which uncertainty and fear shape the logics of security action is determined by one's view of the international system and the rationality of decision makers. Fatalist logics assert a deterministic world in which states want but never achieve 100 per cent certainty and respond to this impossibility with power. Mitigator logics assert multiple different worlds in which the conditions of uncertainty are changeable and strategic action (based on rationality assumptions) is more political. Transcender logics assert the negation of fear through trust but not the eradication of uncertainty. While uncertainty precludes control, it is often responded to by a desire for predictability, the distancing of contingency and the production of seemingly universal strategies for security. This search for control is also found in concepts of risk that are increasingly pervasive in security agendas. While traditional security operates on the logic of threat (intention + capability) and response (strategy), risk operates on a calculus of probabilities and harms. It is more unpredictable, more diffuse, less controllable and, ultimately, cannot be eliminated only managed. This leads to an attempt to colonize and control the future through often depoliticized strategies that rely on logics of management and precaution and seek to build resilience and reduce vulnerability. These different concepts of uncertainty have previously inhabited different political spheres but threat and risk logics are now mixed and the political spheres of domestic and international security are merging. However, this merger is far from complete. The next two chapters explore these issues further by looking at how states enact their strategies by forming security groupings, such as alliances, regimes and other institutions (Chapter 6), and ultimately through war (Chapter 7).

Chapter 6

Global and Regional Security Formations

This chapter looks at the range and roles of what we can term 'security formations'. While much literature speaks in general terms of security institutions, which include formal organizations and regimes, this chapter has a wider focus on the range of ways states come together in more or less durable formations of security relationships, hence the term 'security formation'. These relate primarily to the various forms of cooperative relationships states form with each other to pursue security, ranging from attempts to create global collective and common security to alliances, regimes and security communities. These characterizations and concepts of security formations emphasize the different social logics and practical limits in the purpose, dynamics and durability of security seeking beyond the state. The chapter then looks at regional security in order to show how states' security relationships differ at the regional and global level, with some important implications for the supposedly universal claims put forth by many approaches to security. Such regional security formations include cooperation and conflict in relatively durable configurations. Finally, it draws out the ways in which regional security formations, including security communities and other groupings, may complement or conflict with global collective or common security.

The central theme of the chapter is the construction of cooperation in interstate security relationships. Cooperation is seen as difficult in anarchy, and for realists the logics of competition predominate because of uncertainty (see Chapter 5). However, for liberals, cooperation is not invalidated by uncertainty in anarchy. Rather, institutions of various types 'play a role in security relations *because* states are bedevilled by the problem of uncertainty' (Wallander et al., 1999: 3). Uncertainty means that states invest in information and the institutions that provide it. For constructivists and some critical theorists, cooperative and conflictual relationships are not universal but are constructed through particular social and historical processes. Rather than merely altering the cost–benefit calculations of rational actors, these perspectives view security formations as evolving through processes of socialization. The debate, however, is not as polarized as this picture implies. In particular, debates about security formations problematize the understanding of realism as based on simple cost–benefit power decisions, liberalism on institutions, constructivism on socialization, and critical approaches on cosmopolitanism and change. Rather, all approaches combine varying emphases and interpretations on all aspects.

Global security formations

Collective and common security

'Collective security' is an idea whose time has come, many times. Collective security means the provision of security as a collective good rather than as a national good provided in competition with others. It is often a vague and 'protean' concept, widely deployed, poorly understood and greeted with either exuberant enthusiasm or derision (Betts, 1992; Downs, 1994). It is primarily related to a condition of interstate security in a limited form of the protection of states' rights through collective enforcement in cases of violation, rather than more positive and cosmopolitan themes of peace and justice (Kelsen, 1948).

There are varying degrees of collective security. In minimal forms, international law supports the use of force in self-defence and reprisal for illegal action, but gives a framework in which states acting in line with international law are seen as acting for the collective of law. This does not replace a self-help environment, and the use of force and enforcement is decentralized (Kelsen, 1948). Minimal collective security can be found in regional 'concert' arrangements, such as the Concert of Europe (1815–1914), which prevented bipolar divisions and kept a peace in Europe between Austria, France (after 1818), Prussia, the Russian Empire and the UK for 40 years after the Napoleonic Wars until the Crimean War (1854–56). In concerts, the most powerful states maintain the status quo and avoid war. Consensus decision making is emphasized but often lacks a formal mechanism and flexible, informal arrangements predominate. This allows power balancing to be more subtle and effective rather than an exclusive mechanism for producing stability within the concert (Kupchan and Kupchan, 1991). A middle-level approach is evident when a central body makes decisions about the use of force in enforcement action. States may agree to renounce the use of force on their own initiative and reserve it only to the central organ of governance (Kelsen, 1948). Somewhere between this middle and the maximal view lies Claude's (1962) concept of 'ideal collective security', in which security is provided for all states, by all states, and there is a strong legally binding commitment to respond to aggression. For Kelsen (1948), maximal collective security exists when only a central organization has the means to use force, when the legal and practical monopoly on the use of force rests with a central body, and other actors are disarmed. This is the model of the sovereign nation-state (see Chapter 4). Importantly, no collective security formation at the international level has attempted this and even the UN does not fully reach the middle level.

The issue of self-defence is a primary limit on all forms of collective security. The right to self-defence is enshrined in international law and, in various forms, in domestic laws. Kelsen (1948: 785) argued that this has to be the case, even in maximal forms of collective security, for simple pragmatic reasons:

> Between the moment the illegal attack starts and the moment the centralized machinery of collective security is put into action, there is, even in case of its perfectly prompt functioning, a space of time, an interval, which may be disastrous to the victim.

This limit has beset all collective security relations, and led to the darkest hour of the UN: its failure to act effectively in the Rwandan genocide of 1994.

The first attempt to build collective security at the global level was the formation of the League of Nations (1919–46) at the end of the First World War. This failed due to a lack of enforcement powers and slow decision making hampered by the need for consensus, which meant that each member state had effective veto power over any action. The formation of the United Nations (UN) around the end of the Second World War (1945) attempted to learn these lessons by moving up the scale of collective security. First, its collective security commitment is stronger. Whereas the League committed members not to go to war with each other and to refer disputes to its council, the UN Charter goes further and commits states not to use force in their relations with each other (except in self-defence), or even to threaten to use force. Second, it incorporates a greater centralization of the use of force by having a mechanism through which military action can be authorized to preserve peace and security, and the legitimacy it can convey on the use of force is of primary importance. Throughout its history, the UN has not been asked for its authorization in many cases of war and military intervention, and in many other cases, it has denied it and military force has gone ahead regardless.

There is a deep tension in the structure of the UN between its ostensibly collective goals and the uneven power structures embedded in its primary security organ, the UN Security Council (UNSC). This comprises the permanent five (P5) members (the USA, the USSR/Russia, China, the UK and France) and 10 other members on a rotating basis. The P5 hold veto power, while the other members do not. This veto was utilized regularly during the Cold War (1946–89), which constrained the UN's collective security roles and marginalized it from the central peace and security issues of the day. The third attempt to build collective security has produced change in the UN. It has seen a substantial expansion in peacekeeping activities (see Chapter 10), discussed a growing range of security issues in the UNSC, has made extensive use of sanctions, and is growing collaborations with other international and regional security organizations. Freed from bipolar constraints, the UNSC became a more significant security organ in the 1990s: of the 294 vetoes used in the UNSC from 1946 to 2002, only 7 were cast from 1991 to 2000. The UNSC also became more able to reach consensus decisions more rapidly, increasing from an average of one resolution per month during the Cold War, to one per week since. A far greater proportion of resolutions have been agreed under Chapter VII of the UN Charter (enabling enforcement measures) (Wallensteen and Johansen, 2004). While still often neglected, seeking UNSC authorization has also become a more important political requirement for legitimizing the use of force by states (Voeten, 2005), although this has recently been diminished by a US preference for ad-hoc coalitions and unilateral action. In spite of these practical developments, deeper attempts to reform the formal structures of the UNSC towards more collective forms have consistently faltered (Weiss, 2003).

While collective security is primarily concerned with stability, 'common security' extends similar arguments to more positive and human-centred security. Retaining an interstate foundation, common security is based on the idea that security is best achieved on the foundations of reciprocal relations rather than mutual fear between states. In the latter stages of the Cold War, common security was influential among a network of government officials and civil society groups that extended across the bipolar divide. In particular, the 1982 Palme Commission, which brought together officials from NATO and Warsaw Pact countries as well as some neutral and nonaligned countries, articulated a foundation for common security that recognized that the two sides 'must achieve security not against the adversary but with him. International Security must rest on a commitment to joint survival rather than on a threat of mutual destruction' (Palme, 1982: ix). Importantly, this was premised on the idea that threats arise not just from individual states but 'global problems shared by the entire international community', including nuclear war, but also disparities in living standards and environmental degradation (Buzan and Hansen, 2009: 137). Although mostly disregarded by security theorists, the idea catalysed some confidence and security-building measures (CSBMs) to reduce mistrust, particularly in the nuclear sphere. While there remained diversity among commission members on whether to pursue nuclear disarmament or to see nuclear weapons as a precondition for prudent behaviour, there was agreement that contemporary developments of nuclear war-fighting strategies were potentially dangerous. Fuller notions of common security have expanded since the end of the Cold War. This can be found theoretically in the cosmopolitan hopes for emancipation found in Welsh School CSS, and in some of the policy discourses and practices of humanitarianism and human security (see Chapters 9 and 10). Most notably, in 2004, a High-level UN Panel Report redescribed collective security as the security of all states and peoples against their 'mutual vulnerability' to transnational crime, terrorism, weapons proliferation, disease and poverty (UN, 2004).

Alliances

Alliances form on the basis of collective defence, not collective security: members commit to responding collectively if one member is attacked by an external state, although the form of that response is not guaranteed to include the use of military force. While alliances are sometimes defined as 'a formal or informal relationship of security cooperation between two or more sovereign states' (Walt, 1987: 1), this encompasses any form of security cooperation and most concepts emphasize arrangements focused on military security, particularly the pooling of military resources, in which cooperation has an external orientation (Snyder, 1997; Walt, 1997). These may still be formal, as in NATO, or informal, as in contemporary US preferences for coalitions of the willing (ad-hoc coalitions formed for particular operations or wars).

Since alliances are defined by cooperation *against* another state (or alliance), they are closely related to theories of the balance of power or the balance of threat (Walt, 1987) (see Chapter 2). Realists like Walt (1997) and Snyder (1997) analyse alliance formation as a subset of security behaviours undertaken on the basis of cost–benefit analysis. The benefits of alliances relate primarily to capabilities' aggregation: they increase the military power of a state more cheaply than investment in building up national military forces. Alliances thereby enhance deterrence, to prevent an attack, strengthen defence, if an attack happens, pool resources and spread the costs of military capabilities and/or allow states to engage in preclusion (forming an alliance with a potential enemy, or ally of an enemy, in order to prevent potentially hostile alignment). Alliances are also costly, both internally and externally. Internal costs relate to the risks of entrapment or abandonment. Entrapment is the foreclosure of options incurred in forming an alliance and the risk that allies may draw a state into a conflict it would not otherwise be involved in. Abandonment is the risk that allies will abandon the state in a crisis. These costs are contradictory, but relate not just to alliance formation but its degree of institutionalization: a stronger degree of institutionalization reduces the risks of abandonment but increases the risks of entrapment and vice versa. Snyder (1984) refers to this as the 'alliance security dilemma'. A related internal cost is that alliances require management, and management costs generally fall on the more powerful states such as the USA in NATO. External costs of alliances relate to their effects on wider security relations and uncertainty (see Chapter 5). Forming a powerful alliance runs the risk of prompting counterbalancing, or even a spiral/security paradox. Further, states may wish to retain some secrecy and uncertainty about their intentions and capabilities, but forming alliances often entails giving away some information and reducing rivals' uncertainty and the resultant precautions they might otherwise exercise (Snyder, 1997).

In most theories, states choose their allies on the basis of relative power or threat concerns. While Snyder emphasizes balance of power and Walt balance of threat (see Chapter 2), both locate the prime drivers of alliance formation among the systemic and structural features of global security politics. Domestic factors only feature in specific and limited ways such as how and how quickly an alliance will form (Snyder, 1997). Domestic factors, such as ideology and culture, also have some importance in the choice of allies, but realists argue that these are additional; that is, all other (systemic, power and threat) things being equal, states will tend to form alliances with those with similar political values or ideologies – liberal democracies ally with liberal democracies, Marxist governments with other Marxists and so on (Walt, 1987).

Alliances may fall apart for the same reasons they form: changes in the distribution of power or threat, domestic political and ideological affinities, and changes in the degree to which member states believe an alliance to have 'credibility' – either in effectiveness in countering threat or in the credibility of mutual assurances among members (Walt, 1997). For Mearsheimer (2001: 33), alliances are merely 'temporary marriages of convenience'. Yet NATO, the most studied alliance, clearly does not fit this prediction. NATO has survived, thrived and expanded its membership and its roles since the end of the Cold War, in the absence of the threat against which it was initially formed. Rationalist theorists argue that the persistence of NATO can still be explained by some form of cost–benefit calculation. Some argue that NATO expansion has been a means of reinforcing US hegemony that will eventually wane (Layne, 2000; Mearsheimer, 2001).

Others emphasize that alliances persist due to internal changes rather than falling apart because of external ones. Here, processes of institutionalization and socialization alter the cost–benefit calculations of alliance members. While, in general, security theory institutions are emphasized by liberal scholars and socialization by constructivist scholars, in studies of alliances some realists give these issues some significance. Institutionalization may explain alliance persistence and strength, since liberalism indicates that institutions help firm up expectations, reduce uncertainty and the prospects for cheating, and enable beneficial cooperation (see Chapter 2). Further, since building institutions is expensive, states may choose to use existing alliance institutions to follow wider security goals rather than build new institutions for each new purpose; thus NATO was claimed to have moved from a defensive alliance to a 'security management institution' (Wallander and Keohane, 1999; Wallander, 2000). Institutionalization also builds up bureaucracies within formal organizations, and there is an 'elaborate transatlantic network of former NATO officials, defence intellectuals, military officers, journalists and policy analysts who have both influence and much to lose if the alliance were to collapse' (Walt, 1997: 166). Thus, institutionalization creates both capabilities and interests in the persistence and perhaps expansion of the alliance that do not derive from the initial reasons for its formation. A degree of socialization also accompanies alliance development and may explain their persistence. Members of an alliance may come to see themselves as having common values, goals and even identity. This blurs the distinction between alliances and security communities (see below). However, Walt argues that the concept of security communities is not applicable to NATO, as although some degree of socialization exists, the ties of this regional community are less strong than national ties and interests (not a claim made by security community theories). Further, Walt (1997) argues that state leaders may use the language of common community without really believing it, and that even if an alliance produced socialization, there is little reason to assume that this socialization would outlast the more foundational strategic rationales and contexts.

Regimes

Regimes are 'sets of implicit or explicit principles, norms, rules, and decision making procedures around which actors' expectation converge in a given area of international relations' (Krasner, 1982a: 185). Unlike global collective security or common security, or externally focused alliances, regimes are security formations confined to particular issue areas. While their core functions can be characterized as enhancing the 'detection' of cheating and reducing incentives for 'defection' (Stein, 1985), regimes are social institutions that may contribute to these functions but are not only functional. The concept of regimes introduces a sense of states' interactions shaping behaviour and outcomes rather than simple structural or domestic politics models (Stein, 1982). Importantly, regimes are seen to exist when patterns of behaviour do not fully conform to the model of politics in which states seek short-term gains on the basis of egoism in anarchy. Even realists like Krasner (1982a: 187) argue that 'it is the infusion of behavior with principles and norms that distinguishes regime-governed activity in the international system from more conventional activity, guided exclusively by narrow calculations of interest'. Regimes, therefore, are more than the sum of their parts – norms, procedures and perhaps their embodiment in treaties, agreements and organizations. Many areas of security politics have some or all these ingredients. However, it is the characterization of relations as anomalous to the predicted baseline of conflict that separates regimes from other security politics. It is on this basis that Jervis (1982) indicates that many apparent agreed rules in the security sphere do not constitute regimes but instrumental agreements with a short life span.

Perspectives on regimes follow the broad constellations of assumptions found in realist, liberal and constructivist theories (Hasenclever et al., 1997). Realism's emphasis on anarchy, self-help and security-seeking states as valuing relative rather than absolute gains predisposes realist accounts to posit strong limits to the formation and significance of regimes. Realists tend to view regimes, if they matter at all, as 'intervening variables' that complicate and shape the rational calculations and actions of states but do not supplant or transform the conditions of anarchy, power and fear, although Krasner (1982b) also articulated a view of regimes as having some autonomous importance. Liberal perspectives on shared interests, institutions (of which regimes are one type) and the seeking of absolute gains mean they are more optimistic about regimes. Regimes enable cooperation and the pursuit of longer term goals and have autonomous importance. Constructivists emphasize the importance of regime norms and identity formation in producing different understandings of states' interests and how they are pursued.

However, debates on regimes enable a coming together of realist and liberal paradigms in a focus on the shaping of behaviour that relies neither on pure structure and anarchy nor domestic politics (Haggard and Simmons, 1987). Regimes, then, occupy a middle ground between most theories: they exist between anarchy and hierarchy. Regimes are not merely created by design, but emerge from human interactions and evolve through their internal dynamics and external contextual change (Young, 1982). Thus, they may be less formal than international organizations, less deliberate than negotiated treaties and laws, but more than an expression of power competition. Certainly, most realist and neoliberal theories of regime formation assert a close association between the distribution of power and the formation of regimes: regimes tend to be formed by the most powerful states to pursue the forms of cooperation they wish to see. However, whether regimes require a hegemon to create and sustain them is more debated (Keohane, 1984). The structures of power within regimes, much as the special status of the P5 in the UNSC, tend to reflect the distribution of power at the time of their formation. Yet, regimes may persist when the distribution of power changes.

As with alliances, regimes persist when the distribution of power that created them changes because of institutionalization and socialization. Krasner explains this in terms of 'lags' and 'feedback'. Lags are when the distribution of power or the interests of the most powerful change but the regime does not. This means that regimes are slower to change than power distributions. This may be for reasons of custom (states and policy makers become used to doing things in a particular way, and will continue to do so out of habit), or cognitive reasons (states may be dissatisfied with a regime but cannot articulate an alternative). Krasner also highlights the issue of uncertainty (see Chapter 5). States continue to participate and invest in regimes when power distributions change as there is uncertainty about the future durability and strength of a change in power. The metaphor here is not one of states as billiard balls colliding on an anarchic table (as in basic realism), but of tectonic plates shifting: in regime formation, the plates of power and regime are close together, but may drift apart over time. When those incongruities become acute, a regime, or its contents of rules and norms, may change or collapse, but they will not do so quickly and maybe not until a compelling alternative is agreed. At the systemic level, Krasner argues that this explains the endurance of the organizing principle of state sovereignty in international relations even when it doesn't fit as closely with the character of relations as it did in the 18th century.

Feedback is the process through which regimes affect that basic character and distribution of power and the calculation of interests and strategies. Notions of 'feedback' are disruptive of basic realist assumptions, but are emphasized (with different terminology) by liberals and constructivists. For Jervis (1982), regimes are based on rational egoism and participation in a regime does not affect a state's identity and its identity does not affect its interests (there is no feedback). In contrast, constructivists and liberals argue that identities and interests are shaped through regimes, and norms and expectations of international behaviour evolve. This means that regimes are not just built on the foundations of power and interest that they initially reflect, but take on a life of their own and have an effect on power and interests. A middle ground is taken by Krasner's (1982b) realist view, which outlines four basic feedback mechanisms. First, regimes may alter actors' calculations of how to maximize their interests by establishing forms and procedures for the flow of information, communication and decision making that alter the incentives and opportunities for acting in a particular way, that is, mitigating the security dilemma. While establishing regimes has some costs, when they exist it is often more attractive to maintain them and use them than to invent new, untested (uncertain) procedures (Krasner, 1982b). Second, regimes may change actors' interests. Increased transaction flows, connections and understanding between members increase interdependence and raise the opportunity costs of change. For Haas (1982), regimes allow more transactions among states than would otherwise be possible and generate greater amounts of information flow between states. In some cases, regimes also contribute to the development of 'epistemic communities', which are communities of policy makers and practitioners who develop common understandings of the character of cause and effect relationships and the values held within the governing of those relationships (Haas, 1989; Adler and Haas, 1992). Krasner's third and fourth mechanisms relate to power. Regimes that enable greater transactions tend to set the conditions of who benefits; for example, the trade regime based on norms of free trade tends to benefit export industries (and their political allies) rather than import-dependent economies. This creates feedback in two ways: first, by altering the distribution of power among certain actors; and second, by being, in itself, a source of power, as states use regimes to legitimate particular norms and practices (Krasner, 1982b; Duffield, 1994).

Jervis (1982) argued that regimes are both difficult and necessary to achieve in the security field due to the security dilemma (paradox). He argued that few regimes are successful, with the exception of the Concert of Europe. However, Jervis was using the term 'regimes' to apply to more general forms of collective security. Nye (1987) claims that this pessimistic argument does not hold when one views security regimes as issue-based forms of cooperation. Rather, there was a 'mosaic' of 'partial regimes' covering (imperfectly) a wide range of security issues in US–Soviet security relations. Focusing on issue-specific forms of behaviour and outcomes rather than talking of 'security' writ large allows the debate on security regimes to be more productive. While an overly pessimistic account cannot raise questions of how states learn, redefine their interests, or change their behaviour, regime concepts enable exploration of security behaviour's variation in different issues. For instance, there is arguably a nuclear nonproliferation regime, the centrepiece of which is the 1968 Nuclear Non-Proliferation Treaty, but which extends to the role of norms, numerous other treaties, and organizations from the International Atomic Energy Agency to more informal frameworks for cooperation among states that supply nuclear technologies (for peaceful purposes), such as the Nuclear Suppliers Group and the Zangger Committee (see Chapter 8). This regime has long outlasted the distribution of power in which it was set up and has continued to evolve. While evaluations of its success vary (several states have gained nuclear weapons since 1968), and debates remain as to its adequacy for tackling contemporary proliferation challenges, such as the nuclear weapons programme of North Korea or the prospect of nuclear terrorism (see Chapters 8 and 11), this regime continues to articulate norms, solidify expectations, and provide a forum for discussion of these issues that would not otherwise exist. More importantly, for now, the existence and significance of this regime indicates that in certain areas of security policy, including those related to the most powerful of military capabilities, regimes can be a useful way of understanding security formations that alter the logics and limits of security politics.

Beyond nuclear weapons, regimes are present in many other aspects of military security, particularly covering other categories of weapons in the form of arms control and disarmament (see Chapter 8), or the range of CSBMs and forms of regional security cooperation discussed later. As definitions of security have broadened, the range of possible regimes of concern to scholars of security has expanded. It is debatable whether true regimes exist in these issue areas, or just some of the necessary ingredients. Certainly, the politics of issues of transnational crime and terrorism (see Chapters 11 and 12) contain many of the norms, formal agreements and treaties, coordinated forms of action and other things that may characterize them as regimes. Some security fields lack a single regime but encompass areas where wider or narrower regimes are present. Human security, for instance, is not spoken of as a regime but wider economic regimes (such as global trade regimes) and a human rights regime cover some aspects of the problem (Donnelly, 1986) (see Chapter 9). Climate change, which has important implications for environmental security, lacks a single overarching regime, but there can be argued to be a 'regime complex', a 'loosely-coupled set of specific regimes' on particular aspects of the problem (Keohane and Victor, 2011) (see Chapter 13).

Security communities

Security communities are groups of states among which relationships are socialized to the extent that they can be characterized as a 'community' in which war has become unthinkable. For instance, it is difficult to imagine a war among the states of North America or the states of most of Europe. Deutsch (1957: 5) created the concept of security communities in the 1950s, and defined them as a:

> group of people which has become 'integrated'. By *integration* we mean the attainment, within a territory, of a 'sense of community' and of institutions and practices strong enough and widespread enough to assure ... dependable expectations of 'peaceful change' among its population. By *sense of community* we mean a belief ... that common social problems must and can be resolved by processes of 'peaceful change'.

Security communities are formations in which there is profound transformation of security relations between actors beyond a few specific issues. They differ in the extent of integration and the significance of collective identity formation (Adler and Barnett, 1998a). Importantly, Deutsch spoke of a 'pluralistic security community', which differs from the notion of community discussed in relation to the state and domestic security practices (see Chapter 4). In pluralistic communities, member states remain sovereign, unlike national political communities, where sovereignty passes to the state, or formal federalism where it is shared in some ways (which Deutsch called 'amalgamated security communities'). Decision making remains national, but decisions are shaped by a sense of community, thus they have some commonality with medium-level forms of collective security. Security communities are conceptually distinct from purely strategic accounts of alliances but in practice much focus has been on how alliances like NATO can become security communities. Adler (2008: 213) argues that NATO's functional and geographical expansion produced a cognitive change and the development of a community of 'self-restraint', in which it progressively 'replace[d] balance of power practices with security-community practice'.

Deutsch prefigured later constructivist thought that sees security communities as one type of social structure that contrasts with the security dilemma (Adler and Barnett, 1998b; Bellamy, 2004) (see Chapter 5). Since, for constructivists, social structures and identities are produced by states' interactions, both the security dilemma and security communities can be conceived as social systems. Wendt (1995: 73), for example, claims that: 'A security dilemma ... is a social structure composed of inter-subjective understandings in which states are so distrustful that they make worst-case assumptions about each others' intentions, and as a result define their interests in self-help terms.' Security communities, in contrast, are 'composed of shared knowledge in which states trust one another to resolve disputes without war'. It is not that a natural or given order, a foundation of normal conflictual behaviour in anarchy, is supplanted by an anomalous pattern (as in rationalist accounts of regimes), but that one social system is replaced with another. This occurs not only through the alteration of incentive structures but also through processes of normative development and social learning; that is, states develop norms about not going to war with each other, or not even preparing for war with each other, and they learn to abide by them. Deutsch pointed out that most norms and laws are adhered to voluntarily not merely by threat of punishment, as found when such voluntary compliance was lacking in the USA under prohibition (Bellamy, 2004). Thus, the realist appropriation of the Hobbesian account of order relying on a single sovereign is mistaken, since rule-based order is learned as much as it is enforced.

For Deutsch (1966: 77), it is communication that produces communities: 'Communication alone enables a group to think together, to see together, and to act together.' He took inspiration from communication theory and the work of his friend and colleague, Norbert Weiner, on cybernetics to speak of complex networks of interaction, transaction and communication (Adler and Barnett, 1998b; Alker and Biersteker, 2011). Formed beyond the strategic relations of states that dominate alliances and regimes, the process of integration and the creation of a sense of community relate to the development and implications of a wide range of mutual transactions that are international and transnational, such as trade, migration, educational exchanges and so on, which produce a range of channels of communication (beyond those addressed in Chapter 5's discussion of communication in the security dilemma). It thus goes beyond rationalist accounts of cooperation, or of alliance or regime persistence and evolution, since these emphasize instrumental logics within the socialization of policy-making elites in the formal institutions of alliances, or the changing cost–benefit calculations related to the widening utilization of institutional resources. While institutionalization matters in the formation of security communities, levels of institutionalization vary in practice and the growth of community is not conceived solely as a result of this.

Deutsch's research programme faltered in the shadow of classical and neorealist projects that envision an atomistic world of autonomous states rather than transactionally connected and produced communities. The rise of constructivism and the end of the Cold War enabled a resurgence of the concept, and Adler and Barnett (1998b: 4) argued that amid the broadening of security issues, there was emerging a:

> transnational community of *Deutschian* policy-makers ... who are challenging the once nearly hegemonic position of realist-inspired policy makers and offering an alternative understanding of what is possible in global politics and a map to get there.

They refined and systematized the Deutschian model by identifying multiple types of security communities – 'loosely coupled' and 'tightly coupled', the latter going beyond expectations of peaceful change to more structured forms of governance and mutual aid. Adler and Barnett (1998a) also produced a three-stage model of their development through 'nascent', 'ascendant' and 'mature' phases, which shows the difficulties and characteristics of the process of development. In generating this linear model, they identified the need for 'precipitating conditions' of some significant change that prompts the development of community, such as changing technological, demographic, economic and environmental contexts, changing interpretations of social reality, or changing external threats. These are added to by factors conducive to mutual trust and collective identity, including structural factors of power and knowledge, and 'process' factors, including Deutsch's emphasis on transactions as a form of bounded communication between actors, be that symbolic, material, economic, political or other forms of transaction, as well as an emphasis on international organizations and social learning processes. Together, these factors may produce mutual trust and collective identity to varying degrees (discussed in terms of tight or loose coupling), which are the necessary conditions for identifying a security community as existing (Adler and Barnett, 1998a). Recent practice theories (see Chapter 3) have further developed understandings of security communities, emphasizing how the daily practices of security professionals constitute and embed 'self-restraint' and the sense of community that shapes security (Williams and Neumann, 2000; Bjola and Kronprobst, 2007; Williams, 2007; Adler, 2008; Pouliot, 2008). Here, it is not just that norms of restraint develop in interstate processes and are then embedded in institutions and become internalized. Rather, such theories also emphasize 'background' or 'tacit' knowledge – forms of knowledge that arise within practice.

Regional security

In collective and common security, there is a foundational political claim that the geographic extent of security politics and institutions should match that of the security threats encountered – global problems require global solutions. While most theories of security seek universal claims, much security practice arises not at the global systemic level but in distinct regional formations. Security communities largely emerge regionally rather than globally. Many alliances and regimes are also regional rather than global. Further, many conflicts have strong regional dynamics not attributable to the relative position of states in a global distribution of power: the long-standing rivalry and conflict between India and Pakistan set the scene of regional security dynamics that are not just a function of the global distribution of power. Thus, it is important to explore how security practices and formations differ in specific geographically defined locations.

What is a region?

Defining regions may seem easy: one simply looks at a map and can see continental formations that group states together. However, a map is a poor guide to the regional character of security relations, as shared borders would place Russia and China in the same region, and shared neighbours would mean China and Finland are part of the same region, when it is self-evident that they are not. While simple geography is insufficient, geography matters in more specific ways. Regions are conceived as subgroupings of the global relations of states where there are regular and intense relations among members that are qualitatively different to those with non-regional states: most notably, a degree of interdependence as well as geographical proximity (Nye, 1968). In addition, some argue that regions should be recognized as such by those within and outside them, and some degree of political, economic, cultural and linguistic similarities is also emphasized. In security studies, it is the existence of interlinked systems of power distribution or security interdependencies that is most prominently emphasized. Security regions are therefore theoretically informed constructs that apply and often modify global understandings of security. Indeed, many combine a neorealist emphasis on the distribution of material capabilities and polarity with some elements of constructivism (Lake and Morgan, 1997; Morgan, 1997; Buzan and Waever, 2003; Frazier and Stewart-Ingersoll, 2010).

Some rationalist approaches view regions as merely a level of analysis, a subset of the globe but reflecting the same purportedly universal patterns and logics of behaviour that are posited globally. For Mearsheimer (2001: 44), hegemony is only really possible at the regional level, in part because conventional military force projection is limited by the importance of land forces and the associated 'stopping power of water'. Similarly, Walt's (1987) balance of threat concept includes geographical factors as determining whether the power of one state will be interpreted as a threat by others, thus imposing some limits of geographical scale on the intensity of security relations. Other realists view regions as systems in their own right that contain their own distributions and balances of power, their own polarities and even hegemons. For Lake and Morgan (1997: 7), these are not simply smaller areas where the global logics of security are 'played out in miniature', nor are regions so unique that they require completely different theories. Rather, regions modify realist predictions. Regions are open systems (open to developments, dynamics and actors from the global system and other regions), whereas the global system of structural realism is closed (it already encompasses all actors and processes). This means that Waltz's globally framed argument that bipolar systems are stable (see Chapter 2) does not work at the regional level because regional powers can always draw in resources from external (non-regional) states: bipolarity produces 'internal balancing' and stability at the global level, but 'external balancing' and possible instability at the regional level (Lake and Morgan, 1997: 10).

Regional security complex (RSC) theory, developed by the Copenhagen School, is one of the most influential concepts of regional security. Regional security complexes are groups of states whose security problems are so closely linked (interdependent) that their national security concerns cannot be considered or resolved apart from one another (Buzan, 1991; Buzan and Waever, 2003). In other words, security concerns, and the processes of securitization, manifest in regional clusters marked by intense interdependence within and 'security indifference' with those outside (Buzan and Waever, 2003: 48). RSC theory echoes Walt's balance of threat concept, as Buzan and Waever (2003: 4) claim that 'insecurity is often associated with proximity' and 'most threats travel more easily over short distances than long ones'. But it combines this with constructivist relational understandings of securitization. Important regional power relations and patterns of 'amity and enmity' constitute durable 'sub-global, geographically coherent patterns of security interdependence' (2003: 45). While durable, these patterns evolve so that regional security complexes may expand or even merge. In Europe, for example, the end of the Cold War brought new geographical distinctions characterized more by interdependence than by difference and opposition, as 'Eastern Europe moved West and became Central and Eastern Europe (CEE), and the former Soviet Union (FSU) became a new international sub-system of states' (Buzan and Hansen, 2009: 180). Likewise, Northeast Asia and Southeast Asia have become part of a single East Asian complex, drawing in Australia and New Zealand. This is important, as it implies that seemingly permanent lines of division in global politics are deeply malleable above the level of the state, and in ways that are not merely about changing global distributions of power.

Constructivist accounts emphasize the importance of regional identity. For Adler (1997), regional security communities can be seen as 'imagined communities', just as nations are. Regions, here, are less tied to geographical proximity, so Australia is part of a Western security community and the US–Israel relationship can be characterized as a security community in spite of the vast distance between them (Higgott and Nossal, 1998). Williams and Neumann (2000) draw on Bourdieu's concepts of symbolic power to argue that institutions like NATO can be viewed as a field of practice in which identities are produced, forms of capital (such as symbolic capital) are accumulated and used, and forms of power (symbolic, cultural and so on) are exercised. In this way, NATO articulated the 'West' as a liberal democratic security community (Williams, 2007). Combining constructivism with particular normative perspectives articulates 'regionalism' as a political project that sees regions as a preferable level for providing governance and security (Hettne, 1999; Fawcett, 2004). Rather than defining security regions solely by the intensity of security relations, these perspectives combine economic and security regionalization and emphasize an increase in wider processes of regional integration within which security operates.

Regionalization and difference

It is often claimed that security and other interstate relations have become regionalized since the 1980s (Hurrell, 1995; Söderbaum and Shaw, 2003; Fawn, 2009). Certainly, many security issues tend to manifest regionally. Most interstate conflicts occur between regional neighbours, and the most protracted geopolitical rivalries are regional, such as that between India and Pakistan, or hotspots like the South China Seas. Civil wars have become particularly regionalized as violence often spills over borders, and neighbouring states are affected by refugee flows and may support one side or another in the conflict. Indeed, one of the major security roles of regional organizations has been forms of peacekeeping and peace enforcement. However, it would be a mistake to assume that all security issues are regionalized in the same way. Buzan and Waever (2003) acknowledge this when they indicate that the geographical and material foundations are not the same for all 'sectors' of security and are less consistent for the economic sector than others, as global rather than regional relations are more significant. Beyond this, however, assuming that threats have a regional character masks important geographical differences. While some issues, such as aspects of poverty and disease, encompass the whole of a region, or at least the states responsible for governing the territory and population of a region, others are transnational in various ways, from cross-border but localized resource issues and illicit trafficking to wider migration flows, natural disasters, transnational crime and so on. The spatiality of these issues may all be considered 'regional', but there are wide differences between them: one cannot assume that competition over water resources has the same spatiality as the transnational flow of narcotics (see Chapters 12 and 13). Thus, amid the diversity of security issues, it is the state as a fixed territorialized political actor that underlies the relative geographic stability of the regional level. Regions remain primarily conceived as groups of states, combining to tackle security issues that are in some way regional.

The key contribution of studies of regional security is showing that there are greater differences in security interactions than can be accounted for in universalist or global understandings. For instance, RSC theory has been used to show that different sectors are securitized in different regions:

- In East Asia, the Middle East and post-Soviet states, military and political issues are securitized.
- In South Asia, military and political issues and some economic issues are securitized.
- In Africa, political and societal sectors are the most securitized, with major arguments around the economic sector.
- In South America, there is variation, with the Southern Cone seeing political and economic issues securitized, and the Andean north seeing military, political, economic and societal sectors securitized.
- In North America, the primary security sectors are the political, societal and economic, plus issues pertaining to military dynamics for the USA as a global actor.
- In Europe, political and societal issues are often securitized.

This shows that in areas viewed as security communities (Europe and North America), economic and societal issues are most prominent, but in 'conflict formations', military and political security are emphasized (Buzan and Waever, 2003: 476–7). Further, there are different types of regions based on differing degrees of integration. For Morgan (1997), various types of conflict management systems can develop at the regional level ranging from a balance of power, great power concert, forms of multilateral collective management undertaken by all members, pluralistic security communities to full regional integration. In other words, all the types of global security formations discussed earlier can manifest regionally.

Where does regional integration come from?

Although there are no universal processes of regional security integration, some scholars claim relatively universal explanations for the degree of security integration within regions. These relate to the significance of particular powers, regional organizations, or wider processes of integration.

Power

Power-centric explanations argue that the great powers, and the patterns of enmity between them, shape the character and degree of regionalism. In the Middle East and South Asia, conflict between powerful states has limited regional cooperation. In Southeast Asia, powerful states have used the regional organization, Association of Southeast Asian Nations (ASEAN), to enhance stability. Lake (2009) argues that peaceful regional orders arise when a dominant state produces something akin to a Hobbesian security bargain by providing security to less powerful states. This does something at the regional level that is deemed impossible globally: the ordering principle of relations shifts from anarchy to a degree of hierarchy. For Lake, this remains an emergent order based on functional and cost–benefit calculus rather than socialization: dominant states provide some security for a subordinate that has the effect of diminishing the security dilemma for other states. This is strengthened by economies of scale in which the costs of building military capabilities sufficient to provide stability for one subordinate may be substantial, but the costs of extending that security to others are much lower. Finally, subordinate states may grant authority (informally) to the dominant state by participating and granting legitimacy to their conflict management actions as members of the Organization of American States have done for US military actions. Differing degrees of hierarchy may then explain the variation in regional security formations, from the security communities of North America and Western Europe (both due to US dominance) to the degree of order (and lesser hierarchy) provided by Russia in the post-Soviet space. Similarly, the lack of dominant powers in the Middle East, East Asia, South Asia and Southern Africa may explain why balance of power politics continues to characterize regional security (Lake, 2009). Conversely, there is some empirical evidence to suggest that the ordering role of dominant powers may militate against stronger regional integration. In Central Asia, the influence of Russia and the USA is a stronger influence than faltering attempts to develop distinctively subregional security management (Allison, 2004; Bohr, 2004; Macfarlane, 2004). Likewise, wider regional security cooperation among post-Soviet states in Central Asia and the Caucasus through the Russian-dominated Commonwealth of Independent States (CIS) has not enjoyed the level of regional integration of other regions (Kubicek, 2009).

In RSC theory, power also determines the degree of regionalization of a particular state's security practices in a different way: 'Possession of great power overrides the regional imperative' and so while weak powers will be locked into an RSC with their neighbours, great powers will 'penetrate' several adjacent regions; and superpowers will 'range over the whole planet' (Buzan and Waever, 2003: 46). In this view, security is naturally regionalized and it is the absence of great power that confines security to the regional level, while the presence of great power globalizes security.

Organizations

Liberal approaches emphasize international organizations at the regional level. The growth of regional peacekeeping in Africa and elsewhere indicates an increasingly significant role of regional organizations in conflict management and post-conflict peacebuilding (Chapter 10). Beyond this, the degree to which formal regional organizations lead regional integration is widely debated. The formation of a regional organization does not inevitably produce greater security integration: the oldest regional organization, the League of Arab States formed in 1945, has had only a minimal role in security matters in spite of strong common identities and interests (Barnett and Solingen, 2007). Further, there is no correlation between the presence or age of regional organizations and the degree to which regional organizations acquire supranational powers: for instance, in the Arab League and ASEAN, state sovereignty and nonintervention are reinforced not surpassed by regional organizations. In ASEAN, this relates to a specifically 'ASEAN Way' of producing security that reinforces the principle of nonintervention and engages in private diplomacy that emphasizes shared values of seeking agreement (Narine, 1998; Goh, 2003). While these principles are not always abided by, it is notable that there have been no violent interstate conflicts between its members since its formation in 1967, even as membership has expanded from 5 to 10 states.

Functional integration

Functionalist and neofunctionalist theories argue that integration in one functional area such as trade will produce conditions and interests conducive to integration in others, and predict that economic integration will often precede political and security integration (Haas, 1958). It is notable, for instance, that economic forms of cooperation, such as the North American Free Trade Agreement (NAFTA, founded 1994) in North America, or MERCOSUR, the Southern Common Market (founded 1991), in southern Latin America, have had some effect on interstate security relations and stability. Further, formal regional organizations developed in economic issues have been used for security functions, such as the long history of European integration or the recent history of the Economic Community Of West African States (ECOWAS, founded in 1975) in West Africa. However, security integration does not always follow economic integration. The initial rationale for ASEAN was security, and has only recently expanded into economic and social relations. Even in Europe, security rationales underlay the development of economic integration in the European Coal and Steel Community (1952–2002). Further, while there has been considerable economic and political integration in Europe, security integration remains limited and views of security remain diverse in Europe (Burgess, 2009).

Functional integration theories are criticized for being predominantly based on European experiences and may be of little relevance for other regions. Ayoob (1986) argues that European experiences are based on centuries of state formation that produced the prerequisites of regional integration, such as strong sovereign states in which the population identified with the nation as the referent of security and security concerns relate to external threats. In the developing world, however, these prerequisites are absent, states are weaker and fail to be the dominant object of allegiance, and security threats and violent conflicts arise within the state (see Chapter 10). This implies that different regions have different security logics and limits, to such an extent that the main posited sources of regional integration of security are less relevant in some regions than others. Additionally, in a broader security agenda, regionalization in some areas militates against regionalization of security production overall. In Europe and North America, for instance, open borders may facilitate social and economic transactions and communication, which support the development of pluralistic security communities, but also limit the scope and strength of controls over transnational flows of migrants, criminals, terrorists and drugs.

Regional–global relations

In spite of the lack of unambiguous explanations for regional security integration (or the lack thereof), there is greater diversity in the logics and limits of security within regions than the apparently universal truths that much security theorizing implies. What does this mean for global relations, or at least for relations outside the region? Simply put, is security practised and produced in one world or many worlds (Hurrell, 2007)? For Buzan and Waever (2003), the world has shifted from a post-Cold War '1 + 4 world' (1 superpower and

4 great powers) to a contemporary '1 + 4 + regions' world. For Katzenstein (2005), this depends on which region we are talking about: Europe and Asia are more open systems, where the power and involvement of the USA are significant, while other regions are more 'closed' and have their own regional security logics. In the early part of the 21st century, there has been a return of an overarching global narrative of security with the global 'war on terror'. However, this has not reversed the regionalization of security. Current US counterterrorism strategy has distinct regional priorities (US Government, 2011), and UN action on counterterrorism is supposedly shaped by a principle of partnerships with regional and other organizations on the basis of comparative advantage. Thus, the uneven regionalization of security cannot produce a universal picture of how global and regional security orders and practices are related. Perhaps the more important question is: Where this is going? Is regionalization a stepping stone or a stumbling block to globalization and global collective or common security?

Viewed as a stepping stone, the expansion of political communities beyond the nation-state, greater interdependence, communication, organization and common identity are loosening the chains of territory for security politics. Critical IR theorists claim that 'intimations of the post-Westphalian world are apparent in Western Europe' (Linklater, 1998: 9) and that the territorial and exclusionary basis of political and security community may be changing (Ruggie, 1993). Critical security studies views security communities as exemplifying the prospects for changing the nature of security, and Booth and Wheeler (2008) argue that they are a model of how even global transcendence of the security dilemma might be achieved. In this view, collective and common security can be found beyond the UN system and emerging through the regionalization of security. This is supported by the recent history of the peaceful expansion of regional organizations and their growing roles in other geographic areas. The European Union has expanded from an initial 6 Western European members to the current 27 members, while ASEAN expanded from 5 to 10 and, in 1994, developed the 25-member ASEAN Regional Forum, to engage in confidence building and security discussions with wider regional and global powers. Further, many regional organizations have operated 'out of area', particularly in areas where regional institutions are weak, such as NATO's role in Afghanistan or in tackling piracy off the coast of Somalia, or the EU's conflict management roles in the Congo and southern Europe (Fawcett, 2004: 434).

In contrast, regionalization may be viewed as a stumbling block to global security formations. While regionalization expands the geographic scale of security politics, it has not produced deterritorialized cosmopolitan security and still relies on and reinforces the sovereign state as the dominant form of political community. The relative success of regionalism in Europe and North America and the more muted successes in Africa have been argued to point to one common feature: 'a successful move beyond the state depends on the existence of reasonably well-functioning states' (Hurrell, 2007: 143; see also Ayoob, 1986). It is doubtful that regionalization expresses a trajectory towards global cosmopolitan governance and security. First, many regionalizing projects, from Pan-Arabism to Pan-Africanism, frame a different political community other than traditional models of state and global system, but still rely on exclusionary and geographically demarcated identities (Hurrell, 2007: 138). Second, Falk (2004: 37) warns that regions may be 'enclaves of reaction', which undermine universal human rights and take resources and energies away from the UN system, such that 'regionalism works against the sort of human solidarity needed to take on such global challenges as global warming, ocean pollution, and the militarization of space'. Finally, some regional action can be seen as undermining global security formations: there was no UN mandate for the 1999 NATO air strikes against Serbian forces in Kosovo, and this is often claimed to have undermined UN authority.

Perhaps the more common view is that global and regional political institutions complement each other in emerging networks of global governance. Within the UN system, there is a sense that regional organizations should contribute to a division of labour in the maintenance of peace and security, particularly the conduct of peacekeeping and peace support operations (Brahimi, 2000; Pugh and Sidhu, 2003; Fawcett, 2003). The delegation of action from the UNSC to regional organizations is codified in Chapter VII of the UN Charter, and since the 1990s, the UN has increasingly acted within and through a series of partnerships with regional and nongovernmental organizations (NGOs) (Smith and Weiss, 1997). Just as security provision within many states involves partnerships with the private sector that reconfigure the distinctions and relations between the public and private (see Chapter 4), so the global governance of security increasingly takes place in evolving partnerships between states, regional organizations, the UN, private actors, NGOs, specialized agencies and others, in ways that reshape but do not eradicate their distinctiveness. There are practical advantages to subcontracting global security in this web of partnerships: it may be politically easier to gain agreement to take action on a problem within a regional organization than it is to garner sufficient interest in the wider international community (or among the P5 of the UNSC). However, it is not necessarily the case that regional states will be more interested than others in intervening in other's security problems (Hurrell, 2007). When powerful regional actors are interested, they may be motivated by enhancing their hegemony rather than humanitarian concerns, as has been argued in relation to Russian dominance of the CIS and its war in Georgia in 2008, and the domination of West African ECOMOG (Economic Community of West African States Monitoring Group) peacekeepers by Nigeria (Macfarlane, 1997; Smith and Weiss, 1997). Moreover, while the notion of burden sharing or devolution is pragmatically attractive (Alagappa, 1997), there is an unresolved, and maybe irresolvable, tension between a claim that authority derives from universal principles (such as human rights) and global institutions (the UN), but that practical and political capacity resides at the regional level (Bellamy and Williams, 2005; Hurrell, 2007).

Conclusion

States cooperate, and sometimes conflict, in and through security formations. These formations are subject to varying explanations; some posit universal causes, logics and limits, while others highlight the specificity of different types of formations. The implications of uncertainty, discussed in Chapter 5, pose challenges for cooperation, but they also produce the need for it. From attempts to build global collective or even common security, to collective defence through alliances, cooperative issue-based regimes and pluralistic security communities are indistinct formations. Indeed, the same formations (such as NATO) may be described using several of these titles. Each identifies a degree of institutionalization and socialization as important, although the extent to which this is supplementary or integral to functional cost–benefit calculus is debated. Increasingly, the regional and the global dimensions of security are seen as intertwined in a multi-level system of security governance. The regionalization of security shows that the material (and especially territorial) and ideational foundations of political communities and security relations are in flux and thus cannot be seen as eternally given. Regions, security communities and regimes show that there may be radical differences in the logics and limits of security in different places and different issues. Overall, the formations produced for, and through, security may transform security or reinforce a status quo. Whether this indicates an overall trajectory towards peace or merely some occasional anomalies to predicted patterns of security behaviour is more debatable. To understand this, we must explore the politics and practice of security in a range of issue areas. Chapter 7 begins this exploration through engagement with the central issue of war and killing.

Chapter 7

War and Killing

Violence and war are perennial features of security relations. As realists, like Walt (1991), claim, the use of military force has far-reaching effects on states and societies. As critical scholars, like Huysmans (1998) argue, security seeks to intervene in human relationships with death and particularly violent death. The sources and limits of war and killing are, therefore, central to understanding security. This chapter explores these through engaging with the philosophy of modern war, the transformation and limiting of warfare, contemporary manifestations of war, and issues of killing and violence beyond the confines of war. In doing so, it explores different understandings of war that all, in some way, articulate themselves in relation to the dominant theorist of modern war, Carl von Clausewitz (1780–1831). Specifically, it addresses the basic philosophical conceptualization of war found in Clausewitz and the varying ways this has been appropriated or critiqued by scholars of security. It outlines differing arguments about the causes of war and then addresses the logic, intensity and scale of warfare, particularly in the 20th and 21st centuries. It thus engages with various proposals about war, from those that claim it is eternally present to those liberals who argue it is increasingly obsolete. It then looks at contemporary forms of war, including the high-tech, 'virtuous' wars of liberal Western states, the growth of private military actors, and the 'new' civil wars embedded in the globalizing structures of governance and capital. Finally, it briefly engages with the question of the political utility of violence beyond war, particularly in relation to genocide.

Clausewitz and understanding war

War inspires diverse opinions that combine explanatory and normative claims. For some, it is celebrated as a means of social evolution that tests the strength of nations, for realists it is an inevitable feature of security relations in anarchy, while for others it is often necessary but its use should be limited, as in the Christian just war tradition that informs much international law, or even something that should be eliminated, as in the numerous religious (Mennonite, Quaker, Buddhist) and secular pacifist traditions that advocate practical strategies of nonviolence from Gandhi to Martin Luther King (see Pick, 1993; Nabulsi, 2005; Atack, 2005). Within security theory and practice, the dominant philosophy of war is an instrumental and political one: war is a tool put to political use.

The view of war as a political tool is most famously expressed in the Prussian general and military thinker Carl von Clausewitz's claims (2008:

75) that war is 'an act of force to compel our enemy to do our will' and therefore 'war is merely the continuation of policy by other means' (2008: 87). However, Clausewitz's thought and its legacy are much contested, partly because he never finished the book, *On War*, which was published posthumously by his wife in 1832 (Gray, 1999, 2012; Clausewitz, 2008; Howard, 2008). Further, the translation from the original German varies, with some referring to a continuation of political relations, others to policy, and still others to statecraft (Honig, 2007), thus introducing ambiguity over whether the use of political violence by non-state actors is covered by his claims (Bassford, 2007; Strachan and Herberg-Rothe, 2007). Nevertheless, for Clausewitz, war is always connected to politics and is in a subordinate relationship to political decision, it is merely an instrument. This situates war as a strategy, a means to an end that is politically defined. It thus makes no sense to approve or disapprove of war, or to seek to understand it in isolation from its political purpose.

War is violent but it is not unrestrained violence – for Clausewitz, this would be 'pure war' rather than 'real war' (Paret, 2008). For Clausewitz (2008: 605), war is a means of political relations, not the end or failure of political relations as many of his contemporaries argued:

> Do political relations between peoples and between their governments stop when diplomatic notes are no longer exchanged? Is war not just another expression of their thoughts, another form of speech or writing? Its grammar, indeed, may be its own, but not its logic.

Thus, 'policy converts the overwhelmingly destructive element of war into a mere instrument' (Clausewitz, 2008: 606). This does not, however, mean that war must only, as many realists think, be understood as always serving a significant and rational political purpose: for Brodie (2008: 706): 'Clausewitz did not deny that war could become "something pointless and devoid of sense." He only argued that it should not.' This view can be seen as articulating a dialectic between violence and reason (Howard, 2008), although Clausewitz (2008: 89) himself prefers a trinitarian view in which war must be understood 'like an object suspended between three magnets'. These elements were 'primordial violence, hatred, and enmity ... a blind natural force', combined with 'the play of chance and probability within which the creative spirit is free to roam' and 'its element of subordination, as an instrument of policy, which makes it subject to reason alone'. These three elements interact with each other, and are not found in identical balance or measure for each war. For Clausewitz, these aspects mainly relate to the people, the military and the government, respectively.

The role of politics in war, then, is to subsume the irrational and violent passions of the people and to direct the art of the soldier. While war as a strategic means to political ends is highlighted by most realist readers of

Clausewitz, this relationship between passion and politics contrasts with rationalist views that see war as only a rational instrument in which passions play no part, and the people as the peace-loving, war-averse, cost-bearing publics of liberal democratic peace theory. Indeed, Clausewitz (2008: 89) expressed the most vehement criticism for theories of war that were partial or rigid in their application of the trinity: 'a theory that ignores any one of them or seeks to fix an arbitrary relationship between them would conflict with reality to such an extent that for this reason alone it would be totally useless'. By this measure of ignorance or fixity, then, many understandings of war are 'totally useless'. More importantly, though, the flexibility of the trinitarian view enables debate on changes in the causes (political aims) and conduct of war.

Rationalism and explaining the causes of war

Rationalist security theories adopt an instrumental view of war as merely a tool. They have tended to look at the conditions and causes of particular wars and attempted to discern a picture of regularities of the causes of war that eschews historical variation. For example, the Correlates of War Project (www.correlatesofwar.org), an academic study of war that began in 1963, explores the correlations between war and key variables, ranging from measures of national power as diverse as military expenditure, energy consumption and urban population, to relational variables such as alliances and colonial relationships, and geographical factors from resource locations to land borders, among many others (Singer, 1972; Vasquez, 1987). However, such studies have not yielded strong consensus on the causes of war. This is not surprising since war is a diverse phenomenon, and each war is subject to varying explanations. Further, raw data alone cannot produce an explanation of causes and so most explanations for war articulate some form of the major issues and relationships explored in this book, from human nature or global anarchy as underlying explanations, to processes of state formation and the construction of an interstate system, to the specifics of the distribution of material capabilities, alliances, misperception, the offence-defence balance, the absence or failure of regimes or the limits of security communities, and geographical factors of proximity and the ability of threats to travel shorter or longer distances. Indeed, rather than posit universal causes of war, the most advanced rationalist studies tend to frame their debates in terms of levels of analysis: Is war a product of the particular perceptions and decisions of political leaders, the nature of the state, or the nature of the system (Cashman and Robinson, 2007; Levy and Thompson, 2010) (see Chapter 1)? Beyond these posited general conditions that enable or restrain the resort to war, specific propositions exist that war is more likely in certain specific contexts, such as when conquest is easy, when power shifts quickly and strongly, and when political leaders have a 'false optimism' about its outcome (van Evera, 1999). Such questions and approaches characterize the study of interstate and intrastate wars. These three primary foci of rationalist accounts of the causes of war are also three primary features of the concept of politics in much realist thought: instrumental rationality, power, and territory/resources.

Rationalist explanations view war as a deliberate choice made by states or state leaders on the basis of an instrumental rationality of cost–benefit analysis showing its 'expected utility' (Bueno de Mesquita, 1981, 1985; Nicholson, 1992). They have imported assumptions from economic theory in which the self-serving decisions of *Homo economicus* lie behind many explanations of war (Cramer, 2002; Malesevic, 2010). This fits with the methodological individualism of most rationalist theories (see Chapter 1) and reduces the nature of war to a single object with a fixed (and natural) relationship to politics and its conditions. Thus, while Clausewitz cautions against fixity and ignorance in understanding war, this view downplays, or ignores, the 'passions' in favour of a pure utility calculus, and establishes a fixity of relations between 'ends' and 'means'. For instance, 'fear' is a term often used but seldom given much attention in understandings of security, even in relation to the security dilemma (Booth and Wheeler, 2008). For the most part, fear is viewed as a result of uncertainty in which its operative importance is not as an emotion but as a metaphor for prudence where the emotional is absent or at least downgraded to a reaction to threats that can militate against rational decision making (Buzan, 1991). Hatred, too, is distanced by the rhetoric of rationality, although it reappears in some accounts of civil wars in the developing world that implicitly locate hatred as primordial and irrational – a feature denied space in accounts of Western wars past and present. The separation of reason and emotion, then, posits war as an instrument of reason, chosen and controlled on the basis of rationally defined political aims – themselves set by the logics of competition and limits of cooperation in anarchy.

A purely instrumental view of war, which separates ends and means, and then links them via rationality, fits well with most rationalist theories of security. Although Clausewitz emphasized war as an instrument subject to reason, he avoided the crude rationalism of many of his later appropriators. For Clausewitz, war was an art not a science, and so was an imprecise instrument that encountered 'friction' and unpredictability of reactions. Although embedded in Enlightenment thought and later invoked as a source of realism, Clausewitz can also be read as having eschewed the 'hyper-rationalism of the Enlightenment that had its strategic correlates' both in his time and the contemporary period (Vega, 2007: 131). The rationalist fixing of relations between ends and means, and the tendency to base this on permanent features of international life (human nature, anarchy), leads rationalist accounts of war to focus on the perennial material dimensions of security: power, territory and resources.

Power and security are entwined in war and so the potential for war varies according to the view of power. If states seek security they may seek to avoid war, but if states seek power for its own sake then war may be more common. While the distribution of power is a primary emphasis of realist thought, widely varying and opposed conclusions can be found in realism. For instance, Morgenthau argued that multipolar systems tend to be stable, while Waltz argued that they are more war-prone than other distributions of power. Some argue that parity in power has encouraged great power war (Lemke, 2002; Moul, 2003), while others say that rapid shifts in power distribution make war likely. War is often precipitated by a decline in the relative military power of a rival (Levy, 1987), and sudden changes in power present 'windows of opportunity and vulnerability' that explain many wars (van Evera, 1999).

Since power is conceived in primarily material terms for most rationalists, resources and territory matter in their understandings of war. Indeed, from realists to Marxists and a variety of critics, states are often motivated to start a war for access to resources such as oil or territory. Approximately half of all wars in the past two centuries arose out of the escalation of territorial disputes (Vasquez, 2012; Hensel, 2012). Indeed, Senese and Vasquez (2008: 407) claim that disputes between states over contiguous territory is the 'single issue that is most likely to result in inter-state war'. Some argue that it is characteristic of territorial issues that war becomes a significant possibility because domestic support is easier to mobilize for territorial claims, particularly relating to the 'homeland' (Goertz and Diehl, 1992; Huth and Alee, 2003). Conversely, Senese and Vasquez (2008) argue that the likelihood of war derives not from something inherent in territorial issues or the wider structure of the international system, but that territorial disputes tend to form a series of mutually reinforcing 'steps to war', which follow realist prescriptions about the formation of alliances, military build-ups and so on that often lead to war (see also Levy and Thompson, 2010). States go to war for more than territorial claims, but many accounts highlight material motives. This is unsurprising in a field founded on the myth of the Westphalian rationalization and secularization of politics, in which conflicts over material interests rather than ideas fuel violence. For instance, the 'resource curse' and the management and exploitation of natural resources are common explanations for regional interstate conflicts and civil wars (Homer-Dixon, 1994) (see Chapter 13).

Power and territory combine in some wider patterns in war. Most wars have historically occurred in the relatively confined global geographic areas of temperate climates (Keegan, 1993). In 1904, Halford Mackinder, the father of modern geopolitics, proposed a view of the world that divided the earth's land surface into a 'world-island' in Eurasia – with Eastern Europe being the most important heartland – marginal lands of the rest of Europe and Asia, and 'outer continents'. For Mackinder, and others, control over this heartland would mean control over the world, and, indeed, most major bids for hegemony, the two world wars and the Cold War can be viewed as vying for control of this particular area (Gray, 2012). However, recent critical forms of geopolitics provide a less deterministic and naturalized view of the relationship of territory, states and war. These argue that rather than the fixed view of preformed states interacting in anarchy and conflicting over territory, the world and its wars are better understood as processes of territorialization, deterritorialization, and the understandings and production of territoriality (Agnew and Corbridge, 1995; Ó Tuathail and Dalby, 1998; Ó Tuathail et al., 2006). War remains central in these discussions, and they argue that war has made and unmade particular understandings and values of territory. While the territorialization of politics and security may be seen to be declining through globalization, the values and attachments states and societies place on territory remain important for war. In other words, people are willing to fight for territory because of its symbolic value for belonging, citizenship and identity, rather than, primarily, the material resources found in particular territories (Kahler and Walter, 2006; Cowen and Gilbert, 2008).

The transformation of war and killing

War has both enduring and changeable characteristics. Gray (2012: 346–7) argues that 'war, warfare and strategy have not changed over the course of more than two millennia'. This seems like an odd claim. The form of political units that wage war has changed, the method and manner of war-fighting has altered, and the political, social, economic, technological, historical and geographical contexts of war have all changed significantly. Gray's argument does not deny these changes, but says that they do not change the nature of war as a political instrument. In contrast, others argue that the history of war is one of transformation, and these transformations have deeper implications for understanding and explaining when and why wars occur and the form and scale of killing they involve. Three transformations are particularly prominent: first, the long historical trend towards the totalization and limiting of war among the most powerful states; second, the contemporary continuation of limiting focused on how Western states wage war; and third, the emergence of 'new wars' within states that show very different characteristics.

The totalization and limitation of war

Total war

The long history of war and war-fighting can be seen as a process of 'totalization' until the Second World War and a period of limitation thereafter. 'Total' war relates to the mobilization of all a nation's military, political, economic, social and human resources for the purposes of war. That is, the pursuit of war becomes the core political goal. In the era of modern wars, from the Peace of Westphalia to the Second World War, war underwent enormous changes in its organization, social function, scale, destructiveness, location and position in the field of forces identified in Clausewitz's trinity. The organization of military forces developed from forces made up of a few professionals and a large proportion of hired mercenaries, to professional armies and then, in the Napoleonic era, the development of mass mobilization through ideology. The locations and forms of war-fighting shifted from sieges and skirmishes to large-scale battlefields in which numerical superiority reigned and eventually, in the 20th century, to the growing significance of air power and totalization of the spaces in which wars were fought, beyond battlefields, to include the skies and the target cities below (Calvocoressi et al., 1990; Buckley, 1999; Chikering and Förster, 2000; Sheehan, 2010).

The lethality of war changed considerably over the era of modern wars. The numbers of war casualties are often unreliable, politicized and hotly debated (Greenhill, 2010). However, it is widely held that the scale of casualties increased through this totalization, partly as a result of technological changes that allowed killing from a greater distance (the development of rifling allowed rifles and artillery to shoot further and more accurately) and chemical weapons that allowed mass casualties in the First World War. Likewise, the type of casualties shifted as mass conscript armies exposed entire generations to war. In the Second World War, all industrial, agricultural, human, economic, social and other state resources were mobilized in the war effort. Such total mobilization makes all such aspects of life part of what Clausewitz called the enemy's 'centre of gravity' and legitimated the mass killing of civilians through blanket bombing of cities and eventually the use of two nuclear weapons in 1945. As a result, 20th-century wars are claimed to have resulted in over 100 million direct deaths due to 'death dealing armaments' and 'state-backed extermination of civilians' (Tilly, 2003: 55). This reflects a millennium of increasing death rates rising from tens of thousands in the 10th and 11th centuries (Malesevic, 2010). Of course, populations have increased dramatically too, but Tilly (2003) estimates that death rates have risen from 90 people per million of population per year in the 18th century, to 150 in the 19th and 400 in the 20th century. Such killing was particularly marked by increasingly high proportions of civilian deaths.

Limited war

The post-1945 period and the Cold War were an era of limited wars. Direct 'hot' wars between the superpowers and their European allies did not occur, instead global political rivalries involved the use of military force by proxies and allies. From the wars in Korea (1950–53) and Vietnam (1959–75) to the

Arab–Israeli War (1967), the superpowers sought to limit the violence and destructiveness of war (although the use of napalm and Agent Orange in Vietnam may militate against this view) and attempted to manage the risk of escalation. A range of civil wars, such as in Afghanistan (1979–1989), Angola (1975–2002) and Nicaragua (1981–89), involved the superpowers supporting one side or the other with weapons and training rather than direct combat roles. Thus, war shifted from the relations of the great powers to the relations of their allies and proxies, and did not achieve the levels of industrialization or totality of the European and world wars of the early 20th century. Indeed, throughout this period and beyond, intrastate civil wars rather than interstate wars have accounted for the majority of major armed conflicts in any given year.

Overall, the number of interstate conflicts has fallen significantly since the 1970s, and even civil wars have declined since the mid-1990s. Importantly, however, recent research indicates that even in this era of limited war, the states involved in most international wars between 1946 and 2003 were the UK (21) and France (19), particularly in relation to anti-colonial struggles, and the USA (16) and Russia/USSR (9) (Human Security Centre, 2005). There is also some evidence that war is becoming less lethal (Lacina et al., 2006). By one estimate, the number of battle deaths per conflict has dropped from an average of 38,000 per conflict in 1950 to 600 per conflict in 2002 (Human Security Centre, 2005). Empirically, such declines remain questionable, since records of battle-related deaths in many areas of conflict are weak and tend to underreport by a significant amount. But the primary explanation is that the wars of the 1950s were superpower and great power wars, with high-tech, large-scale killing, while the majority of conflicts now are either Western wars with limited (Western) casualties, or civil wars with different characteristics of killing (see below).

What explains this limiting of war? Most accounts posit some kind of limiting of the utility of war; that is, war was not used because it was not an effective tool to achieve strategic aims. Three basic form of this explanation predominate: war is not useful under the conditions imposed on international relations by the presence of nuclear weapons; war is becoming obsolete; and the norms and laws against war have restrained it.

Nuclear weapons and deterrence

Many realists claim that stability in the Cold War and the limiting of war derive from the nuclear standoff and resultant deterrence (see Chapter 5). This was the ultimate test and triumph of reason over war in Clausewitzean thought. First and foremost, the scale of destruction wrought by nuclear weapons was potentially so great that it negated any political goal for which war might be used. Thus, war between nuclear powers became irrational and so did not occur, and wars that could escalate into nuclear weapons use were avoided. Indeed, nuclear war could have approximated 'pure war'

(war free to pursue its own logic of destruction without political restraint) and nuclear weapons radically altered war from Clausewitz's time. When Clausewitz was writing, between 1816 and 1830, the art of the solider lay in overcoming the fog and friction of war and the limits of technology and politics; for Howard (2002), the nuclear era conditions of potential absolute war were those in which the human challenge was to control the opportunities of technology and constrain absolute war.

Nuclear weapons not only promised massive irrational destruction, but were also increasingly embedded in strategies and capabilities that would deliver nuclear warheads to their targets within hours of the start of nuclear war. Simply put, this meant there was very little time for politics to occur and assert the rational control over war that Clausewitz predicted and desired. Clausewitz (2008: 79) argued that 'if war consisted of one decisive act', it would tend towards totality and begin and end without politics asserting control. Weapons' developments in the 1950s 'inhumanly compressed the time available to make the most terrible decisions' and further concentrated nuclear decision making in the hands of a few (Schelling and Halperin, 1961: 3). Since nuclear war would be irrationally destructive, and escalation could occur so quickly as to be uncontrollable, the only means for politics to control war was to avoid the prospect of war. Thus, strategist Edward Luttwak claimed in 1983 that 'we have lived since 1945 without another world war precisely because rational minds ... extracted a durable peace from the very terror of nuclear weapons' (cited in Mueller, 1988: 55).

While there was a broad consensus among strategic thinkers that there was a need to find ways to use conventional military force without escalation into nuclear confrontation or total war, debate circled around whether nuclear weapons were useful in this form of war (Osgood, 1957; Kissinger, 1960; Halperin, 1961, 1963). Rather than seeking to avoid war, some realists argued that nuclear weapons can be militarily useful and so can be integrated into conventional (political) war (Klein, 1994). In 1980, Gray and Payne argued that 'victory is possible', as nuclear weapons could be used early in a war to destroy Soviet nuclear weapons and political and military targets and enable a conventional military victory. This idea of rendering nuclear weapons militarily useful in pursuit of political goals fed into the development of new weapons, forms of targeting and the ambitious Strategic Defense Initiative known as 'Star Wars' pursued by President Reagan from 1983. Since that time, the goal of nuclear war-fighting was periodically resurgent, and contemporary US nuclear weapons strategy envisions integration with conventional forces.

Obsolescence

The scholarly response to total war is often either to call for the abolition of war, as in early idealist liberal scholarship in the interwar years, or to again render war as a useful political tool, such as expounded by military theorist B.H. Liddell Hart in the same period (Larson, 1980). The latter perspective was adopted by early realists in the shadow of total war and impending nuclear confrontation. Liberal, constructivist and other perspectives on the limiting of war since 1945 make very different arguments. Some liberal scholars argue that nuclear weapons are largely irrelevant (Luard, 1988; Mueller, 1988). However, greater focus is placed on the claim that, since 1945, and in a long historical trend over the past few centuries, war has become unusable, because it cannot serve political and economic purposes and anti-war norms and sentiments have grown stronger among nations and people. Indeed, the role of economic interdependence in contributing to the declining utility of war has a long history in liberal thought, from Bentham and Cobden in the 18th and 19th centuries to early 20th-century thinkers like Angell, who claimed in 1910 that war was economically and socially futile and governments needed to realize this. In the contemporary period, many liberals believe that war has become all but useless (Rosecrance, 1986; Luard, 1988; Fukuyama, 1992). Other liberals and constructivists argue that war has become obsolete among certain groups of states (among democracies or within security communities) that are growing (see Chapters 2 and 3). Among the most prominent scholars claiming the obsolescence of war, Mueller (1989, 2004) argues that interstate war has largely become obsolete and civil wars and wars against non-state actors are merely the 'remnants of war'. For Mueller, the modern history of states and state-building established the political control over war, and on this foundation, over the past century, a disenchantment with war has arisen, even an 'aversion to war'. This is embedded in the development of international laws limiting war, and is following a similar path to the abolition of slavery – making it an obsolete institution and practice.

Laws and norms

More widely, liberal, English School and constructivist scholars have emphasized the significance of the development of international laws and norms that seek to limit war. Limiting the scale of war has been central to older traditions of warfare: the ancient Greeks valued battle and face-to-face killing in order to confine killing, and some disdain was reserved for archers and others who fought from a distance and thus relative safety (Shaw, 2005). Likewise, the efforts to control military technology through international treaties and agreements can be viewed as an attempt to civilize war and war-fighting (see Chapter 8). The international law of armed conflict, known as 'international humanitarian law', has evolved in close and reciprocal relationship with the character and use of war (Neff, 2005). Medieval controls on war derived partly from Christian just war traditions that specify conditions of *jus ad bellum* (the legitimacy of a war) and *jus in bello* (the legitimacy of conduct within war). However, from the 17th century, war became viewed less as promoting and policing a just order and more as a normal practice of interstate relations, and questions of just cause became less politically relevant. As Neff argues, contemporary legal frameworks relate to the legitimacy of war largely in terms of the UN Charter (and before that the League of Nations), the right to self-defence enshrined in Article 51, and the authorization of the use of military force by the UN Security Council. This reflects only some elements of the need for a just cause and legitimate authority found in *jus ad bellum* criteria. Contemporary debates have seen a resurgence of this question in relation to the legitimacy of pre-emptive military action (de Goede, 2008) and humanitarian intervention (see Chapter 10), and wars are now justified in liberal terms of promoting democracy and freedom.

Standards of conduct within war, in contrast, are subject to more detailed legal frameworks that evolved through the Hague Conventions (1899 and 1907), the Geneva Conventions (1949) and their Additional Protocols (1977 and 2005). These instruments codify standards of behaviour in the conduct of warfare, most notably inheriting *jus in bello* criteria of proportionality of violence to its aims, the outlawing of *deliberate* targeting of civilians and civilian infrastructure, as well as establishing standards of treatment for prisoners of war and some limits on the types of weapons that can be used. Such instruments are an attempt to civilize war, to make its conduct more limited and more humane. The provisions of this body of law are challenged, frequently, by practices that target civilians, destroy non-military targets, torture prisoners, and other states practices, from nuclear standoffs to brutal mass killings in civil wars. However, this body of law and its principles remain central to the politics and practice of war, even if they are notably broken in many cases. Further, there are some signs of growing legal accountability for crimes in breach of these legal principles, such as the founding of the International Criminal Court in 2002, the ongoing prosecution of Serb leaders Radovan Karadzic and Ratko Mladic in the International Criminal Tribunal for the former Yugoslavia in The Hague, and the April 2012 conviction of former Liberian President Charles Taylor on 11 counts of war crimes pertaining to his material support for the brutal Revolutionary United Front (RUF) in neighbouring Sierra Leone.

Contemporary Western ways of war

War viewed merely as an instrument is often so abstract that the lived experience of killing, victimhood and fear are neglected. Feminist accounts do much to question this, viewing the experience of practices related to killing as central to understanding war (Sylvester, 2012). As Elaine Scarry (1985: 67) argues, 'reciprocal injuring is the obsessive content of war', and not an 'accidental and unfortunate entailment of human injury' during operations represented as eliminating weapons or strategic resources. In her *Intimate*

History of Killing, historian Joanna Bourke (1999) demonstrates that the production of effective soldiers is a complex phenomenon that includes fear, guilt and pleasure, which is often unsuccessful (with a fraction of soldiers being willing to shoot on command in the heat of battle), and thus draws out the complexities of killing in war that strategic accounts of war neglect. More broadly, contemporary Western ways of war show that war is a social institution, and some argue that it can now be characterized as postmodern, virtual and virtuous.

Some observers argue that Western military powers have cultivated, and been seduced by, a dream of 'clean' and 'civilised' warfare (Robertson, 2003). This sanitization and civilization of war are clearly represented in the development of what can be viewed as a particular American or Western way of war. Shaw (2005) argues that a new Western way of war developed from the US war in Vietnam (1965–73) through the British–Argentine war over the Falklands/Malvinas in 1982 to the first Gulf War in 1991, and later uses of military force in Kosovo (1998–99), and recently Afghanistan (2001–present) and Iraq (2003–11). The central feature of this way of war is very low numbers of military casualties, at least for Western forces. Notably, while US/Western military casualties number mostly in the hundreds or less, enemy military deaths number in the thousands or tens of thousands, as do direct and indirect civilian deaths (Shaw, 2005). Shaw (2005) refers to this as 'risk-transfer war', which centres on reducing the life risks to the military and organizes war in such a way to reduce that risk and transfer it to others, both enemies and civilians. In addition to low casualties, fast victory is also central to Western wars; for example, the first Gulf War involved six weeks of combat, the second only three (Shaw, 2005).

Technology and Western killing

Technology is central to the limiting and distancing of killing in the Western way of war. Air power is often particularly crucial to the aims of limited casualties and quick wars. It was used almost exclusively in the early weeks of the first Gulf War and more recently as the predominant Western form of action in the early phase of war in Afghanistan (with US bombing supporting ground warfare by Afghan opposition groups). Since its advent in the First World War, the use of air power has promised to avoid the horrors of trench and ground war (Robertson, 2003). However, the use of air power in the Second World War saw even greater mass killing. The reasons for this lay in the technological limits of targeting bombing and the decision to use indiscriminate 'area bombing' in British attacks on German cities and the US use of nuclear weapons on Japan in order to damage civilian morale. Thus, the desire to limit war may be constrained by technological challenges and strategic decisions to engage in what can be seen as total war. This 'inhumanity of airpower' later continued in the use of napalm in the US war in Vietnam and extensive bombing of Cambodia (Shaw, 2005).

The promises of technology to deliver more precision in killing, to minimize civilian casualties, and to do so from a distance to minimize military casualties are argued to have underlain the development of a 'liberal militarism', especially in the USA and the UK, that relies more on high-tech weapons than mass armies (Shaw, 2005: 4). So-called 'smart' weapons and precision-guided munitions promise accurate killing from a great distance, with greater invulnerability to military personnel and the possibility of lower civilian casualties. In the 1991 Gulf War, the US use of such weapons meant that while 88,000 tons of bombs were dropped in 43 days of the air campaign, the number of civilians killed was the lowest of any major bombing campaign. This number remained significant, at around 3,000, but great emphasis was placed on the precision of these weapons that supposedly allowed greater compliance with international humanitarian law (Rizer, 2001). Since then, the use of precision-guided munitions has become more routine. Indeed, 90 per cent of the bombs dropped in the first few weeks and 35 per cent of all used in NATO air strikes on Kosovo in 1999 were 'smart' weapons (Arkin, 2001). However, this is not merely technological enhancement. Cohen (2001: 55) argues that 'as precision becomes technically possible, it quickly becomes politically imperative' for domestic and international public opinion and diplomatic reactions.

Perhaps the clearest embodiment of the technological sanitization of war through distance and precision is the use of drones (unmanned aerial vehicles, UAVs) by the USA. While the political use of assassination by states is illegal, 'targeted killings' through use of UAVs have increased in recent years and are said to be a contemporary manifestation of this virtualized and virtuous killing in war and beyond war (Gregory, 2011). Again, this may be an illusory precision, while official US figures note a small number of civilian deaths, others suggest up to a third of casualties may be civilians (Bergen and Tiedemann, 2010; Williams, 2010). Indeed, one database indicates that the 355 US drone strikes in Pakistan since 2004 (until mid-2013) have killed up to 3,336 people, with up to 637 of these either civilians or unknown (New America Foundation, 2013). Beyond the political and legal imperatives to be precise in war, the technological promise of clean war can be argued to be undoing the disenchantment with war that Mueller and other liberal scholars posit. In particular, developments in cybernetics, biotechnologies, nanotechnologies and information technologies promise a 'post-human' form of war that sanitizes and reduces the risks of war, which, Coker (2004) argues, are producing the re-enchantment of war in the 21st century.

While the USA is at the forefront of this way of war, its key features are found more widely, partly because the USA tends to go to war as the lead in forces composed of allies (either formal NATO allies or coalitions of the willing), rather than unilaterally. The 'clean' war of precision and impunity underlies this and represents the furtherance of longer term trends in the preparation for war within Western states. The decline of mass armies and a growing reliance on technology and capital-intensive preparations for war rather than labour-intensive models of war-fighting is a fairly universal trend among Western states. However, capital-intensive preparations for war are no longer a purely Western phenomenon, as in 2011, for the first time, planned defence spending in Asia (18.5 per cent of global total) exceeded that of Europe (18.3 per cent of global total) (International Institute for Strategic Studies, 2012).

Virtual and virtuous war

Beyond the technological and political dimensions of the sanitization of the conduct of war, the Western way of war extends into the complexity of war's relationship to society. The decline in people's direct encounter with or participation in warfare as a result of capital-intensive and technology-intensive preparations for war and the fact that most wars fought were geographically distant mean that the primary encounter Western people have with war is as a spectacle on the TV news. This led the philosopher Jean Baudrillard (1995) to declare that 'the Gulf War did not take place'. Baudrillard's apparently overstated point is that it was primarily an event oriented towards the media. The Gulf War was the first time TV images were purportedly relayed 'live' from the battle, but also involved a high level of military control over the images presented. Patton (1995: 3) claims that since the Vietnam War, military planners have learned to control the media, by procedures developed and tested in the conflicts in the Falklands, Grenada and Panama:

> As a result, what we saw was for the most part a 'clean' war, with lots of pictures of weaponry, including the amazing footage from the nose-cameras of 'smart bombs' and relatively few images of human casualties, none from the Allied forces.

Similarly, Ignatieff (2001) argued that the 1999 war in Kosovo was a 'virtual war', in which 'the media becomes the decisive theatre of operations'. So, while the advent of air power in the First World War, and its maturation in the second, meant that war took place in the air as well as the land and sea, in recent wars, a key battlefield is the virtual media. It is important to note that for Der Derian (2001), and others, the virtuality of war lies not only in its portrayal and conduct in the media but also the virtual character of the conduct of war: using virtual technologies and UAVs controlled at a distance in which soldiers encounter the enemy (and their death) as a virtual image on a screen. This, it is argued, creates a distancing of the soldier from the act of killing, which reduces psychological barriers and makes the decision to kill easier, particularly when training and preparation for this type of military action are simulation that resembles a computer game. Der Derian argues that the different dimensions of the virtualization of war, when linked with ethical imperatives towards democratization and neoliberal markets and technological capabilities to attack precisely with minimal casualties, constitute not just a virtual war but a 'virtuous war' – a form of war that appears to be less destructive and bloody. This virtuous appearance is, unsurprisingly, a 'sanitization of violence' that is 'still about killing others', including civilians (Der Derian, 2001). Such war can be mapped not just as an instrumental relationship of policy to war, a simple Clausewitzean trinity, or a military-industrial complex, but a military-industrial-media-entertainment network.

The relationship between society and sanitized virtual/virtuous wars has been described as a 'spectator sport'. This originates with historical sociologist Michael Mann, who linked the development of technology-intensive forms of war-fighting and sanitized social encounters with the violence of war. Defining militarism as 'a set of attitudes and social practices which regards war and the preparation for war as a normal and desirable social activity', Mann (1987: 35) argued that Cold War elites had a 'deterrence science militarism', which emphasized elite/private decision making in a confrontation consisting of a quest for nuclear parity or slight advantage combined with limited proxy wars far away from the superpowers. While in Soviet states this was supported by a mass militarized socialism, in the West it was encountered through 'indirect participation' of 'spectator sport militarism' (Mann, 1987). In the new Western way of war, it seems, the first form of militarism may have disappeared, but the spectator sport militarism continued. McInnes (1999, 2002, 2003) took Mann's lead and identified four key features of Western spectator sport wars in the 1990s:

- they are localized in geographically distant areas and not tied to a global-level confrontation
- the enemy is defined largely in terms of a leader/regime of the target state rather than its people or even its military forces (a different 'centre of gravity')
- there is a desire to minimize civilian casualties
- wars are fought by highly skilled professionals on behalf of the West (rather than mass armies) and there is a an intention to minimize casualties among these forces.

Thus, McInnes's concept of spectator sport war combines many elements of Shaw's Western way of war and the wider view of war as an increasingly virtual as well as literal battlefield – at least insofar as Western populations encounter it. While it is notable that the global 'war on terror' may recast McInnes's first point about conflicts lacking ties to a global-level narrative, the point about distancing and localizing conflict remains prescient; also, the leader/regime as the defined enemy was reinforced by the 2003 Iraq War, which was posited to be against Saddam Hussein's regime and not the Iraqi people.

Privatization

More recently, the distancing of states from casualties and responsibility for them and the high demands of capital-intensive military investment have contributed to another shift in ways of war that link the high-tech Western military powers to the new wars into which they often intervene: the return of mercenaries and the privatization of military force. Private companies have long provided support to formal state military forces, particularly through the provision of logistics and other support services. In the 1990s, a number of private military and security companies (PMSCs) arose offering wider military services. Companies such as the South African Executive Outcomes and the British Sandline International provided a range of military services, including the use of force, in conflicts in Angola, Sierra Leone, Papua New Guinea and elsewhere. While some observers saw these companies merely as corporate mercenaries, as guns for hire to weak states (Musah and Fayemi, 2000), the 2003 invasion of Iraq saw such a large number of PMSCs contracted by the USA that they provided the second largest contingent of military and security personnel, rising from one-tenth of deployed personnel during 2003 to 100,000 contractors (local and foreign) working alongside 133,000 US troops in 2006 (Avant, 2005; Kinsey, 2006; Singer, 2007). The growth of the private military industry built on the availability of military personnel after post-Cold War military downsizing, and longer developments of Western neoliberal governance that view the private sector as inherently more efficient than the public (Abrahamsen and Williams, 2011). Now, hundreds of PMSCs operate on all six continents, and generate revenues of hundreds of millions of dollars in a global 'market for force' (Avant, 2005; Singer, 2007). These companies prompt heated debate between those who view them as corporate 'mercenaries' that fundamentally erode the state's monopoly on legitimate violence (Musah and Fayemi, 2000), and those who see them as providing essential services that many states cannot afford to provide for themselves (Shearer, 1998). While mercenarism is illegal under international law, the status of PMSCs is more ambiguous. Most of their roles do not relate to direct combat, and states can, in principle, authorize other actors to use force without destroying their monopoly (see Chapter 4). However, systems for authorizing and holding PMSCs to account are a weak and evolving patchwork; there is no global treaty on PMSCs and national licensing systems are still in their infancy. Beyond legal frameworks, however, a range of voluntary initiatives are developing ranging from codes of conduct formed within the companies to international frameworks, such as the 2008 Montreux Document, produced by the Swiss government and the International Committee of the Red Cross, and a 2010 International Code of Conduct for Private Security Service Providers, which was signed by 211 major private security companies and includes human rights standards and rules on the use of force.

New wars

Most wars are within states rather than between them. This has long been the case, and the conduct of war in civil wars can present challenges to the dominant strategic and instrumental view of war developed for international conflicts. In 2010 (the latest year for which figures are available), 30 wars were ongoing, none of which were purely interstate (Themnér and Wallensteen, 2011). In the 1990s, civil wars in Angola, Liberia, Sierra Leone, Somalia, the Democratic Republic of the Congo, and to a lesser degree in Central Asia and other regions, were understood as contrasting with the supposed sanitization of Western war. The primary forces of these wars were not formal, bureaucratically organized armies but informal 'warlord' forces led by charismatic leaders, without clear rank or uniform, lacking formal military training (sometimes), and accused of co-opting child soldiers and conducting brutal violence against civilians. The violence of such wars did not fit with either the industrialized pattern of Western total war or the law-bound, technologically enabled surgical killing of Western military power. These 'new wars' not only took new forms but were driven by different goals. Varying explanations, popular among the media and policy makers, posited some combination of ancient ethnic hatreds or economic greed as the drivers of conflict. Certainly, many armed groups, such as the RUF in Sierra Leone, did not articulate a political aim in the familiar sense of ideological or territorial claims, but instead appeared to be a vehicle for the economic enrichment of their leaders through the trade in conflict diamonds and other commodities. Likewise, armed groups from Rwanda and Burundi to Somalia were organized on the basis of ethnic or clan divisions. For some critics, this form of war and their characteristics challenge the Clausewitzean paradigm of war that focuses on rational states, professional armies and wars fought on battlefields (van Creveld, 1991; Keegan, 1993; Kaldor, 1999). However, changes in the extent to which war is conducted by formal military organizations on behalf of the people and directed by the state do not necessarily mean that the original trinity (of primordial violence and hatred, the play of chance, and their subordination to reason) is displaced, as critics like van Creveld, Kaldor and others have claimed (Strachan and Herberg-Rothe, 2007; Gray, 2012). Indeed, they may merely disrupt the earlier correlation of these to the people, the military and the state.

There are divergent views on what social and political conditions enable the occurrence and apparently brutal form of the 'new wars'. In many (but not all) cases, a process of state collapse or fragility is seen as underlying conflict (see Chapter 10). This claim, however, is hotly debated. Some rationalist explanations for the 'new wars' argue that collapsing states approximate the conditions of Hobbesian anarchy that produce the security dilemma, and thus, with only slight amendment, the concepts of rationalism can be applied (see Chapter 5). This perspective is not inherent in the assertion of an instrumental account of violence, but reflects wider rationalist and liberal traditions of thought, in which the development of the state and the processes of economic development occur through the processes of pacification of internal relations (see Chapter 4) and national modernization, which posit state collapse as related to the failures of elites to pursue the correct course. This means that the new wars are an expression of pure hatred, either a simple irrationality or a rational Hobbesian fear, and a lack of politics facilitated by anarchy: they are made possible by the weakness and failure of the state in which they take place. In contrast, others adopt structuralist (Marxian), liberal cosmopolitan and poststructuralist explanations, which argue that the processes of global change are what make brutal civil wars possible.

Most prominently, Kaldor (1999) argues that globalization is related to each of the key differences of the new wars from the 'old' and that goals are framed in terms of identity politics, and so the new wars are part of a tension between cosmopolitan forces and those of 'particularism'. This further embeds the new wars in networks that extend beyond the territories of the nation-states in which the fighting itself occurs. Such networks include diaspora networks and the web of trading relations that are formed through the export of conflict commodities, as well as global media networks. While also arguing that the new wars are linked to the new political constellations of globalization, Duffield (2001) claims that they are made possible by changes in the character of global capitalism since the 1970s, particularly the shift from expansion to consolidation of capitalist relations that produces different relationships between the powerful North and the excluded and exploited global South. In both regions, states are challenged by globalization, but the violence of the new wars is not merely the result of state collapse, an absence of hierarchical ordering, but of the ways in which political complexes arise and are compelled to participate in non-territorial shadow economic and political networks. It is the emergence and operation of these networks, not the absence of power structures, that produce the brutal violence of the new wars.

These wider processes of globalization and the emergence of neoliberal forms of global governance shape how the powerful states and societies of the North respond to such violence by viewing it as a threat to their security, and thus seeking to police the circulation of refugees, migrants, diseases and so on that are said to spread from these zones. At the heart of this is the so-called 'liberal peace', in which the solution to conflicts perceived as arising from the weakness and collapse of states, civil society and the absence of liberal market economies is to instantiate such arrangements (see Chapter

10). Importantly, for Duffield (2001), this is not a world of functioning and liberal states combating violence and collapse in weak states, but a world in which the new wars and the liberal peace take similar forms of transborder networks of state and non-state, public and private, actors, social groups, flows and commodity chains.

Early characterizations of the new wars that posited a transformation in motives of war from political 'grievances' to economic 'greed' have given way to more sophisticated accounts of the political economy of war. This characterizes violence not as a means of economic gain but as embedded and active within evolving structures of power and profit that are local, global, regional, transnational – anything but easily mapped onto the national territorial space of traditional war (Keen, 1998; Berdal and Malone, 2000; Ballentine and Sherman, 2003; Pugh et al., 2004). In this context, organized violence in the new wars is not becoming apolitical, but differently political – embedded not in the politics of and between nation-states in pursuit of security and power (at least not as most rationalist theories portray such politics) but in the processes of globalization. Indeed, many sociological accounts of the transformation of war in the contemporary era link the high-tech and (seemingly) low casualty wars of Western powers and the low-tech 'new wars' that escape the systems and standards of international humanitarian law.

It is the phenomenon of globalization that enables, produces and reconfigures war into these forms and so takes us beyond Tilly's (1975: 42) claim that 'war made the state and the state made war', which emphasized that the preparation for war required territorial consolidation, the centralization and bureaucratization of power, and the monopolization of legitimate violence. Thus, in different ways, theorists of the new wars, and others like Barkawi (2006) and Bauman (2001), argue that the changing patterns and practices of war both reflect and produce the interconnections and reconfigurations of power and ordering that constitute globalization, rather than being merely a deepening of the economic and social interdependencies that make war irrational or obsolete in liberal accounts. Indeed, some poststructuralist-inspired scholars of war argue that contemporary wars are related to current manifestations of liberalism and neoliberalism that legitimate the humanitarian and sanitized wars of liberal states as biopolitical wars 'to make life live' and to establish liberal patterns of control with the promise of security and human wellbeing (Jabri, 2006; Dillon and Reid, 2009).

Genocide

It is tempting to assume that killing on a genocidal scale is irrational, that the mass killing of hundreds of thousands, even millions, of civilians for no reasons other than ethnicity, nationality, religion or other group identity can serve no greater political purpose and thus cannot be understood in the same way as war. However, most genocides have occurred in the context of war, and as a central part of war, from the Holocaust, to Cambodia, Rwanda, Bosnia and others. Further, the practice of genocide is still organized political violence, and is generally organized by governments, even in cases like Rwanda where much of the actual killing was carried out by non-state militia. Indeed, definitions of genocide emphasize a deliberate and instrumental dimension to the violence. The 1948 UN Convention on the Prevention and Punishment of the Crime of Genocide defines genocide as acts committed 'with intent to destroy, in whole or in part, a national, ethnical, racial or religious group, as such', by killing members of the group, but also by causing bodily or mental harm, inflicting 'conditions of life' calculated to bring about physical destruction, imposing measures to prevent births (such as sterilization), and forcibly transferring children of the group to another group. Thus, genocide is a much wider set of instrumental acts than just killing or even the use of direct violence, but always has the intent to destroy a group. Raphael Lemkin (1944: 79), the originator of the term 'genocide', also included a cultural dimension. His initial definition was 'a coordinated plan of different actions aiming at the destruction of essential foundations of the life of national groups, with the aim of annihilating the groups completely'. This relates not only to the rapid mass killing of members of a group (particularly an ethnic group) but the destruction of cultural and physical foundations of a way of life. For instance, the deliberate destruction of the built environment of cities, known as 'urbicide', is given scant attention but has profound implications as a form of violence against the constitution of public political spaces (Coward, 2009b). In practice, the use of the term 'genocide' is politically difficult, even in the face of mass killings, since it carries considerable legal and political weight and obligations in the international community.

A growing body of work studies genocide in the same terms as war. Indeed, there are the same debates over the transformation or eternal character of mass killing, its decline over time, its relationship to the era of modernity and so on. More specifically, some liberal scholars extend the democratic peace argument on war to genocide and other forms of mass political killing by the state. Rummel (1998: 367) argues that there is a strong correlation between a lack of democracy and mass political killing and thus that 'power kills, absolute power kills absolutely'. A wider sociological view of violence also shows that the mass killing of civilians in which civilians are a target in and of themselves remains political because, for Shaw (2003: 5), it 'uses the logic of war and can be seen as an extension of degenerate war'. To paraphrase Clausewitz, then, genocide has become the continuation of war by other means, although not in any way that would grant it legitimacy. Other critical scholars, however, deny this. For Booth (2007: 318), blurring the distinction between politically instrumental war and genocide is a mistake. Rather, he echoes some aspects of the new wars thesis and claims that: 'Genocidal acts represent the violent rationality of visible collective madness, not the political rationality of Clausewitz.' Booth (2007: 120) thus disavows accounts like that of Bauman, who views the Holocaust as integral to the project of modernity. Rather, the key to combating the contemporary fertile conditions for further genocide lies not in a rejection of modern progress but in its reinforcement to combat genocidal rationality through more effective international action against those who commit genocide. Clearly, the status of genocide, and other mass killing by states, is a central issue reflecting particular views of the state, modernity, progress and reason.

Conclusion

The logics of war may be conceived as a tension between pure violence for its own sake and the political instrumental view that Clausewitz saw as the only possible real manifestation of war. Caught in some ever changing configuration of his three forces, wars retain their political character even as they vary in many other respects. Yet war has clearly been transformed, in both its political purpose and its utility, and in the totality or limiting of its conduct. While some realists insist that war is an eternally relevant instrument of states in their relations with each other, liberals respond with evidence of its decline and restraint to point to possible obsolescence. Drawing on a wider range of social theories, other scholars point to changing formations of political, economic and social relations in which war is embedded and which war expresses. Further, war is conceived not only as an expression of a set political order or rationality but also as constitutive of the world of states and the world of globalization, the modern and the late or postmodern. Most of us now will encounter war in very different ways than our parents and grandparents, although for all its supposed sanitization and subjection to reason and law, the horrors of war remain barely hidden from view. War, then, is an eternally important question but also a deeply enigmatic one. For all the attempts to render it either usable or obsolete, war remains with us, but explanations based on eternal human nature of structural imperatives can offer little explanation for its wide variance. The political use of violence on an organized and substantial scale, however, is worth addressing not just through such broad historical, social and theoretical analyses as discussed here, but also the complex relations between the politics of violence and the spread and control of the means of violence. It is these complex relations that are explored in Chapter 8's discussion of the arms trade, arms control and disarmament.

Chapter 8

Arms Trade, Arms Control and Disarmament

Weapons and military technologies are integral to the security dilemma and the incidence and conduct of war. Much security theory and practice relate to the acquisition, transfer and control of weapons of various kinds. Broader theoretical debates about whether states can build deep cooperation in security matters, and whether such cooperation has much impact on states' behaviour, are particularly played out in relation to military technology issues. Indeed, we can think about these issues in two related ways. First, as a range of relations between states that are conducted via technology: that is, how and why states relate to each other by exchanging technology with each other, or by restricting the movement and use of technology internationally. Second, relations with technology: Are weapons mere tools or do they shape states' relations with each other? The balance between these views differs not just between states, but between different categories of weapons in ways that are not simple reflections of the destructive power weapons embody.

This chapter looks at how access to arms is structured and managed. It explores the arms trade, a commercial venture and a foreign policy tool, and the reasons why states acquire arms, and how their procurement practices reflect global dynamics and deeper political and social practices. It then looks at the rising concern with the proliferation of so-called 'weapons of mass destruction' (WMD) in order to discuss varying positions on the implications of proliferation for international security. Finally, it discusses the body of practices related to arms control, disarmament and nonproliferation. This explores the logics and limits of international cooperation on arms matters and the evolution and challenges of controlling military technologies. In doing so, it shows how weapons and the politics of arms reflect and produce the global structures within which states seek security.

The arms trade

The global trade in conventional arms is largely understood as a legitimate and essential part of states' military, strategic, political and economic relations. The arms trade is not a completely free market: states exercise some control over what arms companies based in their countries do, or at least which other countries they sell weapons and military technologies to. States also participate in the arms trade as manufacturers and exporters for political and financial reasons. Arms transfers between states have been used to bolster alliances, support friendly regimes, and engineer or alter balances of power within conflicts and in regional systems. However, states do not exercise full control over the arms trade, and like other trade regulations, controls involve a complex mix of competing interests and perceptions. Today, most policy debate on conventional arms relates to what restrictions should be applied to particular weapons or particular recipients: what the exceptions to the general rule of legitimacy of arms transfers should be, and how they should be decided.

This has not always been the case. In the early 20th century, international arms trading was relatively free and largely private. Private companies, such as Vickers and Armstrong in the UK and Krupp in Germany, supplied their own governments and engaged in exports, partly to recoup the research and development costs of new technologies in a period of rapid technological change. This included exports to rival states, and governments were sometimes unable to prevent companies from selling weapons to their enemies. In 1900, the British government introduced the Exportation of Arms Act that gave it powers to prohibit exports to particular countries, although this power was not used until 1914 (Krause, 1992: 63). In the years between the two world wars, there were attempts to rein in the arms trade. States increasingly introduced rudimentary 'export control' laws in order to exercise some control over possible exports that were not in their interest. At the international level, in 1925 the League of Nations produced a draft convention on the arms trade, but this was never adopted. While there are now numerous regional and multilateral agreements on arms transfer controls, it was only in March 2013 that a global Arms Trade Treaty was agreed after many years of faltering negotiations.

Making the market for arms

The development of the arms trade has always been interrelated with global security relations in changing ways. The origins of the current arms market lie in the early post-1945 period when only a few states were significant suppliers. The arms trade expanded from this small base, with 'second-tier' and 'third-tier' producers and suppliers gradually increasing their market share (Krause, 1992). However, the arms market has always been highly stratified, with a handful of countries exporting the vast majority of weapons. Early in the Cold War, the superpowers used arms transfers to solidify the two emerging power blocs. The USA was by far the largest supplier in this period, and has been many times since. It gave arms as part of military assistance packages to allies in Europe and Asia. Likewise, the USSR supplied arms and weapons production technologies to its Eastern European allies. From the early 1960s, the market changed, with US arms transfers increasingly occurring through the commercially motivated Foreign Military Sales programme, and a range of European states that had been rebuilding their arms industries entered the export market, producing a two-tier system. While European states' arms sales were also commercially motivated, there was considerable political control over them: Eastern European states' exports were restricted by Soviet military policy and the Comecon (Council for Mutual Economic Assistance) to such a degree that they were seen as an extension of the USSR's arms industry. Likewise, although less centralized, NATO's CoCom (Coordinating Committee for Multilateral Export Controls) was established in 1950 to ensure that Western states did not transfer sensitive technologies to the Soviet Union, China and their allies. As the arms trade expanded to include growing sales to developing countries, such bloc divisions remained important and often meant that most (but not all) countries could buy arms from only one side. In the mid-1960s and early 1970s, this expanding number of suppliers was augmented by a 'third tier' of arms producers and exporters, such as China, Israel and Brazil, who pursued arms sales for commercial reasons and, especially, to support their own independent arms production capabilities in order to acquire arms free from supplier bloc constraints.

In the 1970s and 80s, as the era of limited wars increasingly took the form of proxy conflicts (see Chapter 7), the political use of arms transfers expanded and the global scale of the arms trade increased. This was not only determined by structural shifts, but also by the views of particular leaders as different US governments had different perspectives on the political utility of arms transfers. In the early 1970s, under President Nixon, concerns about the loss of US lives in Vietnam contributed to a decision to transfer arms rather than troops to pursue wider US national interests. In the late 1970s, President Carter's presidential campaign emphasized restraint in arms transfers. However, after the initial stages of his presidency, arms transfers again became a key tool in 'normalizing' relations with China and in pursuing strategic interests in the Middle East. In the 1980s, President Reagan continued and enhanced the use of arms transfers to pursue strategic interests, through gifts to allies and as part of a strategy of containing the 'evil empire'. Here, proxy wars were particularly important, with civil wars in many parts of the world fuelled by arms transfers from both superpowers and their allies. The USSR sent large quantities of arms as well as money, training and occasionally their own military forces (Afghanistan) or Cuban troops (Angola) to support government forces in Angola, Nicaragua and Afghanistan. In turn, the US government used regional allies (South Africa and Zaire, Honduras and Pakistan respectively) and the CIA to supply rebel groups in these countries. In some cases, these arms transfers were illegal under US law and were pursued in violation of congressional wishes.

The mix of commercial and political motives and the stratification of the arms market among tiers of suppliers remain perennial features of arms trading. However, recently there have been important changes in the defence industry and in what is traded. First, the post-Cold War arms trade became more commercialized and privatized; levels of military aid from the major suppliers to allies in the developing world dropped significantly, forcing many countries to purchase arms on a commercial basis, and state-run arms industries in Eastern Europe and beyond were sold off. Second, the arms market became more competitive in the early 1990s as global defence spending declined and the market for arms shrank. However, the links between defence spending and the arms trade are more complicated than this implies (see Figures 9.1 and 9.2).

Contemporary trends

Global military expenditure rose again from the late 1990s, and particularly after the 9/11 terrorist attacks, although many other countries have followed the US lead in increasing spending (see Figure 9.1). In 2012, US$1.75 trillion was spent on military expenditure, equivalent to 2.5% of global GDP. This increase is unevenly distributed; US, Russian and Chinese expenditure

Figure 9.1 ***Global military expenditure***

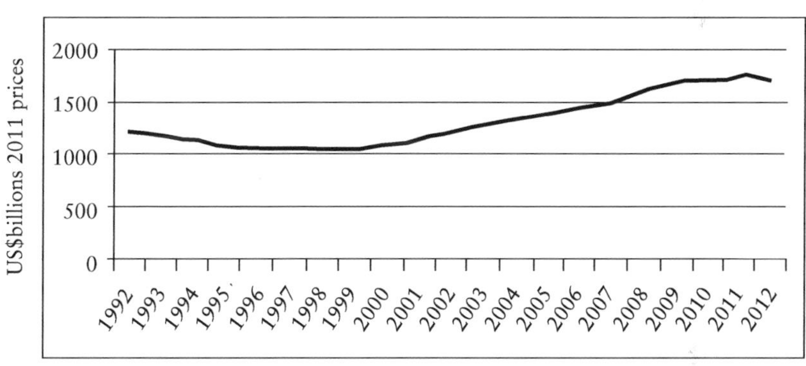

Source: Data from Stockholm International Peace Research Institute, 2013a

Figure 9.2 ***Global arms transfers***

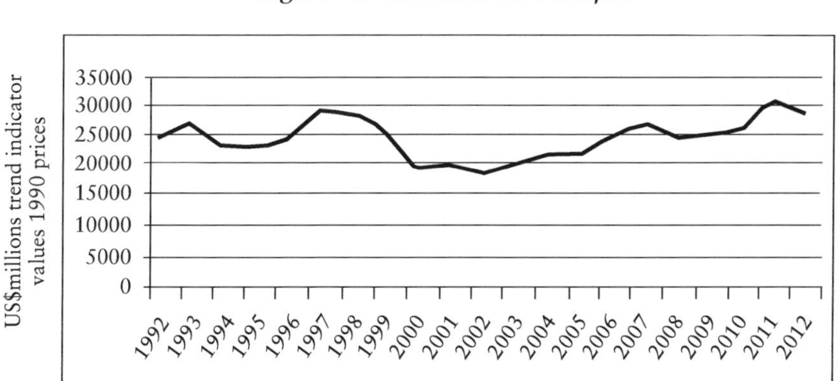

Source: Data from Stockholm International Peace Research Institute, 2013b

is rising significantly, as is spending in Asia, the Middle East and North Africa, whereas spending in Western and central Europe is declining. The USA spends more on military expenditure than any other state, accounting for 45.7% (US$739.3 billion) of global spending in 2011 and 39% in 2012 (Holtom et al., 2011; Perlo-Freeman et al., 2013). The value of military expenditure is debatable. US spending in 2012 was the equivalent of 4.4% of its GDP, and in many countries military expenditure outweighs spending on health, education and other social spending. There is also some evidence that military expenditure decreases other investments, is correlated with corruption, and diminishes economic growth, although these concerns feature little in the politics of arms and are subject to great contestation (Smith, 1980; Deger and Smith, 1983; Gupta et al., 2001).

Expenditure on arms accounts for only a small proportion of military expenditure but the value remains high. The value of the global trade in major conventional arms (tanks, planes, ships and so on) fluctuates each year, but general trends indicate a significant decline towards the end of the Cold War and the immediate post-Cold War period, followed by a dramatic increase since the start of the 21st century. The latest year for which reliable figures are available is 2007, in which the financial value of arms transfers was over $50 billion (in contemporary dollar values, rather than the 1990 values used to calculate trends in Figure 9.2) (SIPRI, 2013c). Since then, while precise figures are not available, the overall value of arms transfers has increased by 17% over the past five years (Holtom et al., 2013). This represents the highest level of arms transfers since the late Cold War. In the period 2008–12, 75% of this was made up of exports from just five countries: the USA (30%), Russia (26%), Germany (7%), France (6%) and China (5%). These recent figures are the first time since the Cold War that the UK has not been in the top five suppliers (Holtom et al., 2013). Thus, in general terms, the world's largest arms suppliers tend to be the P5 members of the UN Security Council (SC) and some others. In 2010, US proposed arms sales (covering a substantial deal with Saudi Arabia to take place over several years) reached a 10-year high at US$106 billion (Liang, 2011). Even more significant increases have been seen from China, which has increased arms exports by 95% over the past decade while also reducing its dependency on arms imports from other suppliers (Holtom et al., 2012).

Politically motivated transfers remain important. While of low overall value, China's politically motivated transfers to African regimes have had some political prominence in relation to conflict and human rights concerns, particularly the 'ship of shame' incident of 2008 when China shipped small arms to the regime of Robert Mugabe in Zimbabwe, as well as equally questionable transfers to Iran, Myanmar and Nepal (Spiegel and Le Billon, 2009). Other leading suppliers continue to use arms transfers as a key foreign policy tool. For instance, the USA increased military aid including arms transfers to key partners in the war on terror, including Pakistan, Indonesia and the Philippines, which had been key allies in the Cold War but had been subjected to restrictions on the basis of human rights and nuclear proliferation concerns in the post-Cold War era.

The arms trade cannot be understood solely through national market shares and motivations. The defence industry has become increasingly 'globalized' in various ways, including foreign ownership of previously national defence companies, joint ventures between companies, and the transnational subcontracting of aspects of production. This raises concerns about declining national autonomy in arms acquisitions and the possible proliferation of sensitive technologies (Markusen, 1999; Bitzinger, 2009). Further, much of the arms trade is not in complete weapons sold to military forces, but in components and dual-use technologies (technologies that can be used in military and civilian industries), and transfers within firms as well as between them. Contemporary joint research and development and production serves similar purposes to the rebuilding of defence industries in the postwar period and many arms transfers throughout the Cold War – the deepening of political integration and the strengthening of key strategic relations. Within Europe, the joint development and production of the Eurofighter Typhoon involve the UK, Spain, Germany and Italy, and the planes are built by a consortium of companies including BAE Systems in the UK, Alenia Aeronautica in Italy, and the pan-European aerospace and defence giant EADS (itself formed by a merger in 2000 of French, German and Spanish companies). Such trends are set to continue and expand, particularly with the activities of the European Defence Agency, founded in 2004 to further the development of a European defence industry and encourage more European states to buy weapons from each other (Keohane, 2008a).

The 'arms dynamic' and procurement

Why do states acquire weapons? Why do they participate in the arms trade? Why do they acquire the particular weapons they do? The main explanations of the 'arms dynamic' include an emphasis on systemic factors and domestic factors (Buzan and Herring, 1998). They also raise questions about how states relate to technological advances, and particularly whether and why they try to make full use of new technologies. In reality, the distinction between these factors is not clear-cut: processes of technological development are not unrelated to domestic political decisions that affect the procurement of particular weapons.

An emphasis on systemic factors in arms procurement and trade often reflects wider structuralist models of security behaviours. In particular, the concept of the security dilemma poses arms procurement as related to the competitive logics that arise from uncertainty and anarchy (see Chapter 5). Arms procurement is seen as subject to an action-reaction dynamic; for example, when one state develops or buys a new fighter jet, other states will view that development with suspicion and therefore respond in kind. Particularly intense action-reaction dynamics in arms procurement are sometimes described as 'arms races', although it should not be assumed that all competitive arms acquisitions are necessarily as intense and difficult to manage as that term implies. While presenting the elegant logic of a simple process with complex manifestations, there are reasons to question this model. First, it can easily become deterministic and imply that each state at any given time had little choice but to make the specific decisions it did, thereby depoliticizing the choices made about arms procurement. Second, while states may be involved in reciprocal relationships, identifying particular actions and reactions is difficult, particularly when new and high-tech weapons systems take many years to develop and build, and even purchasing weapons from foreign or domestic companies can take years between order and delivery.

Domestic factors shaping procurement are more diverse. They include everything from the concerns of particular politicians with employment issues in their constituencies, the influence and interests of military organizations in securing a share of the defence budget, to a range of economic issues. Indeed, many economic arguments for exporting arms take the security issues around arms transfers and procurement for granted and focus on economic benefits such as export revenues, the reduction of unit costs of national procurement, contributing to good political and trade relations with other states, and helping to maintain a defence industry that is necessary for national procurement (which tends to be sporadic). These arguments cannot be taken at face value. For instance, the economic benefits become questionable when one factors in the considerable costs of government subsidies and assistance to arms companies. Further, for some observers, it is important to note the political influence of arms companies and the military institutions that seek out new equipment and a greater share of government defence spending. For example, US President Eisenhower's 1961 farewell speech warned of the influence of the 'military-industrial complex' that he believed was growing, in part because of the increasing role of government in conducting or contracting military technological research.

Procurement decisions are not necessarily the product of rational calculations trying to balance all these interests and find the most effective weapons systems. In some cases, economic interests have combined with the typical conservatism of military institutions towards the adoption of new technologies, so that old weapons platforms were amended with new technologies rather than replaced with totally new weapons systems. This produced what Kaldor (1982) calls 'baroque' weapons, which are increasingly complex and expensive to maintain but actually have little military utility. More broadly, constructivists and poststructuralists argue that states do not engage with arms issues on purely rational grounds, reacting to the actions of others or particular domestic political and economic interests. Rather, the symbolic value of particular weapons may overshadow these factors (Suchman and

Eyre, 1992). Indeed, some studies indicate that much weapons procurement involves a particular culture of technology that centres on high-tech weapons. Wendt and Barnett (1993) argued that while 'third world' states have huge differences in their security context and the nature of state formation, they have still adopted a strikingly similar military model to Western states: a 'capital-intensive' model reliant on skilled soldiers and high-tech weapons rather than large labour-intensive people's armies that some could have developed more easily. Combined with the broad increase in the unit costs of weapons in evidence in the postwar period (Krause, 1992), a situation arose in which weapons systems that are too expensive, too high-tech to maintain or use, are bought by states that cannot afford them.

Beyond such cultural factors affecting procurement, it is notable that the politics of armaments is framed in particular ways that legitimates some weapons and transfers and delegitimizes others. Thus, in the 1990s, growing concern with the possible spread of nuclear, chemical and biological weapons and missile technologies was framed in terms of 'proliferation', which poses any spread of those weapons to any states as potentially destabilizing and dangerous. In contrast, the spread of conventional arms (tanks, planes, ships, rifles and ammunition) is usually described in terms of 'trade', which portrays the overall movement of weapons in what Mutimer (2000) calls a 'commercial frame', an economic and largely legitimate process within which only a few specific dangerous and destabilizing transfers can be identified and excluded. Indeed, contemporary measures seeking to control the conventional arms trade do not try to reduce the arms market, but only to limit the risk that particular transfers might contribute to destabilizing accumulations of weapons, worsen regional security, or affect human rights and development.

Proliferation

Far greater and more amplified security concerns relate to the proliferation of nuclear weapons, and to a lesser extent, biological and chemical weapons. While such weapons were a high-profile concern in Cold War security politics, their proliferation became increasingly identified as a threat in the 1990s. In 1992, the first ever summit meeting of the UN Security Council (1992: 4) made an unprecedented statement that the 'proliferation of all weapons of mass destruction constitutes a threat to international peace and security'. Contemporary proliferation concerns related particularly to the acquisition of nuclear weapons by terrorists (see Chapter 11) and what some have called 'rogue' states, such as concerns over North Korea's testing of nuclear weapons in 2006, 2009 and 2013 and the ongoing development of enrichment facilities for highly enriched uranium (HEU, a key part of developing nuclear weapons) by Iran.

The contemporary nuclear weapons map includes nine states that possess nuclear weapons – the USA, Russia, China, France and the UK (the P5 members of the UNSC, recognized as nuclear weapons states, NWS, under the 1968 Nuclear Non-Proliferation Treaty), as well as Israel, India, Pakistan and North Korea, although North Korea is not yet believed to have a nuclear warhead capable of fitting onto a missile. There are also suspicions over the nuclear ambitions and development of reactors and enrichment facilities in Iran and Syria. Nuclear proliferation concerns relate primarily to 'horizontal proliferation' (the development of nuclear weapons' capabilities by states that previously did not have them), and to a limited degree to 'vertical proliferation' (the accumulation and modernization of nuclear weapons, stockpiles by existing nuclear armed states). While total global nuclear warhead stocks increased throughout the Cold War, reaching around 80,000, significant cuts by Russia and the USA have reduced numbers to around 19,000 (5,500 in Russia, 5,000 in the USA, 300 in France, 240 in China, 225 in the UK, up to 200 in Israel, and around 100 each for India and Pakistan). Many of these are more powerful than earlier warheads and while there is continuing nuclear disarmament, this is often accompanied by force modernization.

Biological and chemical weapons are now banned by international conventions. While several states (China, India, Libya, Russia and the USA) have declared that they have stocks of chemical weapons, which are due to be destroyed, Egypt, Israel, Iran and Syria are also believed to have chemical weapons' stocks. Biological weapons are held by Israel, Russia and North Korea, and covert programmes are believed to exist in China, Egypt and Syria (Carnegie Endowment for International Peace, 2009). These types of weapons are also seen as a major concern for mass destruction terrorism (see Chapter 11).

Debating proliferation

While most states accept, in some form, that nuclear weapons' proliferation is damaging to international security, security theorists have more diverse opinions. Most academic debate has been polarized between so-called 'proliferation optimists' and 'proliferation pessimists'. In an exemplary debate, conducted in the early 1990s and reconvened in 1998, regarding Pakistan's nuclear tests, and recently regarding the possibility of Iranian proliferation, structural realist Kenneth Waltz and organizational theorist Scott Sagan articulated starkly opposing views. Waltz argued that 'more may be better', pointing out that a small number of nuclear weapons are enough to establish deterrence, as even a few warheads prompt circumspection by rivals. Thus, even if the number of states with nuclear weapons increases, this may bring about more stability. This reinforces a view in much deterrence theory that caution in the security relations with nuclear armed states derives from the strong rationality assumption of realism (see Chapter 5) and the realist view of limited war in the Cold War, since nuclear weapons' use renders war irrational (see Chapter 7). In contrast, Sagan has pointed out that nuclear weapons are embedded in systems of control that are always imperfect, even for the USA and the USSR. For Sagan, the spread of weapons to countries like Pakistan and others, which may be unable to build effective security and safeguards, risks a range of nuclear accidents, including accidental launch, and thus more countries with nuclear weapons 'will be worse' (Sagan and Waltz, 2003). Importantly, a central dimension of the disagreement relates not to whether nuclear deterrence can work – both sides agree it can – but whether the nuclear peace between the superpowers during the Cold War can be, or will be, replicated in regional and global security relationships of new nuclear armed states (Karl, 1996/97).

Private proliferation

Other concerns about proliferation go beyond the possibility of stable deterrence. For instance, the possible terrorist acquisition and use of chemical, biological, radiological and nuclear weapons is viewed as undeterrable (except perhaps for deterring states that might assist in this proliferation) (see Chapter 11). More broadly, proliferation concerns have been privatized such that deterring states may only be part of the equation. Thus, some observers point to a growing nuclear black market that could supply technology and nuclear materials to terrorist groups or states that would sponsor them. In relation to nuclear technology, observers point to the global network of front companies and middlemen created by Dr Abdul Qadeer Khan to procure technology for the Pakistani nuclear programme. Established in the 1970s, this network shifted from procurement to selling nuclear weapon technology after the late 1980s, including transferring nuclear weapon designs and missile technology to Libya, Iran and North Korea (Russell, 2006; Fitzpatrick, 2007; Boureston and Russell, 2009). This network was dismantled after 2003, but fears remain that future nuclear proliferation could take place through private networks that are harder to control. In relation to nuclear materials, experts also point to the thousands of cases of the smuggling of nuclear materials since the 1990s. Most of these relate to nuclear junk and contaminated scrap metal, but some involve HEU and plutonium. However, much of the HEU has not been weapons grade, and would need further enrichment for weapons use, and the plutonium is often trace elements found in smoke detectors. While the total amounts of HEU and plutonium ever seized from smugglers would not be enough for a nuclear weapon and the trade is highly disorganized, comprising amateur thieves, there are fears that what is known of this trafficking is the tip of an iceberg in which terrorist groups or their state sponsors might be able to acquire nuclear materials (Zaitseva and Hand, 2003; Frost, 2005; Fitzpatrick, 2007).

Motives for proliferation and deproliferation

States may try to develop nuclear weapons for a combination of reasons, including international security, deterrence, power balancing, domestic political reasons, and the international prestige and power that accompanies being a nuclear armed state. Supply side factors are also important, such as the supply of sensitive technologies and materials by other states (Kroenig, 2010), or the supply of civil nuclear technologies that enhance the proliferation capacities of states (Fuhrmann, 2009). Perspectives on proliferation are dominated by assumptions of simple cost–benefit calculations. However, recent scholarship has identified psychological and normative dimensions of political leaders' sense of national identity as shaping the decision to pursue nuclear weapons (Hymans, 2006). Domestic political factors may even predominate in many cases of proliferation. Thus, Solingen (2007) argues that those states that have pursued nuclear weapons (North Korea) are a rare exception, due to focusing on internal political matters rather than worrying about the international political and economic costs of breaking with nonproliferation norms.

The reverse process of 'deproliferation' is often neglected. While most theories of proliferation view it as an inevitable process of the spread of advanced technology, it is notable that nuclear weapons have not spread as much, or as quickly, as many predicted in the early part of the Cold War. Indeed, 37 states have developed some nuclear weapons activities since 1945, but while only half these countries actively pursued nuclear weapons, 10 acquired them and 1 (South Africa) acquired them and then gave them up. Many other states faltered in technological development or gave up nuclear ambitions before completing weapons, and the total number of states undertaking related activities has declined significantly since the late 1980s (Müller and Schmidt, 2010). While the technological challenges of proliferation are high, political explanations also play a role. Realist explanations emphasize restraint in proliferation through the provision of security assurances by superpower allies. However, this does not explain all cases of deproliferation, and constructivist scholarship emphasizes the development of a nonproliferation norm and its codification in a complex nonproliferation regime centring on the 1968 Treaty on the Non-Proliferation of Nuclear Weapons, commonly known as the Nuclear Non-Proliferation Treaty (NPT), and a range of regional nuclear weapons-free zones. The existence and effects of an international norm of nonproliferation are debated, and some constructivists argue that the stronger 'taboo' is against the use rather than the possession of nuclear weapons (Tannenwald, 2007). Wider international political relations, sanctions and hidden diplomacy are also crucial for explaining Libya's renunciation of WMD in 2003, and South Africa's unilateral nuclear disarmament in 1989. At times, military action has also slowed the development of nuclear weapons, such as the Israeli bombing of Iraq's Osirak reactor in 1981, and such action remains part of the possible response to perceived Iranian nuclear ambitions.

Arms control, disarmament and nonproliferation

International efforts to manage weapons and military technology take the form of arms control, disarmament and nonproliferation. These relate largely to forms of international cooperation through the agreement of formal treaties and wider regimes, as well as bilateral negotiations and looser politically binding frameworks. Such efforts are often discussed in a highly technical discourse that can make it difficult to discern the underlying political processes and dynamics. Indeed, debates about arms control have tended to combine authoritative statements about technology with assertions of the immutable laws of states' behaviour in anarchy (Cooper and Mutimer, 2011). Thus, it is important to understand the different perspectives on technology that form part of the debates on arms control, and then to explore the differing debates on what arms control and disarmament can achieve, and finally the types of challenges and opportunities that exist for this area of security practice.

Theories of technology embedded in understandings of security may be broadly categorized as 'instrumental' and 'substantivist' (Wyn Jones, 1999). These cross the boundaries between rationalist and critical perspectives on security (see Chapters 2 and 3). Most arms control theory is based on instrumentalism, although substantivist accounts of nuclear weapons and technological change are also influential. While the two are opposed understandings of technology, both tend to be invoked as limiting the potential for arms control and disarmament.

'Instrumentalist' views of technology predominate in Western political and social thought and view technology, including weapons, as neutral tools subservient to political and cultural values. Instrumentalism in security studies is exemplified by Gray, Mueller and others who, within otherwise widely differing perspectives, adopt similar arguments about the essential irrelevance of weapons and technological change in relation to war and violence. Instrumentalism is present in some critical security studies too. Booth (2005b: 266) disavows a theoretical concern with technology as merely 'hardware dimension of realism'. Rather, he locates the emancipatory dimension of concerns with nuclear weapons firmly among the cultural, moral and psychological aspects of the 'genocidal mentality' of 'nuclearism' (Booth, 2007: 267). Much constructivist work also emphasizes the priority of intersubjective norms attached to weapons rather than the weapons themselves. Thus, Price (1997: 6) claims that the reasons why some weapons are subject to traditions of non-use and others capable of similar indiscriminate killing and cruelty are not 'lie not simply with the objective and essential characteristics of the weapons themselves but with how civilizations and societies have interpreted those characteristics and translated them into political and military practices'.

'Substantivist' views, in contrast, see technology as determining social and political relations, not as a mere tool within them. For substantivists, technological progress has an autonomous logic that subsumes and shapes society, politics and economics. Forms of substantivism are prevalent in discussions of nuclear weapons. Waltz's proliferation optimist position is based on a substantivist reading of nuclear technology, in which, regardless of the context of political relations and regional security, the presence of nuclear weapons determines a high degree of caution and instantiates stable deterrence. The pessimist position highlights that military and political factors present in the archetypal nuclear standoff of the Cold War are not present in many other regions and thus nuclear stability is unlikely, thereby incorporating a degree of instrumentalism in the debate.

Arms control and disarmament

Arms control theory is a strange thing. Traditionally, it has articulated itself not against arms but against disarmament. The so-called 'golden age' of arms control theory was also the era in which strategic studies was developing in the 1950s and 60s. Early arms control theorists, such as Hedley Bull, Thomas Schelling and Morton Halperin, were keen to distance their ideas from what they perceived as naive proposals for 'general and complete disarmament' and the failed disarmament conference of the interwar years. Thus, they used the term 'arms control' to dismiss disarmament, or at least to make it one tool among many in the arms control toolkit. Part of the rationale of the distinction was not just one of different techniques but a deeper philosophical distinction between ends and means: for early and recent theorists of arms limitation, 'arms control' is about ensuring stability and security through the judicious control of military technology; 'disarmament', it is claimed, views the reduction in weapons as a goal of value in itself (Larsen and Wirtz, 2009). The notion that those in favour of disarmament are guilty of confusing ends and means is frequently used by many scholars to dismiss the practice. For Buzan (1987: 250), for instance, within an anarchic international system, 'the logic of disarmament is so obviously flawed that except for propaganda purposes, and for limited reductions in the context of arms control, the idea is, as the historical record indicates, a non-starter'. Here, then, many thinkers are guilty of a rather duplicitous rejection of disarmament – conceptually it is deemed utopian and unachievable, so when it exists, and therefore cannot be utopian, it is not counted as disarmament but as 'arms control' (Cooper, 2006).

Early arms control theory quickly reached a consensus on the three main objectives that arms control could contribute to, which still dominate discussion – reducing the likelihood of war, reducing the political and economic costs of preparing for war, and minimizing the scope and violence of war if it occurred (Schelling and Halperin, 1961; Bull, 1961). It is worth noting, however, this early consensus masks significant differences between early arms control theorists; Schelling, an economist, sought to ignore 'political context' as much as possible, while Bull asserted a unity of strategy, arms control and politics. Assertions of instrumentalism against substantivism were particularly influential in forming arms control theory. Bull (1959) criticized his former employer, the disarmament advocate Philip Noel Baker, by claiming that arms are a consequence not a cause of political tension and disarmament is only possible in the wake of political agreement. Nevertheless, Bull, Schelling and Halperin all saw some of the danger of war as residing in the nature of weapons, especially the incentives for pre-emptive war that nuclear weapons produced. Later realist thought, however, disavowed even this limited substantivism.

Early theorists emphasized that arms control could only play a modest role in building security. For Bull (1961: 5), arms control was one tool among many for achieving 'peace through the manipulation of force'. This family of techniques also included engineering a balance of power, assuring security through world government, building a system of collective security, or a system of 'mutual deterrence or general terror'. Bull (1961: 95) claimed that all these have some merit, but that each on its own, pursued in abstraction from political considerations, would 'become absurd'. However, advocates of the latter views of power balancing and/or deterrence became dominant in the field of strategic studies and tended to restrict the contribution of arms control to a technique for stabilizing nuclear deterrence.

The combination of particular views of security politics with particular views of technology establishes the major contours of debates about arms control. Gray (1992) argued that not only is disarmament irrationally and dangerously utopian, but so too is 'arms control' – it is a 'house of cards' that is doomed to fail. Gray's central argument is that arms control is caught in a paradox: it is only needed when it is impossible, it is only possible when it is not needed. He claims that if strategic relations between states are at risk of moving into war, no real arms control can be agreed as the tensions between the states will make agreement impossible; and if they are not at risk of war, arms control may be agreed but would be irrelevant. Clearly, Gray could not deny that arms control agreements were a feature of global security relations. Rather, this paradox means that the history of arms control, as he saw it, was littered with insincere offers to negotiate, broken promises and poorly negotiated deals that could leave one side (the USA) vulnerable to the duplicity of the other (the USSR). Thus, Gray (1992: 5, 221) claimed that 'history, logic, and common sense all point to the futility of arms control', that it is like 'a chocolate diet to chocoholics', superficially attractive but also 'really bad for us'. Making the ultimate instrumentalist argument about arms control, Gray (1992: 68) claimed that: 'Peace and war are political; they are not technological or administrative via apolitical and astrategic theories of arms control and stability.' This is hardly surprising from a defender of a Clausewitzean paradigm of war (see Chapter 7) and an academic who worked as an adviser on arms control with the Reagan administration. However, it presents a challenge to arms control supporters to counter his argument.

Croft (1996), in contrast, has an optimistic view of arms control and disarmament. He criticizes Gray for focusing on a limited range of arms control, by focusing only on a part of Cold War arms control with the purpose of preventing superpower war. Croft also claimed that Gray neglected the changing nature of security politics even in that period, and since, for Gray, interstate relations are irredeemably and unchangingly competitive, it is hardly surprising that he sees little role for arms control. However, Croft argues, if one accepts the possibility of significant political change, and looks to a longer historical view in which arms control has been used for wider objectives, a different picture emerges. Most notably, various forms of arms control have been used to produce strategic stability within particular interstate relationships – to manage the proliferation of weapons, create and consolidate a peace after war, and others. Over time, Croft argues, arms control has evolved and undergone a process of 'widening' and 'deepening'.

By 'widening', Croft means that since the Cold War, arms control has tackled a far wider range of types of weapons, from landmines to small arms as well as nuclear, chemical and biological weapons, and that these processes have pursued a broader range of goals. Thus, since the 1990s, it has become commonplace for the UN to impose arms embargoes on countries involved in civil wars to signal the international community's disapproval, and to conduct disarmament operations as part of post-conflict peacebuilding (see Chapter 10). By 'deepening', Croft means that arms control agreements have become stronger, longer and more detailed. While for Gray, long detailed commitments were a sign of how technical and obscure much arms control was, for Croft, the level of detail reflects a deeper commitment to enforcement. For example, in the early post-Cold War period, the Conventional Forces in Europe Treaty (1990), the Chemical Weapons Convention (CWC, 1993) and START I (Strategic Arms Reduction Treaty, 1991) were all 'very deep', and included detailed commitments on how the principles they contained could be implemented. Agreements were also getting stronger through the establishment of systems of 'verification', ranging from information exchange to inspections to monitor implementation. Earlier, during the height of the Cold War, the intrusive nature of verification commitments meant that there were few really 'deep' agreements. But the 'very deep' agreements of the early post-Cold War period had stronger verification systems. This is not to say that short arms control documents no longer feature; the 2002 Strategic Offensive Reductions Treaty on nuclear disarmament between the USA and Russia is two pages long, with the main commitment (to reduce warheads to 1,700–2,200 each) contained in two sentences totalling 89 words. So, size doesn't always matter, but content does, and this – Croft argues – has improved.

If one accepts this view of the widening and deepening of arms control and disarmament, it is difficult to see how, as Gray claims, history, logic and common sense point to its futility. Certainly, there can be no role for arms control in changing politics in particular strategic relationships when, for definitional reasons, arms control is excluded from politics, and politics is viewed as unchanging anyway. However, Croft's view is rather teleological, arguing for a progressive strengthening of arms control across history without looking in depth at the role of power relations in shaping what is and is not subjected to rigorous control, or what its overall implications are for world order (Cooper, 2006).

Other critics of arms control and disarmament go even further, arguing that it has not yet lived up to its potential to provide security because in practice it has tended to be conservative, reflecting and reinforcing existing international order rather than transforming it. While Bull based his views of arms control on 'general grounds of historical pessimism' about grand designs, he was deeply critical of an assumption that arms control could only marry with the status-quo orientation it had found in US and Soviet practice, which obscured its possible role in promoting a challenge to world order (Bull, 1976; O'Neill, 2008). Cold War arms control was 'meant to denote rules for limiting arms competition (mainly nuclear) rather than reversing it' (Goldblat, 2002: 3). More recently, critical security scholars have criticized the way in which arms control and disarmament continue to play a role in legitimating and preserving an unjust world order. In a critical view, it is not that the realities of power politics mean that arms control is impossible, as Gray claims, but rather that power operates through arms control. Cooper (2006) argues that arms control has tended to reinforce an 'asymmetric' system of arms limitation. Going beyond Croft's broadening and deepening, he argues that traditional models of arms control typified by Cold War practices were about interstate processes of negotiation oriented towards the military security of particular states that produced cumbersome bureaucratic processes and detailed formal verification systems. New forms of arms control tend to have much in common with these older paradigms of arms control practice, even so-called 'humanitarian' arms control that includes the 1998 Ottawa Treaty that banned anti-personnel landmines, the 2001 UN Programme of Action on Illicit Small Arms and the 2008 Convention on Cluster Munitions. These processes differ from purely interstate processes as they have often involved many nongovernmental actors in the broad discussions – but these actors only have a significant voice on these few categories of weapons (Stavrianakis, 2010). While many new arms control issues are articulated around human security concerns, such as landmines, cluster munitions and small arms, these tend to have little verification. For Cooper (2006), this produces a series of asymmetries in the arms limitation system, in which much nonproliferation is oriented against 'rogue' states and preserves the hypocritical distinction between those that are permitted to have nuclear weapons and those that are not, and those that are subject to verification inspections and those that have the right to refuse inspections (the USA in the case of the CWC).

Much empirical support can be found for this critical view of a hypocritical and asymmetric arms control system. Controls are tight on nuclear, biological and chemical weapons, but much weaker on conventional arms. Conventional arms control does not seek to reduce the scale of the arms trade, and does not target the high military expenditures and multi-million dollar high-tech weapons systems of Western military power. Instead, it focuses on regulating trade, and stronger controls are only present for a limited range of weapons, such as anti-personnel landmines and cluster munitions – that are of little military importance to the powerful states – or the illegal trade in small arms that fuels crime and conflict. Cooper (2006) argues that the overall effect of these asymmetries is that while the USA and other powerful states have the largest military budgets and conventional military power, and the right to nuclear weapons, it is other states that are the targets of arms limitation. Thus, arms control is oriented towards preserving Western military hegemony.

The development of nuclear arms control

The development of nuclear arms control demonstrates some parts of all three perspectives: the difficulty of establishing strong arms limitation in situations of security competition, the gradual expansion and (sometimes) strengthening of arms control, and the hypocrisy and asymmetries that are embedded. Nuclear arms control began in the early postwar years with bilateral efforts among the former allies. In 1946, the USA proposed the Baruch Plan for the international management of nuclear technology, the abolition of nuclear weapons and other WMD, and a system of verification to ensure compliance. This faltered at the early stages of consideration in the UN, and was among the supposedly naive plans for disarmament that early arms control theorists condemned. Bilateral and multilateral measures continued, however, as did the major powers' own nuclear weapons programmes.

Bilateral arms control measures between the USA and the USSR generally served the purposes of ensuring deterrence rather than reducing arms competition. The first major treaty was the 1972 Strategic Arms Limitation Treaty (SALT I), which set limits on the number of intercontinental ballistic missiles (ICBMs) for each superpower. These limits were set at 1972 levels rather than reducing them. In the same year, the Anti-Ballistic Missile Treaty established stronger limits on missiles that could be used to defend against ICBM (or other) attacks. This sought to preserve deterrence by ensuring that both sides could maintain an effective 'second-strike' capability. If either side had an effective 'missile shield', as Presidents Reagan and George W. Bush have wanted at different times, they could, in theory, launch a first strike and defend against a nuclear retaliation, thereby negating the notion of mutually assured destruction and making nuclear attack a rational option. This shows clearly how arms control played a limited role in managing deterrence: arms control was not the means to security, it was a tool to maintain the means to security – even though that meant ensuring that their populations remained vulnerable to nuclear attack.

Wider nuclear politics, however, were given a different goal: nonproliferation. In 1963, the Partial Test Ban Treaty established controls on most (but not all) ways in which a country developing nuclear weapons could test them. This encouraged further negotiations, leading particularly to the centrepiece of the nuclear nonproliferation regime: the 1968 Nuclear Non-Proliferation Treaty (NPT). This established the central hypocrisy of the arms control system that served the status quo: its central bargain was that the five states that had nuclear weapons were declared 'nuclear weapons states' (NWS) and were permitted to keep them, and indeed to build up their arsenals to bewildering levels. Other states, however, committed themselves not to develop nuclear weapons. Two major aspects of the trade-off are worthy of note. First, the NPT agreed that non-nuclear weapons states should be given assistance to pursue peaceful nuclear technologies, such as for power generation, and second, the NWS committed themselves to eventual nuclear disarmament. However, limited progress on both commitments has been a perennial problem for the NPT and the regime as a whole. Nevertheless, the NPT remains in force, as in 1995, after 25 years (it entered into force in 1970), it was extended indefinitely. It remains a nearly universal instrument, and although several states (Israel, India, Pakistan and North Korea) have developed nuclear weapons since 1968, most were not NPT signatories, and North Korea withdrew in 2003 before conducting a test in 2006.

Controls on some other weapons are less riven by hypocrisy and contradictions and are embodied in absolute prohibitions, although this norm is not necessarily matched by full implementation. Thus, the 1972 Biological and Toxin Weapons Convention (BTWC) prohibited the development, production, stockpiling or other acquisition or retention of BTW. This built on earlier international law that prohibited the use of such weapons. Since the late 19th and early 20th century, the weaponization of chemical and biological agents has been deemed repugnant. The use of such weapons was prohibited in the 1899 Hague Convention, which included a declaration prohibiting projectiles for spreading asphyxiating gases, the 1907 Hague Convention, and the 1925 Geneva Protocol for the Prohibition of the Use in War of Asphyxiating, Poisonous or Other Gases, and of Bacteriological Methods of Warfare, which are seen as codifying ancient Greek and Roman standards against the use of poison and Qur'anic prohibitions. Similarly, in 1993, the Chemical Weapons Convention (CWC) was agreed after 13 years of negotiations (and entered into force in 1997). This prohibition includes commitments to destroy existing chemical weapon stockpiles; currently, just over 60 per cent of the global stock of 71,194 metric tons of chemical agents have been disposed of. While similar in their central norms, the BTWC and CWC are often contrasted in debates about verification. The CWC has a fairly robust system of verification, with a permanent organization (Organisation for the Prohibition of Chemical Weapons, OPCW) and the ability to conduct inspections. This includes 'challenge inspections', in which a member of the CWC who is suspicious of another can demand the OPCW to undertake an inspection at any site – and that state has no right to refuse the inspection. To date, over 4,000 inspections of all types have been carried out. In contrast, the BTWC lacks a verification mechanism, and the 1990s saw revelations that the USSR had maintained a covert biological weapons programme in spite of it.

The challenges and opportunities of arms control and disarmament

Attempts to manage arms dynamics may include unilateral measures such as shifting emphasis and spending to defensive technologies, tacit bargaining (in which one state seeks to avoid escalation and seeks reciprocity), or formal negotiated arms control (Downs et al., 1985). Thus, arms control, as Bull highlighted, falls into a wider family of efforts to manage military security. However, the challenges and opportunities for arms control are largely conceived in terms of formal (and sometimes informal) negotiated agreements. In this regard, arms control practice has predominantly taken the form of an incremental process that operates by parsing issues into constituent technical problems amenable to manipulation by experts (Krause and Latham, 1998). Progress in the processes of arms control thus often operates by making key problems into technical rather than political issues. However, the wider logics and limits of arms control experience combine political and technical issues.

Much debate about arms control relates to the limits of possibility for trust and cooperation in the international political sphere. This is often framed in terms of those who see the security dilemma and arms competition as requiring flexible decision making that militates against arms limitation, and those who argue that negotiated restraint may manage but not transform those relations. Even for those critical scholars adopting less pessimistic accounts of the potential for trust and cooperation to be built through arms control, the challenges remain significant (Ruzicka and Wheeler, 2010). However, constructivist work highlights how the evolution of norms about particular types of weapons is important in understanding how arms control controls arms: it is not simply a case of legal restraints that are kept or broken. Rather, the norms of states' behaviour in relation to weapons and violence evolve, which means that even unsuccessful arms control negotiations (of which there have been many) and treaties with loopholes can be argued to play a part in establishing a norm that has an effect.

Important challenges do not derive solely from the anarchic nature of the international system but result from the requirements for consensus built into the procedures of negotiating fora. The 65-member Conference on Disarmament (CD), for example, after early post-Cold War successes, such as the Comprehensive Test Ban Treaty (opened for signature in 1996, but still not in force) and the CWC, has only been able to agree once (2009) in the past 13 years on a programme of work. Likewise, it is frequently disappointing to note that, due to the structural features of negotiations, success in review conferences for existing treaty regimes is often seen in terms of whether or not an outcome document was agreed, rather than in terms of more far-reaching criteria for success.

A major challenge noted since the early days of arms control theory is that technological development outpaces regulatory innovation (Kahn, 1960; Whitman, 2007). Rapid developments in biotechnology since the 1980s have the potential to undermine the BTWC and have featured significantly in debates at BTWC review conferences (Wheelis and Dando, 2000). Likewise, some types of chemical agents, notably those used to incapacitate rather than kill, are not clearly defined in the CWC, allowing some continued research and use. For instance, unknown chemical incapacitants were used by the Russian authorities in the Moscow theatre siege of October 2002 – supposedly non-lethal agents that resulted in the deaths of 120 people. Similarly, the emerging militarization of nanotechnology presents challenges for future arms control (Altmann, 2006). In addition to outpacing regulatory frameworks, technological development is seen as taking its own direction, generating uncertainties about what capabilities will result. According to Farrell (2007), this places further pressure on states to favour short-term, self-help measures in arms control.

Given that much technological development is of 'dual use' and is undertaken by private companies and universities rather than just governments, a range of practical, political and economic considerations driven by technological development also impact on the strength of arms control agreements. Both the BTWC and CWC have a 'general purpose criterion' that applies an open-ended prohibition against certain types of science and technology processes. In the late 1990s, an ad-hoc group attempted to negotiate a system of inspections that could be added on to the BTWC. This was ultimately unsuccessful due to US reluctance to allow inspections in biotechnology facilities, which would include commercially sensitive labs of pharmaceutical companies. Dual-use technological developments also open up new arenas for potential conflict and militarization that present new challenges for arms control. For example, while the 1967 Outer Space Treaty prohibited the deployment of nuclear and other WMD (not conventional arms) in space, contemporary technology developments raise the spectre of the militarization and weaponization of space. In particular, the development and deployment of dual-use space technologies for communications, surveillance and other military applications and novel conventional weapons are seen as requiring new forms of control. Indeed, proposals for new missile shields include space-based elements of these systems, and both China and the USA have demonstrated a capability to attack satellites in orbit (Sheehan, 2007; Peoples, 2008; Moltz, 2011). Outer space combines dual-use technologies and arms control aims in a new and challenging arena of potential weapons and conflict.

Contemporary arms control opportunities

The instrumentalism and incrementalism of arms control theory and practice have rendered it largely a 'problem-solving' rather than a transformative project. This has evolved from seeking to add stability to deterrence to seeking to engage in 'global counterinsurgency' in an asymmetric system of arms limitation aimed at pariah states and terrorists and at controlling pariah weapons that have no place in 'civilized warfare' (Krause and Latham, 1998; Cooper, 2006). Indeed, much arms control, and particularly prohibitions and disarmament commitments for 'indiscriminate' or 'inhumane' weapons, reflects the self-identification of the West as civilized military powers engaged in the civilizing of warfare. This characterizes the broad process of arms control as one of achieving instrumentalism of warfare, through what Walker (2007) has described as an 'enlightenment' project to establish political mastery over science and technology that gives modern mastery over nature.

A changed proliferation environment and rising concern about rogue states and terrorism, however, have produced pressures not only to maintain the asymmetric status-quo system but also to revitalize interest in nuclear disarmament. Reminiscent of the Baruch Plan, current interest in nuclear weapons disarmament and the control of nuclear materials includes such measures as a new START agreement (START I expired in December 2009), and a broader explicit commitment by states, made at the 2010 NPT review conference, to aim for the eventual elimination of all nuclear weapons. There have been high-profile calls for a move towards 'nuclear zero' by President Obama and other senior officials and experts, including Henry Kissinger and George Schultz, former US secretaries of state, and William Perry, former US secretary of defense. More immediate and definite plans are being developed to bring all vulnerable stocks of fissile material (HEU and plutonium) under control by 2014. While the path to nuclear zero is not yet clear, and much fissile material security work is taking place through bilateral agreements, formal multilateral arms control negotiations remain central. In particular, over the past 13 years, there have been efforts to begin negotiations on a Fissile Material Cutoff Treaty (FMCT) to prevent further production of plutonium and enrichment of uranium to weapons grade (energy generation requires lower levels of enrichment). The home of the FMCT process is the CD in Geneva, the main UN-related arms control negotiation forum in which the CTBT and CWC were negotiated. However, this has been hampered by the consensus rules of the CD enabling one state (Pakistan) to have an effective veto that has deadlocked any attempt to begin negotiation.

Amid resurgent prospects for nuclear disarmament, critical perspectives remind us to ask questions about other categories of weapons. What of the conventional arms trade that seems so integral to security and commercial practices of states? This generally has a much lower political profile and aims for much less restrictive systems of control. However, here too, there is renewed hope for some forms of global control measures. In March 2013, a global Arms Trade Treaty was finally agreed, after more than a decade of preparatory informal discussions and formal negotiations in which a handful of states (this time the USA) prevented agreement in the face of broad consensus until 2013. This treaty prohibits arms transfers if they would breach UNSC obligations or would be used in genocide, war crimes or crimes against humanity. States also agreed to assess the potential that conventional arms transfers might undermine peace and security, be used to break international humanitarian law and human rights laws, or be used in terrorism or transnational crime. This treaty adds to regional and other multilateral approaches that have established similar standards among EU member states and the Wassenaar Arrangement (an arms exporters' organization that was the successor to the Western CoCom after the end of the Cold War). However, since the major arms exporters such as the USA, the UK, France, Italy and Germany already use similar criteria (enshrined in common EU standards) and still engage in transfers many consider ethically dubious, the extent to which this will lead to greater restraint in the arms trade as a whole remains an open question.

Conclusion

The security politics and practices related to weapons and military technology are complex. As a set of relations with others through technology and relations with technology, differing perspectives on procurement, the arms trade and arms control do not merely derive from broad theoretical perspectives on security (there is no one realist view or one constructivist view). In practice, access to arms is shaped by various pressures on procurement practices, the structuring effects and developments in the conventional arms trade, and by partial and incomplete arms control and disarmament. The arms trade does not supply all equally, and while military capabilities may be a major element of states' power and security, the means by which capabilities are acquired are structured by more than an anarchic free market. Likewise, the extent to which arms control agreements may impact security, and whether such impacts are beneficial, is hotly debated. Much discussion of arms control and disarmament, however, relates to the limits to its potential agreement and implementation.

Questions of what, if anything, is to be done about particular types of weapons are more than technical questions, although they are often given technical answers. As it has been practised, arms control offers an ambiguous empirical basis for assessing its potential future role. Currently, it seems that numerous arms control and disarmament practices are somewhat revitalized, but this remains a partial and fragile development. Academics will probably never agree on whether these developments reflect progress in the sophistication of arms control, a continued preservation of hegemonic relations, or a risky house of cards on shaky conceptual foundations. However, the direct and indirect human costs of the spread and use of arms remain important questions. Chapter 9 turns to 'human security' in its many forms.

Chapter 9

Human Security

Security has increasingly been discussed in terms of fostering human security. The language of human security and, perhaps more widely, its ethical underpinnings and the scope of security it implies have become pervasive, particularly in relation to interventions in conflicts or the conduct of military interventions (see Chapter 10). The concept of human security shifts the referent object of security to the human rather than the state (see Chapter 1). While previous chapters have explored states' security roles and behaviours, this chapter explores the politics of defining security on the basis of a different referent object. Does this imply a wider range of security issues or a different type of security politics and practice? Does the change in referent object necessarily imply a change in who provides security? What role do states have in pursuing human security? Is human security really as ethically sound as it presents itself? All these questions arise within the debates on human security and the various analyses of the political fortunes of the concept.

What happens when the referent object of security shifts to the human? This chapter is primarily concerned with the fortunes of the concepts of human security in practice, and the theoretical interpretations and implications of its political career. It offers an opportunity to explore how transformative or conservative forces shape the fortunes of seemingly radical ideas, how debates over the character of security can affect practice, and how practices and ideas evolve together. The chapter begins with a discussion of the political origins of the concept of human security in practice rather than in political theory. It then explores the different views of the scope of human security and outlines the main aspects of what we may call the 'political career' of the concept from its radical youth to its mainstream contemporary existence. Finally, it explores some of the most prominent arguments made by academic analyses of human security.

Origins of contemporary human security

Human security discourses are rooted in the insecurities that millions of people encounter in their everyday lives. This immediately takes security beyond the condition of war. In recent years, direct deaths from conflict have averaged 55,000 per year, a similar figure to unintentional homicides, and a fraction of the nearly 400,000 (75 per cent) attributable to intentional homicide. Indeed, from 2004 to 2009, the countries with the highest violent death rates (per 100,000 population) included Iraq's conflict deaths (59.4 per 100,000), but only in second place after El Salvador's high levels of crime-related deaths

(61.9 per 100,000), closely followed by many Latin American states with significant narcotics crime linkages (Geneva Declaration, 2011). However, human security goes beyond the prospect of violent death, from forced displacement and refugee flows caused by conflict and natural disasters, to the millions of deaths each year from diseases ranging from HIV/AIDS to malaria, or even the preventable deaths of children and adults that derive from conditions of poverty, which are claimed to account for one-third of all deaths each year and go alongside economic insecurities, illiteracy and poor quality of life (Pogge, 2008). Such insecurities have existed, and on similar scale, in eras when the politics of security was not explicitly connected to those lives but only to the international power of the states that coincidentally governed them.

Human security arose as a concern articulated against the neglect of individuals' everyday insecurities. The contemporary politics of human security is very much a post-Cold War politics. The term 'human security' appeared in passing in UN Secretary-General Boutros Boutros-Ghali's *An Agenda for Peace* (UN, 1992), which set out the UN's role for the post-Cold War era and called for an 'integrated approach to human security'. Most discussions of human security begin with the coining of the term by the UN Development Programme (UNDP) in its 1994 annual report on human development. Criticizing traditional security concerns and practices of the Cold War, it claimed:

> Forgotten were the legitimate concerns of ordinary people who sought security in their daily lives. For many of them, security symbolized protection from the threat of disease, hunger, unemployment, crime, social conflict, political repression, and environmental hazards. (UNDP, 1994: 22)

The UNDP report drew an initially stark contrast between the Cold War standard practice of security and a human-centred approach whose time had come. The former, it said, focused on the security of states, and so security was seen as the protection of national territory from external aggression and of selfish national interests in international relations, and global security was dominated by the threat of nuclear holocaust. Shifting the referent object of security was, for the authors of this report, a deceptively simple move that had profound implications for the scope and practice of security. The report claimed that:

> In the final analysis, human security is a child who did not die, a disease that did not spread, a job that was not cut, an ethnic tension that did not explode in violence, a dissident who was not silenced. Human security is not a concern with weapons – it is a concern with human life and dignity. (UNDP, 1994: 22)

Human security has many different definitions. In the UNDP report (1994: 23), it is seen as difficult to define with precision, but easier to identify by its absence (security is the absence of insecurity). It is conceived in terms of daily life, living in peace or conflict, access to social and market opportunities, and 'how people live and breathe in society'. In more concrete terms, it relates to 'safety from such chronic threats as hunger, disease and repression ... it means protection from sudden and hurtful disruptions in the patterns of daily life – whether in homes, in jobs or in communities' (1994: 23).

The UNDP report highlighted seven overlapping dimensions of human security – economic, food, health, environment, personal, community, and political. In some respects, these are similar to Buzan's (1991) five sectors of national security (see Chapter 1), but are defined somewhat differently:

(1) *Economic security:* having an assured basic income either through work or a social safety net – a condition only a quarter of the world's population had in 1994.
(2) *Food security:* the security of physical and economic access to food supply and protection from famine, and thus integrates threats arising from economics, environment, politics and so on.
(3) *Health security:* includes protection from diseases like HIV/AIDS and malaria but also heart disease and access to healthcare.
(4) *Environmental security:* defined somewhat more specifically than in Buzan's sectors, and is local and global, including security from local environmental disasters and pollution to global climate change.
(5) *Personal security:* freedom from physical harm arising from violent crime, conflict, rape, child abuse, and sometimes even harms arising from the self such as drug abuse and suicide.
(6) *Community security:* relates to the non-national communities of which people are part, such as families and ethnic communities, since it is through such groups as well as the state that people make themselves secure, protect their identities, conflict with each other, and may be subjected to abuse.
(7) *Political security:* viewed particularly in relation to human rights abuses perpetrated by governments and inappropriate priorities, such as spending more on military expenditure than on health or education – it thus shows how a wide range of government actions produce insecurity.

The most far-reaching implication of human security, however, is not the longer list of issues that enter the realm of security, but the character of the condition and practice of security that is thereby envisaged. The UNDP report identified 'essential characteristics' of human security that go beyond the shift of referent object. First, in a cosmopolitan move, it claimed that human security is a matter of *universal concern.* Human insecurity may be more acute, or take on different forms in different places, but unlike national security that is tied to national interest, it is universal. Importantly, each of the issue areas of human security, including the health and economic forms, are not just issues in poor countries, although they may appear more acute there. The insecurity of incomes, housing, the threat of heart disease, and uneven and insecure access to healthcare systems are features of the daily lives of many in even the richest countries. This was explicit in the UNDP report, but has become a more muted concern in recent human security politics, which associates much human insecurity with poor countries. Human security is also *interdependent*, which echoes the notion of interdependence found in liberal thought but asserts an interdependence of humans rather than just states: human insecurity travels the globe, it relates to issues that are often transnational and not contained by state borders (see Chapters 11 and 12). Further, these issues tend to be achieved better through *early prevention* rather than 'later intervention'. This is obviously the case with disease and deaths from hunger, but is also a claim made about the types of crime, civil war and human rights abuses that characterize much human insecurity.

Taken at face value, these point to a different notion of human community, ethical responsibility, and the purpose and possibility of political action. Here, security is not just related in complex interdependence but is indivisible, it is more akin to a common good, and it cannot be pursued in ways that the critical theorist Booth (2007) refers to as the 'business as usual' of security politics. For Thomas (2000: 6), this indivisibility means it 'cannot be pursued by or for one group at the expense of another'. Thus conceived, it is an alien concept to political realism, which posits zero-sum competition as foundational to political and social life. Of course, human security doesn't need to be interpreted that way, and it is perhaps unlikely that the authors of the UNDP report intended to call for global cosmopolitan governance, but the early scoping of human security demonstrates a radical potential. However, this potential has lost much of its force in a set of practices and debates in which the scope of the application of the term 'security' forms the major distinctions. While this is a long list of sets of issues, each containing numerous security problems, two dimensions form the main elements of human security: 'freedom from fear' and 'freedom from want'. A third, 'dignity', is sometimes added to further widen the concept to include a more positive dimension (Thomas, 2000). This shorthand can be loosely applied to the two major approaches to human security found in academic literature and the global politics and practice of human security.

Conceptual analysis of human security, however, yields a different set of distinctions. Newman's (2001) constructivist analysis shows four major strands that combine in different ways in discussions and practices of human security:

(1) A *basic human needs* focus, strongly emphasized in the UNDP report and 'freedom from want' approaches. Here, the focus is on human welfare at a basic level, with foundational needs for safety, freedom, food and shelter.

(2) An *assertive/interventionist* focus, which seeks to alleviate gross human suffering, abuses of human rights, genocide and so on through interventions in weak states and conflicts (see Chapter 10).
(3) A *social welfare/developmentalist* focus, which goes beyond the basic minimums of safety and survival and seeks sustainable development and peace through partnerships rather than just intervention.
(4) A *new security* focus, which emphasizes the interconnectedness of a wider range of security issues (disease, migration, conflict, crime) – the negative side of globalization (see Chapters 11–13). Here, state security and human security are articulated and built together through reconstructing security in weak and failing states.

These four strands of thought are expressed together in varying combinations that show differing degrees of modification of the understandings and practices of security, with some seeking to re-establish a status quo of interstate order and the containment of transnational threats, and others seeking wider reform of global structures of inequality and global governance (Newman, 2001). Understanding human security in this way enables discussion of how, and in what ways, human security is operationalized and what limits on its radical potential are established.

The political career of 'human security'

The political career of the concept of human security since 1994 has been a rocky and divided one. The term 'human security' has been found in many major policy debates and at times it has been widely cited (and perhaps pursued) in discussions of related issues in all major intergovernmental fora, from regional organizations such as the African Union and the EU to rich country clubs like the G7/G8, to global institutions, particularly the UN. Versions of it have found their way into the foreign policy actions of states such as Canada, Japan, Norway, Switzerland and others. However, its appearance has been sporadic, rising in the late 1990s, declining in the early part of this century, and recently growing in prominence again. Further, while it has a profile in political talking shops, it is questionable whether net human security has increased significantly in the two decades since the term was coined. There are two major dimensions of the political career of the concept: its scope and its institutionalization.

Scope

Some approaches to human security have a narrower 'freedom from fear' understanding. These focus attention on political violence from civil wars to human rights abuses and are particularly concerned with issues of conflict prevention, humanitarian intervention, state-building, international humanitarian law, and humanitarian arms control (the banning of landmines and cluster munitions and the control of small arms and light weapons) (see Chapters 8 and 10). This narrower view may also include crime, drug trafficking and some wider issues like HIV/AIDS, but is primarily concerned with security as freedom from the fear of physical harm arising from violence. It therefore emphasizes some combination of the 'interventionist' and 'new security' strands identified by Newman. In political practice, this narrower view characterizes the use of human security by the Canadian government in the 1990s and early part of this century.

Two international initiatives adopt this narrower view. First, the Human Security Network is an informal group of states, formed by Canada and Norway in 1998, that seeks to bring together interested states to discuss human security issues and act as a coordinator among those states in international negotiations (producing joint statements and so on) on key human security issues. It combines a rather unusual mix of states – Austria, Canada, Chile, Costa Rica, Greece, Ireland, Jordan, Mali, the Netherlands, Norway, Slovenia, Switzerland, South Africa (as an observer) and Thailand – that seem to share little in common politically, geographically, or even in their global power or history of conflict. Second, the 2001 International Commission on Intervention and State Sovereignty (ICISS) developed the idea of the Responsibility to Protect (R2P), in which sovereignty was redefined not just as the right not to be intervened in but as a responsibility to protect their citizens (from human rights abuses, genocide and so on). This reconfiguration of sovereignty, one of the organizing principles of international political life, is potentially one of the most important implications of an assertion of the value of human security, which the ICISS (2001: 6) claimed was 'increasingly providing a conceptual framework for international action'. This process and its implications have been used to legitimate a wide range of international interventions in conflict and post-conflict states, including military interventions and state-building operations, and prompts some observers to claim that the narrower view has particularly come to emphasize the interventionist approach Newman identifies (see Chapter 10).

A wider approach, including freedom from want as well as freedom from fear, retains a 'new security' strand, and occasionally the 'interventionist' view, but is primarily based on 'basic human needs' and 'social welfare/developmentalist' focuses (Newman, 2001). While Canada is prominent in the narrow view, it is Japan that has been a leading figure in the wider approach, and has explicitly oriented its development policy in human security terms. In 1999, Japan established a Trust Fund for Human Security within the UN system to support human security projects. At the political level, most notably, Japan sponsored the UN Commission on Human Security (CHS) that reported in 2003. The CHS (2003: 4) adopted an even broader view, in which human security was about survival, livelihoods and also 'dignity', and entailed 'protect[ing] the vital core of all human lives in ways that enhance human freedoms and human fulfilment. Human security means protecting fundamental freedoms – freedoms that are the essence of life.'

The CHS (2003) identified a different security politics based on two mutually reinforcing things: protection and empowerment. Protection is protection from 'critical and pervasive threats', but this carries through elements of the UNDP approach by arguing that this should be addressed in ways that are systematic, comprehensive and *preventive*. The key task here lies in developing strong international and national norms and is seen as a form of 'top-down' action, in which the primary responsibility lies with states. Empowerment, on the other hand, envisions a less state-centric politics, a bottom-up process in which people become participants in defining and implementing their vital freedoms, demand respect for their dignity, and publicize the insecurity of others by mobilizing for the prevention of famine, protesting human rights abuses and so on.

Institutionalization

Human security is not a regime (see Chapter 6), but it does have a variety of forms of institutionalization and adoption. There are four discernible positions among states and institutions on human security: to ignore it, as many do; to adopt some of its issues but not all its essential characteristics and not to use the term, as many countries like the UK and some early EU actions did; to use the term in the narrow version as Canada did and many academics do; or to seek to support the broader version, as has increasingly been the case within the UN system.

Within the UN, a broad version of the concept of human security has generally been used. The CHS (2003) definition has fed into key documents like *In Larger Freedom* (UN, 2005a), which set out the future role of the organization, and more recently, the UN has reaffirmed the importance of the concept (and the broader version) in a series of General Assembly debates (in 2008, 2010 and 2011), reports and resolutions. There has been some limited institutionalization in the UN system. After the CHS reported in 2003, a Human Security Unit was established within the UN, tasked with promoting human security throughout the UN and running the Trust Fund for Human Security. Thus far, the Unit's activities have largely related to spreading the norm of human security. The Trust Fund continues to derive most of its funding from the government of Japan, but there have been attempts to broaden this basis. It has supported over 200 initiatives in over 70 countries, from demand reduction programmes on illicit drugs in Afghanistan, to programmes to empower women and girls at risk in Latin America, building energy services in rural African communities, expanding access to education, working on refugee issues and so on. These all tend to be small-scale local projects. This can be interpreted in two ways: either a handful of small projects indicate a lack of political support for greater investment in human security, or projects are small and local because human insecurity is locally specific and does not always require big budgets.

Within regional organizations, the concept has been less institutionalized, but much of the scope of security it produces has been influential. Thus, when the African Union launched its Peace and Security Council, it claimed that a comprehensive vision of human security was foundational to peace and security in Africa. Some regional organizations have shifted from the ad-hoc inclusion of some issues towards more extensive use of the concept. In Europe, the EU's 2003 European Security Strategy begins with highlighting human security issues, such as the deaths of 45 million people per year from poverty, the destructive effects of HIV/AIDS on societies, the notion that security is a precondition for development, and that the status quo is not working since Africa is poorer than it was 10 years earlier. However, this important document does not mention the term 'human security' at all. Indeed, according to some observers, while containing elements of human security, it is sufficiently ambiguous on the principles that it presents a strategy that could be endorsed from a realist and a human security perspective (Keane, 2006). In 2008, a report by the Council of the EU did use the term as underpinning the EU approach to security, and the term has been increasingly used in the European Parliament and the work of the European Commission since, although largely in the narrow purview of conflict management and the links between security and development. As yet, it remains to be seen whether what Martin and Owen (2010) call the 'second generation of human security', the growing use of a crisis management and human rights-centred version of the concept within the various EU institutions, reaches the level of a unifying strategic concept to the EU's external roles, as a group of academic and policy experts recommended in 2004 (Study Group of Europe's Security Capabilities, 2004).

At the nation-state level, few states have whole-heartedly adopted human security, but 'new security' perspectives of interconnected threats and interdependent state and human security are commonly noted, as in the national security strategies of the USA, the UK and others. Even among its most prominent supporters, the endorsement of human security has had a rocky history. For instance, Canada's extensive role in peacekeeping operations in the early 1990s expanded into wider political articulation of the value of human security. Thus, in 1997, Canadian Foreign Minister Lloyd Axworthy (1997: 185) claimed that human security provided 'a uniquely Canadian identity and a sense of Canada's place in the world'. Canada initially adopted a wider view of human security but became more focused on issues associated with the narrower 'freedom from fear' variant. The centrality and level of effort in human security in Canadian policy has become more vulnerable since a Conservative government was elected in 2006. Indeed, the use of the term was reportedly banned within government soon after (Martin and Owen, 2010). Japan, by contrast, has remained wedded to the wider approach.

Interpretations and critiques of human security

Human security is difficult to locate in any single theoretical perspective. It is commonly appropriated by variants of liberalism, although it can also accord with the normative preferences and arguments for emancipation found in some critical approaches. However, realists and critical scholars alike have articulated similar arguments that criticize human security for being captured by liberal states (Booth, 2007; Newman, 2010; Christie, 2010), and many scholars express deep concern about the implications of securitizing issues such as poverty and human rights. While human security may be framed initially as a radical, cosmopolitan, human-centred approach to security coming up against a traditionalist, conservative, amoral national security approach, recent theorization of human security goes beyond debating that normative impetus to a deeper assessment of the potential and actual forms of transformation or conservation of the practices of security. This includes continued debate over the potential utility of the concept through definitional debates, critiques that argue that human security is either inherently conservative or has been captured by states, and the degree to which human security produces different forms of security politics and practice and different modes of governing threats and risks.

Definitional politics

If there is no agreement on what human security is, how can it be achieved? Many assessments of human security conjoin questions of political utility and explanatory power to raise concerns about the utility of the concept. Numerous authors argue that the wider definition is nothing more than a wish list that makes setting policy priorities difficult (Paris, 2001; Thomas and Tow, 2002; Krause, 2004; Mack, 2004; Macfarlane and Khong, 2006). King and Murray (2002) criticize the initial UNDP version for failing to produce an integrated single concept, while Krause (2004: 367) argues that the broad version is merely a 'shopping list' and becomes a 'synonym for bad things that can happen'. Going further, Paris (2001: 88) claimed that human security as a whole is 'slippery by design', arguing that its advocates have cultivated its ambiguity to ensure that it is flexible enough to hold together a disparate range of perspectives among the otherwise inchoate network of actors that use it. While this has proved a successful strategy for important gains like the Ottawa Treaty banning anti-personnel landmines, Paris argues that it also diminishes the utility of the concept for guiding academic research and policy making. The imprecision of human security is further augmented by the lack of reliable measures of human insecurity. Some basic thresholds and indices have been suggested to yield more precise measures, such as the under-fives mortality rate, or an indicator based on life expectancy and poverty, but few seem likely to attract significant support and most have their own measurement problems (King and Murray, 2002;

Owen, 2004; Roberts, 2008). Even if reliable measures can be found, clear indicators still do not themselves offer clear explanations and so human insecurity will remain a matter of debate in scope and explanation.

Academic demands for limiting definitions to create coherence for analysis and policy partly reflect behaviourialist and positivist preferences for testing tightly delimited sets of variables. In contrast, some critical authors prefer to emphasize the political import of an open definition. McDonald (2002) argues that not only is defining human security a political act, but that the debate over the utility of definitions gets at a deeper issue of how human security functions. Human security is not a policy agenda, which would require some precision in definition to set some practical boundaries on what action was intended to achieve, but a set of norms and values, which does not require the same specification. Indeed, this may mean that debate on definition is to be welcomed as it enables deeper questioning and subversion of dominant power relationships, even as the quest for certainties through precise measurement reinforces those relationships (Grayson, 2008). This argument, however, is not entirely opposed to the narrowing of definitions, since some argue that human security denotes certain shared values in its narrow form and that its broader form is unhelpful (Mack, 2004).

Assertions of the value of narrow definitions can sometimes miss the central difference in the concept of human security as something that enables more complete realization of the relationships *between* issues. For instance, some argue that human security is so broad that it is unable to provide an explanation of causal relations: 'a concept that aspires to explain almost everything in reality explains nothing' (Mack, 2004: 367; see also Macfarlane and Khong, 2006). If defining human security was the first stage of a causal analysis that sought to explain everything, this would be fair. However, it is not generally the aspiration of advocates of a broad concept to produce a single theory of everything. The counterargument is that human security not only adds to the range of issues but is also an integrative concept (UNDP, 1994; Hampson, 2004; Thomas, 2004; Uvin, 2004). Thus, Uvin (2004) argues that human security provides a link between various fields of political action and different organizations within them, including human rights, development assistance, humanitarian relief, and conflict management. It does not merely multiply the range of issues, but recognizes links between 'fields of social change'. So, human security is no disparate list of 'bad things that can happen', but the inheritor of peace research's interdisciplinary concern for human welfare and the recognition that academic and practical divisions of the world into social, economic and political spheres tends to neglect the violence done by structures and processes beyond war (see Chapter 3). For instance, Nef (1999: 13) argues that human security provides an understanding of the bridges that link economy and environment, society and economy, and so on in a complex world system. It thus draws attention to the ways in which the wealthy North are tied up in mutual vulnerabilities with the poor that are 'a multifaceted systemic echo of the premise of mutually assured destruction in the era of nuclear stalemate'. Thus, for Tadjbakhsh and Chenoy (2007: 237), a broad, integrated approach is necessary because without it 'it would be impossible to efficiently counter threats which are intrinsically linked. The concept is resolutely ambitious and this is one of its strongest points.' This notion of integrated, interdependent threats rather than a list of disparate desires has had some significant political purchase. In 2004, a UN report (UN, 2004) identified common security threats to states and peoples as relating to their 'mutual vulnerability' to transnational crime, terrorism, weapons proliferation, disease and poverty.

The integrative potential of human security, however, does not diminish the political challenges of definition, as much of the politics of human security has become bogged down in definitional issues rather than progress on substantive issues (Ewan, 2007). At the 2005 World Summit, UN member states called for further discussion of the concept of human security within the General Assembly (GA). At the three GA thematic debates on human security (2008, 2010 and 2011), many countries said the term was too imprecise and/or that their primary interpretation of it was through the protection of territorial integrity and national sovereignty. Other countries emphasized that a broader version like that of the CHS (2003) is flexible and forward-thinking. At the 2010 GA debate, UN Secretary-General Ban Ki-moon noted that in the previous year 'more than 200 million people were affected by natural disasters, while violent conflicts drove a record 42 million people from their homes' (UNGA, 2010). He re-emphasized the key elements of the initial concept such as the interconnected nature of security, and called for 'people-centred, comprehensive, context-specific and preventive strategies at every level' (UNGA, 2010). Nevertheless, the most concrete action relates to definitional issues, with a 2012 UN Resolution tasking the secretary-general to seek the opinions of states on the concept and the possibility of finding an agreed definition. While these definitional processes seem to have little connection with the lived insecurities of many millions, they represent a continuation of the political importance of the concept, even in its broader form, in spite of academic predictions that a narrow definition is needed.

Conservatism, capture and effectiveness

If human security is a set of values, rather than an assertion of causal explanations, and an integrative concept rather than a sector of security, then it does not have its own logics and limits. Rather, the potential and realization of human security combine with wider understandings of security that yield varying assessments of its success. Here, a key question is whether human security has been taken on as an agenda-setting move or merely provides a humanitarian veneer for the same old security politics, or has it been captured and overtaken by a different mode of governing and practising security that corresponds to neither.

Some critics are sympathetic to the values of human security but are deeply disappointed with the ways it has been taken on. While holding considerable radical potential, human security practice has often demonstrated a tendency towards limited 'problem-solving' agendas rather than transformative projects (Newman, 2010). Indeed, Christie (2010) argues that the concept has become a new orthodoxy and lost its radical potential, and while it may have led to some greater political and economic resource for aid budgets and so on, it merely amplifies certain aspects of policy and is unlikely to produce counter-hegemonic moves. Human security often falls into the 'interventionist' and 'new security' foci identified by Newman, and thus fails to question existing power structures, and has legitimated forms of interventionism that reinforce existing power structures and apply one-size-fits-all approaches rather than locally designed solutions (McDonald, 2002; Conteh-Morgan, 2005). For example, international organizations, such as the OECD DAC (the Development Assistance Committee of the Organisation for Economic Cooperation and Development, a group of the major development donors from rich countries), have engaged with the need to tackle the root causes of conflict and to engage in development in ways that are attentive to the potential impacts on conflict dynamics, but have been reluctant to engage with any critiques of the underlying neoliberal orthodoxy that views market liberalization as the route to long-term development (Hampson and Daudelin, 2002).

This conservatism may relate to the lack of causal specification inherent in the concept in either narrow or broad versions. The values of human security do not establish a clear preference for particular causal explanations for insecurity (see Chapter 1). Civil war, crime and poverty may be caused by poor decision making, weak governance, global structural inequalities and pressures and so on. For instance, advocates of treating poverty as a human security concern include those who adopt a position derived from structuralist perspectives in development studies (Thomas, 2000), which emphasize unequal global trade structures, and those associated with a liberal and modernization theory approach, which views poverty as the result of a lack of modern liberal values and practices requiring privatization, open markets, limited state spending, and foreign investment. Each explanation leads to wholly different policy prescriptions with their own logics and limits. So, there is a wider division in human security politics between those whose explanations for insecurity and prescriptions for security lie in the prevailing neoliberal consensus (or some modified version thereof) and those for whom human security is a more ambitious political project open to differing explanations.

Thomas called for human security to be a more radical project; for her, human security was defined in the broadest terms, including dignity. This was not, however, to be thought of in contemporary neoliberal terms. Rather, Thomas (2000: 6) argued that human security:

> differs fundamentally from notions of 'security of the individual', conceived in the currently fashionable neoliberal sense. Human security is very far removed from liberal notions of competitive and possessive individualism (that is, the extension of private power and activity, based around property rights and choice in the market place). Rather, human security describes a condition of existence in which basic material needs are met, and in which human dignity, including meaningful participation in the life of the community, can be realised.

This called into question the conduct and politics of international trade and economic development and the wider global structure of the capitalist world economy. The human to be secured was not the neoliberal individual or the citizen of the nation-state but the person pursuing security as part of various collectives, ranging from the household (a significant level of analysis in development studies but rarely in security studies), the village, or religious, caste or ethnic community (Thomas, 2000: 7). In this view, ensuring 'basic human needs' is insufficient for security, rather it requires that decisions of significance for people's lives involve their participation. This goes far beyond the securitization of particular issues, like poverty. Indeed, the participation of those affected is not a feature of the exceptional politics of securitization posited by the Copenhagen School. This is more akin to the emancipatory politics of inventing humanity that Booth's CSS advocates. Although human security has many normative and analytic parallels with emancipation-oriented CSS, Booth (2007: 323) argues that it has been co-opted by Western governments to appear to be 'good international citizen[s]', without really changing their behaviour.

While human security as an integrative security agenda may raise the prospect of questioning global structures that give rise to insecurity, the predominance of 'new security' and 'interventionist' practices has led to it being much more conservative. Chandler (2008) describes human security as 'the dog that didn't bark' and claims that it has been relatively easily integrated and accommodated within mainstream security agendas. He offers three reasons for this: political elites and human security advocates share a tendency to overstate threats and claim that they are mutually reinforcing; most of the new threats to security are easily located within the developing world; and human security has compensated for the lack of clear strategic vision since the end of the Cold War by arguing that threats are so intertwined that clear strategic prioritization is futile. In doing so, however, it has clearly ignored the full implications of interdependent insecurities posited by the early concept. While the initial concept of human security was indivisible and applied to the insecurities of people in rich and poor countries alike, the way in which this has been translated into 'mutual vulnerability' has easily morphed into an assertion of the interconnectedness of dangers (drugs, crime, migration and terrorism) that move one way – from poor and failing states to the developed North/Western states (Cooper, 2005; Bourne, 2011a). Seemingly humanitarian concerns for the wellbeing of conflict-affected communities have become conjoined with the security and economic concerns of wealthier and more powerful people and states (Cooper, 2005). This conjoining, reflecting the uneven character of the merger of security and development more broadly in this period (Duffield, 2007), produces a colonization of apparently cosmopolitan concerns with human security, such that debates are framed in terms of concerns over securing and protecting the wealthy from particular types of circulation (drugs, disease, refugees, terrorism and so on). This posits a symbiosis of Western state security and the security of the poor in the South that enables a problem-solving and interventionist agenda (see Chapters 10 and 12). However, it is important not to overstate this limiting of human security. As Owen (2008) argues, while realist scholars have adopted some aspects of human security issues and located threats to Western security as originating in the developing world, advocates of human security do not make such claims and view the insecurity of people in weak and failing states as the prime concern, not the (often spurious) assertions of threats to the West.

It is true that some states and organizations have sought to profit from the idea of human security. In the cases of the leading state proponents of the concept, Canada and Japan, Bosold (2011) notes that each state's focus was a continuation of their earlier foreign policy expertise (peacekeeping for Canada and development assistance for Japan) rather than a radical shift. In Canada, for instance, Neufeld (2004) argues that the issues and values that became defined as human security were part of the 'counter-consensus' of NGOs in Canada since the 1970s, which the government then took on, constrained and captured without significantly changing their security orientation away from states and towards humans. Likewise, in the UN, from its founding conferences to the 2000 Millennium Summit, issues of human rights and security have been articulated as interlinked, and freedom from fear and freedom from want have been defined as the twin goals of the UN.

The fact that human security is used by middle powers and institutions to enhance their political goals and roles need not mean that it is merely an ethical veil for selfish action, but may have limited the ways in which it can be pursued (Suhrke, 1999; Hampson and Daudelin, 2002; Liotta, 2002a). The importance of middle powers in human security politics may indicate that realist assumptions that major powers set security agendas and weaker powers follow are flawed (Behringer, 2005). Hampson and Daudelin (2002) argue that the coalitions of like-minded states, generally middle and small powers, which have arisen can deliver human security public goods as they also provide a political middle ground. Such middle powers lack the power to (re-)structure international politics and cannot provide human security on their own, but they often have strong bargaining and negotiation skills that enable them to bring competing interests together. Thus, 'middle power multilateralists' can utilize soft power to produce a political space for providing human security. However, this has not been fully realized: in the informal multilateral politics of the Human Security Network, the concept of human security has enabled significant agenda setting but the Human Security Network has not been able to institutionalize the interactions of its members nor fully embed human security in the national policies of its member states (Krause, 2008). Similarly, many advocates of human security are sceptical of the ability of international organizations, especially the UN, to provide for human security, since they are often characterized by paralysis due to conflict among powerful members and suffer from collective action problems, encounter significant financial limitations, are slow to act due to bureaucratic and political constraints, and have set mandates that restrict their scope of action (Hampson and Daudelin, 2002). Nevertheless, the limited but sustained institutionalization of human security within the UN system, and particular initiatives such as the interventionist R2P, may indicate significant alterations in the conditions for intervention and a broader evolution of the dominant relationships between individuals, states and international society in frameworks that may enable the deterrence of gross abuses of human security (MacFarlane and Khong, 2006) (see Chapter 10).

A key feature of the 'soft power', consensus-oriented politics of human security is that a wider range of political actors and voices are legitimated (Hampson and Daudelin, 2002). Thus, developments in the global human rights regime in recent decades have been significantly affected by transnational civil society organizations, such as Amnesty International and others, becoming involved in setting and monitoring standards for human rights conduct (Dunne and Wheeler, 2011). Although not all civil society groups promote human security (some have been opposed to the provision of contraception to prevent HIV/AIDS or tackling illicit small arms flows), it is notable that human security conceptually legitimates civil society organizations' political voices more than a national security paradigm would permit. Nevertheless, even when NGOs have played a significant role in the politics of human security, several observers indicate that this has tended not to challenge the dominant structures and practices in issues like poverty and HIV/AIDS (Shittecatte, 2006; O'Manique, 2006; Chandler, 2008).

While broader concepts of human security emphasize the principles of dignity and bottom-up participatory forms of security politics, the practices of ensuring 'local ownership' of peacebuilding and development programmes on the ground are beset with tensions and have had mixed results (see Chapter 10). For example, EU assistance to sub-Saharan Africa for conflict management and prevention has enhanced African capacities and ownership of conflict management through supporting regional organizations, in spite of the ambiguities in EU member states' motives, which combine realist and human security approaches (Keane, 2006). In the realm of development, there has been something of a change in the way in which developing countries are dictated to by international financial institutions when structural adjustment programmes were replaced with Poverty Reduction Strategy Papers, in which poor country governments set more of their own targets and priorities; in reality, many recipients did so in line with the neoliberal development orthodoxy, knowing that little else would receive funding. Similarly, by comparing two different international interventions in Haiti, one that took place without a human security framing and one informed by it, Muggah and Krause (2006: 115) note that there has not been a radical shift in practical approaches to, or outcomes of, intervention, countering the assumption of many critical and constructivist approaches that discourses, like that centring on human security, are 'significant themselves without examining the link to actual practices'.

A different security?

How differently is security conceived in human security? The answer to this relates not only to broad claims about the potential or capture of the concept, and the ways in which the global politics of human security reinforces or goes beyond interstate power competition, but also the extent to which the condition of security is conceived and the manner in which it can be produced. Indeed, in this regard, human security may represent a stronger challenge to traditional security paradigms than it does through the debate on the scope or referent object of security.

Scholars from diverse theoretical perspectives view human security in ways that do not alter the basic understanding of what security is. Freedom from fear approaches, new security and interventionist approaches view human security largely in terms of protection and the absence of threats. For others, human security also denotes a positive condition of welfare that includes but extends beyond the satisfaction of basic needs to participation and dignity. In these latter approaches, human security may do more than extend the issues to which the title 'security' is attached and the range of actors involved in its politics. However, feminist scholar Annick Wibben (2008) has argued that human security has not engaged with the wider questions posed by many poststructuralist-inspired scholars about why the invocation of security is powerful or how some formulations of security have enduring meaning while others decline (see also Der Derian, 1995; Rothschild, 1995; Dillon, 1996; Huysmans, 1998, 2006; Campbell, 1998c; Burke, 2002). By failing to open up this line of enquiry, human security and many critical approaches remain wedded to an understanding of security that is concerned with:

> (1) threats that locate danger; (2) referents to be secured; (3) agents charged with providing security; and (4) means by which threats are contained and – so the tale is told – security provided. (Wibben, 2008: 457)

While issues may move around within this framework, this broad structure endures, such that a discourse that does not function with these four elements is not recognized as 'security talk' (Wibben, 2008). By conforming to these rules of what security is, human security has not engaged in an examination of the meaning of security as such (Wibben, 2008). Likewise, many critical scholars debate human security within the parameters of their paradigms. Buzan (2004) has raised the concern that human security represents a dangerous form of 'political pandering' that securitizes human rights issues when a desecuritized politics is preferable. The notion that securitization universally means an enhancement of political resources and urgency but a dangerous embedding of issues in logics of exceptionalism and short-termism is thereby unchallenged. Human security issues merely get securitized or desecuritized the same way others do.

The understanding of positive conditions of human security has been largely framed, and limited, by viewing it in terms of risk, vulnerability and resilience (see Chapter 5). Indeed, Chandler (2012) argues that the real contest in human security lies between the preventive dimension (through intervention and other means) that seeks to build resilience to risk by empowering the vulnerable, and the liberal paradigm in which intervention lies in a liberal mode of protecting civilians. Nevertheless, the locating of human security in a risk discourse alters the political logics of security. As Liotta (2002a: 478) argues, while state security issues pertain to large-scale threats from other states and the protection of territory, many human security issues 'are often more tenuously related to issues of vulnerability and only involve direct threat in the most extreme circumstances'. While threats relate to clearly identifiable, immediate and potentially military responses, human security is a realm of vulnerabilities and amorphous risks: 'A vulnerability is often only an indicator, often not clearly identifiable, often linked to a complex interdependence among related issues, and does not always suggest a correct or even adequate response' (Liotta, 2002a: 479). Security analysts tend to view security issues as relating to conditions of 'extreme vulnerability' that are clearly evident. Thus, it is easy to identify human insecurity in refugee camps, natural disasters, famine events and war zones. However, this misses the importance of long-term vulnerabilities created by environmental change, wider economic issues, population growth and so on – issues that do not present a clearly identifiable response. When the UNDP argued that prevention was better than response, it was getting at the same issue. This longer term politics necessary for human security is clearly different to the short-term emergency politics of much national and human security practice today. However, it may also subject human security to the managerial practices and depoliticized forms of action that characterize other risk approaches.

It is perhaps surprising that little attention is given to how the 'human' is understood in human security. Tadjbakhsh and Chenoy (2007: 13) argue that: 'Elevating the person as the ultimate end is made possible by defining this new actor in terms of his/her vulnerabilities on the one hand, and his/her capacity to affect change on the other.' Thus, human security defines the human as a set of vulnerabilities and capacities to affect change. While the referent object 'human' is largely seen as the single individual, political action can only be seen as collective actors involved in collective decision making and trade-offs (Chandler, 2008). Certainly, there is a tension between the fact that human insecurity has important local dimensions and is experienced locally and the fact that its politics is a global and largely international politics (Lemanski, 2012). However, it would be unfair to assume that all human security works on the basis of a neoliberal individualism. Human security is still conceived in terms of a public good, much as security within the state is in traditional theories (see Chapter 4). Some analyst advocates of human security, including Hampson and Daudelin (2002) and Tadjbakhsh and Chenoy (2007), argue that it is best conceived as a global public good. That is, it relates to the provision of a good on the basis of membership of a public, rather than on membership of a club (club goods) or ability to pay (markets). While normally conceived in national terms, such that they are not pure public goods since they are excludable along lines of citizenship, the public good of human security is (in principle) global. It is part of a universal public. Yet, to produce this public good does not require fully cosmopolitan (post-international) governance. Rather, the issue is the underprovision of a public good.

If human security is a public good provided for humans conceived of as vulnerabilities and capacities for change, then the implications of human security for the state may be profound. The state remains central as the provider and main political actor in much human security. The key question, therefore, is whether this role of the state now occurs in a different political configuration than the politics of (inter-)national security. For the most part, it seems not. Certainly, the role of the state has come to feature more strongly in the politics of human security, as the 2003 CHS report reinstated the state as the prime provider of security and the major actor in security politics (along with civil society groups and individuals) (Wibben, 2008). Liotta (2002a, 2002b) argues that human and state security interests are increasingly converging. This is primarily an argument that human insecurity in the South has a 'boomerang effect' on national security in the North, in which human security is reduced to recognition of a changed security environment. However, this does not have to imply the short-term politics of securitization. Indeed, true recognition of this should lead to more long-term action. For Liotta, human security issues need not be met by military means, and if military means are to be used, this requires a different sort of military action than that associated with Cold War interstate security (see also Smith-Windsor, 2002). This blending of state and human security and military and non-military, short term and long term is increasingly visible in national security strategies and postures, as in the USA and the UK, and in wider practices of humanitarian intervention (Thomas and Tow, 2002).

Combining many of the critiques of risk-based logics and state capture of the concept, some poststructuralist scholars argue that human security is associated with a shift in the logics of governing (through) security towards what Foucault (2004, 2007) called 'biopolitics'. Biopolitics is a form of power that operates on populations rather than governing and protecting national territory. Most easily understood as a shift from geopolitics to biopolitics, from governing territorial relations to governing populations, a key aspect of this distinction is that the 'sovereign' power of the former enacts the right to kill, while as Dillon and Lobo-Guerrero (2008: 265) argue, 'biopower is a form of power over life whose vocation is to "make life live"'. For Foucault, and other theorists adopting and adapting the concept, sovereign power and biopower may coexist and clearly do so in human security (De Larrinaga and Doucet, 2008). It is obvious, then, that human security has many resemblances to biopolitical governance. At its most basic, as De Larringa and Doucet (2008: 528) argue: 'The target of human security, whether broad or narrow, is to make live the life of the individual through a complex of strategies initiated at the level of populations.' Much biopolitical governance operates on the governing of circulations and is embedded in practices of enabling some flows (information, investment) and combating others (drugs, weapons, disease), even if such controls are not explicitly justified in terms of 'human security' (Duffield, 2007; De Larringa and Doucet, 2008; Dillon and Lobo-Guerrero, 2008) (see Chapters 10 and 12). Biopower tends to be expansive, operating on ever more areas of daily life and bringing them under the purview of dispersed systems of governance. Indeed, since it is based on reducing vulnerabilities, calculating risks and probabilities, and operating on populations, human security can be seen to engage and expand security logics in fields dominated by this calculus, such as public health, poverty reduction, environmental sustainability, insurance and so on (see Chapter 5). For Duffield (2001, 2007), human security, particularly the unequal merger of security and development and the growing emphasis on building effective states (see Chapter 10), is part of a shift to global biopolitical governance that does not articulate the universal cosmopolitan values some claim, but polices a distinction between rich and poor, the 'insured' and 'uninsured', and governs not territory but populations and circulations, through complex networks of public and private power. This further reveals the dangers of securitization, since development becomes a technology of security rather than (primarily) poverty reduction. Beyond the dangers of securitization, however, critics of the biopolitics of security argue that while it claims to make life live, its operation in contemporary liberal governance entails considerable violence and killing – particularly through interventionism (Duffield, 2007; Dillon and Lobo-Guerrero, 2008).

Conclusion

As with all concepts, human security is defined in two ways that take us beyond simple technical definition. First, it is defined through its relations with other concepts. While national security is closely related to territory, external threat and so on, human security relates to community, human rights, human development, risk and vulnerability (as well as threats from wars). Second, it is defined through its changing use in practice. By exploring both of these, it becomes clear that while much debate over human security appears dry and definitional, such definition is not preliminary to a deeper theorizing of human security or enactment in a politics that is yet to come but is integral to an ongoing theorization and political action that does not correspond fully either to the pessimists' assertion of the limits of international politics and naysaying of human security's radical possibility, or the optimistic liberal or critical logics of progress. There has, however, been a limiting of human security in many ways: its scope has been restricted (but expanded again); its relationship to state security has become increasingly symbiotic to a degree that can be interpreted as capture; and its notion of the interconnectedness and universality of its issues has morphed, to a degree, into a global system of biopolitical governance that focuses on particular weak states and circulatory problems. These limits and the political and security practices in which they are enacted in the management of conflict and the building of states and peace are the subject of Chapter 10, and the governing of circulation in the name of security is addressed in Chapter 12.

Chapter 10

Weak States and Intervention

The greatest levels of human insecurity are often found in states that are weak, failing, or collapsed. Such states are increasingly viewed as the source of threats to powerful states since they are believed to be associated with conflict (Chapter 7), terrorism (Chapter 11), and transnational crime, disease and refugee flows (Chapter 12). This links human and state security (Chapters 4 and 9) in a changing international system. This chapter first explores the rise of weak and failing states as a central concern in global security politics. It then explores the various forms of intervention that other states undertake in relation to state weakness and associated violence and conflict. This relates to the debates over whether it is justifiable for the international community to intervene in the domestic affairs of other states and the implications of intervention for sovereignty and international order. It also relates to the conditions under which intervention may be deemed legitimate, and whether it actually works to produce security and for whom. Finally, the chapter explores the contemporary liberal peace and the practical and political challenges of 'fixing failed states' and building post-conflict security (Ghani and Lockhart, 2008).

Weak and failing states

Human and state security are increasingly linked through notions of weak and failing states, which are states that cannot provide public order and security for their populations, control territory and borders, and sustain political institutions or have their legitimacy and authority challenged by other forms of social and political authority. It is common to speak of a spectrum of state weakness ranging from collapsed and failed states, to failing states, to weak states. Thus, state weakness is not just a condition but a process of weakening, even to the point of failure and collapse. This process is often understood as a cause and an effect of civil war. State formation has ceased to be a historical curiosity (Chapter 4), and become a central preoccupation of security politics.

In 1990, Robert Jackson coined the term 'quasi-states' to refer to those states whose governments lacked strong territorial control or bureaucratic systems of governing. He showed that internationally recognized juridical sovereignty and practical sovereignty were often not as closely linked as most theories of security assumed. Instead, many states in Africa and elsewhere utilized the benefits of juridical sovereignty to access diplomatic fora, secure international aid, and negotiate trade arrangements, while presiding over undeveloped state structures or systems of governance based on the dominance of private elites rather than any wider social contract (Jackson, 1990; Reno, 1999; Duffield, 2001). Initially viewed as anomalies to dominant theoretical expectations, the 40–60 failed or failing states have become central to security agendas. It is now conventional wisdom among governments, and some realist and liberal scholars, that weak and failing states are the origin of terrorism, transnational crime, ethnic conflict, poverty, disease and genocide (Fukuyama, 2004; Krasner and Pascual, 2005; Patrick, 2006; Cockayne and Lupel, 2009).

Weak and failing states significantly alter understandings of insecurity. First, the sources of insecurity derive from within states rather than in relations among them. Kaplan's (1994: 8) dystopian vision of 'coming anarchy' pictured an emerging 'last map' of global power and (dis)order: a neomedieval set of shifting power centres in which 'city states and the remaining nations' would be 'confused in places by shadowy tentacles, hovering overhead, indicating the power of drug cartels, mafias, and private security agencies'. While this hyperbolic prediction posits an undoing of Westphalian order and pacification (see Chapter 4), a marginally toned-down version is presented as a description of the contemporary map of insecurity. For instance, Rotberg (2002: 128) argues that failed states like Afghanistan, Sierra Leone and Somalia are 'incapable of projecting power and asserting authority within their own borders, leaving their territories governmentally empty'. In earlier periods, such emptiness may have resulted in security concerns only within states, but the era of global interconnection makes insecurity harder to contain (Rotberg, 2002, 2004; Krasner and Pascual, 2005).

Second, understandings of state power and its relation to security are reoriented. Traditional rankings of superpowers, great powers, major powers and so on are no longer measures of security or threat. Security/insecurity is measured by internal strength or weakness. Thus, the annual Failed States Index ranks states differently (Fund for Peace, 2012). Somalia is the world's weakest state and Finland is the strongest. While internationally powerful states like the USA, the UK and France are viewed as internally strong, none are stronger than Luxembourg. China may be a rising international power, but as the 76th weakest state, it is ranked as significantly less strong than Barbados, as is Russia, ranked as 83rd weakest. States whose military power is viewed as threatening Western interests are weak: North Korea is 22nd weakest and Iran 34th.

In this context, the logics and strategies of security shift towards the 'interventionist' and 'new security' views espoused in human security (Newman, 2001) (see Chapter 9). Notions of mutual vulnerability become Western-centric with interconnected transnational dangers threatening powerful states viewed as originating in weak state control in the South (Cooper, 2005). Thus, the logics of security shift from deterrence strategies in interstate relations to a modified form of containment, clearly expressed by US Secretary of State Condoleezza Rice (2005):

> Absent responsible state authority, threats that would and should be contained within a country's borders can now melt into the world and wreak untold havoc. Weak and failing states serve as global pathways that facilitate the spread of pandemics, the movement of criminals and terrorists, and the proliferation of the world's most dangerous weapons.

While these changes are important, the foundational understandings of security they articulate are merely a reconfiguration of earlier assumptions. First, the security functions of the state remain its core definition. For Rotberg (2004: 3) and others, 'there is a hierarchy of political goods. None is as critical as the supply of security, especially human security', and other public goods (political participation, access to healthcare and education) can only be provided once security has been attained. This reflects a continued dominance of liberal and Hobbesian logics of social contracts and security bargains. Second, while a spectrum of strength and weakness does not fully conform to Waltz's notion of two organizing principles for political life (hierarchy and anarchy), traditional associations of insecurity and anarchy are re-emphasized in a new form and new locations. Indeed, this has recently expanded to include other 'ungoverned spaces', where any geographical or functional gap in governance is understood as potentially breeding insecurity (Arquilla and Ronfeldt, 2001; Clunan and Trinkunas, 2010).

Criticisms of the failed states discourse

There are numerous empirical and conceptual critiques of the failed states discourse and how it has functioned. The empirical challenge to the overarching association of transnational dangers with weak and failing states is strong. Some accept the basic premises of the argument but argue that terrorism and crime require a degree of order and governance in which to flourish, so weak but not collapsed states are the most threatening (Patrick, 2006; Mair, 2008). Others point to a dearth of empirical evidence for the associations of anarchy and transnational dangers (Patrick, 2006; Patrick and Brown, 2007; Cockayne and Lupel, 2009). The assumption of a correlation between terrorism and failed states is actually rather weak, with the obvious exceptions of al-Qaeda in Afghanistan and Sudan (Newman, 2007; Elden, 2007) (see Chapter 11). Likewise, the associations with crime and drug trafficking are more reflective of the wider political and geographic assumptions of the nature of international order than they are of the empirical evidence of illicit flows (Bourne, 2011a) (see Chapter 12). The resulting understanding that state-building is an antidote to terrorism, crime and human insecurity is also undermined by the poor record of state-building generally, and by detailed empirical accounts of the significant contradictions between the aims and processes of state-building, counterterrorism and counternarcotics (Felbab-Brown, 2005; Goodhand, 2008).

Conceptual critiques largely reject the foundational assumptions of the failed states discourse. The equation of state weakness with emptiness and anarchy neglects the existence and emergence of other forms of social and political ordering not associated with Weberian ideal types of bureaucratic, rational states (Menkhaus, 2006). This neglect is reinforced by an essentialized notion of the state that reduces the diversity of existing state forms and processes of formation to a singular essence of sovereign hierarchy in functional control of territory, population and processes therein (Milliken and Krause, 2002; Eadie, 2007). Likewise, it ignores the specific forms and conditions of state formation in an evolving set of global relations, and assumes a universal transhistorical process of state formation and functioning (Morton and Bilgin, 2002; Bøås and Jennings, 2005; Jones, 2008). Paradigms of state strength and weakness naturalize the Western model of security and order, posing strength as the natural condition of the state and end point of state-building processes and weakness as sickness (Hagmann and Hoehne, 2009). Weak states are viewed as simply not mature and modern enough (Berger, 2007). This localizes the dynamics of state failure, viewing it as the outcome of bad government decisions in the weak state rather than global structures or the actions of powerful states, even as it globalizes the threats they pose (Newman, 2009). For a minority of critics, understanding the diversity of state forms and processes of formation leads to a different prescription: 'let them fail' rather than seeking to reimpose a form of Westphalian territorial ordering that never worked since artificial territorial boundaries were imposed by imperial and then Cold War international orders (Herbst, 2004). This is ethically uncomfortable, but may imply that the state collapse that accompanied African civil wars is a process of building new types of states rather than a descent into chaos (Niemann, 2007).

This combination of empirical and conceptual critique leads some to suggest that the failed states discourse is not a neutral description of state strength or security, but an ideological support for interventionist and hegemonic forms of neoliberalism (Morton, 2005; Bøås and Jennings, 2007). Thus, state-building processes invariably seek a Western liberal model of the state (Englebert and Tull, 2008). In this regard, state failure has two dimensions: empirical cases of a decline and collapse of state institutions and functions; and a theoretical/ideological failure, a sense of surprise that existing states do not conform to the expectations of stateness and security provision anticipated by purportedly universal security theories (Milliken and Krause, 2002). There is a degree of hypocrisy here too: if weak states are threatening because governance has receded and become informal, it is odd to view similar informality positively in other states where it is associated with neoliberal privatization and the enabling of private investment (Bøås and Jennings, 2007).

Intervention in conflict and state failure

Insecurity and violence are often perpetuated by states rather than arising out of their incapacity. The 1994 Rwandan genocide did not arise from institutional collapse but as government-orchestrated 'chaos from above' (Longman, 1998). International interventions in conflict and crimes against humanity seek to tackle this in what some argue is a new international security order that enables the pursuit of humanitarian goals rather than selfish realpolitik. This has the potential to reconfigure the relationships between sovereignty, security and authority among peoples, states and the international community.

During the Cold War, interventions in conflicts in Africa, Asia and Latin America were largely justified in terms of furthering Cold War security alliances and containment. Humanitarian motives were downplayed, and the UN Security Council (UNSC), as the main international institution tasked with ensuring international peace and security, was largely stymied by extensive use of vetoes by the two superpowers. Nevertheless, 13 UN peacekeeping missions took place during the Cold War, beginning with the deployment of unarmed military observers to Palestine in 1948 (Goulding, 1993). Traditional peacekeeping operations in the Middle East, Kashmir, Congo and Cyprus had limited goals, focusing on assisting a peace in interstate conflict rather than creating and enforcing a peace within states. They involved the deployment of relatively small numbers of unarmed or lightly armed peacekeepers (half the Cold War era's peacekeeping forces were unarmed). Importantly, such deployments generally occurred with the consent of the state, and operated on the basis of rigid impartiality and neutrality rather than taking sides in the conflict. The first peacekeeping operation with contemporary parallels was the mission in the Congo conflict (1960–64). This began as a traditional peacekeeping operation but soon evolved into a more ambitious and costly effort as state institutions collapsed and the UN authorized the use of force and moved towards enforcing rather than observing a peace (Goulding, 1993).

In the 1990s, the number and scope of missions increased dramatically: 49 of the 67 UN peacekeeping missions since 1948 began after 1991 (35 in the 1990s and 14 this century). The scale of UN involvement in conflicts has increased from 11,000 military and police personnel deployed at the start of 1992 to a peak of 102,000 in early 2010 (Goulding, 1993; UNDPKO, 2012a). The post-Cold War resurgence of peace operations led to a rapid evolution of the goals, forms and principles of intervention. Traditional peacekeeping has become overshadowed by more ambitious attempts at peace enforcement, including the use of military force in humanitarian military interventions, and a growing dominance of post-conflict intervention in the form of state-building. These practices have raised much debate over whether it is legitimate or desirable to intervene without the consent of the state; when, how, and who should intervene; and the prospects and implications of state-building as building security.

Should states intervene?

Is it ever legitimate and appropriate to intervene in the internal affairs of another state? Traditional peacekeeping took place with the consent, and invitation, of the state or states concerned. Many interventions now take place with military force and without such consent, which raises the dilemma of whether the long-established right of states to noninterference in their internal affairs should continue to trump human security concerns. This is not just a question of power vs ethics, as practical, political, legal and ethical arguments are made on both sides. Such arguments articulate differing understandings of the relationships between order and justice, statehood and security, and the potential for moral action rather than pure power politics and with it the demands of collective or common security (see Chapter 6).

The right of states to nonintervention has a long, if patchy, history. It is enshrined in Article 2(4) of the UN Charter (the foundational treaty of the United Nations, signed in 1945), which commits states to refrain from 'the threat or use of force against the territorial integrity or political independence of any state'. This seems to disallow unilateral intervention in the affairs of other states. Even the UN does not have a clear right to intervene, as Article 2(7) establishes that nothing in the UN Charter gives the UN the right 'to intervene in matters which are essentially within the domestic jurisdiction of any state'. The only exception to this is under enforcement measures undertaken under Chapter VII (authorized by the UNSC) (see Chapter 6). The authors of the UN Charter were evidently wary of justifying extensive intervention, a position the UN continued to emphasize throughout the Cold War. In 1965, Resolution 2131 (XX) of the UN General Assembly (GA) declared that:

> No state has the right to intervene, directly or indirectly, for any reason whatever, in the internal or external affairs of any other State. Consequently, armed intervention and all other forms of interference or attempted threats against the personality of the State or against its political, economic and cultural elements, are condemned.

Such intervention was then declared in 'violation of international law' in 1970 (UNGA, 1970). In the context of decolonization in the postwar period and the 1960s, many states believed that a clear prohibition on intervention was the only guarantee of the self-determination of peoples, and that the principle of nonintervention was a barrier to a resurgence of colonialism and the pursuance of self-interest through war. This is sometimes called a 'pluralist' position, which argues that international order is premised on maintaining a plurality of political and social forms (democratic, authoritarian, communist) rather than pursuing moralistic goals that confuse cultural preferences for universal values – something early realists also warned against. Thus, nonintervention offers protection against international violence, and intervention weakens the protection of plurality and invites more war (Jackson, 2000; Chesterman, 2001). Indeed, for some pluralists, nonintervention is a 'grand norm' that makes the pursuit of the good life possible (Jackson, 2000: 373). From this perspective, it is not that nonintervention serves the interests of the state and that intervention serves the interests of human security (as is often claimed), but that nonintervention offers protection for states that are not very far down the road of state-building. Nonintervention can be a 'demand for justice by the weaker states against the stronger states' proclivity to impose their preferred view of international order on the weak in the name of justice within states' (Ayoob, 2002: 98–9).

Against the 'pluralist' position are 'solidarists', who argue that there is a degree of solidarity in international society regarding the enforcement of law extending beyond sovereign rights to nonintervention to the guardianship of human rights everywhere (Wheeler, 2000). They claim that the principle of consent for intervention has exceptions in times of 'massive human suffering' (Bellamy, 2003: 5). Intervention to protect others is justifiable for its own sake, for humanitarian reasons and for preventing the security threats that might arise from regional destabilization and state failure. Zartman (2005: 1) criticizes the pluralist argument that nonintervention protects order and claims that it 'pits an actual abuse, the misuse of sovereignty as a cover for a state's neglect and repression of its citizens, against a potential one, the danger of dominating a weaker state through interference in its internal affairs', and for him, 'the real abuse is paramount over the hypothetical one'.

Pro-intervention arguments are also supported by international law. Solidarists argue that Article 2(4) of the UN Charter is concerned with the use of force that damages the territorial integrity and political independence of states, and that many interventions seek to protect rather than undermine these. Further, international laws on human rights, including the UN Charter, the 1948 UN Universal Declaration of Human Rights and the 1948 UN Genocide Convention, give a legal status to the rights of individuals independent of those of sovereign states. Beyond formal laws, customary international law (law that arises through common practice rather than laid down in treaties and charters) is argued to provide a right (but not duty) to intervene (Wheeler, 2000: 14).

Customary rules in support of intervention have strengthened through the authorization of intervention in the name of protecting civilians, such as those in Bosnia and Somalia in the early 1990s. Other necessary interventions did not materialize in time to prevent massive civilian casualties, such as in the Rwandan (1994) and Darfur (2003–) genocides, but these haunting failures lie behind more recent attempts to strengthen international norms on intervention. In some ways, this articulates a social contract understanding of the state as having responsibilities to its population (see Chapter 4). In 1999, UN Secretary-General Kofi Annan emphasized that states should be understood as the servant of the people, not vice versa. Indeed, throughout the 1990s, the responsibility of the state to manage conflict and provide good governance became a central assumption of many donor governments and academics (Keller and Rothchild, 1996; Zartman, 1997; Villalón and Huxtable, 1998). This means that sovereign states have certain responsibilities for which governments are accountable to their own populations and the wider international community. Only by discharging its responsibilities for good governance can a state legitimately claim the protection of national sovereignty (Deng et al., 1996).

In 2001, the International Commission on Intervention and State Sovereignty (ICISS) claimed that a responsibility to provide security (understood as protection against crimes against humanity) was inherent within the notion of sovereignty and in emerging practices and standards of human rights and human security. The ICISS (2001: xi) argued that while states have primary responsibility for the protection of people, where a population is suffering serious harm as a result of conflict, repression or state failure and the responsible state is unwilling or unable to halt it, 'the principle of non-intervention yields to the international responsibility to protect'. This notion of a Responsibility to Protect (R2P) understands human security as implying a shared responsibility and a mutual vulnerability in a world where fragile and failing states and human rights abuses 'constitute a risk to people everywhere' (ICISS, 2001: 5). Thus, human and state security are symbiotic not opposed: 'in security terms, a cohesive and peaceful international system is far more likely to be achieved through the cooperation of effective states, confident of their place in the world, than in an environment of fragile, collapsed, fragmenting or generally chaotic state entities' (ICISS, 2001: 8). In 2005, R2P was unanimously endorsed by heads of government at the UN World Summit, although in a narrow version that emphasized protection against crimes against humanity rather than wider human security. The ICISS argued that R2P contains three related responsibilities: to prevent, to react, and to rebuild. These raise the question of when and how intervention should occur.

When and how should intervention occur?

Debate on when and how intervention should occur, particularly if it involves the use of force and without consent, is shaped by the older tradition of just war theorizing on which much international humanitarian law is based (see Chapter 7). This Christian tradition questioned when it might be permissible for Christians to participate in war, but the ICISS drew on it more broadly when it presented a series of thresholds and conditions in which military intervention is justifiable. While military intervention clearly raises sovereignty concerns, other forms of intervention are also important in the principles this raises.

Perhaps the most obvious question about intervention relates to principles of 'just cause'. These emphasize that military intervention should only be an exceptional and extraordinary measure undertaken when there is 'serious and irreparable harm occurring to human beings, or imminently likely to occur' (ICISS, 2001: 32). This includes large-scale loss of life (but not necessarily genocide) produced through state action, neglect or failure, and large-scale 'ethnic cleansing' through killing, forced expulsion, terror or rape. Thus, it is the degree of actual or imminent violence and the role or incapacity of the state that define the justice of the cause. This sets a more specific, higher bar to intervention than some recent just war theory, such as Walzer's (2006: 107) claim that 'humanitarian intervention is justified when it is a response ... to acts "that shock the moral conscience of mankind"'. The principle here is that it shocks not only political leaders but also the moral convictions of ordinary men and women. In practice, judging when a just cause exists remains a political matter rather than a neutral or popular assessment. Neither R2P nor the older Genocide Convention provides adequately clear criteria for this. Pape (2012) argues that a 'pragmatic' standard is required, premised on the presence of mass homicide (2,000–3,000 people in a short period), with the prospect of greater deaths in the future that can be stopped (rather than aiming to punish atrocities in the recent past), combined with a low-cost intervention strategy and the prospect of building enduring security. This joins just cause with pragmatic questions of whether intervention can actually prevent loss of life effectively and cheaply.

Even when a just cause is found, the ICISS emphasized that precautionary principles should be adhered to. These derive directly from just war theorizing and argue that intervention should be undertaken with 'right intention' (to halt human suffering), as a 'last resort' (only after more peaceful means have failed or there is reason to believe they will), with 'proportional means' (the minimal scale, intensity and duration required to achieve human protection objectives) and 'reasonable prospects' of success, with the action being undertaken not likely to worsen the situation. In addition, debate also centres on the just war and R2P requirement for 'right authority' (who provides the authorization for legitimate intervention). There has long been debate on whether military humanitarian interventions have or can meet these criteria (Slater and Nardin, 1986).

'Right intention': realpolitik, selectivity, misuse and risk

Do states have the 'right intention' when intervening? Intervention to halt human suffering does not preclude other motives on behalf of intervening actors, but to restrict legitimacy to a search for such ethical purity in motives would probably negate all cases of intervention. Most realists and some liberals argue that states will only undertake intervention when there is also a national interest at stake rather than on purely humanitarian grounds. During the Cold War, interventions in situations of genocide, such as India in Bangladesh in 1971, Vietnam in Cambodia in 1979 and Tanzania in Uganda in 1979, were largely justified by concerns about refugee flows or fears of territorial expansion. While post-Cold war interventions are more explicitly justified in humanitarian terms, global and regional security interests, transnational security concerns or resource access are often underlying motives for particular interventions. Taken to its logical conclusion, this implies that humanitarian motives merely serve as a mask for selfish aims. To conclude this, however, may simply be an assertion of basic realist principles, such as a rejection of ethical motivations in international politics, a view of order and security that derives from power-seeking behaviour, and a Clausewitzean view of war as a narrowly defined political instrument. Liberals argue, instead, that states have a national interest in producing a more rule-based international order in which extreme violations of human rights are punished (Holzgrefe, 2003). In this view, Western interventionist states have grown beyond legalistic sovereignty and now pursue the enforcement of some minimal values on 'premodern' weak and failing states 'unwilling or unable to accept them' (Cooper, 2003: 59). Thus, intervention need not pose an absolute conflict between moral principles and realpolitik. Chandler (2004) argues that realpolitik rather than legal standards sustained the principle of nonintervention in the Cold War, and that powerful states' interests now lie in interventionism. However, some constructivists reject the view that intervention is solely predictable on the basis of geostrategic or economic interests. In the early 1990s, the US-led intervention in Somalia had little geostrategic importance, the contributors to the enormous UN mission in Cambodia had little strategic interest in the country, and while the first Gulf War in 1991 is explicable with reference to geostrategic and economic interests (such as oil), the extension of that role to the protection of Kurdish and Shiite populations was not (Finnemore, 2003).

Strategic motivations may explain why powerful states are selective in their engagements and so not all just causes receive intervention. The lateness of intervention in Rwanda and Darfur and the contemporary lack of military intervention in Syria (in the face of at least 60,000, and rising, civilian deaths) are clear indications of this. It is questionable, however, to what degree intervention requires great power support. Chesterman (2001) argues that the failure of protection in Bosnian 'safe areas' arose because of a lack of clear leadership, that the limited UN action that eventually took place in Rwanda would not have arisen without France taking a ready-made plan of action to the UNSC, and that no action would have been taken against the violence that erupted in East Timor after the vote on independence from Indonesia in 1999 if Australia had not taken the lead in a multinational force. Certainly, a basic requirement for great power support precludes military intervention against the great powers themselves. The ICISS (2001: 37) was not naive on this point, and noted that such interventions would probably not be justifiable on utilitarian grounds and they may not be mounted in every deserving case. However, it pointed out that this 'is no reason for them not to be mounted in any case'.

Issues of self-interest and selectivity also arise in pluralists' fears of misuse of a pro-intervention norm (Chesterman, 2001). Even some consensus on the R2P has not diminished the concerns of less powerful states that interventionist agendas may be misused against them. Certainly, naive acceptance of humanitarian rhetoric is inadvisable. In 1938, Hitler wrote a letter to British Prime Minister Neville Chamberlain, invoking the rights of German citizens to self-determination, a growing refugee crisis and the 'security of more than 3,000,000 human beings' to justify the invasion of Czechoslovakia (Goodman, 2006: 113); and the 2008 Russian invasion of Georgia on humanitarian grounds was clearly motivated by geostrategic interests. Yet, advocates of R2P argue that the problematic invocation of humanitarian principles to justify the US-led interventions in Iraq and Afghanistan does not imply that R2P principles are a dangerous pretext for pre-emptive conflict but that they should be more stringently applied (Weiss, 2004). Indeed, Thakur (2004), one of the architects of R2P, argues that the post-hoc justification of the 2003 invasion of Iraq on humanitarian grounds delegitimated humanitarian intervention rather than legitimating the Iraq War.

The human and financial costs of intervention also contribute to the selectivity of intervention in practice. There is some evidence that Western states tend not to intervene unless they are confident of low casualties, as they were in Kosovo in 1999 but were not in Rwanda in 1994 (Wheeler, 2000; Boettcher, 2004). Indeed, even Kofi Annan (1999: 8) argued that this risk and economic costs, and the risk of failure, rather than sovereignty concerns, have tended to prevent intervention. What prevented effective intervention in the 1994 Rwandan genocide was not arguments about nonintervention clauses of the UN Charter (which were not made), but vacillation and difficulty in finding willing interveners so soon after the US intervention in Somalia had resulted in the brutal deaths of US soldiers (Barnett, 2002). An aversion to risking soldiers lives to save strangers reflects the 'new Western way of war', in which the use of military force is expected to produce minimal casualties for the intervening force (see Chapter 7). However, this is neither absolute nor universal and few go as far as Huntingdon's argument that it is 'morally unjustifiable and politically indefensible that members of the [United States] Armed Forces should be killed to prevent Somalis from killing one another' (cited in Holzegrefe, 2003: 30).

This aversion to risking Western lives does not preclude intervention. Indeed, official figures indicate that 3,062 UN peacekeepers have been killed since 1948, with 70 from the USA (UNDPKO, 2012b). The largest contributors of uniformed personnel to UN peacekeeping operations are not the most powerful states but developing countries. For instance, in 2012, of the 113 countries contributing uniformed personnel to UN missions, Bangladesh and Pakistan were the top two contributors, each providing almost 9,000 personnel, while the UK was ranked 46th (284 personnel) and the USA 57th (133 personnel) (UNDPKO, 2012c). In some cases, these states may be interested in regional stability, but many are from far-flung parts of the world and may be more interested in receiving the US$1,028 paid per soldier per month. According to the UN Department of Peacekeeping Operations (UNDPKO, 2012d), the financial costs for peacekeeping operations tend to be provided by powerful states – in 2012, 27% of costs were provided by the USA, 12.5% by Japan and around 8% from France, Germany and the UK. While this cost is substantial, at over US$7 billion from June 2012 to June 2013, and the total costs between 1948 and 2010 were around $69 billion, the current figure remains less than 0.5% of global military expenditures.

The motives for and against particular interventions reflect deeper distinctions in the ethics of intervention. While many pro-intervention arguments espouse a Kantian or cosmopolitan ethics in which there are moral duties to others, restrictions on interventions on the basis of national interest and the risk of casualties tend to accord with a communitarian ethics, in which moral responsibility ends at state borders. In both cases, poststructuralist scholars have pointed out that humanitarian intervention is framed through power asymmetries, in which the West is portrayed as the saviour of the poor and distant foreigners, and debate occurs as to whether 'we' should help 'them' (Campbell, 1998a, 1998b; Edkins, 2003; Owens, 2004).

Last resort and conflict prevention

The human, financial and political costs and dangers of intervention mean that it should be an exceptional measure in response to a just cause (Slater and Nardin, 1986). Some suggest that the humanitarian benefits could be gained at less cost through funding public health, disaster response and assisting refugees (Valentino, 2011). Nevertheless, military forces have been deployed to protect civilians in 20 states since 1990 – including Afghanistan, Albania, Bosnia, Burundi, Central African Republic, Croatia, Democratic Republic of the Congo, East Timor, Georgia, Haiti, Iraq (Kurdistan, 1991), Ivory Coast, Kosovo, Liberia, Macedonia, Rwanda, Sierra Leone, Somalia, Sudan (Darfur) and Tajikistan (Kuperman, 2008).

In the just war tradition and R2P, military action is to be a last resort, once more peaceful methods have failed (UN, 2005b). The international community can use many peaceful tools ranging from mediation to coercive diplomacy, sanctions, or humanitarian and financial aid. The adage that prevention is better than cure is often argued to apply to conflict. In this vein, the ICISS (2001: xi) argued that there is a 'responsibility to prevent' and that 'prevention is the single most important dimension of the responsibility to protect'.

Conflict, genocide and ethnic cleansing may seem like events that are difficult to prevent purely because they are difficult to predict. However, in many cases, the warning signs of impending civil wars in the 1990s were identifiable before the end of the 1980s (Zartman, 2005). There is strong evidence that effective prevention measures are, or would have been, much less costly than later intervention and peacebuilding (Brown and Rosecrance, 1999; Chalmers, 2007). While early warning may be possible, it is difficult to identify clear opportunities for effective action and early response has largely proved elusive. Although there have been numerous failed attempts at conflict prevention (Bosnia, Rwanda, Somalia, Haiti and the first Iraq War), some conflict prevention has succeeded in Macedonia, Slovakia and even had effects once conflict has started in Cambodia and El Salvador (Brown and Rosecrance, 1999).

Preventing the worst forms of state collapse is arguably possible, but conducting such prevention relies on understanding the causes of state failure. For Rotberg (2003: 10), 'failure is preventable, particularly since human agency rather than structural flaws or institutional insufficiencies are almost invariably at the root of slides from weakness (or strength) toward failure and collapse'. While many weak states that have failed have endured long conflicts, so too have many that have not. Rotberg claims that the difference between weak states that have failed (Sierra Leone, Somalia and Zaire) and those that have not (Sri Lanka and Indonesia) is that the former have lost legitimacy among their populations while the latter retain it. Further, in the former category, governments have often preyed on their populations and built security institutions focused on elites and regime security rather than providing security as a public good. This means that preventing state failure is concerned with building effective security and governance institutions and enhancing the legitimacy of the state, but this is usually done after a conflict rather than before.

Institutional capacities for conflict prevention remain limited and patchy. Numerous regional and other organizations have developed conflict prevention capacities: for example, the EU conflict prevention assessment missions in Indonesia, Nepal and Fiji and the ongoing development of a Rapid Reaction Mechanism; the Organization for Security and Co-operation in Europe's (OSCE) conduct of conflict prevention in southern Europe, the Caucasus and Central Asia; and the wider development of 'conflict-sensitive' aid strategies and units for conflict prevention and post-conflict reconstruction by development donors such as the UK. Globally, however, there is a lack of significant investment and institutionalization of conflict prevention. While UN conflict prevention capabilities have expanded on an ad-hoc basis, key statements indicate merely that 'a culture of the prevention of armed conflict' should be promoted (UN, 2005b: 21; Bellamy, 2008).

While prevention is cheaper than cure, the costs are not insubstantial and getting governments to dedicate resources when there is no clear proof that conflict will (only may) erupt or that prevention will work is inherently difficult as it relies on a counterfactual argument. Thus, the UN Trust Fund for Preventive Action had received $33 million by 2005, compared with the annual running costs of peace operations of around $5 billion (Bellamy, 2008). Politically, the fortunes of conflict prevention are also limited by the use of prevention arguments to support pre-emptive military action such as in Iraq (Fierke, 2005; Whitman, 2005; Bellamy, 2008).

Proportional means and prospect of success

In the just war tradition, the conduct of the use of force should always be proportional to the legitimate aims. This means that the scale, duration and intensity of the military action should be the minimum necessary to secure the human protection objective, not the defeat of a state or other national interests (ICISS, 2001). The proportionality principle is intended to limit the negative political effects of intervention and ensure that it is conducted in line with international humanitarian law.

Importantly, proportionality does not restrict the international community from escalating military action, but does have some implications for its form. In particular, states may face a difficult choice between proportionality and human cost. While the ICISS (2001: xiii) argued that 'force protection cannot become the principle objective' in intervention, many interventions have prioritized this. The NATO intervention in Kosovo, for example, began with 11 weeks of bombing, which included 10,484 'strike missions' dropping over 12,000 tons of munitions (Lake, 2009; Webber, 2009). The use of air power limited NATO casualties but resulted in thousands of civilian deaths on all sides and accidental bombings of a refugee convoy and the Chinese Embassy in Belgrade (Shea, 1999; Shea and Marani, 1999; Coady, 2002; Kay, 2004). At the time, there was much public and academic debate on whether air power or the deployment of ground troops was appropriate (and proportional) to the stated moral aims of the intervention. Aferdita Kelmendi (1999: 18), a Kosovan testifying to a US Senate hearing, thanked the USA/NATO for its campaign: 'But bombs cannot stop these men with guns and black masks. Bombs cannot make it safe for me and for my family to return to our homes.' After the bombing campaign, NATO deployed KFOR (Kosovo Force) ground troops, a mission that has continued to the present day in the form of long-term peacebuilding.

Proportionality and the prospect of success are linked by the principle that intervention should not make the situation worse. Booth (2007: 314) commends humanitarian sympathies but argues that they should still be 'calmed by the old injunction about not making things worse'. It is hard to know if intervention has benefited human security, since this relies on a counterfactual argument that if action had not been undertaken, the situation would have been worse – and it is inherently difficult to count people who did not die (Seybolt, 2007; Zehfuss, 2012).

Kuperman (2000, 2004, 2008) argues that intervention can worsen violence, and that genocide might be encouraged by the international community showing itself willing and able to intervene. Most genocides occur during conflicts that begin through rebellion or attempted secession. Anticipating that the international community will come to their aid shifts the cost–benefit calculations of rebels, and they would be more circumspect about launching a rebellion if the international community did not indicate this willingness. For Kuperman (2000, 2004), this 'humanitarian hazard' is exacerbated by the fact that while it may take months for the international community to respond, genocide can happen very quickly. In Rwanda, half the genocide deaths happened in the first few weeks, and in East Timor, government-backed militias displaced a large proportion of the population within a week of the 1999 vote on independence from Indonesia. Kuperman seems to devalue the point that many thousands of lives could have been saved after the early weeks of violence. However, others argue that even effective military intervention may worsen future violence by enabling new actors to seek revenge against their former opponents or oppressors, as happened in Croatia, Kosovo and Afghanistan (the flip side to the risk of misuse by great powers) (Maley, 2002).

In spite of these concerns, most interventions seem to save lives and it is rare for intervention to worsen a humanitarian situation. Seybolt's (2007) analysis of 17 humanitarian military interventions in the 1990s found that only 2 made the violence worse (UN Operation in Somalia II and NATO's Operation Allied Force in Kosovo), and 2 others failed to save lives. These cases are not to be taken lightly, as it is evident that the NATO bombing campaign made Kosovans less secure because Milošević used it as a cover to increase the scale and violence of his ethnic cleansing (Wheeler, 2000). Here, intervention seems to have produced what it sought to prevent and by the end of the conflict, 90 per cent of the ethnic Albanian population of Kosovo had been displaced.

The record of relative success in saving lives does not translate into an equally strong record of political success in producing a lasting peace (Seybolt, 2007). Indeed, some argue that there is a tension between enforcement action, which may stop violence but not lay the foundations for peace, and consent-based operations, which lay those foundations but do not stop violence (Doyle and Sambanis, 2000). Luttwak (1999) goes further and claims that a stable peace only results when a war ends through military victory. For him, intervention and the insistence on producing ceasefires merely serves to provide opportunities for belligerents to reorganize, rearm and begin fighting afresh. Luttwak (1999: 109) claims that 'fighting must continue until a resolution is reached', since it is only possible for accommodation (peace) to become attractive when hopes for military success fade.

The evidence for Luttwak's contention is inconclusive. Toft (2010; Nathan and Toft, 2011) argues that most wars between 1940 and 2000 ended with military victory, and a far smaller proportion of these subsequently reignited than those that ended with a negotiated settlement. However, other studies indicate that this trend is changing, with many more post-Cold War conflicts ending with a negotiated settlement, although still only one-third (Harbom et al., 2006). Recent research also indicates that the majority of conflicts do not fall into any of these categories but end under much less clear situations when fighting stops without a decisive end point (Kreutz, 2010). While most attempts to negotiate a peace agreement collapse, and most successful agreements produce only a limited peace in which violence has declined but positive peace is lacking – a situation MacGinty (2006) calls 'no war, no peace' – these limits may owe more to the failures of peacebuilding than the lack of decisive military victory.

There is no simple choice between military victory or negotiated settlement, and Luttwak's call to 'give war a chance' misrepresents the aims of intervention: increasingly, it does not aim to merely stop violence and ignore the politics that lie behind it, but to recognize that opportunities for political solutions may need to be created. Here, the presence of peacekeepers may have similar effects to military victory in reducing the likelihood of war recurrence by up to 85 per cent compared with situations without them, especially if the conflict parties consent to peacekeeping (Fortna, 2004, 2008; Kreutz, 2010). Contra Luttwak's logic, some argue that military victories lead to genocides more often than negotiated settlements (Licklider, 1995). Indeed, there is some evidence that international interventions that directly challenge the perpetrators of genocide have the greatest chance of success in slowing or stopping the killing and do not make matters worse (Krain, 2005).

Right authority

Who can or should be able to authorize intervention, particularly the use of military force without the consent of the state in which intervention takes place? Under international law, only the UNSC can authorize legitimate military action against a state, yet many military interventions have taken place without UNSC authorization. In the cases of NATO intervention in Kosovo and the 2003 invasion of Iraq, UNSC authorization was sought, indicating a general perception that intervention is better if authorized by the UNSC. However, in both cases, the UNSC did not agree resolutions that authorized the interventions desired by the USA and others, and intervention went ahead. This is widely viewed as undermining the authority of the UNSC and, partly in response to the Kosovo intervention, the ICISS (2001: 48) argued that challenging or evading the UNSC will 'undermine the principle of a world order based on international law and universal norms' (see also Lang, 2009).

The UNSC is clearly an imperfect organization and its authorization of military intervention, sanctions and other measures is beset with difficulties of slow decision making and the veto power of the P5. Further, the problems of the UN system extend beyond the UNSC, and Western powers' vacillation and unwillingness to sacrifice lives and political fortunes in the mire of Rwanda were shared by some in the UN Secretariat, who wanted 'to make sure that the UN did not go down with Rwanda' (Barnett, 2002: 118). Barnett argued that the institutional culture in the UN conflicted with the good intentions of moral individuals within the organization. While the shame of failure in Rwanda has driven much changing practice on conflict intervention, the question remains whether and which other actors may legitimately authorize intervention if the UN fails to act in a timely and effective manner.

Regional organizations have deployed numerous peacekeeping and peace support operations since the 1990s (see Chapter 6). Indeed, from the ECOWAS Ceasefire Monitoring Group (ECOMOG) in Liberia and Sierra Leone, to NATO in the Balkans (and elsewhere), regional missions have been deployed in conflicts, often in greater numbers than UN missions present in the same countries. Further, if one includes ISAF (International Security Assistance Force) in Afghanistan, in recent years the number of peacekeepers deployed by regional organizations has exceeded those deployed by the UN (Center on International Cooperation, 2012). The OSCE and EU have also deployed civilian election monitors and missions to assist in peacebuilding. Increasingly, joint UN-regional organization missions are conducted, although it is debatable whether regionalization challenges UN authority or helps share the burden of peacekeeping costs (Bures, 2006) (see Chapter 6). Regional organizations may be claimed to have greater legitimacy in speaking for the peoples and states of a region, and thus in authorizing intervention, but they often still rely on UN support and authorization. While regional organizations may be claimed to have a greater willingness to intervene, cultural similarities and other advantages, they also raise the danger of self-interested interventions dominated by regional powers (Morris and McCoubrey, 1999; Bures, 2006).

Can individual states, or ad-hoc coalitions, legitimately authorize intervention? While the ICISS argued that 'right intention' criteria were better assured in multilateral operations, many large interventions have occurred unilaterally, or by a coalition of like-minded states. Legitimacy is a combination of legal and moral considerations, and in some cases these appear to conflict. Thus, the UK House of Commons Select Committee on Foreign Affairs (2000) argued that while NATO intervention in Kosovo was of 'dubious legality', it was 'justified on moral grounds'. Self-authorization by states is supported by the orthodox view that failing states pose a strategic threat to global security as well as a humanitarian concern. Here, self-defence can support pre-emptive intervention and trump UNSC authorization. The 2002 US National Security Strategy declared that: 'While the U.S. will constantly strive to enlist the support of the international community, we will not hesitate to act alone, if necessary, to exercise our right of self-defense by acting pre-emptively' (US Government, 2002: 6). Similarly, Russia justified its war in Georgia in 2008 on humanitarian grounds and because Georgia's attack on the South Ossetia town of Tskhinvali constituted an 'act of aggression', even though under international law only the UNSC can make such a determination (Allison, 2008; International Crisis Group, 2008; King, 2008).

If self-authorization permits abuse, is it necessarily illegitimate? Some argue that legitimacy follows from the capability to act, and many Western states echo this when they claim a moral duty to intervene in their selected conflicts. For Pattison (2011), this means that the most legitimate/effective actor is NATO, followed by powerful individual states, and only thirdly the UN and fourthly regional organizations, since the latter still suffer from limited capabilities. This approach is politically problematic, since it cannot address longer term questions of where investment in peacekeeping capabilities should lie. The question of whether the UN can effectively authorize intervention is ultimately a question of whether the UNSC and wider system should be reconfigured and enabled to engage effectively or whether the status quo of fragmented, often subjective, and largely selective forms of authorization is the best that can be hoped for.

State-building and the liberal peace

Responsibility to Protect implies a shared responsibility to rebuild after conflict. Contemporary liberal interventionism pursues this by 'fixing failed states' as the symbiotic key to peace, human security and global security (Ghani and Lockart, 2008). This builds on the wide international consensus on peacebuilding that emerged through the experiences of the 1990s known as the 'liberal peace', since it centres on liberal assumptions that democratic governance and open market economies offer peaceful means of conflict rather than violence and war (see Chapter 2). This means introducing, or imposing, democracy and free markets in post-conflict states. For defenders of the liberal peace, this may be a neocolonial civilizing mission but it is a necessary one (Paris, 2002). Critics point to the variety of conflict and post-conflict situations that contrasts with a common set of approaches and aims for peacebuilding. This consensus has been so strong that many peacebuilding processes are framed as technical and administrative exercises in building governance capacities. However, this hides the inherently political character of what is actually a radically transformative agenda that seeks to stabilize weak states to contain transnational threats (Duffield, 2001; Chandler, 2006; Jacoby, 2007).

The liberal peace has evolved over time. In the early 1990s, peacebuilding focused on rapid democratization, but this was criticized by those like Paris who argued that functional governance capacity and institutions should be built before democratization. Others argue that although democratization is important in the long term, security requirements should be addressed first (Hampson and Mendeloff, 2007). More recent peacebuilding has attempted to combine this institutionalization and security building, but this can mean that technical matters are prioritized over local participation in peacebuilding (Paris, 2010; Barnett, 2006).

The liberal peace has a common set of aims but is not a simple one-size-fits-all model. There are graduations in the precise form of peacebuilding, ranging from the violent imposition of peace, as in Iraq and Afghanistan currently, and Kosovo, Bosnia and Somalia in the 1990s, a conservative version characterized by top-down, state-centric processes imposed by intervening states, which characterized the later stages of peacebuilding in Kosovo, Bosnia and Somalia, to an orthodox version that emphasizes local ownership – the main version of the liberal peace at play in UN and other peacebuilding missions (Richmond, 2007). In practice, what often emerges is a 'hybrid' peace that combines (often uneasily) internationally imposed and locally derived processes of peacebuilding (MacGinty, 2010). While 'local ownership' is an important aspect of much peacebuilding discourse, it poses challenges for identifying and strengthening local partners who may actually be intent on pursuing power for a particular elite, or may legitimate some less than peaceful modes of governance (Belloni, 2001; Pouligny, 2005; MacGinty, 2008).

Contemporary peacebuilding tends to focus on state-building: a transformative process of reversing state weakening and failure. This is a conservative project aimed at reinstating the state rather than questioning state sovereignty (Campbell, 1998b; Walker, 2003). State-building has a poor record of success. While there has been some success in Namibia, Mozambique and perhaps Liberia, the list of states where self-sustaining state institutions have been created is shorter than where they have not – Sierra Leone, Burundi, Ivory Coast, Sudan, Democratic Republic of the Congo and many others (Englebert and Tull, 2008). Thus state-building often fails to live up to its name and produces only 'virtual', 'simulated' 'phantom' states that appear functional from the outside but are – at best – dependent on international supervision in which local politics is subordinate to international donor agendas and practices (Debrix, 1999; Chandler, 2006; MacGinty, 2006; Richmond and Franks, 2007; Heathershaw, 2008). Further, like peacebuilding, state-building is a liberal project of 'modernising' or 'civilising' weak and failing states (Fukuyama, 2004). It does not just build 'states' but is a vehicle for the globalization of a particular type of state (Paris, 2002). While this may conflict with the pluralist worldview, which seeks to accommodate different internal political orders among juridically equal nation-states, defenders of the liberal peace argue that it also reflects a combining of the best tools at the international community's disposal (Quinn and Cox, 2007; Paris, 2010). Indeed, most state-building assumes that international actors and local political elites share the same understanding of the state and state failure (Englebert and Tull, 2008).

In spite of the variety of post-conflict security situations, there has been a gradual process of standardization and institutionalization of the forms and functions of internationally supported security building (Colletta and Muggah, 2009). This increasingly occurs through two related strategies: medium-term security building through disarmament, demobilization and reintegration (DDR); and longer term processes of security sector reform (SSR).

Disarmament, demobilization and reintegration (DDR)

Most post-conflict security building now begins with a formal disarmament, demobilization and reintegration (DDR) process. This entails the disarmament of ex-combatants, their demobilization (removing them from the structures of rebel- and sometimes government-armed forces) and reintegrating them into civilian life (often through job training and financial assistance). Since the UN first undertook DDR in Nicaragua in 1989, more than 60 DDR operations have been run by the UN or others (Muggah, 2009). Indeed, some argue that DDR has become 'the main business' of most contemporary UN peacekeeping operations (Berdal and Ucko, 2009). DDR was initially pursued in ad-hoc ways until the mid-1990s, when the UN and others began to solidify DDR as an integrated strategy involving all three elements, as earlier programmes had often focused on demobilization but with little disarmament or reintegration. By the early part of this century, DDR had become a common practice and the UN developed Integrated DDR Standards in 2006 that tried to learn lessons from past experiences and ensure stronger coordination between international actors. Some of these lessons are worth noting as they reveal the challenges of each element of DDR.

Disarmament has had varying success. For instance, in Liberia, over 100,000 combatants were demobilized but only 25,000 weapons were collected (Spear, 2006). This means that supplementary forms of weapons' collection are often needed in later periods. Disarmament processes often attract the submission of old and unserviceable 'junk' weapons, while better weapons are hidden for future use or sale. Further, if payments are made for weapons, they run the risk of stimulating a black market. In general, disarmament is done by consent, and combatants often have to submit a weapon to be able to qualify for demobilization benefits. Forced disarmament has been tried but has largely failed, as in Somalia in the early 1990s and Colombia more recently. In spite of these challenges, even partial and problematic disarmament can have positive symbolic effects, as it signifies a commitment to peace – particularly when accompanied by public ceremonies of weapons' destruction.

Demobilization often takes much longer than initially planned and sometimes raises concerns for the security of ex-combatants and others in demobilization camps, and can reinforce rather than reduce the strength of command structures or produce frustration that leads to remobilization, as happened in Nicaragua. Further, while rapid demobilization is desirable from the point of view of 'macro-security' (dismantling armed forces so that war cannot easily restart), if it is done too quickly, or in an unmanaged way, it can stimulate 'micro-insecurity' as demobilized soldiers turn to crime to support themselves (Knight and Özerdam, 2004).

Perhaps most importantly, reintegration has often been poorly designed and is commonly underresourced. Reintegration is a long-term process, and unlike finite processes of disarmament and demobilization, it has no clear end point (Ngoma, 2006). As a result, it often suffers from 'donor fatigue', in which donor governments lose interest or are unable to commit the resources needed to fund long-term projects. There have been numerous attempts to learn from these experiences, and many programmes now have dedicated separate programmes to focus on the specific needs of children and women (Dzinesa, 2007).

Security sector reform (SSR)

Security sector reform (SSR) seeks to build an effective and democratically accountable security sector, on a broadly Western model. It developed not only in relation to post-conflict situations but also in transitions from authoritarian rule to democracy (Cawthra and Luckham, 2003a; Hänggi, 2006). SSR integrates the reform and reconstruction of numerous security actors from military forces, police, prisons, the criminal justice system, intelligence and border security. As with DDR, this practice began in an ad-hoc fashion but has expanded to take on more aspects of security governance. It solidified later than DDR, with concerted strategies being developed from around 2002, and the UNSC finally endorsing and promoting SSR in 2007/08. SSR typically begins later in the post-conflict period than DDR, and many of the more difficult aspects of SSR are often postponed, although evidence suggests that early engagement and planning are crucial to their success (Bourne and Greene, 2012).

There are many tensions in the SSR process. First, it seeks effectiveness and democratic accountability and these goals sometimes conflict, such that much practice has focused on the former at the expense of the latter (Cawthra and Luckham, 2003b; Bernabéu, 2007; Knight, 2009). Second, recent donor policy espouses a 'holistic' approach to SSR (OECD, 2007), because there is little point in building an effective police force if the judiciary and prison systems are not functioning. However, such approaches have more often been emphasized in policy rhetoric than realized on the ground. They also require that donors should adopt 'whole of government approaches' (OECD, 2007) to supporting SSR (where development, defence and other ministries coordinate their activities), but these have not been well developed (Patrick and Brown, 2007). Finally, SSR imposes Western liberal models of the structure and functioning of the security sector on countries where this may not fit, such as the separation of the police and military. Indeed, donor models of security institutions are explicitly derived from the 'normative Western template of how security systems should operate' and influenced by human security and technocratic approaches to public sector reform (OECD, 2005: 62). Further, in many developing countries, informal (non-state) mechanisms provide 80–90 per cent of justice and dispute resolution, but these are often neglected or negatively impacted by the formalized, state-centric process of SSR (Albrecht and Kyed, 2011).

Both DDR and SSR seek sustainable security, but are often undermined by the high levels of armed violence and insecurity that characterize many post-conflict situations. Such violence often exceeds levels during conflict, for complex reasons that are not explicable merely as a continuation of conflict or a descent into crime. Much formal security building does not recognize or effectively tackle these different forms of violence (Muggah and Krause, 2009; Steenkamp, 2011). DDR and SSR also have wider political implications since they reinforce the assumption that the roots of insecurity are domestic to the conflict state itself rather than related to global structures or the actions of other states (such as supplying weapons) (Cooper and Pugh, 2002; Ebo, 2007). The expansion of donor involvement in SSR also reinforces the failed states discourse and the broader securitization of development and neoliberal good governance agendas that tend to reinforce unequal global power relations (Duffield, 2001; see Chapter 9). In Afghanistan, for instance, SSR has increasingly been utilized as a means of tackling insurgency rather than building long-term peace or human security (Mackay et al., 2011).

Conclusion

Since the bodies of US soldiers were dragged through the streets of Mogadishu in 1993, Western security concerns have come to focus on the seeming collapse of state-based forms of order. The collapse of Somalia into clan-based violence, the demise of Yugoslavia, and the rise of intrastate conflicts, characterized by the persistence of legal statehood in the absence of practical government, called into question the territorial assumptions of Westphalian political order and the Hobbesian or Lockean bargains at the heart of the state. Categorizing a spectrum of states from strong to weak, failing to failed reorients theorizing of the state, power and security away from an assumption that states are singular, unitary rational actors towards a practical security logic that seeks to make them so. The failures of security theory are recast as failures of political order, and the task has been framed not as retheorizing security in the light of evidence of a different world but as building the world in the image of the old assumptions.

The practices and politics of international intervention in conflicts and crimes against humanity have evolved significantly over the past two decades, and have become increasingly entangled with the discourses of containment and modernization in weak and failing states. Older debates between pluralism and solidarism have reconfigured into debates over whether there is a practical responsibility to protect the citizens of other states and what the implications are for the international order based on rights to nonintervention. Echoing, but only partly realizing, the standards of the just war tradition, political and theoretical debate has focused on whether, when and how intervention should take place. The motives of states and the prospects of creating a sustainable peace through external intervention set the scene for a security politics in which the familiar categories and concepts of security, anarchy, order and ethics are relocated into the territorial boundaries of weak states and the civilizing missions of liberal interventionists.

Through this process, the forms of sustainable security building have standardized around donor-led practices of DDR and SSR. These and wider conflict intervention practices suffer from limited successes (or unrealistic expectations). There are internal contradictions within the processes between the need for external support and the need for sustainable local capacities, between long-term and short-term goals, between local specificities and purportedly universal Western models. In the process, many lives have been lost, and many lives have been saved. We now turn to the two primary strategic security concerns that the Western consensus on weak states identifies most prominently: terrorism (Chapter 11) and transnational crime and migration (Chapter 12).

Chapter 11

Terrorism and Counterterrorism

Terrorism and counterterrorism have become defining features of security practice this century. Whether it is the changing threat of terrorism or the practices of counterterrorism that are responsible for altering security is open to contestation. Certainly, the 'war on terror' has killed far more people than terrorism has in recent years, but the future of terrorism rouses the greatest fears and uncertainties. This chapter begins with a discussion of definitional issues and the problems of conceptualizing terrorism. It then explores the relationship between terrorism and states by asking whether states can be terrorists and how states have provided support to non-state terrorist actors. It explores the major transformations in terrorism that have produced the greatest concern about seemingly fanatical, powerful terrorist networks, enabled by globalization, with the means of mass destruction at their disposal. Finally, it explores different approaches to counterterrorism and the related developments of international cooperation.

Defining and conceptualizing terror

Terrorist violence has existed for centuries, but the term 'terrorism' is surprisingly new. Acts of political violence, such as bombings, assassinations, hijackings and so on, were described using these terms rather than the all-encompassing 'terrorism' until the late 1960s (Zulaika and Douglass, 1996). While earlier uses of the term 'terror' related to the activities of states, from the post-revolutionary Reign of Terror (1793–94) in France to the repressive violence of Stalin and Hitler, since 'terrorism' began, it has been used primarily as a label for political violence by non-state actors.

Discussions of terrorism are replete with cliché and hyperbole, with the most pervasive combination of both being the claim that 'one person's terrorist is another's freedom fighter'. While this reveals the selective and subjective use of the term 'terrorism', taken too far, it implies that terrorism is in the eye of the beholder (Weinberg et al., 2004). Such ambiguity enables the use of the term to denote any use of violence that is disapproved of; as Sir Jeremy Greenstock, UK ambassador to the UN, claimed in the wake of the 9/11 attacks: 'terrorism is terrorism ... what looks, smells, and kills like terrorism is terrorism' (quoted in Schmid, 2004). Two aspects of this claim should be refuted. First, it emphasizes the legitimacy, or not, of the political cause of the actor using terrorism, which is not a definition of terrorism per se. Second, it posits that the difficulty is in determining which actors are terrorists, implying that there is something about an actor rather than an act that constitutes terrorism. Academics differ on whether an objective definition is possible. For some, the diversity of existing definitions does not preclude the production of an objective definition, it merely highlights the need for one (Schmid and Jongman, 2005); while for others, there can be no such thing as an objective definition that removes all subjective judgement, but this does not mean that anything goes (Jackson et al., 2011).

It is more helpful to define terrorism by identifying its common elements than by the perceptions of those applying the label. There are hundreds of definitions of terrorism to choose from, which partly reflect their origins: academics tend to prefer narrow definitions to apply in research, while government agencies use more all-encompassing definitions to permit flexibility of interpretation and application in the light of their own roles and mandates (Jackson et al., 2011). Schmid and Jongman (2005: 28) combined the most common elements of 109 major definitions to argue that:

> terrorism is an anxiety-inspiring method of repeated violent action, employed by (semi) clandestine individual, group or state actors, for idiosyncratic, criminal or political reasons, whereby – in contrast to assassinations – the direct targets of violence are not the main targets.

By accommodating the broadest range of common elements, this definition is not likely to attract universal acceptance but does highlight a number of key themes. The aim of violence is primarily about creating fear, rather than the destruction that is wrought or the lives that are lost. Thus, Jenkins (1975: 15) argued that 'terrorists want a lot of people watching and a lot of people listening and not a lot of people dead'. The victims of terrorism are 'message generators' and violence is a form of communication (Tuman, 2003; Schmid and Jongman, 2005: 28). Terrorism may be perpetrated by a well-organized group or by an individual 'lone wolf'. Most view terrorism as politically motivated, rather than economic and criminal, although most terrorist acts are illegal, or motivated by idiosyncratic reasons.

The diversity of definitions reflects not just subjective judgement but the diversity of terrorism itself. Laqueur (1999: 99) claims that there has been 'no "terrorism" per se, only different terrorisms'. Perhaps the most useful reminder of this diversity is the argument that we should focus on terror not terrorism. An 'ism' implies a relatively unified phenomenon and belief system (as in liberalism, realism, Marxism). Tilly (2004: 11–12) expressed this best with his claim that:

> Properly understood, terror is a strategy, not a creed. Terrorists range across a wide spectrum of organizations, circumstances and beliefs. Terrorism is not a single causally coherent phenomenon. No social scientist can speak responsibly as though it were.

Terrorism, then, is a type of act, not a type of actor, and not a political cause. This is more intellectually appealing in many ways. First, it mitigates the pejorative implications of labelling, since it is more commonly acceptable to consider particular violent means as potentially justifiable or inherently illegitimate than to apply such judgements to a particular actor and thereby all their actions. Coady (2004) argues that terrorism should be defined as a tactic of violence against 'innocents' (noncombatants) or their property, rather than any anti-state violence. Second, there are political implications of actor-based definitions that should not be replicated. The designation of the African National Congress (ANC) in South Africa as a terrorist organization, for example, was not shared by many anti-apartheid protestors. Third, the question of definition always raises the question of who gets to define terrorism. Much academic work on terrorism implicitly takes the position of dominant states and so functions as a problem-solving discourse that simply accepts the discourse of the state and seeks to find a new solution or identify a new trend or element, such that it is 'counter-insurgency masquerading as political science' (Schmid and Jongman, 2005: 182).

An action-based approach conflicts with much terrorism discourse that views terrorist violence as inherently amoral. For Wilkinson (1974: 17), what distinguishes terrorism from other violence is its 'amorality' through which terrorists are 'implicitly prepared to sacrifice all moral and humanitarian considerations for the sake of some political end'. Others emphasize the passions and dogmatism of terrorists: 'Every terrorist is driven by burning impatience coupled with an unswerving belief in the potency of violence' (Griset and Mahon, 2003: 191). These are subjective judgements and pejorative statements, not descriptions of acts or actors. It is presumptuous to speak for the motives and beliefs of 'every terrorist'. Certainly, some people using terrorism may fit this profile, but others do not; they may operate on different ethics than those held by Western liberal scholars, but that does not imply either amorality or that terrorists simply think that the political ends justify all violent means. Further, much counterterrorism invokes a similar consequentialist ethics (the ends justify the means) in combination with inchoate elements of communitarian ethics and just war theory, rendering a black and white distinction between the amoral terrorist and the moral counterterrorist deeply problematic. The assertion that terrorist violence is driven by passion and counterterrorism by rationality also creates a false distinction that is increasingly articulated around religious terrorism.

However, there are still problems with some tactical or strategic approaches to defining terrorism. First, it is possible to define terrorism as a tactic and assume that only non-state actors use it. Arguing that terrorism is a weapon of the weak, Hoffman (2006: 22) claims that:

> Cast perpetually on the defensive and forced to take up arms to protect themselves and their real or imagined constituents only, terrorists perceive

themselves as reluctant warriors, driven by desperation – and lacking any viable alternative – to violence against a repressive state, a predatory rival ethnic or nationalist group, or an unresponsive international order.

Second, tactics and strategy are the products of rational choice. This implies that the choice of terrorism is viewed as potentially successful. Certainly, there is some evidence that it can be successful, from the FLN (National Liberation Front) attacks that led to French withdrawal from Algeria, or the Zionist attacks on British rule that contributed to the formation of the Israeli state. But more than 90 per cent of terrorism does not achieve its full political aims (Cronin, 2008). However, perhaps it is not the prospects of success but the perception that success is possible that can make terrorism a rational strategy. Even suicide bombing can be explained through a rational choice perspective, since while it may be irrational at an individual level, it can be cost-effective and rational at the group level (see below). While countering a problematic tendency in the media and some governments to dismiss terrorism as irrational fanaticism, there are dangers in applying rational choice models to any forms of violence, since this leads to a neglect of many contextual, social, psychological and emotional aspects of action. For instance, critical scholars of terrorism note a profound lack of historical analysis of the development and conduct of terrorism (Gunning, 2007). Indeed, this lack of historical analysis and assertion of rationality tends to assume that 'people are essentially alike' (Ilardi, 2004: 218) and that the interests of states and terrorists are broadly fixed, and thus engages in reductionist analysis (Ilardi, 2004; Gunning, 2007). In recent years, a new approach to understanding terrorism has developed in the form of critical terrorism studies (CTS). This builds on Welsh School CSS (see Chapter 3) and is critical of the positivist epistemologies, objectivist ontologies, and conservative, problem-solving, political agendas of 'orthodox' terrorism studies. Most CTS scholars emphasize the historical and discursive construction of terrorism, and condemn all acts of terror whoever the perpetrator, instead seeking emancipatory approaches to tackling terrorism (Gunning, 2007; Breen Smyth et al., 2008; Jackson et al., 2011).

State terrorism

Viewing terror as an action rather than a type of actor calls into question the dominant habit of most governments and scholars of portraying terrorism as an action undertaken by non-state actors (Norris et al., 2003; McDonald, 2009). If terrorism is a tactic or strategy of violence, then much of the violence perpetrated by non-state actors is not terrorism. Conversely, much of the violence conducted by states may be considered terrorism, even when it is conducted in the name of counterterrorism. While this resonates strongly in CTS, orthodox terrorism scholars, like Wilkinson (2011: 10), have also argued that 'the tendency of modern governments to apply the terms terror and terrorism exclusively to sub-state groups is blatantly dishonest and self-serving'.

Even if states are not defined out of the scope of the phenomenon, they are fairly thoroughly neglected. While many are comfortable in describing the actions of Hitler's Germany or Stalin's Russia as terrorist, such terms are not generally applied to democratic regimes. Indeed, Wilkinson (2011) viewed much of the current problem as a contest between terrorism and democracy. CTS has sought to 'bring the state back in' to terrorism studies by highlighting the extent and significance of state terrorism (Blakeley, 2007, 2009; Jackson et al., 2009b). State terrorism has a long history that is considerably bloodier than the non-state equivalent. It includes the use of assassination, extrajudicial killing and disappearances that were common in the Latin American Dirty Wars in the 1970s and 80s and used more recently in Sri Lanka (Menjivar and Rodriguez, 2005; Wright, 2007). It also includes the use of torture, wider political repression and even genocide. Such actions may be undertaken directly by the state or through government-supported, non-state 'death squads', vigilantes and militia.

There are some objections to calling repressive violence by the state 'terrorism'. In Weberian understandings, the state has the right to use violence domestically and, in certain conditions, internationally (see Chapter 4). This implies that the state use of violence is of a different legal status to that used by non-state actors. However, this does not imply that state violence is always legitimate: violent political repression, human rights abuses, torture, forced disappearances, or genocide and certain forms of violence in war (such as the targeting of civilians, or blanket bombing) are not deemed legitimate internationally. Some argue that CTS's highlighting of state terror entails a crass relativism, in which 'we are all terrorists now' (Jones and Smith, 2009). However, this is not a point accepted by CTS or by Wilkinson. Jackson (2007: 18) argues that 'CTS is not an anti-state or anti-Western project, a discourse of complacency or an appeasement of tyranny', but simply 'views civilian-directed forms of violence as inherently illegitimate, regardless of what type of actor commits them, in what context or to what purpose'. Likewise, Wilkinson (1981: 468) argued that 'the only consistent moral position for a liberal democrat must be unequivocal opposition to both the terror of regimes and terrorism by faction'.

Perhaps more compelling is the argument that many forms of state violence already have other names (genocide, repression) that do not have positive ethical and legal connotations and so there is little need to apply the concept of terrorism to states. However, to argue that states may use terrorism is not to argue that all state use of violence is terroristic. Further, this objection downplays the political and normative roles of labelling. For Jackson (2005, 2008), echoing wider constructivist and critical theory, language is more than representative of reality, it is also constitutive of how we understand something. Thus, to insulate state violence from this terminology serves to legitimate much violence done to maintain a particular status quo of liberal international order, or the interests of major powers, while delegitimizing the counter-hegemonic use of violence (Jackson, 2008; Jackson et al., 2011).

Terrorism is more than illegitimate violence. Some argue that state violence is qualitatively different to non-state violence because states use violence in order to preserve a particular order, and non-state actors use it to challenge that order (Hoffman, 2006). Of course, state terrorism does not conform to Hoffman's argument that terrorism is a weapon of the weak. However, this is not a common defining feature of terrorism, even if it is a common assumption in many understandings. Further, some of the greatest state terrorism has been used in pursuit of revolutionary goals, from the Terror after the French Revolution, to Stalin in Russia and the Khmer Rouge in Cambodia (Jackson et al., 2011). Beyond this, if terrorism is a tactic or strategy of violence intended to engender fear among those who are not the direct targets of violence, then the extensive use of torture and violence by European states in their colonies can be considered state terrorism.

State terrorism differs from non-state terrorism in form and extent. State terrorism has been more lethal, not least because it is undertaken from a position of legal, bureaucratic and military superiority. On lethality, for instance, even a conservative estimate of state violence against their own populations would give a figure in the millions of deaths (particularly if one considers genocide a form of state terrorism) compared with tens of thousands produced by non-state terrorism. Indeed, recent estimates of the number of deaths caused by non-state terrorism indicate figures in the hundreds each year, with the obvious exception of the almost 3,000 killed in the USA in 2001 (Lutz and Lutz, 2008: 44). Further, the fear generated by state terrorism is more lasting and pervasive than non-state terrorists have achieved. From Stalinist Russia to Chile under Pinochet or Cambodia under Pol Pot, a situation of fear existed pervasively since no one could ever know they were safe from violence, imprisonment or disappearance (Rapin, 2009; Jackson et al., 2011).

State sponsorship of terrorism

States also sponsor terrorist groups by providing essential financing, training, materials and logistical support. Historically, major terrorist organizations have received some form of state support at some stage. Sponsoring terrorism is a cheap form of strategic action since the financial, political and human costs of providing training and weapons to terrorists are lower than engaging in war or intervention. Byman (2005) argues that states sponsor terrorism for strategic reasons, with ideological affinity being a common but not sufficient motive. Such strategic goals have included the overthrow of a rival regime or undermining stability in a rival state. This has frequently become a reciprocal relationship between neighbours: Sudan and Uganda hosted and equipped rebels in each other's conflicts; in the 1980s, Iraq supported the Mujahedin-e-Khalq in Iran (in spite of ideological differences since they were a Marxist group) and Iran supported Shia groups in Iraq and elsewhere. Sponsorship is also a means of projecting power beyond the reach of states' conventional military power, such as Libyan support for the Provisional IRA in Northern Ireland, or Iranian support for attacks on Iraqis in Europe. While often condemned in the West, international prestige has been a secondary motivation in many cases, such as Arab states' support for Palestinian groups, which is seen as a means of enhancing their credentials as regional leaders (Byman, 2005).

The US State Department has an official list of state sponsors of terrorism, which includes a small number of states that have been on the list for a long time:

- Cuba (since 1982) for providing safe haven to members of ETA (Euskadi Ta Askatasuna/Basque Homeland and Freedom) from Spain, and FARC (Fuerzas Armadas Revolucionarias de Colombia/Revolutionary Armed Forces of Colombia) and ELN (Ejército de Liberación Nacional/National Liberation Army) from Colombia
- Iran (since 1984) is deemed the 'most active state sponsor of terrorism' and has provided finances, weapons and logistics to groups in the Middle East (particularly Hizbullah) and Central Asia (the Taliban)
- Sudan (since 1993) for hosting al-Qaeda, Palestinian Islamic Jihad and Hamas at various times
- Syria (since 1979) for hosting Iraqi insurgents and cooperating with Iran to sponsor Hizbullah.

Iraq, Libya and North Korea have all been on the list in the past. This is neither an objective nor comprehensive list. Cuba, for instance, is on the list partly because it has criticized US counterterrorism and has harboured criminals wanted in the USA, although the USA has hosted Cuban dissidents too. Others are on the list due to weakness as much as intentional strategic action. Sudan is included in spite of being a strong partner in US counterterrorism efforts in Africa, and Syria is highlighted for having a financial sector that is vulnerable to terrorist financing as it is largely cash based and often uses informal banking services. Further, while the list runs the gamut of 'rogue' and 'failed' states, there is also a long history of Western states supporting insurgent groups that some governments see as terrorists. Covert US support for the contras in Nicaragua, the mujahideen in Afghanistan and UNITA in Angola during the 1980s was substantial, indeed, probably larger than that provided by Iran to terrorist groups in recent years. More recently, while not designated terrorists, Western states have sent arms and provided military support to rebel forces in Libya, Syria and others.

Responses to state sponsorship have taken many forms. Official US designation of being a state sponsor of terrorism leads to a ban on US arms exports, added scrutiny for dual-use goods exports, prohibitions on economic assistance and opposition to World Bank loans. Sanctions are also often used, although some studies suggest they are ineffective, with a 17 per cent success rate for unilateral sanctions and slightly greater success for multilateral sanctions (Byman, 2005). However, this ineffectiveness may be due to poor design rather than sanctions being inappropriate to the task (O'Sullivan, 2003). The use of force is increasingly common, particularly following scepticism about economic sanctions. The invasion of Afghanistan is the most obvious example here but it is also notable that Syria reduced its support for the PKK (Kurdistan Workers Party) in Turkey after it prompted rising interstate tensions between the two states and a threat of invasion. In some cases, a combination of strategies has proved effective. In 1986, the USA applied unilateral economic sanctions on Libya combined with some air strikes on terrorist training camps. This preceded a decline in the number of Libyan supported terrorist attacks, although their lethality remained high and had a higher proportion of American deaths. In 1992, the UN applied sanctions on Libya in response to its sponsorship of aircraft bombings in 1988 and 1989. These multilateral sanctions preceded an overall decline in Libyan support for terrorism and insurgency (S.D. Collins, 2004).

Such measures seek to alter the cost–benefit calculus of sponsorship and so are not well suited to many dimensions of state sponsorship. First, the growing phenomenon of 'passive sponsorship' (support by deliberate inaction) enables terrorists to operate within a state's territory, such as turning a blind eye to al-Qaeda financing operations in Sudan, or the funds and arms collected in the USA by the Provisional IRA (Byman, 2005, 2008). Passive sponsorship involves varying degrees of complicity by the government and the ruling elite, and often carries far lower political costs internationally (Pillar, 2003; Byman, 2005). While no state openly supports al-Qaeda, the limited and inconsistent actions against it by Pakistan, Saudi Arabia and Yemen are all viewed as passive sponsorship. Second, many weak states lack the capacity to effectively combat terrorist organizations based in their territory. For Byman (2005), this makes them victims rather than sponsors of terrorism, but the basic phenomenon is similar: terrorists operate with relative impunity and establish safe havens. Third, much sponsorship is not centrally organized and approved by the state, but conducted by semi-autonomous state agencies, such as intelligence organizations. For instance, the Pakistani Inter-Services Intelligence is believed to have some independent links with jihadists (Byman, 2008). Iranian support for terrorist organizations is largely run by the Iranian Revolutionary Guard's external operations branch, the Qods Force. Likewise, the CIA's support for the contras and the mujahideen was organized fairly autonomously and sometimes illegally. Finally, if states can be terrorists, then sponsorship from other states may also be important. For example, within the logic of the war on terror, the USA increased military aid including arms transfers to key partners such as Pakistan, Indonesia and the Philippines that had been key allies in the Cold War, but were then subjected to restrictions on the basis of human rights and nuclear proliferation concerns in the post-Cold War era. Further, under the rubric of the 'war on drugs', the US government has supported the Colombian government in its conflict with FARC, including its tacit and sometimes active support for rightwing paramilitaries (Stokes, 2005).

Fortunately, state sponsorship is said to be declining in scope and significance. The end of the Cold War, the rising use of sanctions and the wider context of the war on terror has reduced the number of states with the strategic interest in supporting terrorism. However, much of this decline has also been viewed as a negative sign: terrorism is changing and, in general, requires less state support to gain access to money, weapons and safe havens (Tucker, 2001).

Trends in terrorism

In the 1990s, some scholars began speaking of a 'new terrorism' on the basis of perceived trends that amplify the terrorist threat (Laqueur, 1996, 1999; Carter et al., 1998; Lesser et al., 1999; Hoffman, 2006). These trends relate to how and where terrorists are organized, supposedly becoming more networked and transnational and so harder to combat; the primary motives for terrorism, becoming more religiously motivated; and changing tactics towards a greater propensity for mass destruction. For each trend, al-Qaeda has become the emblematic threat, and so they have become important assumptions in the global politics and practice of counterterrorism. However, these trends are all questionable in terms of their extent and novelty. Most terrorism remains domestic rather than transnational, is focused on territorial and political issues not religious goals or motives, and uses conventional tactics that aim to produce spectacle and fear not mass destruction (Duyvesteyn, 2004). So, these trends may reflect a change in the fear of terrorism, but not its basic nature (Guelke, 2008).

Towards transnational terror networks

Terrorist organizations are said to have become more dangerous because they are harder to combat, or even identify. Much like legitimate businesses, they have adapted to the advantages of new information technologies, enhanced international mobility and other globalizing trends by adopting networked forms of organization, which contrast with the earlier hierarchical models that still characterize states (Sageman, 2004; Hoffman, 2006). While hierarchies have clear leaderships and functionally differentiated structures that are vertically integrated, networks are horizontally integrated, 'flat' structures that lack the need for direct control and even leadership and operate through communication and coordination of more or less autonomous actors. Numerous organizational models can be considered networks, ranging from a hub-and-spoke model to 'all-connection' networks, in which all members are linked to all others but there is no clear hierarchy or authority structure (Lesser et al., 1999; Arquilla and Ronfeldt, 2001). In networks, decision making, such as planning or executing an attack, is dispersed rather than concentrated.

Networks have a number of advantages. They are a flexible structure that enables rapid adaptation due to the relative autonomy of small groups and the limited bureaucracy of decision making (Jackson, 2006; Kenney, 2007a; Eilstrup-Sangiovanni and Jones, 2008). Networks are resilient to disruption; since there is no central point, no single leader, killing or capturing powerful leaders may not undermine the network the way it can in hierarchies. In some cases, terrorist groups are characterized as 'leaderless networks' that operate more as an ideology motivating and guiding the action of autonomous terrorists rather than directly controlling them. These are particularly difficult to infiltrate effectively, since one 'terrorist' cannot lead law enforcement to many others. The Earth Liberation Front is said to operate in this way, and it is claimed al-Qaeda does too (Hoffman, 2006). While some networks may be 'leaderless', others are hybrids of networks and hierarchies, with multiple forms of leadership dispersed around a 'hydra-headed' network (Lesser et al., 1999).

There are several important points to note about networks. First, terrorist networks are not new; 19th-century anarchist groups were organized as loose networks, often with strong transnational dimensions (Bergesen and Lizardo, 2004; Jensen, 2008). Many traditional terrorist groups, like the Provisional IRA in Northern Ireland, had a structure of semi-autonomous cells. Second, many terrorist groups are not networks. Hizbullah is hierarchically organized (Ranstorp, 1994), as are many if not most rightwing, leftwing and nationalist terrorist groups. Third, and perhaps most importantly, while networks have some advantages, they also have limitations. They may be less durable since, for example, 'all-connection' networks require a lot of dense communication that is hard to sustain over the long term even in an age of instant virtual communication (Lesser et al., 1999). Further, the lack of centralized command authority enables affiliates to engage in activities that were previously off limits and restrained by leadership, such as forming alliances with criminal groups (Dishman, 2005). While networks are said to expand easily, in practice the relationships that sustain them are often based on familial, ethnic or religious ties that enhance trust but limit recruitment and scale. Also, networks run on communication, but the more dispersed the network, the harder efficient and secure communication becomes. A lack of central organization and a compartmentalized structure also inhibits effective organizational learning and adaptation that are supposed advantages of network forms (Kenney, 2007a). Finally, while network structures inhibit disruption by states, the lack of

- Don't think above is that relevent.
- Just note that networks are increasingly seen, not hierarchical structures.

clear leadership may make them more likely to fragment when attacked and to engage in excessive risk taking (Eilstrup-Sangiovanni and Jones, 2008).

It would be a mistake to view the adoption of network structures as a choice made on the basis of these abstract advantages and disadvantages. It may be a response to government action disrupting hierarchies rather than inspired by the opportunities of globalization (Pillar, 2004). Before 2001, al-Qaeda was organized more centrally than today. Although never fully hierarchical, a core group close to Osama bin Laden were the main planners of attacks, and groups in different countries cooperated with that central group and were provided with finance and technical assistance. This varied, of course; the 1993 attack on the World Trade Center received technical and financial support, but more direct involvement was seen in the 9/11 attacks and the attacks on the US embassies in East Africa in 1998. Since 2002, al-Qaeda has been compelled to adopt a progressively looser structure, making it unable to mount an attack on a similar scale and at a similar distance to the 9/11 attacks. Indeed, what Sageman (2008) has called 'leaderless jihad' has evolved with a 'third wave' of jihad, in which the foreign professionals and highly educated radicals of earlier years are replaced by amateurs and home-grown terrorists. The extent of this transformation is debated, with many noting continued elements of hierarchy (Gunaratna, 2002; Hoffman, 2008), and others arguing that al-Qaeda has never been a network in the traditional sense of the word, but is more of an ideology (Burke, 2004). Since the status and strength of al-Qaeda is much debated, it is unsurprising that the implications of the death of Osama bin Laden in 2011 and other key figures are as yet unclear.

Partly due to network structures, terrorism is also viewed as becoming more transnational, with organizations based and operating in multiple countries (Heupel, 2007). In the early 1990s, a decline in Soviet sponsorship of terrorist organizations and a strengthening of Western governments' counterterrorism produced a decline in transnational terrorism (Enders and Sandler, 1999). The post 9/11 focus on al-Qaeda, and networked terror more widely, has seen a resurgence of interest in the transnational aspects of terrorism. It has long been the case that terrorist organizations can be based in one country but attack in another. Black September's abduction of Israeli athletes during the 1972 Munich Olympics, Hizbullah's suicide bombing of the US Marine barracks in Beirut in 1983, attacks on airliners such as that by Hindu extremists on Air India flight 182 in 1985, or the attack on Pan Am flight 103 in 1988, as well as al-Qaeda's truck bombing of the World Trade Center in 1993, and the near-simultaneous hijackings of four passenger airliners on 11 September 2001 all had strong transnational dimensions. However, much of the global war on terrorism has focused on key transnational aspects of terrorism by seeking to counter terrorism where it is based (for example Afghanistan).

Weak and failing states are often assumed to be safe havens in which terrorists can base themselves, train and organize attacks (Piazza, 2008). Here, terrorist networks are portrayed as geographically flexible and assumed to choose their global location on the basis of searching out the impunity state weakness offers (Brafman Kittner, 2007; Elden, 2007; Howard, 2010). Certainly, the presence of al-Qaeda in some weak and failing states seems to support this, as does the widening presence of jihadist networks from North Africa to West Africa and beyond (Howard, 2010). However, the correlation between weak and failing states and terrorism is not actually very strong. First, the correlation conflates the violence that arises in weak states from local insurgent groups with transnational terrorists choosing their location. Second, prominent al-Qaeda-related attacks, such as the bombings in London and Madrid, and the 9/11 attacks were not organized in weak and failing states, but within the target countries and other parts of Europe (Patrick, 2006; Newman, 2007). When al-Qaeda has been based in weak states like Sudan and Afghanistan, it was government support as much as weakness that facilitated this, and it moved from the first to the second in 1996 when the Sudanese government came under international pressure to expel it (as well as having strategic reasons for shifting its focus from the 'near enemy' in the Middle East to the 'far enemy' of the USA). Third, terrorists need more than anarchy and the impunity it provides, they also rely on a degree of order and infrastructure. For instance, al-Qaeda moved to Somalia in 1993 after it was unable to operate in Saudi Arabia. While it anticipated easy recruitment and impunity due to the absence of government, clan-based groups and criminality in Somalia meant that it achieved neither. Indeed, local security situations in weak and failed states have limited al-Qaeda activities to the extent that no major al-Qaeda attacks have been organized from Afghanistan, Iraq and Somalia since US military operations began (Menkhaus and Shapiro, 2010).

Contemporary transnational violence is attributed to globalization shifting the distribution of violence and power towards non-state actors (Davis, 2009). However, transnational violence has historically been closely related to processes of state formation and the consolidation of state power (Thomson, 1994; Löwenheim, 2007). In some cases, state terrorism has functioned through informal transnational networks between state agencies rather than formal interstate political processes. In Latin America's Dirty Wars in the 1970s and 80s, Operation Condor was a form of semi-official coordination and cooperation among the rightwing military governments of Argentina, Chile, Uruguay, Paraguay, Bolivia and Brazil, and later Ecuador and Peru, with the knowledge and some facilitation of the US government. State agents shared intelligence and military and paramilitary forces hunted down other states' dissidents and even conducted assassinations in a sustained campaign of state terrorism. Tens of thousands of men, women and children are believed to have perished in the operation of this parastatal network that extended beyond Latin America and into the USA and Europe (McSherry, 2005). More recently, Blakeley (2009) has characterized the conduct of 'extraordinary rendition' by the USA and its allies in similar terms, as European allies cooperated, or turned a blind eye, to the kidnapping of terror suspects and their rendition to countries where torture could be used against them. This has also been argued to contribute to an erosion of the international norm against the use of torture (McKeown, 2009).

Terrorists motives

It is common to use four categories of terrorism: leftwing, rightwing, ethnonationalist/separatist, and religious/sacred (Cronin, 2002/03; Lutz and Lutz, 2008). Religiously identified or motivated terrorist groups are seen as growing in relative importance since the 1990s. Leftwing groups, such as the Red Brigades in Italy and the Red Army Faction in West Germany (1970s and 80s), or Naxalite groups in India (ongoing), and rightwing groups, such as neo-Nazi groups in Europe or the Ku Klux Klan in the USA, were the prominent form of terrorism in earlier periods. Ethnonationalist and separatist groups, from anticolonial movements in the 1960s to Republican terrorist groups in Northern Ireland (the Provisional IRA and now dissident republican groups), and Basque separatists (ETA) in Spain, seek a territorial political goal related to a particular ethnic or other social grouping. Cronin argues that most leftwing groups in Western Europe were brutal but relatively ephemeral, and most rightwing groups have been less cohesive than those on the left. Others note that ethnonationalist groups tend to be longer lasting, with most terrorist groups that last more than a decade falling into this category (Crenshaw, 1991).

From the Zealots in the Roman Empire to the Thugees in India, religious motives and inspiration have been a prominent form of identity and driver of political violence (Rapoport, 1984). While leftwing and rightwing terrorists and ethnonationalist terrorists have broadly secular motivations, many argue that religious terrorism is again growing in significance (Hoffman, 1993, 1995; Laqueur, 1996, 1999; Jurgensmeyer, 2000; Cronin, 2002/03; Ramakrishna and Tan, 2002). According to Gurr and Cole (2000), in the 1980s, only 2 out of 64 terrorist organizations could be identified as religious, a figure that increases to 25 out of 58 by 1995. For some, this shift means that 'new' terrorists have radically different values, morals and worldviews (Hoffman 2006). Indeed, Hoffman (1995) argues that religious terrorism is more lethal, accounting for 60 per cent of deaths but only 25 per cent of attacks.

There are many reasons to be sceptical about this claim and its implications. First, while some aspects of the identity and aims of terrorist groups may be couched in religious terms, the political goals of many terrorists remain related to particular forms of governance, territory, or other more familiar political issues (as can be seen among most al-Qaeda affiliated groups such as those in North Africa and the Maghreb). Second, many groups and individual terrorists have multiple dimensions of identity and it is difficult to reliably isolate whether the political or the religious predominates (Quillen, 2002). Those members of al-Qaeda who perpetrated the 9/11 attacks were not particularly religious when they were radicalized and many al-Qaeda jihadists seem to have moved into radical groups out of personal conditions of loneliness and alienation, combined with political causes as well as religious motivations (Holmes, 2005; Sageman, 2006). Finally, this is not unique to terrorism and some observers claim it is linked to a wider growth of religion in politics that is sometimes a resistance to globalization but also often inherent in late modernity and processes of globalization (Neumann, 2009).

Current fears of 'religious terrorism' may say more about our understandings of security than the motives of terrorists. Much of the tenor and assumptions of this fear reflect a European post-Enlightenment notion of religion as inherently irrational and private (Toros and Gunning, 2009). Here, it is not just the prospect of violence that is deemed threatening but the demand for a politics different from that divested of religion in the purportedly neutral secular space of modern politics. Many terrorist groups espousing a religious view tend not to accept the secular Western view that politics and religion are separate (public and private) spheres. This is more disruptive of understandings of security as relating to a politics in which the development of the state rationalized and secularized violence (see Chapter 4). However, this does not mean that the growth of 'religious' terrorism is less rational and so less understandable. First, it is clearly a nonsense to argue that religion is inherently more violent than secular ideology, when most 20th-century terrorism and most major wars of the past few centuries have drawn on secular ideologies. Second, this has important political effects: portraying religious terrorism as 'irrational', or even just differently rational, enables the counterterrorism discourse to assert the impossibility of some strategies (negotiation or deterrence for example) and to legitimate more aggressive and militarized strategies against an enemy that cannot be understood. It also enhances the false sense that terrorists are radically different to states; since states may be driven by fear that results from strategic uncertainty about other states, but terrorists are deemed to be driven by hatred rather than fear of the state.

Tactics of terror

Most terrorist attacks use conventional weapons (Lutz and Lutz, 2008). Explosives are particularly common, because they are cheap and relatively easily procured. Approximately half of all terrorist attacks involve bombs of some kind (Sandler and Enders, 2004). Indeed, the most deadly terrorist attacks have used conventional weapons, or in the case of 9/11, innovative tactics such as the use of aeroplanes as weapons (Griset and Mahan, 2003).

There is some evidence that terrorist attacks are becoming less frequent but more lethal. However, contrary to some claims, this does not derive from apocalyptic religious logics but is a wider trend actually associated with nationalist terrorism (Masters, 2008). Trends in terrorist tactics reveal the combination of logics of rationality and risk in contemporary understandings of security.

CBRN terrorism: weapons of mass destruction

The growing lethality of terrorist incidents raises the spectre of mass casualty terrorism. While mass casualties were produced by aeroplanes and bombs in the most lethal terrorist attacks, greater fear arises about terrorist use of chemical, biological, radiological or nuclear (CBRN) weapons. The founding document of the US Department of Homeland Security (2002: 8) stated that: 'Today's terrorists can strike at any place, at any time, and with virtually any weapon.' While the omnipresence of terrorist threat is questionable (Mueller, 2006), the accessibility of 'virtually any weapon' has become an operational certainty in the politics of counterterrorism. This is couched in terms of risk that asserts a low probability of attack, each year, but an eventual certainty that CBRN weapons will be used. Indeed, the US government Commission on the Prevention of Weapons of Mass Destruction Proliferation and Terrorism claimed in 2008 that: 'It is more likely than not that a weapon of mass destruction will be used in a terrorist attack somewhere in the world by the end of 2013' (Graham et al., 2008: xv). In particular, nuclear terrorism is repeatedly identified as the 'single biggest threat' to US security (Spillius, 2010).

While terrorism has been referred to as 'the politics of uncertainty' (Ericson, 2007: 36), the precautionary principle inherent in many Western approaches to risk is what lies behind the relative certainties attached to the threat of CBRN terrorism. The probabilities of nuclear terrorism are incalculable, but some academics have used abstract mathematical models to posit a 3% chance per year of nuclear terrorist attack (meaning 30% over 10 years) (Bunn, 2006). As Jenkins (1999: x) points out:

> The analysis of 'dream threats' is filled with pitfalls. It is easy to begin by identifying vulnerability ... positing theoretical adversaries ... then reifying the threat – a subtle shift of verbs from could to may happen. 'Could' means theoretically possible while 'may' suggests more.

This creates a danger that speculation becomes the basis of political action. Indeed, this is a defining feature of the 'risk' paradigm (see Chapter 5), in which uncertain futures are acted on in the present, even in the absence of clear evidence of a contemporary threat. In November 2001, when he was the US vice president, Dick Cheney argued that if there is a 1% chance of Pakistani scientists helping al-Qaeda to build a nuclear weapon, this small chance has to be treated as 'a certainty in terms of our response ... It's not about our analysis, or finding a preponderance of evidence, it's about our response' (quoted in Suskind, 2007: 62).

To date, there has been only one successful use of CBRN weapons by an organized terrorist group. On 20 March 1995, Aum Shinrikyo, the Japanese apocalyptic cult, released sarin nerve gas on the Tokyo subway. Attacking at rush hour, this attack killed only 12 people, although it resulted in many thousands of injuries. Added to this attack are some cases of terrorist organizations attempting to acquire CBRN-related technologies or materials, the use of chlorine bombs in Iraq, and some attacks by 'lone-wolf' terrorists such as the anthrax letters in the USA in 2001. However, terrorist use of CBRN agents is less deadly than conventional explosive attacks, and 90 per cent of incidents resulted in no fatalities (Rapoport, 1999; Ivanova and Sandler, 2006).

Traditionally, it was assumed that since terrorists seek spectacle, mass slaughter would be counterproductive as it would alienate their support base (Jenkins, 1975). Since 9/11, this assumption has been reversed in political and theoretical discussion. Some posit that religious motives shift the rationality of violence towards mass destruction, since religion tends to view the world in terms of good and evil that dehumanizes opponents and legitimates indiscriminate violence (Hoffman, 1993, 2006; Laqueur, 1996; Jurgensmeyer, 2000; Cronin, 2002/03). While secular terrorism is viewed as engaging in strategically limited violence proportionate to its political purposes, which also leaves open opportunities for political dialogue, religious terrorists freed from the need for state sponsorship are understood as lacking proportionality (Guelke, 1998; Smith and Benjamin, 2000; Tucker, 2001). For instance, al-Qaeda is believed to have pursued various CBRN capacities, especially nuclear weapons, even before the 9/11 attacks. In 1998, Osama bin Laden declared that 'acquiring WMD for the defense of Muslims is a religious duty' (quoted in Mowatt-Larssen, 2010: 2). However, such claims are selective in their evidence: while al-Qaeda in Iraq used chlorine as a chemical weapon (although only the conventional explosives used caused deaths), shortly before his death, bin Laden expressed concern about possible Yemeni terrorist use of chemical weapons, and warned them to be 'careful of doing it without enough study of all aspects, including political and media reaction' (Bergen, 2013).

Since it is assumed that terrorists now have few inhibitions in using CBRN weapons, debate focuses on technical feasibility (Stern, 1999; Perry, 2001). In relation to nuclear weapons, the debate is frequently polarized, with critics arguing that the threat is overblown alarmism (Frost, 2005; Mueller, 2006) and others labelling those critics as 'complacent' (Pluta and Zimmerman, 2006). Those who argue that nuclear terrorism is possible, even a near certainty, highlight the loose controls on stocks of weapons-usable fissile materials (HEU and plutonium) in many countries, particularly those of the former Soviet Union (Ferguson et al., 2005). They point to numerous cases of smuggling of nuclear materials, including this most powerful type, although the empirical record shows that all HEU and plutonium seized from traffickers would be insufficient for even a basic weapon. Further, the designs of crude nuclear weapons are widely available in unclassified documents (Allison, 2006; Bunn and Wier, 2006). Unemployed nuclear scientists may also offer their services. Of particular concern, however, is the prospect of state sponsorship – giving a nuclear weapon or related technologies and materials to a terrorist group. This prospect is debatable and many argue that it is unlikely that states would give nuclear weapons to unreliable terrorists, especially since technological improvements in forensic science enable detection and thus deterrence (Levi, 2008). Perhaps more concerning is the risk that a terrorist group, or organized criminal group, might steal a complete nuclear weapon from a state. Here, the weak security on nuclear weapons stockpiles in several countries is cause for concern, although there has been significant investment in tackling this since the end of the Cold War. Considerable international cooperation has been fostered to tackle these issues, partly by amending and extending traditional arms control frameworks (see Chapter 8).

Importantly, while the different aspects of building a nuclear weapon may be available to terrorists, such as fissile material, technological know-how and so on, each carries risks of detection and combining all these elements amplifies these risks – a plot needs to be clandestine to avoid detection but needs to reach out to other states and criminals to acquire the necessary components. To succeed, nuclear terrorism must succeed in every aspect of the process. For Levi (2007), this means that current policies that focus largely on securing fissile materials and seeking complete security may be misplaced. Instead, a multilayered response is better, in which each policy response alone may be imperfect but combines to produce a strong web of prevention.

Biological terrorism is often seen as more likely, due to cheaper and easier access to materials from laboratories and pharmaceutical companies, more widespread technical know-how, and smaller infrastructure for production (even in home laboratories). The biotechnology revolution also means that techniques for modifying and synthesizing biological agents have developed rapidly and become diffused (Chyba and Greninger, 2004; Kellman, 2007). Unlike nuclear terrorism, there is less debate on technical feasibility of some form of biological attack, since there is no reliable guide from experience as to what broad capabilities are required. For example, with over 40,000 members, 20 university-trained scientists, and up to $1 billion, Aum Shinrikyo failed to successfully develop effective biological weapons (Dolnik, 2007). In contrast, however, the anthrax letter attacks in the USA in 2001 that killed five were believed to have been conducted by a single perpetrator (Heyman, 2002).

Suicide terrorism: weapons of self-destruction

In addition to mass destruction, the supposed fanaticism of the new terrorism is reflected in concern over the growth of suicide terrorism. While suicide terrorism has a long history, it has been a resurgent tactic since the early 1980s, when it was used extensively in Lebanon. It has grown in use in the context of civil war and terrorism in Afghanistan, Chechnya, Iraq, Palestine/Israel, Sri Lanka, Turkey and, of course, the 9/11 attacks in the USA (Crenshaw, 2007). Atran (2006: 128) shows that the scale of suicide terrorism has increased significantly this century; averaging 4.7 attacks per year in the 1980s, 16 in the 1990s, and 180 per year in the first five years of this century. Some argue that this is linked to the rise of religiously motivated terrorism that legitimates suicide (Gambetta, 2005; Atran, 2006).

Suicide terrorism articulates a logic of sacrifice that is not wholly different from that present in state-based war and counterterrorism. Indeed, many scholars now argue that suicide terrorism is a wholly rational strategic form of violence (Crenshaw, 1981; Sprinzak, 2000; Pape, 2003). Pape argues that religion does not explain the rise in suicide terrorism: the leading user of suicide terrorism were the Tamil Tigers in Sri Lanka, a Marxist-Leninist organization articulating an ethnic claim to independence, not a religious identity or justification. Even among Islamic groups, a third of suicide attacks are from groups with secular orientations. Further, individual suicide terrorists are not, as early explanations thought, drawn from the ranks of poor, uneducated, unemployed teenagers and young men, but may also be socially integrated, college-educated men and women, ranging from 13 to their late 40s (Sprinzak, 2000). For Pape, suicide terrorism has a strategic rationale and its growth is explained by the fact that groups have learned from the experience of others that it works, at least if used moderately, since the experience of many terrorist organizations is that political concessions to their cause have been greater since the use of suicide terrorism began (Sprinzak, 2000; Pape, 2003). Others disagree with Pape's claims of success, but argue that part of the strategic rationale for using suicide terrorism is that it increases the 'market share' of the particular organization in popular support: it is part of their strategic competition with other political groups (Bloom, 2004).

Cyberterrorism: weapons of mass disruption

Many possible terrorist tactics, ranging from 'dirty bomb' radiological weapons, through attacks on critical infrastructures such as chemical plants, nuclear power stations, or transport systems, to the prospect of cyberterrorism, are sometimes referred to as 'weapons of mass disruption' (Levi and Kelly, 2002; Bunker, 2007). Such attacks may not cause high levels of casualties but are viewed as having substantial negative effects on the flow of daily life. Indeed, the view of critical infrastructure as a symbiotic network (see Chapter 4) means that states, like their terrorist adversaries, are networks composed of connections and vulnerabilities (Homer-Dixon, 2002). These networks of critical infrastructure increase the concern about cyber-attacks. While criminal cyber-attacks are increasingly common and prolific, most are small, disorganized and, at worst, disruptive. There is no evidence that lives have been lost as an intentional result of cyber-attacks. Rather, cyber-security is understood through the probabilistic technologies of risk and the assertion of vulnerabilities (Dunn Cavelty, 2007) (see Chapter 5).

Eric Schmidt, executive chairman of Google, described the internet as 'the largest experiment in anarchy that we have ever had' (CNET, 1997). The internet has grown from a limited government network established in the late 1960s, through military development in the 1970s and 80s, to privatization and dispersal of the technology in the 1990s. Some now assert a 'virtual battlespace', in which cyberterrorism and the prospect of an 'electronic Pearl Harbour' are articulated (Manjikian, 2010). Terrorist organizations have certainly used the internet for propaganda, recruitment and financing, with many thousands of terrorist organization and supporters websites (Weimann, 2006). To date, however, while there have been many terrorist attacks since the 1990s, and cyber-attacks are a daily phenomenon, these have not combined as cyberterrorist attacks in which the internet has been either the means or the target of an attack (Dunn Cavelty, 2007). This may be because cyber-weapons are not very appealing to terrorists as they do not create fear or spectacle or because national critical infrastructures are less vulnerable to cyber-attacks than is commonly thought (Lewis, 2004).

While cyberterrorism remains a future threat, politically motivated cyber-attacks have occurred. Some have been disorganized protest attacks, such as the 2007 attacks on Estonian political organizations in the wake of the removal of a Soviet war memorial statue (Wilson, 2008). However, it is states that have invested in the most sophisticated cyber-warfare capabilities, including China, North Korea, Russia and the USA. For instance, the USA attacked Iraqi computer networks at the start of the 2003 war, and considered similar attacks in the 1999 NATO intervention in Kosovo (Graham, 2010). The Chinese government is believed to engage in widespread cyber-espionage, and may have been the origin of the 2003–05 Titan Rain hacking incidents against US Pentagon computers, European governments, and defence companies. The most prominent political cyber-attack, however, was the Stuxnet worm incident in 2010. This worm was detected on Siemens computers that controlled enrichment centrifuges at Iran's Natanz nuclear fuel enrichment plant, and may have disrupted or even damaged its functioning (Farwell and Rohozinski, 2011). After much speculation, in June 2012 it was revealed that the worm was developed and deployed by the US government in collaboration with Israel.

Overall, for weapons of mass destruction and weapons of mass disruption, the contemporary record is of state use and the contemporary fears are of future terrorist use. There is no clear tactical divide between the methods of terrorism and the methods of war or counterterrorism, even in the form of suicide. Popular discourses portray (religious) irrationality and risk as characteristics of terror, but there is no uniquely terrorist tactic of political action absent from the actions of states, even in the field of counterterrorism.

Counterterrorism

Since terrorism is diverse and changing, there can be no one-size-fits-all approach to counterterrorism (Cronin, 2008). States have used varying approaches to counterterrorism, ranging from military strategies to policing approaches and attempts to tackle the underlying causes of terrorism. However, it is important to note that terrorism often ends as a result of factors inside the terrorist organization that cause it to fragment, collapse or cease violence (Crenshaw, 1991; Cronin, 2008, 2009). For instance, many leftwing and rightwing terrorist groups found it difficult to continue over generations, as decentralized network structures militate against their durability, and internal factional and ideological divisions often precipitate their effective demise (Cronin, 2008).

The fact that terrorism ends, however, does not mean that a 'war on terrorism' is winnable. The average lifespan of a terrorist group is 5–10 years, although there are examples of much longer lived organizations (Cronin, 2008). However, terrorism as a general phenomenon is persistent, and the ill-advised label 'war on terror' and the associated rhetoric of defeating all terrorism everywhere posits an unachievable aim. Like a war against war, a war on terror makes no sense if terror is a tactic. As English (2009: 120) states, there is as much a need to 'learn to live with it' and have realistic goals about particular terrorist campaigns and issues, as there is to come up with ever stronger counterterrorism strategies that can cost more money and lives than those they seek to defeat.

Approaches to counterterrorism

One common approach is to attempt to 'decapitate' a terrorist organization by arresting or killing its leaders. It is still too soon to tell what the long-term effect of the killing of Osama bin Laden will be on al-Qaeda. While decapitation has a mixed record, some argue that it can work, since terrorist groups often struggle with leadership succession (Price, 2012). Indeed, the capture of Abimael Guzman, the leader of Sendero Luminoso (the Shining Path), a Maoist group in Peru, precipitated a 50 per cent decline in violence, and in Japan, Aum Shinrikyo collapsed after the arrest and trial of its leader Shoko Asahara. Cronin argues that arresting rather than killing leaders tends to be more effective. Assassinations of terrorist leaders, a strategy pursued by Israel against several groups and by the Russian government against Chechen leaders, did not end those forms of terrorism. Treating leaders as criminals also has the advantage of denying the terrorist group political legitimacy and not creating martyrs or more recruits for terrorist organizations. In Turkey, the 1999 arrest of Abdullah Öcalan, the charismatic leader of the PKK, led to a decline in attacks and a five-year ceasefire, until wider regional events such as the 2003 Iraq War revitalized the hard-line faction within the PKK (Cronin, 2009).

Military strategies of counterterrorism have a mixed record. It has worked for limited reasons. The PKK were defeated militarily before the capture of Öcalan; Russian military intervention in Chechnya did a lot to reduce violence there; and after several decades of often brutal war and repression, the Sri Lankan government was victorious over the Tamil Tigers. In these and other cases, this involved extraordinary levels of violence that can be counterproductive, sometimes becoming prominent cases of state terrorism. Further, while military action may defeat a terrorist organization, it does not necessarily lay the foundations for a long-term peace (see Chapter 10). Of course, the converse is even more true: only about 6 per cent of terrorist groups have successfully achieved their main political goals, and where they have (such as the ANC in South Africa), this has been in spite of the use of terrorist tactics (Cronin, 2008).

Between military defeat and terrorist success lies one of the most controversial strategies – a negotiated settlement. Opponents of negotiating with terrorists often argue (with some validity) that engaging in negotiation legitimates terrorism as a political tool and the specific political aims of the group (Toros, 2008). This is always a risk, and the principle of not giving concessions or making deals with terrorists has been stated US policy for many years (Pillar, 2003). However, successful negotiated settlements have produced relatively strong peace, such as the secret negotiations with the Provisional IRA in Northern Ireland, and efforts to support a peace by the Irish and American governments, which underlay the successful negotiation of the Good Friday Agreement in 1998. Such negotiations work best, it seems, when the terrorists are already losing ground or are persuaded that formal democratic processes offer more political or economic benefits than continued violence. Negotiations do not, therefore, drive the demise of terrorism, but can facilitate it (Cronin, 2008). Further, much like wider peace agreements in civil wars, many attempts at negotiation end in failure, or in a ceasefire or agreement that does not hold for very long (see Chapter 10).

Each approach has a mixed record of success. It is also notable that many of the more effective measures for traditional terrorism are less effective, or at least less widely tried, for new terrorism. For example, one study found that while 43% of terrorist campaigns ended by the groups joining the mainstream political process, only 11% of religious terrorism ended this way. While only

10% of terrorism ended through military force, and 40% by police and intelligence agencies arresting or killing leaders, the superiority of policing was even more marked for religious terrorism, for which 16% ended by military force, and 73% through police and intelligence action or splintering from within (Jones and Libicki, 2008).

International cooperation on counterterrorism

Understanding terrorism as becoming increasingly transnational has meant that international cooperation is emphasized in contemporary counterterrorism. There has been extensive transatlantic cooperation in counterterrorism, particularly between the USA, the EU and EU member states. This has developed from ad-hoc bilateral arrangements towards stronger multilateral cooperation at the broad political level and in interagency cooperation (Rees, 2006). The USA has had significant influence in shaping European responses to terrorism in many areas (Kaunert et al., 2012). Nevertheless, there have long been significant differences between US and European approaches, with the former tending towards more militarized approaches and the latter favouring a policing and intelligence approach.

At the regional level, the EU has a more developed strategy and greater coordination than other regions like Africa or Asia. Further, NATO has expanded its counterterrorism roles, in Afghanistan and beyond; and the collective defence provision of the NATO founding treaty was invoked for the first time on 12 September 2001. While regional approaches are important, global counterterrorism still relates to the power of individual states. The development of international counterterrorism has been argued to reflect and reinforce hegemonic relations in which the USA's approach to counterterrorism shapes the approaches of other states and organizations (Beyer, 2010). For instance, US approaches to detention and the handling of terror suspects have been exported to African countries (Qureshi, 2010). Likewise, in Europe, while cooperation has improved in the wake of bombings in Madrid in 2004 and London in 2005, transatlantic relations and bilateral relations among EU member states, and between some EU member states and key countries (like Pakistan) are all stronger than EU-level relations (Keohane, 2008b).

At the global level, the UN has significantly increased its role in counterterrorism since 2001. Before 2001, the UN General Assembly had produced 12 major conventions on particular types of terrorist activity, ranging from taking hostages, making plastic explosives, bombings, and terrorist financing. Before 9/11, only two states (the UK and Botswana) were a party to all these conventions (Ward, 2003). As with NATO's rapid political response, the UNSC passed a far-reaching resolution (UNSC Resolution 1373) within weeks of the 9/11 attacks, which required states to sign and ratify these other conventions. Now, most states are parties to each of these conventions, and further conventions have been added, such as two in 2010 concerned with civil aviation and the unlawful seizure of aircraft. This has since been strengthened further, particularly by extensive action on terrorist financing, and UNSC Resolution 1540 (2004), which aims to combat terrorism with CBRN weapons by criminalizing the supply of these technologies to non-state actors. As with its evolving wider roles (see Chapter 6), the UN's strategy on counterterrorism emphasizes partnerships with other organizations. But, in spite of some successes, UN attempts to develop a Comprehensive Convention Against International Terrorism, ongoing since before 2001, have continually faltered over the difficulties of definition.

Draining the swamp and the liberal peace

Much global counterterrorism currently seeks to 'drain the swamp' of potential recruits (Piazza, 2007). In doing so, it focuses on a particular set of medium- to long-term strategies influenced not only by the forms and threats of contemporary terrorism but also on the basis of assumptions found more widely in the liberal peace (see Chapter 10). This pertains particularly to the promotion of democracy and development.

Democracy has an ambiguous relationship with terrorism. Many studies argue that democracies tend to be more vulnerable to terrorism, since they have open political systems and government security provision based on the rule of law and respect for human rights and are therefore 'soft targets' (Eyerman, 1998; Wilkinson, 2011). Unlike autocratic regimes, so the logic goes, democracies cannot crack down on terrorists to the same extent. Of course, in many Western democracies, concern about terrorism has produced extensive expansion of surveillance and detention powers, changes to legal statutes to enable imprisonment without trial, deportation, and the expansion of police and intelligence agencies' powers. Further, there is evidence that democracies tend to experience more intense and destructive terrorist incidents (Sandler, 1995), more suicide terrorism (Pape, 2003), and that new democracies suffer more than established democracies (Weinburg and Eubank, 1998). Yet, while democracies may be more vulnerable to non-state terrorism, democratization is posited as a cure for terrorism, since it produces an open political system where there are opportunities for the peaceful resolution of political grievances that diminish incentives for the resort to violence (Windsor, 2003).

Poverty and underdevelopment also have an ambiguous causal relationship with terrorism. While poverty may be part of the grievances and conditions terrorist leaders use to recruit supporters and members of their groups, there is no statistically significant correlation between poverty levels and terrorism (Testas, 2004; Piazza, 2006; Kreuger, 2007). In many cases, the leadership of terrorist groups, from al-Qaeda to left- and rightwing terrorists, are drawn from middle-class or affluent backgrounds, as are many of their supporters (Kreuger, 2007). Lower ranking members of terrorist groups, however, are commonly drawn from the poorer and disenfranchised sectors of a society. Further, significant economic disparities may be related to terrorism when they overlap with other social divisions (Piazza, 2006; Stewart, 2008). Most Western governments deny that there is a clear causal link between poverty and terrorism, but use development assistance and poverty reduction to strengthen weak states, reduce public support for terrorists, and support alternative forms of education (Cragin and Chalk, 2003; Testas, 2004; Piazza, 2007).

Such efforts are characterized by inconsistencies. They have often failed to address the root causes in practice and some argue they have reinforced securitized states or 'virtually liberal' states, which replicate the conditions of conflict (Richmond and Tellidis, 2012). Politically, this also means that democracy and development are no longer merely goods in their own terms but have become valued as a means to produce security that extends the wider securitization of development (Duffield, 2007; Keohane, 2008b; Al-Sumait et al., 2009; Aning, 2010). In some cases, this securitization of relations has worked to downplay democracy. Normative pressure for democratization and human rights were downplayed when EU external relations with North Africa and the Euro-Mediterranean Partnership were securitized in relation to terrorism and migration (Joffé, 2008). In other areas, a stronger emphasis on democratization has had negative effects, including shifting local power structures or creating resentment against Western powers, which have led to radicalization that produced a resurgence of the PKK in Turkey after EU-sponsored democratization (Tezcür, 2010), and the growth in support for Islamists after US democracy promotion in Uzbekistan (Crosston, 2009).

More broadly, there are considerable problems with seeking universal root causes to a phenomenon as diverse as terrorism (Newman, 2006). First, terrorist campaigns may begin with particular ideological goals or political grievances but generate their own logics – revenge, group consolidation, retaliation and so on. Second, terrorist organizations themselves may evolve out of terrorism, such as FARC in Colombia, which evolved from a Marxist political group to one increasingly characterized by drug trafficking (Makarenko, 2004). Further, the fact that much use of terrorist tactics occurs in civil war means that defeat or success often relates to insurgent strategies rather than terrorism per se. Third, the aim of reducing public support is often achieved not by state action but by tactical errors by terrorists. Republican groups in Northern Ireland lost much popular support after the Omagh bombing by the Real IRA (a splinter faction of the IRA) in 1998, which killed 29 people, including 9 children (Cronin, 2008, 2009).

Conclusion

Terror is a tactic, a form of violence, directed against noncombatants (or property) to generate fear in an audience. Terrorism is used by a range of non-state actors and by states. States have an ambiguous relationship with terrorism: they may be victims, perpetrators, active sponsors, passive supporters, and are the primary counterterrorism actors (sometimes all at once). While varying in lethality, motive and form, terrorism has become a dominating security issue, with implications that go way beyond specific counterterrorism strategies. Trends in terrorism are much disputed, and the supposed movement towards new forms of networked, transnational, religiously motivated and highly destructive use of terror tactics is far from universal or monolithic. Terrorism does end, but often not because of counterterrorism. Counterterrorism can make terrorism worse, and can even constitute terrorism itself. The politics of definition is pervasive in discourses of terrorism and lies behind many of the major differences in perspectives, be that on whether states can be terrorists, or what the long-term causes and conditions that facilitate terrorism may be. Terrorism and counterterrorism raise particular challenges for understanding security as they are both pervasive and polarizing, subjective and silencing of debate. While this chapter has explored the character of terrorism and the main dimensions of counterterrorism, which have much in common with understandings of conflict and the need for intervention (see Chapter 10), much effort in counterterrorism has also focused on transnational crime and illicit flows that may be related to the financing of terrorism. This is explored in Chapter 12.

Chapter 12

Migration, Crime and Borders

Most security theory concerns itself with static targets – other states. However, concerns about the proliferation of weapons of mass destruction, the spread of pandemic disease or the harms of drugs trafficking cannot be understood solely in national and international terms. They, like many concerns about terrorism, are deemed potentially threatening because *they move*, and because of *how they move*. Thus, security increasingly takes aim at moving targets. Some movements of people and some commodities (arms, drugs and so on) are increasingly securitized – particularly when they are conducted by transnational criminals. For some critics, in contemporary security, all movements of people and things are encountered as potentially dangerous, as possible bombs (Packer, 2006). The way states, as security providers, encounter mobile people and commodities has become complex. No longer are people encountered solely as citizens in need of protection, but also as criminals, victims and potential terrorists. Flows of goods may be viewed as beneficial to wealth and economic development but also as threats to state, societal and human security.

This chapter begins by exploring how flows have become a preoccupation of security and how this challenges our understandings of security. It then explores the ways in which security practices understand forms of migration – the voluntary or involuntary movements of people. It examines key themes in the rise of transnational organized crime and its relationships with security, globalization, states, markets, networks and the apparent association of crime with anarchy and state incapacity. Finally, it discusses trends in security practices aimed at moving targets by exploring the implications of the internationalization of policing, and particularly the expansion and redistribution of border controls and surveillance practices.

Flows, mobility and security

Much social and political life is now mobile, and the boundaries of political communities, economic production and security provision are multiple and changing. As a result, flows rather than territory are becoming a defining feature of many contemporary security issues. Flows of people, commodities, information and finance characterize social and political life under conditions of 'globalization'. This is a fundamental shift in the geopolitical configuration of the world in which security is produced. In what Bauman (2000) calls 'liquid modernity' and Castells (1996) calls the 'space of flows', it is flows and complex exclusions rather than territorial places and boundaries that characterize the spatiality of security. The control of flows has long been part of security. For Hardt and Negri (2000: 332–3), 19th- and 20th-century governance was characterized by 'striation, channelling, coding, and territorializing the flows of capital, blocking certain flows and facilitating others'. However, this is giving way to a new world market that requires 'a smooth space of uncoded and deterritorialized flows'.

These complex trends, sometimes problematically described as homogeneous 'globalization', have enabled and shaped the rise of transnational criminal flows as well as legal trades (Ruggiero, 2003; Aas, 2007). In some places, forms of protection emphasize flows over and above the dominant territorialized perspectives of the protection of individuals within the state through policing and the protection of the state through national defence (Bigo, 2006). It is not that security is no longer connected to territory, but that security is provided unevenly, with different connections to territory and people, in particular local sites, from gated communities to airports. This also reconfigures the relationships between public and private security provision (Abrahamsen and Williams, 2011) (see Chapter 4).

This challenges many of the basic assumptions of understandings of security, which, like much social science, tend to be 'static' (Sheller and Urry, 2006). Recent social and political theory has turned to focus on the mobilities of 'society on the move' (Lash and Urry, 1994: 252; see also Urry, 2000). A fuller recognition of the mobile character of politics requires a focus on 'how sociality and identity are produced through networks of people, ideas and things moving rather than the inhabitation of a shared space such as a region or nation state' (Cresswell, 2011: 551). As Sheller and Urry (2006: 220) state:

> the mobilities of money laundering, the drug trade, sewage and waste, infections, urban crime, asylum seeking, arms trading, people smuggling, slave trading, and urban terrorism, all make visible the already existing chaotic juxtaposition of different spaces and networks.

However, security studies has not fully realized this requirement and has tended to associate flows merely with a threat to territorialized forms of politics and security. In particular, there has been a growing focus on migration as a potential threat to societal and economic security and transnational criminal organizations (TCOs) as a threat to state sovereignty and security.

Migration

Migration has become increasingly associated with security concerns and has itself become securitized. Of particular concern are 'illegal' or 'irregular' migrants, officially estimated to reach levels of 10.8 million in the USA and 8 million in the EU, although independent estimates are far lower, at between

1.9 million to 3.8 million, in the EU (Squire, 2011). Legal migrants are also deemed a security concern in relation to societal and economic security. The conventional understanding is that migration has grown as a result of globalization enhancing transportation and mobility, combined with economic changes and population growth in the global South compelling people to move. Most migration is voluntary, but many people move as refugees fleeing conflict or natural disasters, or as 'asylum seekers' escaping political persecution.

The fact that the perpetrators of the 9/11 terrorist attacks were all migrants is invoked to amplify the sense of vulnerability of states to violence crossing borders (Rudolph, 2003; Adamson, 2006). This securitization of migration builds on longer term developments in which Western states viewed migrants as potentially dangerous in the context of war or other crises (Adamson, 2006). While European states encouraged migration in the 1950s and early 1960s to bring much needed labour to the economy, since then Western states have enacted increasingly 'hostile' policies towards migrants in an attempt to 'regain control' over their borders (Rudolph, 2003: 604). Henceforth, migration became politicized in relation to the supposed burden on welfare systems and articulations of a destabilization of civic order and belonging (Huysmans, 2006). The subsequent securitization of migration amplifies these concerns and serves to reproduce a mythic notion of a homogeneous national society that must be reinforced and re-established through the exclusion of others (Huysmans, 2000). The growth of concern about what Buzan (1991) calls 'societal security' (see Chapter 1) as well as economic and political security underlies this securitization.

The claim that migrants may be a threat to ways of social life produces a discourse that operates on the basis of a covert ethnocentrism that draws and hardens distinctions between 'them' and 'us'. In the contemporary period, the suspicion that falls on Muslims is a clear example of this, although the concern that migrants may resist assimilation into Western society and alter practices of family values, religion and community is far wider than this (Huysmans, 2006). It is not that overtly racist policies are justified, rather there is a growing sense that states should be able to distinguish between the legitimate, economically beneficial migrant and the potentially threatening migrant. Amplified by fears of religiously motivated terrorism (see Chapter 11), this requires the identification of 'good Muslims' and 'bad Muslims' (Mamdani, 2002). Amplifications of fear relate not just to terrorism but also derive from migrants asserting different and multiple identities, and particularly problematic assertions of migrants as potential carriers of disease or as criminals (Buzan et al., 1998; Voelkner, 2011). While not all migrants are identified as security threats, the claimed associations of migration as a general phenomenon with other threats legitimates exclusionary distinctions that are erected and policed in intensified border controls operating against 'illegal immigrants' and 'asylum seekers' (Squire, 2009). In this regard, the securitization of migration is argued to be 'heavy' and 'uneven':

'heavy' because states' powers of surveillance, detention and expulsion have become stronger, but 'uneven' because most Western travellers do not experience this full weight and restriction on mobility that targets refugees, asylum seekers and – particularly – undocumented migrants (Nyers, 2006).

Critical security scholars highlight how framing migration as a security issue subjects it to the statist, exclusionary and managerial logics of security practice and reinscribes and strengthens the limits of political community and conceptions of agency. The securitization of migration blurs the distinction between internal and external security and threats. For Bigo (2001a: 111), this does not reflect an objectively true increase in the level of threats, but a 'lowering of the level of acceptability of the other'. The framing of migration within a field of national security or human security claims also often means that the experiences of individual migrants get lost. Individual migrants are encountered through different categories that filter out many important experiences of migration. Viewing migrating women as victims of human trafficking, for instance, locates them in a criminalized context that strengthens exclusionary practices and downplays their agency as passive 'victims' rather than identifying the impact of personal ambitions, family relations or economic developments (Aradau, 2008; Huysmans and Squire, 2009). Critical migration studies show how migrants, including 'illegal' and 'trafficked' migrants, exercise agency rather than disappearing into 'an undifferentiated flow of people' (Guild, 2009: 5). Indeed, the agency of migrants in their movement and their 'becoming political' through moving are important features of human mobilities (Huysmans and Squire, 2009; Aradau et al., 2010). More broadly, securitizing migration means migrants are caught up in a discourse of managing circulation – either to protect the state and societal security or in humanitarian terms to protect refugees and trafficked persons (Huysmans and Squire, 2009). This managerialism downplays the political character and implications of migrating, which relate to struggles over conceptions of citizenship (Aradau et al., 2010). For instance, the deportation of illegal immigrants and failed asylum seekers is not just a logical consequence of contemporary notions of citizenship but a key area where such distinctions are produced and enacted (Walters, 2002a; de Genova, 2007).

The politics of migration produce multiple shifting categorizations of people that problematize notions of citizenship and the protections it is assumed to afford (Avci, 1999; Nash, 2009). Running through the discourses of migration as a security issue are notions of the protection of societal values and practices, tensions between national identities and cosmopolitan aims, which serve to concretize not just categories of the domestic and the foreign but a range of grey areas such as 'super-citizens' (rich mobile people with full legal citizenship), 'marginal citizens' (legal citizens whose access to the benefits of citizenship are restricted by economic conditions or racial marginalization), 'quasi-citizens' (who have some legal rights and protections but not the right to vote and often no permanent status), and 'sub-citizens' (those lacking employment or a determined legal status like asylum seekers), whose status depends on legal designations and economic opportunities and access to benefits. Each has a different relationship with the protection of human rights (Nash, 2009).

Beneath these operational categories lie vast numbers of 'un-citizens' who fall out of most legal protection and have no clear status, such as undocumented migrants unable to apply for asylum, prisoners in Guantanamo Bay, and others (Nash, 2009). Such people often lack formal political participation or status, but still struggle to assert different forms of belonging. For instance, the 'sans papiers' in France are 'irregular' migrants who are outside the primary logics of political belonging in liberal states (tied to relations with the state, citizen and territory) but are still economically integrated as migrant labour (McNevin, 2006). It is the 'irregular' or 'illegal' migrant, who enters a state's territory without permission or papers, or breaches the conditions of their stay, who is the target of particular securitization (Squire, 2011). This serves to conflate the potentially dangerous with the legally unrecognized, a conflation lacking in clear evidentiary basis. For instance, the 9/11 terrorists were legal migrants with visas. More importantly, such designations have concrete effects. Those designated 'bogus' refugees are made 'abject', confined to holding zones in airports, camps and other sites where they are stripped of citizenship rights and human rights and treated as outsiders, as aliens, and are ultimately subject to expulsion or long-term detention (Isin and Rygiel, 2007; van Munster, 2009). They are denied formal political agency, although their struggles against deportation may reveal a different agency (Soguk, 1999; Nyers, 2003).

A different status is given to those who move across borders involuntarily. Many are designated as refugees. The 1951 Refugee Convention defined a refugee as someone who

> owing to well-founded fear of being persecuted ... is outside the country of his nationality and is unable or, owing to such fear, is unwilling to avail himself of the protection of that country ... or is unwilling to return to it.

Refugee status is generally temporary, and the preferred strategy for managing refugees is voluntary repatriation (Zieck, 1997). State-centric notions of security often reduce the human security of refugees and neglect the underlying causes of refugee flows (Poku and Graham, 2000; Newman and van Selm, 2003; Edwards and Ferstman, 2009). Refugees have a complex relation with states and borders. In one way, refugees are created by state borders: the crossing of borders distinguishes refugees from internally displaced persons, a difference in designation that affects how the international community responds to them. In another way, their status as refugees is an ambivalent one: they are neither citizens nor foreign citizens but an 'other' category offered a form of quasi-citizenship prior to being reintegrated within the 'normal' logic of the state system through voluntary repatriation (Haddad, 2008).

Other supposedly involuntary migrants are trafficked. Trafficking in human beings has increasingly been identified as a serious crime and referred to as the 'slavery of our times' (EU, 2012). Traffickers are believed to target the most vulnerable women, men, boys and girls and use force, coercion or fraud to generate billions of dollars in profits. The UN Global Initiative to Fight Human Trafficking (UN GIFT, 2012) estimates that 2.5 million people are in forced labour (including sexual exploitation) at any given time as a result of trafficking. This accounts for a small but significant proportion of the 20.9 million people (including 5.5 million children) involved in forced labour and sexual exploitation (International Labour Organization, 2012). In Europe, 76% of victims are trafficked for sexual exploitation, and many others for labour, forced begging and so on, and 79% of victims are women (including 12% girls) (EU, 2012). Industrialized countries account for only around 10% of trafficking cases but 49% of profits (UN GIFT, 2012). Some data indicates that 95% of victims are subjected to physical or sexual violence during trafficking (UN GIFT, 2012). These terrible figures of victimization are amplified by low detection and conviction rates. Detecting human trafficking is difficult and faces the challenges of balancing detection with the needs of enabling the free movement of people. As a result, many border agencies in Europe and the USA report low levels of detection of trafficking victims among the tens of millions of people crossing borders. In spite of the scale of the problem, prosecution and conviction rates are low, and in 2006, global figures equated to one conviction for every 800 people trafficked (UN GIFT, 2012). More broadly, however, the predominant framing of human trafficking by states emphasizes border control, and some feminist scholars argue that this downplays the complex conditions that promote and enable it and reduce trafficked women and children to victims while doing little to tackle the causes of victimhood (Lobasz, 2009).

Transnational criminal organizations and illicit flows

The global profits of crime are estimated to be between US$500 billion and US$1.5 trillion each year (Friman, 2009a; Jojarth, 2009). Drugs are by far the most lucrative illicit commodities, accounting for around one-fifth of all criminal proceeds (UNODC, 2013). Total illicit drug markets were valued at US$320 billion in 2003, and recent estimates indicate that cocaine generates US$85 billion and opiates US$68 billion (UNODC, 2013). The most lucrative drug markets are in developed countries, with North America accounting for 44 per cent of global sales and Europe 33 per cent. Estimates of the value of other illicit trades are far lower, such as US$32 billion for human trafficking or US$1 billion for illegal small arms trade (Friman, 2009a). These figures are, however, problematic. Many lack a clear evidential basis, such as the estimates for human trafficking and small arms flows, which are rough figures extrapolated from limited data. Additionally, there is always political pressure to produce high estimates that serve to highlight a substantial and growing threat. Indeed, 'numbers often have more to do with political imperatives and bureaucratic incentives' than practical utility (Andreas and Greenhill, 2010a: 5). While of limited accuracy, numbers are like rumours, they often take on a life of their own through continual repetition and rounding up, in which initial caveats on their reliability are left behind (Andreas and Greenhill, 2010b).

While lucrative, the security implications of illicit flows are not measured in dollars. Criminal organizations and flows may challenge the security of the state or at least its ability to provide security (Matthew and Shambaugh, 1998; Mandel, 1999, 2010; Berdal and Serrano, 2002; Williams, 2002a; Edwards and Gill, 2003; Thachuk, 2007). For instance, in Mexico, Colombia and elsewhere, drugs production and trafficking have created structures of power that rival or even capture the state. More broadly, criminal flows are associated with other issues that challenge national and human security. Illegal migration raises societal and economic security issues, human trafficking raises human security concerns, illicit arms transfers fuel wars, genocide and rampant criminality and raise concerns about nuclear terrorism and proliferation, while illicit flows of oil, drugs, diamonds and natural resources have funded rebel groups and created economic incentives to resist peacebuilding, and raise fears of alliances between criminals and terrorists (Shelley, 2005; Dishman, 2005; Picarelli, 2006; Hutchinson and O'Malley, 2007; Cockayne and Lupel, 2011) (see Chapters 7–11).

Violence is often seen as inherent in illicit flows and organized crime. Unlike legal trades, black markets lack legally enforceable contracts and often rely on violent means to enforce agreements (Fiorentini and Peltzman, 1997; Andreas, 1998). As pure markets, they are akin to the formative assumptions of traditional security theories in which anarchy produces self-help situations and violent strategies (Andreas and Wallman, 2009). This is often overstated. Some illicit trades, like heroin and cocaine, are often associated with violence, while those of cannabis, ecstasy, engendered species, counterfeit goods and even weapons are generally not. Even at the domestic level, there is considerable variation, with US drug markets experiencing high levels of violence, but not Japanese markets (Friman, 2009b). Levels of violence are often more explicable by social, economic and political contexts than an assumption that violence is inherent in criminal activity (Naylor, 2009). Indeed, even where violence is high, as in Mexico over control of drug routes, it partly targets state authorities, but also can relate to the fragmentation of criminal groups (Williams, 2009). Overall, the extent to which an illicit trade is shaped by the 'visible hand of violence' or the invisible hand of the market is much debated (Kenney, 2007: 235; see also Reuter, 1983; Paoli, 2003). Further, violence is not the only means by which criminal groups establish and maintain themselves, and some argue that it is family and ethnic ties rather than violence that help build trust when contracts cannot be legally enforced (von Lampe and Johansen, 2004; Morselli, 2005; von Lampe, 2006).

The most securitized illicit flows tend to be those that contribute to deaths in some direct way. Here, it is debatable whether the death tolls stem from the commodity itself or the conditions of illegality that states create. Estimates of drug-related deaths average 200,000 per year, around half of which derive from overdoses. There are many millions of people living with HIV/AIDS or hepatitis C as a result of injecting drugs (UNODC, 2013). However, it is highly questionable whether these are related solely to the drugs themselves or the negative effects of drug prohibitions, such as the resultant social and economic exclusion that limits access to healthcare. Similarly, the illicit trade in small arms that fuels hundreds of thousands of deaths in civil wars and crime (see Chapter 7) creates conditions of economic deprivation, intercommunal conflict and geopolitical rivalry, which cannot be disconnected from state policies and global power relations; and the sexual exploitation of victims of human trafficking does not exist in isolation from the social and legal dimensions of the sex trade. Nevertheless, most responses to illicit flows focus on controlling supply to a greater degree than demand or harm reduction.

Understanding transnational crime merges the concerns of criminology and security studies. A degree of theoretical convergence between the two disciplines has been easy to achieve since both share state-centric views and rely on reductionist rational choice assumptions (Aas, 2007; Sheptycki, 2007). While in criminological realism, rational choices are based on a 'hedonistic calculus', and in IR realism on survival and security, there is a convergence of the two in recent scholarship that argues that criminal organizations seek to balance the interests of profits and security (Kenney, 2007a). While the securitization of illicit flows and transnational crime is relatively recent (with the exception of the long and unsuccessful history of wars on drugs), these issues have found a sympathetic home in international relations and security studies because they fit within some of the wider assumptions and concerns of these fields. In particular, the debates and assumptions of understanding transnational crime mirror many aspects of understanding terrorism. They are viewed as being closely related to themes of globalization, states, sovereignty and the power of markets, and similar trends in organizational form and associations with anarchy and weak states are asserted. As with terrorism, each association tends to assert a simple relationship or trend that is challenged as much as it is supported by the empirical evidence.

Globalization

The globalization of crime is viewed as a profound challenge to states and the security order they produce. Naim (2003) has declared the fight to control the illegal markets in drugs, arms, intellectual property, people and money to be the 'five wars of globalisation' that pit governments against 'agile' criminal networks. Indeed, TCOs have been argued to potentially challenge states to such a degree that they might come to represent a 'new authoritarianism' to replace Russia as a threat to Western states' security (Shelley, 1999). While predictions of a new 'pax mafiosa' (Sterling, 1994) have not come to pass, globalized crime, what Glenny (2008) calls 'McMafia', is still argued to form a profound challenge to world order.

Globalization has enhanced crime by reducing the effectiveness of borders and increasing opportunities for smuggling (Naim, 2005). Developments in information and communications technology have opened up new modes of coordination and spheres of activity for criminals, for example cybercrime, the trade in child pornography or credit card fraud; and trends towards the containerization of shipping in international trade have vastly expanded the speed and scale of both legal and illegal trades, with many illegal goods transported hidden in cargo containers (Andreas, 2002; Galeotti, 2005). In addition, understandings of crime are globalized, as peculiarly US ideas of organized crime are represented in films (most clearly in Mario Puzo's Godfather trilogy) and policy statements that circulate the globe and drive cultural globalization (Findlay, 2000; Woodiwiss, 2003a). Both benefiting from globalization and integral to it, criminal networks have 'become central aspects of the world order' (Aas, 2007: 125).

There is a danger in positing a simple globalization of crime. Crime is often simultaneously local and global (Hobbs, 1998). This varies a lot between illicit trades. Cocaine is the most globalized illicit drugs market, while heroin is somewhat more concentrated, but other drugs like cannabis and amphetamines are decentralized but also often localized. Firearms trafficking is predominantly local and regional, while trades in cigarettes, counterfeit medicines and child pornography all have more complex relationships.

States and criminal flows

Most understandings of transnational crime and illicit flows rely on simple oppositions between borders and flows, and between states and criminals. Borders are portrayed as fixed and visible, while illicit flows are seen as moving, flexible, unpredictable, hidden, undetectable and unknown (van Schendel, 2005). States are supposed to control flows into their territory. Krasner (1999) referred to this as 'interdependence sovereignty' – a key defining feature of what it is to be a state. As this control is diminished in the face of 'international thugs and thieves', state sovereignty and security is thought to be eroding (Thachuk, 2007: 3–4). This view is prevalent in understandings of crime that adopt a position of thinking and talking 'like a state' (Gootenberg, 2005), of assuming that the state is always in opposition to crime. However, such dominant views are challenged by the complex ways in which states and borders are constitutive of illicit flows.

First, since states create the laws and regulations that make the supply and demand of some goods illegal, they create black markets (Nadelmann, 1990; Andreas, 1999; Serrano, 2002; Andreas and Nadelmann, 2006). Other laws create spaces where illegal activity flourishes, such as tax havens that facilitate money laundering (Abraham and van Schendel, 2005). Further, laws are not evenly enforced by all countries and so states create variations in 'effective illegality' that have shaped the heroin market (Paoli et al., 2009), and cocaine trafficking has evolved in relation to changing market opportunities and regulatory constraints (Kenney, 2007b). Some illicit flows are not in internationally criminalized commodities like narcotics, but relate to other forms of taxation (cigarettes) and regulation (firearms). Since states have different laws, some criminologists propose that these differences produce criminal flows. Passas's (2001: 23) concept of 'criminogenic asymmetries' captures this idea: criminogenic (meaning productive of crime) differences between states create 'structural disjunctions, mismatches and inequalities in the spheres of politics, culture, the economy and the law'. These create demand for illicit flows, and opportunities and motives for criminal action. Whether it is the creation of laws, their uneven enforcement, or wider asymmetries between states and societies that produce illicit flows, the underlying explanation is the same. The 'market' will always respond to states' actions and inefficiencies and, legally or illegally, suppliers will fill a vacuum (Passas, 2002). This argument derives from neoclassical economics, which asserts markets' inherent tendencies to find an equilibrium of supply and demand.

Second, while crime and criminal actions are constituted by laws and regulations, many such laws are not very clear. There are not just illegal 'black markets' and clearly legal markets but also many 'grey markets'. Illicit flows tend to comprise numerous different activities – from drug production, refining, trafficking and distribution, to financial transactions, money laundering and protection. Since numerous elements are involved, it is unsurprising that some are clearly illegal while others exist in a more complex relationship with the law and legal trade. Drug production, for instance, relies on a ready supply of chemicals. While often subject to regulation, these are also widely traded legally. Cocaine production uses potassium permanganate, which is often diverted into Colombia from international trade. The production of methamphetamine uses pseudoephedrine, an active ingredient in decongestant medicines available on domestic legal markets. In contrast, the chemicals used to produce ecstasy and amphetamines are often manufactured illegally and then smuggled (International Narcotics Control Board, 2007).

Third, states may be criminals too, and have often had official and semi-official involvement in conducting illicit trades (Chambliss, 1989; Thomson, 1994; Friman and Andreas, 1999; Gallant, 1999; Löwenheim, 2007). Indeed, for some critical theorists, like Cox (1999), transnational crime is part of a wider 'covert world', which includes TCOs but also state intelligence services, terrorist groups, the arms trade, money-laundering banks and others. Some state officials are enriched through corruption and provide false documentation, such as visas, passports or forms of certification used in illicit trades (Andreas, 1998). Beyond corruption, in some illicit trades, like those in arms and military technologies, states have been far more organized and effective traffickers than non-state actors. The networks built by states to break UN arms embargoes and other restrictions tend to be more centrally organized, more extensive and more long-lived than networks created by criminals or terrorists (Bourne, 2007, 2011b).

Finally, in many cases, it is not globalization that empowered the growth of transnational crime, but relationships with state agencies pursuing other goals. In the Cold War, covert wars fought by the CIA were instrumental in empowering and protecting allies in ways that allowed them to build their power in illicit drugs networks, even when this conflicted with operations of the US Drug Enforcement Administration in the same countries (McCoy, 2003). This included the provision of arms, air logistics and banking services that significantly empowered 'criminal' actors in the Golden Triangle, Central Asia and Central America (Scott and Marshall, 1998; Bull, 2008). More recently, CIA aid to local Afghan leaders was recycled into loans to farmers to finance the next spring's poppy crop (Goodhand, 2008).

Mafias, markets and networks

How are illicit flows organized? As with the study of terrorism, many understandings of organized crime focus on the actor rather than the action, and blur the distinction between the two such that crime is what criminals do (Paoli, 2002; Paoli and Fijnaut, 2004). The 2001 UN Convention against Transnational Organized Crime defines an organized criminal group as 'a structured group of three or more persons, existing for a period of time and acting in concert with the aim of committing one or more serious crimes' for financial or other benefit. Since this requires only three people and more than one crime, it is exceptionally broad. This contrasts with the popular imagination of organized crime consisting of mafia-type organizations. Certainly, these exist as hierarchical secret societies that engage in violence and corruption to operate protection rackets and smuggling, such as the Italian and Russian Mafias or the Japanese Yakuza. However, other TCOs are looser groupings like the Camorra in Naples or the 'Ndrangheta in Calabria. Rather than monolithic mafia hierarchies, much transnational crime is small scale and entails cooperation among criminal organizations rather than control by one (Den Boer, 2002; Williams, 2002b).

For many criminal activities, according to the UNODC (2010a: 19), 'the organizing principle is the invisible hand of the market, not the master designs of criminal organizations'. The fact that much transnational crime is not very organized is sometimes explained by a claim that illicit markets do not tend to produce large-scale criminal enterprises (Paoli, 2002). For example, the 'constraints of illegality' (the threat of legal action and so on) militates against the formation of large hierarchical organizations and monopolistic market structures (Reuter, 1983). Even the drugs cartels in Medellin and Cali in Colombia were not as powerful or centrally organized as popular myth and Hollywood films suggest. These myths of mafia-style hierarchies in control of the drugs trade underlay the US Drug Enforcement Administration's 'kingpin strategy', which had many parallels with attempts to combat terrorism through decapitation. This strategy was ineffective, as it targeted loosely coupled networks as if they were hierarchies. As a result, the main effect of the dismantling of the 'cartels' in the 1990s has been to produce a more dispersed drugs trade, with estimates of up to 300 'kingpins' identified by the Colombian police (Kenney, 2007b).

Networks are a key form of organization that lies between hierarchies and markets. TCOs, like terrorist organizations, are said to be adapting to globalization by organizing themselves more as flexible, adaptable, resilient transnational networks that contrast with the bureaucratic and hierarchical nature of states (Castells, 1998). By doing this, criminals can become more transnational, while states struggle to cooperate across borders (Williams, 2002b; Naim, 2005). This is a common view, but often relies on contrasting powerful criminal networks with hierarchical states. Yet, networks have significant limitations, which make it difficult to sustain and expand them (Eilstrup-Sangiovanni and Jones, 2008: see Chapter 11), while states and their regulatory powers have been enhanced by globalization (Friman and Andreas, 1999; Andreas and Nadelmann, 2006; Friman, 2009c).

Importantly, mafia hierarchies, the invisible hand of the market, or the trend towards flexible networks do not explain all illicit trades. One of the most concerning from the perspective of security is the trafficking in nuclear materials, raising fears of terrorist acquisition of nuclear weapons. This, however, is not hierarchical, not much of a network, and not really a market. Markets mean more than just action motivated by economic gain: they are complex systems in which price determines the distribution of goods and services and follows from the structuring effects of the interaction of supply and demand. The illicit trafficking in nuclear materials, however, is not organized by such pressures, but constitutes a number of individual transactions and incidents in which price does not appear to be a major factor and supply is not clearly connected to demand. There is limited evidence of organized criminal involvement in smuggling nuclear materials; most trafficking is disorganized (both in obtaining the material and trafficking and selling it), and there is usually no clear connection between individual suppliers (corrupt insiders from nuclear facilities and so on) and criminal or terrorist customers (Zaitseva and Hand, 2003). The fear of nuclear smuggling asserts a precautionary logic, in which the large amounts of radioactive junk and small amounts of sensitive nuclear materials that have been smuggled are deemed to be the 'tip of the iceberg' underneath which may be some TCOs that have yet to be discovered (Zaitseva, 2002; Lee, 2006; Shelley, 2006; Fitzpatrick, 2007). While it is difficult to dismiss these fears with certainty, nuclear smuggling does not conform to models of hierarchies, networks or markets.

Anarchy and power

The dominant view of transnational crime in security discourses is that crime inhabits the anarchic gaps in liberal governance, in weak states and 'ungoverned spaces' (Clunan and Trinkunas, 2010; Williams, 2010). Earlier assertions of the unpredictability of transnational crime have been replaced by assertions of their concentration in weak and failing states (Ó Tuathail, 1999; Bialasiewicz et al., 2007; Mair, 2008). Thus, the UK's 2008 National Security Strategy argued that transnational criminal flows 'emanate' from failed and failing states (Cabinet Office, 2008: 14). In 2010, Antonio Maria Costa, the UN Office on Drugs and Crime (UNODC, 2010a: iii) executive director, claimed that: 'vulnerability attracts crime, and crime deepens vulnerability ... What is striking is that if you take a map of global conflicts, and then superimpose a map of global trafficking routes they overlap almost perfectly.' In addition to weak states, on a smaller scale, other ungoverned spaces are identified as breeding grounds and organizing spaces for organized crime, including prisons, ports, some parts of some cities, and borderland areas (Fiorentini and Peltzman, 1997; NATO, 2009a; Williams, 2010). In such a view, any limit in coordination among law enforcement organizations, states and so on 'leaves gaps which are ruthlessly exploited' by criminal organizations (NATO, 2009b).

There is some correlation here. The increasing geographical concentration of previously dispersed stages in the production of heroin in Afghanistan and cocaine in Colombia seems to point to geographical and organizational consolidation of these illicit trades in 'ungoverned spaces', and a recent survey of Afghan provinces highlighted a link between opium cultivation and 'insecure' areas (UNODC, 2010b). Beyond illicit flows, there is also an association between weak states and transnational crime in the form of piracy, most notably between the failed state of Somalia and piracy in the Gulf of Aden, and the weak state of Indonesia and piracy in the Strait of Malacca.

However, the real picture is far more complicated than this. As noted earlier, strong states have contributed to the creation of illicit trades through regulation and direct material involvement and support. Indeed, some illicit activities thrive in strong states, such as the production of amphetamines and methamphetamine, or the significant piracy problems encountered by India and Brazil (Murphy, 2011). A focus on weak states neglects the significance of global legal trades in the chemicals used in drug production or the role of demand in strong states in stimulating supply (Bourne, 2011a). While a lack of government capacity is sometimes important, state-building processes can create the foundations of stability that enable TCOs to flourish, as occurred in Bosnia (Andreas, 2008; Schroeder and Friesendorf, 2009).

Even if the weak enforcement of national and international laws is central to explaining illicit flows, this is not just because states lack the capacity. The flourishing of illicit trades is also associated with the deliberate neglect of enforcement. Global prohibitions have been created by powerful states exerting hegemonic leadership that states have then not sought to fully enforce (Andreas and Nadelmann, 2006; Friman, 2009c). Instead, powerful states have been selective in enforcing prohibitions on drugs and human trafficking, and have tended to prefer actions that externalize the costs of adjusting to and enforcing prohibitions such that poorer and weaker states bear the highest costs (Friman, 2009c). State legitimacy matters as well as functional strength, and even when states do attempt to enforce prohibitions, they are often met with wider resistance from societies that view smuggling as a form of resistance to state power and imperial rule (Hobsbawm, 1981; van Schendel, 2005; Blumi, 2010; Tagliacozzo, 2010).

Responses: policing, borders, surveillance and suspicion

Many contemporary changes in security practices are claimed to be a response to the problems of migration and transnational crime. As many states' security paradigms have shifted from 'warfighting to crime fighting' (Andreas and Price, 2001), military and policing practices have overlapped. Some critics view this as a rearticulation of security threats by intelligence and security agencies in order to secure and expand their powers and budgets (Naylor, 1995). In the process, policing has become internationalized, changing the boundary between internal and international security (see Chapter 4). The protective practices of states have sought to reinforce that boundary by strengthening and transforming borders. But since the threats to security that these flows represent are already inside the state, expansive surveillance powers and the exercise of control through suspicion have been enacted. Across all these areas, it is evident that, as the historian of Andean cocaine Paul Gootenberg (2009: 13) claims, 'for objects-in-motion ... statist languages of "control" underlie their construction and maintenance as illicit and criminalized flows'.

Policing

The apparent globalization of crime has been invoked to support the considerable internationalization of policing. Of key importance here has been the movement towards the harmonization of legislation on transnational criminal offences, pursued through the 2000 UN Convention against Transnational Organized Crime and growing networking and collaboration between police forces. Andreas and Nadelmann (2006: 3) argue that the internationalization of crime control has evolved from ad-hoc forms of policing cooperation to a 'highly intensive and regularized collection of law enforcement mechanisms and institutions'. While posed as a response to the transnationalization of crime, this arose out of a longer history of Western powers exporting their definitions of crime and their moral codes (such as those against narcotics) to the rest of the world. In Europe, for example, early cooperation on drugs trafficking expanded into a wider transnationalization of European policing practices and the strengthening of Europol (the EU's law enforcement agency) – a process significantly enhanced recently by terrorism concerns (Den Boer, 2002; Sheptycki, 2005).

Critical criminologists have expressed concern about these moves. First, they do not reflect the complexity of transnational criminal activity but are based on the spread of a particularly US-based conception of organized crime, in the form of mafia myths that draw attention away from the vast illegal profits gained by politicians and multinational companies in illegal or semi-legal activities (Woodiwiss, 2003a, 2003b, 2005). Second, they portray localized criminal activities as resulting from universal globalization (Hobbs, 1998; Sheptycki, 2005). Third, the securitization of transnational organized crime militates against crime prevention or harm reduction strategies and enables the expansion of measures that constitute more 'intrusive, authoritarian and muscular forms of law enforcement' (Abraham and van Schendel, 2005: 4; Sheptycki, 2005). Thus, as security agendas have shifted 'warfighting to crime fighting', crime fighting has become more warlike.

Beyond formal policing, the internationalization of crime control also encompasses considerable expansion, harmonization and integration of surveillance practices, including at borders, ports and airports, and involves both state and private actors (Zuriek and Salter, 2005; Ericson, 2007). For Ericson (2007: 1), these practices are linked to the securitization of uncertainty in the risk paradigm and a growing trend in Western societies to treat 'every imaginable source of harm as a crime ... rooted in neo-liberal political cultures that are obsessed with uncertainty' (see Chapter 5). Thus, while national security and crime were relatively distinct fields of action, risk-based securitization and criminalization are now intimately linked and indistinct processes.

It is argued that the internationalization of policing and the rising concern about migration are reconfiguring and linking previously separate security practices. As national, international and transnational policing and security practices articulate themselves against transnational threats, they blur the inside-outside boundary that arose from the territorial trap (Sheptycki, 2005) (see Chapter 4). Threats that are perceived as arising from outside are now encountered inside political communities. The spatial blurring of threats has entailed a functional blurring and convergence between the military and the police (Bigo, 2001b). Ironically, the professionalization of policing and military roles that – through long historic processes – established a clear distinction between inside and outside now operates on the basis of blurring that difference.

Borders, control and perfect security

States have traditionally monopolized the decision on permitting or denying access to territory at their borders, indeed, this is a defining aspect of sovereignty (Krasner, 1999; Andreas, 2003). Borders are traditionally conceived as simple two-dimensional lines in the sand, 'thin' places where inspections take place and entry or exit is permitted or denied. The securitization of migration and illicit flows often highlights the decline in border controls in a globalizing world. This discourse has led to a reassertion of borders as the key to security against mobile threats, with many states investing in stronger border controls since 2001. Here, borders are not declining but being reformed. Andreas (2003, 2009) argues that there has been a complex mix of erosion and strengthening of different border functions. Economic borders may be declining, with the reduction of trade tariffs and economic globalization, and military borders that deter invasion and create buffer zones are generally declining in importance with the lessening of the threat of great power war, although this should not be overstated, but 'police borders' that seek to exclude certain non-state actors and flows are expanding and strengthening. Thus, the US–Mexico border has seen a growth in security, with over 700 miles of fencing being built and an expansion of US Border Patrol agents from less than 3,000 to more than 20,000 (Alden and Roberts, 2011). While internal borders within the EU have been reduced, the EU's external borders have been hardened and in 2004 an external border agency, Frontex, was created to promote more integrated border security among members by adopting common risk assessment models and enhancing cooperation among border control agencies. However, these and similar developments are not just a simple hardening of borders but a significant transformation of what they are and how they function.

Critical scholars note wider changes that mean that borders are no longer what or where they are supposed to be (Balibar, 1998; Vaughan-Williams, 2009a). Borders are no longer simple two-dimensional expressions of the limits of sovereign political authority, the lines where one political territorial authority ends and another begins. Rather, they are extending in time and space. In the past, borders used to be where people were inspected when trying to cross. Now, various forms of pre-assessment enable states to decide on admissibility and risk before travellers depart their country of origin. In space, a correlate of this is that state agencies have a presence beyond their own territory. The US border has been transformed by mechanisms such as the US-VISIT programme that uses biometric data to assess travellers before they depart, and the expanded deployment of US border controls abroad (Amoore, 2006). Such pre-emptive assessments are valued by states because they make physical borders and border guards 'the last line of defense, not the first, in identifying threats' (Accenture Digital Forum, cited in Amoore, 2006). This temporal and geographical extension of borders has numerous implications for understanding security.

First, borders are not simple lines but increasingly are networks. The adage that 'it takes networks to fight networks' (Arquilla and Rondfeldt, 1996: 81) finds a home in border security. In Europe, for example, borders are becoming a 'diffuse, networked, control apparatus' (Walters, 2002b: 573). The UK Border Agency has an international presence based on the hub and spoke model, with about 80 decision-making hubs and 250 visa application centres/spokes.

Second, the extension of borders in this way operates primarily on the logics of risk assessment and risk management (Amoore, 2006). They operate on the basis of collecting, analysing and acting on information from a range of sources, such as data on economic transactions (dataveillance), expanded systems of surveillance, and biometric data (Bigo, 2001a; Amoore, 2006; Huysmans, 2006; Vaughan-Williams, 2009b). The development of biometrics is particularly expansive and creates an operative assumption that body measurements are a reliable guide to identity and intentions (Amoore, 2006). Indeed, through the use of biometrics, borders are said to be becoming not just geopolitical but biopolitical (at least in relation to human migrants). Politics no longer acts on territory but on bodies and through technologies of risk that render everyday lives and movements of travellers amenable to intervention and management (Amoore, 2006; Muller, 2010).

Third, risk logics and the expansion of controls relate particularly to the development of new technologies for surveilling, identifying and sorting movements of people and goods, particularly those that claim to produce 'smart borders' (Andreas, 2003). This technologization of security is present (in somewhat different forms) across the range of issues referred to as a new 'security continuum linking together drugs, immigration, asylum, crime and terrorism' (Ceyhan, 2008: 102). The use of full-body scanners, iris scans, profiling techniques, radiation scanners, CO_2 detectors, information exchange systems and so on are all increasingly important features of border security, although relatively low-tech features such as the building of large fences and walls continue.

Fourth, borders are no longer just lines but sites and spaces of politics: that is, politics is enacted at these diverse sites rather than just deciding what goes on there. Some scholars now seek to study not borders as lines in the sand, but 'borderlands' as indistinct but wide areas of territory where lines of authority of states and societies are contested (Abraham and van Schendel, 2005; Zartman, 2010). More specifically, airports are increasingly seen as sites of political action and the construction of distinctions between us and them, safe and dangerous (Salter, 2008a; Adey, 2009). Importantly, this entails a reconceptualization of the border from a simple noun, an object, to a verb – the practice of bordering (Lapid, 2001). It is this that is more dispersed. For some critics, through surveillance practices, the sharing of information and the reliance on quantification and risk management, 'ever-expanding areas of life ... are colonized by "security" and "risk"' (Salter, 2008b: 243).

Fifth, it is no longer just state agencies that enact border controls. In some places, civilian vigilante groups have taken on the tasks of patrolling borders and in the process articulate a new society and identity that they claim to be protecting (Doty, 2007). In other settings, private companies are involved in collecting and sorting information and producing risk assessment and management technologies. Further, in relation to flows of goods rather than human migrants, the independent intergovernmental World Customs Organization (WCO) has developed the SAFE Framework of Standards to Secure and Facilitate Global Trade, a set of standards adopted in 2005 that seeks to produce an 'authorized supply chain' in which customs-to-customs and customs-to-business partnerships ensure supply chain security. This includes preferential arrangements with 'authorised economic operators' – companies that do a good job on supply chain security are then subject to less oversight.

How much security can these borders really provide? Reinforcing the trend of seeing crime as inhabiting anarchic and ungoverned spaces, crime is said to flourish where control is less than total. Some aspects of changing border technologies seek perfect control and security. While many security theorists, from early realists to Hedley Bull and others, argue that perfect security is unachievable, Muller (2010: 14) argues that contemporary attempts to govern the uncertainty of risk are integral to how border security is framed and claims that 'mobility itself becomes potentially threatening ... as the porosity of borders is assumed away, and what Agamben refers to the "originary fiction of sovereignty" is forgotten'. In relation to flows of goods, in the USA the Container Security Initiative began in 2002, which places US customs officials at 58 major ports around the world. National authorities agree to screen shipping containers destined for the USA before they leave foreign ports. Additionally, the Implementing Recommendations of the 9/11 Commission Act of 2007 require that, by 2012, 100 per cent of all US-bound cargo containers should be scanned before being put on a ship. This was, however, found to be unfeasible. Nevertheless, 86 per cent of US-destined cargo is screened (Caldwell, 2009) – a risk assessment is conducted, which may or may not include scanning the container.

Borders not only restrict movement but enable it: they are better thought of as filters than barriers. Contemporary bordering practices emphasize not only the profiling, detection and containment of concerning movements of people and goods, but also the facilitation and enhancement of mobility for trusted subjects and objects (Peoples and Vaughan-Williams, 2010). They function to sort and select mobility in ways that enhance some people's mobility and restrict others' (Adey, 2004). A central element of this capacity has been the international standardization of travel documents and passports (Salter, 2004), whereby states increase their power to control and select movements (Mau et al., 2012). This also occurs for flows of goods. In 2005, the EU adopted 'security amendments' to the Community Customs Code, which extended the security roles of customs organizations and supported the harmonization of risk assessment (European Commission, 2006). More widely, the WCO has been integral to the spread of harmonized procedures and standards in trade facilitation and valuation among its 176 members. Chalfin (2006: 248) argues that these harmonization efforts constitute 'comprehensive ordering practices' that 'play a decisive, albeit largely hidden, role in defining the administrative rationalities of modern statehood and the character of the late capitalist economic order'. In particular, Chalfin (2006: 251) highlights how customs organizations, and the WCO, materialize World Trade Organization commitments and promote 'self-regulating markets' that serve as a 'cover' for the 'routinization of new modes of state intervention, enlarging and reworking the source, substance and scope of state sovereignty around the globe'. Amoore (2009: 58) suggests that the domains of geopolitics and geoeconomics cross over as security is sought and the techniques of governing objects are extended to governing people, as sensor technologies used to track 'mobile things, objects, animals and vehicles' are introduced 'into the domain of the tracking of mobile people'.

Not only are national territories or homelands made secure through such bordering, ordering and filtering processes, but they also seek to produce secure legal flows of commodities in the form of 'supply chain security' (van de Voort et al., 2003; Caldwell, 2009). Since 2001, 'supply chain security' has been redefined beyond simply preventing the entry of contraband (narcotics, firearms, counterfeit goods and so on) to also preventing terrorists from targeting the containerized supply chain or transporting weapons in shipping containers (Willis and Ortiz, 2004). This has entailed a shift in the site and nature of state-led security practices associated with the movement of goods to an emphasis on making the global trade system more secure. However, developing supply chain security not only distributes responsibility for security to private companies but also produces significant extra costs for companies (Grainger, 2007).

A related criminal threat to the security of trade is the growing phenomenon of piracy on major shipping routes, such as the Gulf of Aden and the Strait of Malacca. Levels of pirate attacks have increased substantially since the 1990s (Chalk, 2008). Pirates operating from bases in Somalia have attacked hundreds of ships in the Gulf of Aden. Piracy is a threat to the lives and wellbeing of ships' crews and has a costly and disruptive effect on global trade (through theft and ransom). As global shipping has increased, accounting for 77 per cent of global trade movements, lucrative targets are presented to pirates (Chalk, 2008; Lobo-Guerrero, 2008). As with other responses to transnational crime, countering piracy has taken place at numerous sites and through partnerships and practices that extend well beyond the state. It has been subject to substantial militarized responses, with naval actions by multinational task forces, such as NATO's Operation Ocean Shield in the Gulf of Aden, which provides escorts and deterrence and helps others to tackle pirate trends and tactics. International organizations like the UNODC, the International Maritime Organization and others also play key roles in developing counter-piracy practices. Increasingly, counter-piracy has also taken place on-shore, with a focus on failed states like Somalia that are bases for pirates (Bueger, 2011; Hansen, 2012). Responses to piracy incorporate substantial roles for private security companies and the management of piracy risk by insurance companies and others (Lobo-Guerrero, 2008; Bueger et al., 2011; Hansen, 2012). They also involve the development of 'best practices' for commercial shipping companies to aid in prevention and deterrence (Himes, 2011).

Surveillance and suspicion

Enhanced and expanded border controls carry social and political costs. For instance, the expansion and diffusion of surveillance practices in domestic societies and international mobility regimes raise important questions about privacy and civil liberties. While these are not necessarily best posed as trade-offs between security and liberty, they are extensive and often deeply problematic. For some, they are a rewriting of the social contract between people and states (Chesterman, 2010), and for others they represent a significant diminution of the freedoms (and thus human security) of many people (see Chapter 4). The development of biometrics is therefore intimately related to risk technologies that operate on the basis of profiling the characteristics of threatening persons (Ceyhan, 2008). Such profiles can be problematic in how they reinforce ethnocentric, covertly racist and discriminatory assumptions.

Perhaps the most pervasive forms of contemporary global surveillance and the attendant production of suspicion relate to growing controls over financial transactions intended to combat terrorist financing. Before 9/11, only 36 states had signed the 1999 UN International Convention for the Suppression of Terrorist Financing, and just 4 had taken formal steps to ratify it. Now, 185 are parties and only 2 have not ratified it. At the forefront of much of this effort has been the intergovernmental Financial Action Task Force (FATF), created in 1989 on the initiative of the G7 to combat drug trafficking finance. The FATF covers 34 member states, two regional organizations (the European Commission and Gulf Cooperation Council) and has seven regional versions covering most regions of the world. In 2003, the FATF agreed new recommendations to cover terrorist financing as well as money laundering and drug trafficking finance. Of particular concern is that these recommendations suggest a focus on the financial transactions of charitable bodies and forms of 'informal value transfer systems'. Both are regarded with greater suspicion than other financial transfers. Importantly, traditional financial transfer systems like the hawala system have become a focus, because they do not rely on formal record-keeping systems and so present a relatively unregulated sphere of financial activity. Since they are more difficult to regulate, the logic of control emphasizes that they are more vulnerable to misuse for terrorist financing. Thus, suspicion falls on the 'other', the unfamiliar (to Western eyes) systems of interaction (de Goede, 2003). Some critical scholars point to a stereotyping of hawala systems that construes 'Arab and Muslim money as illegitimate and criminal' (Atia, 2007: 449) and 'implicitly constructed Western banking as the normal and legitimate space of international finance' (de Goede, 2003: 513). Much like the discourse linking failing states to terror and crime, there is limited evidence that such systems are used in terrorist financing, and the US$0.5 million used to finance the 9/11 attacks moved through formal bank transfers and the use of ATMs. Instead, by effectively criminalizing hawala and other non-formal systems, these responses have cracked down on the systems used by migrants to transfer wages to their families in their countries of origin (Vlcek, 2007), and fall into what Passas (2006) calls 'fighting terror with error'.

Conclusion

Globalization has brought a new age of flows in which security practices are increasingly articulated against movements of people and goods. Indeed, Biersteker (2003: 161) claims that 'control over flows and networks is becoming more important than hierarchical control over physical territorial space'. Most mobilities and flows are viewed positively: trade, tourism, and flows of culture, information and communication are all beneficial to states and societies. But flows of *some* people and *some* material objects are viewed as potentially dangerous. The securitization of flows, then, is uneven and selective. In this way, security practices instantiate new fragmented identities and notions of citizenship, rights and protection. People are now not just citizens but victims to be protected, criminals to be detected, and terrorists to be combated.

Far from the mafia myths of popular culture, transnational crime is a disparate and dispersed phenomenon and often not very organized at all. In tackling such a phenomenon, internationalized and militarized policing has been augmented by even more widely dispersed practices of bordering and surveillance. Across the range of issues, policy responses and dominant understandings emphasize the supply side of the trade rather than the wider demand. This serves to locate the source of the problem, and the adjustments required for control, in other places. It is thus a globally expansive control agenda. However, the dispersal of bordering and surveillance practices seeks to enact security in an ever wider range of sites and partnerships that alter understandings of security as something that states provide for citizens. Instead, public and private sectors blur, national and international spheres interconnect, and individuals, companies, banks, international organizations, military forces and alliances, and private security guards all participate in the securing and filtering of flows. Thus, security practices have become much more dispersed and expansive and operate more like the networks they claim to fight.

Flows present a substantial theoretical challenge to understandings of security based on fixed territorial notions of political community and identity and rigid distinctions between inside and outside. However, understandings of flows and responses to them often fall back into familiar categories and assumptions about states, anarchy and violence. So, the dispersed security practices articulated against flows reconfigure rather than replace familiar assumptions, and reassert a strong notion of security as premised on control. This can also be seen in the security concerns articulated around other flows of goods, particularly natural resources, that arise in issues of environmental security, explored in Chapter 13.

Chapter 13

Environmental, Energy and Resource Security

This chapter looks at security relations with and within the natural and human-made world. What is the relationship between natural resources and conflict? How does environmental change affect security? How does the meaning of security change when environmental issues are emphasized? These questions are central to contemporary security practices, but are also issues that most approaches to security were not designed to tackle. Clearly, environmental issues resist the division of security problems along national territorial lines, since the boundaries of political communities do not fully describe the contours of environmental issues. However, the politics of the environment remains partially wedded to the territorial division of power and community. While environmental security arose as a key issue in the 1980s, rather than focusing on the environment as a referent object for security, the dominant concern has been to integrate environmental issues – such as resource scarcity and the implications of global population growth – into traditionalist assumptions about the causes of violent conflict. First, the chapter explores the broad debates over the securitization of the environment. It then looks at how the prospects for resource conflict are understood and the debate over how resource scarcity is related to conflict. It then examines radical alternatives to this debate that posit the environment as a referent object to be secured. Finally, it explores these different ways of understanding security in and of the natural world by focusing on the rising concerns of climate change and the security of energy, food and water supplies.

The issues covered in this chapter may seem disparate. Some are global, others are local, some relate to violent deaths, others relate to the economic wellbeing of states and societies. Here, security practices run the gamut, from the prospects of great power competition and conflict to the banal daily practices of consumption and the satisfaction of basic needs for food and water. However, they all relate to the security of material support systems on which human life relies. So, they relate to the protection of life and the production and protection of ways of life based on established, but perhaps unsustainable, patterns of consumption and interaction. The security of ways of life alters the central understanding of security away from one associated with mitigating threats from other actors and towards one conceived in terms of reducing vulnerabilities and enhancing resilience and sustainability. In this context, the role of the state as security provider does not disappear, but is changing. As national and human security combine with complex natural and technological systems, states, societies and the private sector come to share in the production of security in ways that profoundly challenge understandings of security premised on the relations of the great powers in an anarchic international system.

Securitizing the environment

Many supporters of the broadening of the scope of security issues in the 1980s and 90s included environmental issues (see Chapter 1). Buzan (1991: 19–20) identified environmental security as one of his five sectors, which, for him, relates to the maintenance of the biosphere (both locally and globally), which is 'the essential support system on which all other human enterprise depends'. Similarly, Tuchman Mathews (1989) argued for including resource, environmental and demographic issues in the remit of security, since these held the potential to create human suffering and turmoil. Indeed, emphasizing the environmental foundations of all political life could mean that the security of the environment is the 'ultimate security' (Myers, 1993).

The securitization of environmental issues is more recent than other sectors, dating back only to the 1970s, and most extensively since the 1980s (Buzan et al., 1998). Since then, most views of environmental security have not taken the environment as the referent object to be secured. They have not been as concerned with the security of 'our entire interactive and interdependent planetary environment' (Matthew, 1999: 13–14) as with some combination of national and human security concerns. National security concerns have focused on the potential for population growth and related resource scarcity to prompt violent conflict, or the security of energy supplies. Human security concerns also relate to the potential for violent conflict and access to food, clean water and the satisfaction of basic needs. In each case, the environment is conceived in terms of resources to be exploited rather than an ecosystem to be secured, so the securitization of the environment has been very uneven. While the hole in the ozone layer presented a threat that yielded relatively effective international measures, wider climate change has been even more neglected since the measures required to address it imply significant transformations of existing patterns of consumption and global economic structures. In some ways, this uneven securitization is not surprising: for the Copenhagen School securitization relates to the articulation of an existential threat that requires urgent action (see Chapter 3). While some environmental disasters, such as Bhopal and Chernobyl, meet this criterion, global climate change is often seen as a failed attempt at securitization since exceptional measures have not been justified (Buzan et al., 1998; Buzan and Waever, 2003). Indeed, while much environmental security is discussed on the basis of apocalyptic visions of the future that articulate some existential threat, such a discourse of 'macro-securitization' is not met with the logic of exceptionalism of much security politics, but with the logics of prevention and management of risk-based approaches, particularly in relation to climate change (Trombetta, 2008; Methmann and Rothe, 2012; Oels, 2013). This may mean that environmental securitization operates differently from the notion of securitization inherited from the exceptionalist logics of war.

It may not be desirable to securitize environmental issues. While attempts to raise the profile of these important issues have resulted in a higher degree of political attention, securitization (as understood by the Copenhagen School) tends to produce short-term measures rather than long-term consensual decision making, perhaps undesirable for environmental problems that may call for more radical transformations of world order (Deudney, 1999). Certainly, if understandings of security remain tied to the assumptions and concepts derived from national security, viewing environmental issues in the same way is problematic. Environmental security and national security issues may produce great harm, but are of a different type. For Deudney, environmental issues are not contained in national borders, and while national security concerns relate to the international actions of others, environmental security concerns arise from the natural world and the unintentional effects of action. If national security is about intentional violence and environmental 'security' about unintended harms, the two issues are different and distinct. Indeed, as Gwyn Prins (1993) argues, environmental security concerns are 'threats without enemies'. Deudney (1999: 201) argues that environmental problems require a different approach: national security is associated with military responses by centralized organizations and an emphasis on zero-sum competition, whereas environmental issues require long-term solutions based on a 'green sensibility' that offers a different worldview that is not well served by attempts to securitize.

Environmental security may relate to a different conception of security. Rather than an association with territorial political violence and the intentional threats of other actors, environmentally induced insecurity pertains to issues of vulnerability and resilience. Vulnerabilities are clearly context specific. For instance, while natural disasters may not be caused by politics, the degree of damage they inflict is: more people die from the effects of environmental degradation when it is combined with situations of poverty, limited access to food and clean water, and weak healthcare systems. The effects of earthquakes and tsunamis are not only a function of the raw power of nature but also the strength of buildings, infrastructure, healthcare systems and so on. Resilience has two major dimensions: the ability to prevent and mitigate losses, and then the ability to maintain 'normal living conditions' and manage recovery (Buckle et al., 2000: 13). This is often couched in terms of adaptive capacity: how can societies, economies and so on adapt to catastrophic events or changed contexts (Lonergan, 1997). In this view, vulnerability rises when resilience, as adaptive capacity as well as preventive capacity, diminishes (Brauch, 2011;

Singh, 2011). This concept relates less exclusively to the risk of conflict, but also encompasses energy supplies, the harm potentially caused by floods, earthquakes, disruptions to clean water supplies, pollution, and other environmental 'threats without enemies'. Security defined in terms of vulnerabilities and resilience rather than threats is therefore security to be practised by means other than deterrence, compellence or reassurance, which rest on the interactions of mutually threatening intentional actors (see Chapter 5). This is most clearly revealed in the critical approaches that seek to treat the environment as a new referent object of security. In practice, however, wider reform-oriented discourses have not won out over those that view environmental issues as a threat to the continuation of current patterns of consumption and resource control.

Resource conflict, scarcity and distribution

What is the relationship between natural resources and conflict? Some argue that scarcity is increasing and likely to cause conflict within and between states, others that the presence of resources constitutes a curse for many societies that can cause or sustain conflict. Perhaps the dominant view of resources is that their scarcity causes competition that can at times lead to violent conflict. This accords relatively well with rationalist theories of security that posit competition for power conceived in material terms. However, rather than military resources, natural resources, food, water and so on are emphasized. Scarcity here relates to three things. First, a quantitative or qualitative reduction in resources through the degradation of water supplies, the decline of fisheries, the decline of high-quality agricultural land and so on will reduce the stock of available renewable resources. Second, demographic trends that will further heighten competition for those resources. The global population has expanded exponentially, from around 5 million people in early hunter-gatherer communities, to 1 billion in the late 18th century, 2.5 billion in 1950 to just under 7 billion now, and a predicted peak of 9 billion in 2050 (Barnett, 2010). Third, resources are unevenly distributed, so furthering conflict. Indeed, while the consumption of resources has increased with population growth, it is unevenly distributed, with the 20% of the population that lives in developed countries consuming 57% of oil, 43% of meat and 40% of steel (Barnett, 2010).

More than two centuries ago, the Reverend Thomas Malthus (1766–1834) predicted that demographic changes would produce food scarcity that would be accompanied inevitably by vice, misery and war (Peluso and Watts, 2001). For Malthus, population growth increases at a far higher rate than the ability of the earth to produce food (this was written well before the discovery of new chemical fertilisers). The inheritors of Malthusian views differ little from this pessimistic view. Kaplan's article, 'The coming anarchy' (1994: 58), which posited migration and conflict from weak states as centres of global disorder (see Chapter 10), emphasized population growth combined with environmental degradation (soil erosion, water depletion, overcrowding and disease) as the key drivers of instability, making environmental security 'the national-security issue of the early twenty-first century'. Malthusianism tends to reflect an integration of environmental issues within a broadly realist set of overarching assumptions about competitive relations between states tending towards violence (Klare, 2002). Such authors posit relatively straightforward, deterministic relationships between environmental change and violent conflict. They suggest that resource inequalities can cause conflicts (Gleick, 1991), or that exponential population growth in developing countries degrades environmental resources and holds the potential to produce violent conflict (Myers, 1987). However, while the understanding of conflict remains similar to rationalist theories of security, it may imply a new geopolitical map of conflict. For Klare (2001: 52), 'resource flows rather than political and ideological divisions constitute the major fault lines' of contemporary security.

Malthusian thinking became influential in the Clinton administration in the USA in the 1990s, which accepted views that civil wars in Africa were caused by environmental factors as well as economic ones, and that population control was imperative to security. Populist dystopian visions found such political allies in part because of the work of academic 'neo-Malthusians'. Neo-Malthusians add many other factors to the simplistic Malthusian view of population growth-related scarcity causing violence. Patterns of consumption, extractive technologies and wider political and social contexts are also viewed as important (Kahl, 2006). Here, resource depletion and scarcity do not automatically produce violent conflict, but may be a strong contributory factor. While it might be logical to assume that resource scarcity produces interstate competition and ultimately war, there is little evidence that this is actually the case (Homer-Dixon, 1994). For Homer-Dixon, the most prominent neo-Malthusian scholar, civil wars are more closely linked to environmental degradation and resource conflict, since they produce economic deprivation and undermine social institutions and can cause a descent into civil war. In particular, when these factors are found in strong states they are relatively manageable, but in weak and failing states they place great strain on societies and may produce violent conflict. While absolute levels of poverty may not cause wars, severe economic disparities can create grievances that – if a well-organized opposition arises – lead to violent conflict. Overall, Homer-Dixon (1994: 36) claims that:

> Environmental scarcity has insidious and cumulative social impacts, such as population movement, economic decline, and the weakening of states. These can contribute to diffuse and persistent sub-national violence. The rate and extent of such conflicts will increase as scarcities worsen.

Other approaches reject this prediction and argue that resource scarcity is not often a cause of war between states or a major cause of civil wars (Barnett and Adger, 2007).

Against neo-Malthusianism, other scholars draw on wider liberal hopes and faith in human reason and ingenuity to avoid the deterministic and pessimistic fears of future resource conflict. Sometimes called 'cornucopian' or 'eco-modernization' approaches, they accept that scarcity can lead to conflict, but assert and anticipate that societies adapt to and manage the pressures of population growth and resource scarcity rather than being compelled inexorably towards violence (Gleditsch, 2003; Gleditsch et al., 2006). Here, a liberal faith in markets and technology is often asserted, and rather than exhausting resources, they may be more abundant as price rises in scarce commodities produce adaptations: 'we continuously find new resources, use them more efficiently, recycle them, and substitute them' (Lomborg, 2001: 143). Indeed, for Simon (1996: 580), the 'ultimate resource' is human imagination, and as population grows, problems may increase but so too does the number of people who may solve them. Thus, 'there is no physical or economic reason why human resourcefulness and enterprise cannot forever continue to respond to impending shortages and existing problems with new expedients that, after an adjustment period, leave us better off than before the problem arose'.

Deudney (1990, 1999) argues that interstate war is not likely to arise from environmental scarcity, because the functioning of the global trade system means that states do not rely on territorial control for access to resources on which their national military and political security depends. This makes territorial conquest an unnecessary means of securing resources and global conquest is also now too costly a means of obtaining resources, particularly due to greater economic interdependence. Further, Deudney (1990: 471) argues that technologies have altered the relationship between states and resources as they have entered an 'age of substitutability', in which more plentiful resources (iron, aluminium, silicon and hydrocarbons) are now capable of being made into 'virtually everything needed'. Likewise, the association of rare natural resources with wealth and power is no longer what it was in the 19th and much of the 20th centuries, as the wealthiest states – like Japan – are resource poor, but technologically rich. This has had the effect of driving natural resource prices down, rather than up, which is what would be expected if resource scarcity were really as acute as neo-Malthusians argue. Nevertheless, as Homer-Dixon (1991) responds, contemporary resource issues are complex, with many arising simultaneously and particularly among poor states and societies, so there may be little reason to assume that past capacities for adaptation and improvement will be replicated.

Neo-Malthusian and cornucopian perspectives share a common rationalist sense that resource scarcity can cause conflict, but differ on the extent to which it will do so. More broadly, liberal approaches argue that population growth and environmental degradation need not produce conflict.

This stems from a liberal preference for identifying cooperation as a means of managing conflicting or common interests; that is, political adaptation as well as technological and market-driven adaptation can manage the strains of scarcity. For instance, while water resources are argued to hold among the greatest potential for violence, others claim that shared water resources tend to produce intense negotiation rather than violent conflict (Yoffe and Wolf, 1999). Some constructivists also argue that whether resource scarcity results in conflict or cooperation is not simply a result of material conditions but is socially constructed (Litfin, 1999).

Others argue that the presence and distribution of natural resources correlate with violent conflict rather than absolute scarcity. Since violence requires resources, as Brodie observed many years ago, 'the predisposing factors to military aggression are full bellies, not empty ones' (cited in Deudney, 1990: 473). In contrast to the view of scarcity producing conflict, it is also common for an abundance of some natural resources to contribute to human insecurity, poor governance, state weakness and, ultimately, conflict. The so-called 'resource curse' has meant that in many developing countries where there are natural resources such as diamonds, oil, coltan and other mineral wealth, they have been captured by governing elites for their own enrichment. This has built weak states, since governing elites need not rely on taxation revenues and thus fail to build strong legitimacy or bureaucratic institutions (Humphreys, 2005). So, the resource curse contributes to fragile political orders, in which legitimacy is limited and grievances may arise, and where effective security institutions are not built, making rebellion and conflict cheap (Collier and Hoeffler, 2005; Collier, 2010). This is particularly so when economies are reliant on natural raw materials, since these are readily exploitable and the economy is vulnerable to shocks when prices for such commodities drop. While the presence of natural resources, then, does not make war inevitable and is never the only cause of conflict, it is conducive and productive of wider political and economic conditions that make civil wars more likely and potentially more damaging (Ross, 2003). Reinforcing the resource curse, natural resources can be viewed as a 'honey pot', where greedy groups and faction leaders seek profits through war. This is seen as being particularly the case when mineral resources exist and are 'lootable' (de Soysa, 2000, 2002). Not all resources hold the same potential for conflict, and Homer-Dixon emphasizes that nonrenewable resources (minerals, oil and so on) have produced more conflict than renewable resources (forests, fish and so on). He argues that, of the renewable resources, water is most likely to produce conflict because it is so fundamental to survival and upstream actions by one state (such as dams or pollution) will have negative effects on those downstream. Many argue that the global trading system reduces dependency on territorial control of most resources, although water and energy have been argued to be exceptions likely to promote violent conflict (Gleick, 1991). In relation to adaptation, it is also notable that there has been greater adaptation in some nonrenewable resources than in others (agricultural land) or renewable ones (water and so on) (Kahl, 2006).

Critical approaches have often emphasized that the resource wars focus of environmental security serves to ignore important aspects of political economy. For such views, scarcity is not primarily or solely a product of natural resource shortages or population growth but is produced in a structured political economy. This means that the problems of the environment and related conflict are distributional not natural. Even in conditions of global and local abundance, scarcity can be experienced by the poor and less powerful, since global markets, the expansion of capitalism and so on have tended to organize resource access to serve the consumption of the powerful. In this view, resource scarcity is distributional not natural. The violence that sometimes arises in relation to environmental concerns is therefore context specific, rooted in local histories and social relations as well as broader global power relations and divisions that constitute specific systems of accumulation and fields of power and their shifts (Peluso and Watts, 2001). Indeed, as Le Billon (2001: 568) argues, 'the transformation of nature into tradable commodities is a deeply political process; involving the definition of property rights, the organization of labour, and the allocation of profits'. This political process combines with the form of resources to yield diverse conflictual or cooperative relationships. For Le Billon, if natural resources involve extraction (such as minerals), violence over territorial control (of the state or a smaller area) may occur. If resources are productive (crops), structural violence and relations of domination may predominate that may occasionally result in grievances that yield war. Further, the geographical location of resources matters – if resources are close to the capital of a weak state they may not be open to rebel capture, but if resources are in remote areas rebel groups can more easily capture and integrate them into their war economies. Thus, there can be no crude relationship between conflict and the abundance or scarcity of resources in national terms, but only a more specific set of territorial, political and economic relations that may be conducive to war. Further, this means that even when wars are not motivated by resources, resources become integrated into evolving systems of power and profit through which warring factions support themselves (Keen, 2001). Such war economies are not reducible to simple national-level relations. They are both highly local, as Le Billon claims, but also often deeply regionalized, with neighbouring governments frequently involved in facilitating and profiting from the export of goods (Pugh et al., 2004). These networks, however, cannot merely be attributed to the greed of warlords and corrupt neighbours. They are also inherently entwined with demand and consumption in more powerful states; whether the demand is for cheap diamonds and gold, coltan for mobile phones, exotic hardwood timber for furniture, or even rubber and metal, all have fuelled wars and insecurity in Angola, the Democratic Republic of the Congo, Liberia and Sierra Leone.

From resources to radical ecology

If security is taken to mean the sustainability of current ways of life, existing geopolitical and economic power distributions and patterns of consumption, then environmental change and resource distribution may have far-reaching implications. If, conversely, the environment is the referent object of security, then contemporary ways of life, consumption and power are revealed to have negative effects on resources, such as the environmental effects of oil production and the effects of industrial emissions on local and regional environments. Further, the use of military force in pursuit of security aims often has negative environmental impacts, from the anticipated 'nuclear winter' that could have taken hold after nuclear war to the more fully realized effects of nuclear testing or the use of depleted uranium munitions and the effects of anti-crop warfare or airborne drug crop eradication efforts.

For some more radical perspectives, environmental security requires a shift in the referent object of security, towards the security of the biosphere. These 'ecological' perspectives understand security in different ways, which may offer some prospects for tackling environmental issues without falling into the state-centric, short-term, problem-solving orientation of securitization. This rests on a significant shift in the ontological foundations of theorizing security (see Chapter 1).

Most Western political theory is 'anthropocentric' in its ontology; that is, it sees politics and action as deriving from and among human beings and collectives. It gives no importance to environmental issues or other material things, other than viewing them as a resource within human relations. This rests on a separation of human and nature (or human and technology), and views much of human history as a story of the progressive domination of nature by man. As poststructuralist scholar Walker (2006: 190) claims:

> to imagine that modern man can protect nature or that he can be protected from nature is already to work within a dualism that is at once the great glory of modern accounts of what it means to a proper, mature, and free human being and the source of great angst and alienation.

This modern hope of mastery and fear of its failure underlies both the dread of natural environmental limits on national security asserted by Malthusian and neo-Malthusian approaches, and the optimism of cornucopian and liberal technological hopes for adaptation. Likewise, distributional explanations for resource conflict are social rather than natural explanations for violence that invert the neo-Malthusian relationship between societies and the environment, but maintain the categorical separation and domination of human and natural (Kahl, 2006).

Ecological approaches seek to develop an alternative environmental security politics by challenging this ontological paradigm. They do not assert a simple dominance of politics/social factors or natural/environmental factors, seeing both as reductionist, and instead propose a view that emphasizes how human societies are entangled with biological ecosystems and environmental systems. In this context, security pertains to humans as *part of* an environment (Pirages and DeGeest, 2004), and thus enables a different way of understanding the environment as a referent object of security that goes far beyond the resource dimensions of interstate and intrastate conflicts.

This has two major implications for understanding security. First, it offers a different 'geopolitical imagination' of security, since the referent object is neither, principally, the nation-state nor the individual human but a complex system of humans, nature and technology. This means that since environmental issues do not have a clear inside and outside defined by traditional views of territorial sovereign political communities (states), operating on the basis of those divisions is misplaced. Rather than divisions, ecological views assume that everything is potentially connected with everything else. Political communities, forms of insecurity and transnational threats cannot therefore be isolated and contained. Second, it emphasizes not just how human states and societies are affected by the material world conceived as resource, but how the environment is entwined with and affected by human action. The disposal of waste, pollution, the clearance of agricultural land and so on all have effects on 'nature' – there is no 'free lunch' (Dalby, 2002: 128). Environmental security cannot, therefore, be thought of and achieved through the mindset of modernist separation and mastery or the derivative limiting of politics to human-created political communities defined by territorial divisions. While for Deudney, the first of these meant that environmental issues were not national security issues, for Dalby (2002), both mean that security must adapt its thinking towards an ecological paradigm of complex interrelated systems. He speaks of the 'anthropocene' as a new understanding of humanity within the biosphere to take account of human impacts on the environment.

Ecological approaches argue that traditional ways of thinking about security politics have not just misunderstood the environment (as a mere resource) but that 'modern anthropocentric and utilitarian cosmology is responsible for environmental degradation' (Barnett, 2001: 2). There is a connection between anthropocentric political theory and human actions that puts human beings first (and exclusively) as those to be secured. Green theory offers a different view that avoids separating the human and natural worlds and offers an explicitly normative project that echoes that of human security but seeks not to achieve human security at the expense of environmental insecurity. Instead, ecological security is 'a positive security that seeks to maintain ecological equilibrium in the long term' (Barnett, 2001: 109). This conceives security in terms of sustainability and resilience to environmental (or other) shocks. What is to be made resilient in this view, though, is not fixed national identities, economic systems, or states but diversity, and some argue this diversity conflicts with state-centric approaches to governance and security (Barnett, 2001; Trombetta, 2008).

Some critical approaches to security also problematize the assumptions of the resource conflict debate. While the dominant framing of environmental security treats the term 'security' as a universal and static value, critical security scholars argue that approaches to environmental security are as much a contestation and rearticulation of the meaning of security as they are the implications of environmental change. Viewing security as emancipation prioritizes different environmental issues and politicizes the relationships that sustain them (McDonald, 2012) (see Chapter 3). Across the range of environmental security issues runs the concern that environmental security measures and agendas seek to secure unsustainable forms of resource consumption and global divisions rather than securing the environment or producing a more emancipatory world order. For Booth (2007: 410), population stress and the destruction of nature are part of the impending new crisis of world security as nature is 'being overwhelmed by the growth, spread, demands, and carelessness of human society'. He argues that while states are aware of numerous environmental dangers, the challenge of the destruction of nature needs to be understood as a whole, not as a series of separate issues. The only rational option, therefore, is to adopt a 'deep ecology' view that Booth (2007: 335) associates with the idea of 'Gaia', which conceives the earth and humanity as an organic whole and reveals simply and forcefully that 'time is running out, but much can be saved'.

Further, some feminist scholars have pointed out that environmental insecurity is experienced differently by different people and this often contains a gender dimension that much environmental security studies ignores due to a focus on state or societal security or the insecurity of undifferentiated 'humans'. They argue that environmental security should be viewed in terms of multiple levels and systems and should engage with feminist perspectives on the nature of security, the causes and experiences of conflict, and the highly gendered implications of environmental security policies; for example, viewing population expansion as a security threat affects women as mothers (Detraz, 2010). Some 'eco-feminist' approaches highlight the limited and gendered approach to security inherent in variants of Malthusian security thinking, and seek to resist their gendered anthropocentrism – based on viewing men as dominating both nature and women but portraying women as carers. Instead, they assert a dynamic relationship between human and nonhuman nature that incorporates complex power relations, and cast 'radical ecology' as a 'search for a livable world' (Merchant, 1992, 1996, 2004). Here, the discourse of 'scarcity' views nature as a 'stockroom of resources that may become depleted' and ignores the deeper relations between the two (Detraz, 2010: 105).

Climate change

Climate change has been raised as a security issue for a decade, and reached great prominence in 2007 with a UNSC debate on the issue. Climate change drives macro-scale, long-term environmental changes such as coastal erosion, increasing intensities of droughts and storms, and precipitation patterns. This may be a national security issue, such as for Pacific atoll states like Kiribati, the Marshall Islands, Tokelau and Tuvalu, which are physically and functionally threatened by rising sea levels (Barnett, 2001). It also has shorter term effects on flooding, heat waves, disease epidemics and other human security problems. However, human security is affected in ways that are not wholly attributable to climate effects: vulnerability and adaptive capacity are shaped by social, political and economic conditions (Barnett and Adger, 2007). The complex causalities of climate-related insecurity may therefore militate against simplistic securitization, although simplification is inherent in the securitization of other issues too. There is certainly no consensus that climate change will increase the incidence of war, not least because the debate on resources and war is divided and so the effects of climate change on the various factors identified in that debate may merely further complicate the issues without yielding resolution (Barnett and Adger, 2007; Salehyan, 2008). Likewise, while it is likely that climate change will affect migration patterns, with estimates of 200 million people migrating due to climate-induced hardship by 2050, the political and security implications of climate change-induced migration are harder to predict (Reuveny, 2007; International Organization for Migration, 2008).

In 1991, Jervis (1991: 64) argued that global warming and environmental degradation were unable to offer a basis for action that would be sufficiently unified to set a US foreign policy agenda since environmental problems are 'too far off, the scientific evidence is too ambiguous, the domestic interests involved are too conflict, and the alternative approaches are too many'. This may no longer be the case, as in 1992, the UN created a Framework Convention on Climate Change that eventually led to the Kyoto Protocol agreed in 1997. In 2007, a report by the UN Intergovernmental Panel on Climate Change (2007) synthesized a wide range of scientific research that strongly concluded that it was over 90 per cent certain that global warming was caused by human action.

This scientific consensus has not, however, produced a political consensus on climate change. In particular, climate change covers a wide range of issues and human–environmental interactions that are not fully understood let alone predictable sufficient for strategic decision making. For Keohane and Victor (2011), the distribution of interests and uncertainty about the benefits of action and whether other states will honour promises have militated against the creation of a single climate change regime. Instead, there may be argued to be a regime complex of smaller issue-specific agreements (that still may not yield concerted action). Thus, the cuts required by the Kyoto Protocol were extensive and had high potential economic costs. It is inherently difficult to decide on the distribution of costs that derive from shared global problems. The Kyoto Protocol took what might be seen as an ethical and reasonable judgement that developed countries that had contributed most emissions should bear the brunt of the costs, but developing states like China and India with rapidly rising emissions agreed to implement cuts but have no binding targets. An intractable issue then arises: Should those that caused a problem in the past bear the costs, or those that are now exacerbating it?

More deeply, the complex causation and ontology of the radical ecological view requires an orientation of climate change and other environmental politics towards fundamental political change that conflicts with the conservatism of security thought (Dalby, 2002). For instance, Booth (2007: 413) argues that human-made climate change requires international agreement that includes the states that constitute an 'axis of pollution'. However, recent US and other political leaders have declared climate change a security issue partly because of the possible long-term effects on the ability of the USA to project military and other power, and partly because such effects are uncertain (Floyd, 2010). While most environmental politics does not explicitly adopt a radical ecological discourse, some scholars note that the ontological claims of climate change-related security have shifted from seeing stable and predictable linear processes of climate change to greater fears of nonlinear unpredictable changes that relate to complex interlinkages between the social and the material worlds (Mayer, 2012).

As noted earlier, climate change politics has not conformed to the exceptionalist logics of Copenhagen School securitization, in which significant shifts in policy are expected to follow from the invocation of 'security'. The partial securitization of climate change relies on apocalyptic imaginations of the future but rather than legitimating an urgent exceptional politics of threat-based security predicted by Copenhagen School securitization, responses have been shaped more by a managerial politics of risk (Methmann and Rothe, 2012). While diverse, these invoke and rely on logics of prediction and precaution and conceive of security in terms of vulnerability and resilience, particularly via notions of adaptation (Trombetta, 2008). This has been affected by developing scientific understandings and uncertainties of the causes and consequences of climate change. While general consensus exists on the origins of climate change in human action, uncertainties about specific causes and particularly about local impacts and thus the requirement for adaptation remain high. While cornucopian thought tends to take adaptation as an inherent value of humanity, the costs of adaptation may be high and the politics of investment and distribution remains complex (Methmann and Rothe, 2012; Oels, 2013). Importantly, this transition to a logic of risk in the securitization of climate change has been entwined with a shift from viewing it as an intensifying and ultimately threatening but far-off challenge to a more amorphous nonlinear phenomenon that conflicts with a belief in long-term market-based adaptation (Mayer, 2012). Cumulatively, this means that the reasons Jervis (1991) gave for dismissing climate change as a security issue are no longer present.

While the political discourse of climate change security has begun to emulate (and seek to limit and channel) the complex ontologies suggested by radical ecological approaches, it also continues to be characterized by a prioritization of traditional conceptualizations of the protection of national political communities. In particular, the politics of climate change and security broadly seek the 'maintenance of achieved levels of civilization' (Buzan et al., 1998: 76). Thus, in 1992 US President George Bush argued at the Earth Summit that 'the American lifestyle is not up for negotiation', a perspective that was expressed practically in the withdrawal of the USA from the Kyoto Protocol (Trombetta, 2008: 596). The debates on energy security as a national security issue and food security as a human security issue reveal that the security of ways of life underlies much contemporary environmental security.

Energy security

Energy security is the reliability and sustainability of energy supply sufficient to meet the demands of economic, societal and military demand. It has become a major strategic preoccupation of many of the world's most powerful states, particularly the USA and European states and rising powers like China and India. Energy security relates to short-term needs for the maintenance of energy supplies and the creation of supply networks that are resilient to disruptions. Resilience against disruption also often means reducing or managing dependency since many energy supplies are global markets. For example, the 1973 restrictions on oil exports imposed by the Organization of Petroleum Exporting Countries produced a sharp rise in oil prices and identified the reliance of major military powers on the fuel that is needed for economic growth and the use of military power (LaCasse and Plourde, 1995). More recently, in 2009, a series of disputes between Russia and the Ukraine on the transit of natural gas to European markets resulted in a decline and even cut-off in gas supplies to some EU countries. EU countries cumulatively import around 60% of their gas, around half of which comes from Russia (Proedrou, 2007), resulting in a degree of interdependence since supplier and recipient rely on each other. However, since 2006, many European governments have been seeking alternative sources of gas and may reinvest in nuclear power generation. Past and contemporary disruptions and dependencies in energy supplies combine with anticipations of future crises as the world is approaching the geological peak for existing types of oil supplies, after which depletion of oil reserves may create a degree of scarcity that calls into question the sustainability of fossil fuel-derived energy consumption and the environmental and economic costs of pursuing other reserves. The potential for a decline or temporary disruption in supply is the main concern of energy security. While this relates to the supply of natural gas and the generation of electricity, it is the supply of oil that most captures the imagination of potential future energy insecurity. Indeed, it has been claimed that 'oil, more than any other commodity, illustrates both the importance and the mystification of natural resources in the modern world' (Coronil, 1997: 49).

Energy security has tended to operate on the basis of two major logics that have intersected but reveal different notions of security. First, the 'logic of war', in which energy supply is crucial to the practice of war and also the cause of resource wars. In this logic, security is understood in the traditional way as the security of nation-states in their relations with each other. Second, the 'logic of subsistence', in which every aspect of political, social and economic life is viewed as reliant on energy and so energy shortages and disruptions are a threat to ways of life. Here, the politics of energy security pervades all aspects of life and brings in many competing claims to and about security from states but also NGOs, international organizations, industries and so on, and security becomes the subsistence of ways of life and consumption not the seeking of survival by states (Ciuta, 2010).

The logic of war predominates in the framing of energy security as a national security concern, since most major consuming countries are not self-sufficient in oil, natural gas or other fossil fuels and must rely on global markets that draw on resources from the global South. Global energy and resource consumption is estimated to be rising dramatically, particularly among developing states and rising economies like China and India. For some, this signals a new geopolitical era in which states rather than companies drive investment in resources and technologies, and new configurations of cooperation and conflict emerge on the basis of the distribution of resources rather than military power (Klare, 2008). In realist views, while new modes of cooperation are called for, contemporary practices and developments are producing a zero-sum competition for energy resources akin to an arms race that can only lead to violent conflict between states (Klare, 2008). For example, the oil-rich regions of Central Asia and the Caucasus have seen the USA, Russia and China vying for influence through military and economic aid, and competition in Africa between the USA and China is becoming increasingly militarized (Klare and Volman, 2006). Rather than the ideological and military proxy conflicts of the Cold War, competition for influence in the global South is now over energy supply. In 1993, China became a net energy importer after decades of self-sufficiency. The implications of this are much debated, with some positing that a rising China dependent on oil markets is likely to engage in destabilizing and military actions to secure supplies, while others view dependency as likely to result in greater moderation and the integration of China into the international trading system (Downs, 2004). While this may be a new phenomenon in those regions, some realist scholars emphasize that access to oil has been a major driver of US strategic interests and involvement in the Middle East from the post-Second World War period to the 2003 Iraq War (Layne, 2006), and that the US national interest now lies in stabilizing the regions of oil production across the globe (Brzezinski, 2003/04). There is, however, a tension between attempts to stabilize oil-producing regions and the growing militarization of national energy security practices of major powers evident in the regional and global effects of the 2003 Iraq War (Peters, 2004).

Longer term concern relates to the increasing scarcity of oil in the major oilfields in use. Dramatic rises in oil prices have been experienced since the start of the 21st century, and some analysts argue that oil reserves in Saudi Arabia and other places that provide most oil are reaching their peak and are about to decline significantly (Campbell and Laherrere, 1998; Simmons, 2005). It is notable that 54 of the largest 65 oil-producing states have already encountered peaks in some of their reserves, and the rate of discoveries of new oilfields peaked in 1965. Thus, peak discovery is argued to have passed and peak production is approaching (Mulligan, 2010). When peak production will be reached is much debated, with oil companies pointing to new and plentiful stocks of a different type to those whose discovery peaked 50 years ago (Owen et al., 2010). The prospect of an oil peak challenges anthropocentric political and social theory that has traditionally posited a separation and dominance of humanity over nature. This separation is encountered particularly through the cornucopian expectation that technological solutions can be found to overcome natural problems. As ecologist and chemical engineer Peet (1992: 155) claimed: 'the standard politico-economic world view denies the possibility that humankind will not be able to achieve any technological feat that may be needed, and in the meantime, resources are being used without any thought for the future'. In this view, there is also a tension in seeing energy security as related to environmental security. Energy security relates to the technology and political astuteness and power of political actors (mostly states), whereas the environment – in its full ecological sense – sets limits on security that derive not from power nor anarchy nor the challenges of technical ingenuity but a rigid natural limit that cannot be mastered (Mulligan, 2010). Thus, the assertions of a peak in oil supply are deeply antithetical to much political theory and liberal assumptions.

The logic of subsistence goes beyond the military implications of the short-term stability of oil access and long-term anticipations of peak oil. In this regard, since energy security is defined in terms of long-term sustainability and resilience to short-term disruptions, energy security strategies involve adaptation of the energy supply system as well as protection of access to current supplies. Here, the modern Western hope for adaptive technological solutions is expressed in the development of more efficient engines and the diversification of energy supplies to more renewable sources. There are some signs of hope here, at least for some states. In the USA, for example, greater investment in domestic production through advanced technologies is yielding significant growth. Similarly, technologies for extracting natural gas from shale and the growing efficiency of gas-powered electricity generation contribute to low prices and growing consumption. The negative effects of energy supply on the environment are also believed to be falling, with CO_2 emissions dropping in the USA, and the growth of renewable sources is increasing, from 13 per cent in 2011 to an estimated 16 per cent of energy generation in 2013, which sounds relatively modest but is a faster rate of increase than that in fossil fuel consumption (US Energy Information Administration, 2013). The diversification of sources is central to sustainable and resilient energy supply (LaCasse and Plourde, 1995). Among the world's richest countries there has been some diversification of sources of natural gas but limited diversification of oil supplies. This implies an overall increase in energy security, given the growing reliance on gas. However, it is experienced differently by different wealthy states (Cohen et al., 2011). Further, there are diverse approaches to energy security in practice, with European countries seeking cooperation and liberalization through a common energy policy and the USA and NATO holding out the prospects for more antagonistic approaches involving the possible use of the military to secure supply routes (Trombetta, 2008).

These two logics of energy compete with each other and conflict with wider human and environmental security. The security of energy supplies and the dependence on fossil fuels for economic development are limiting factors in the global politics of climate change. Strategies of diversification for oil production may help mitigate the peak oil threat, particularly since the peak oil thesis relates only to the types of oil extraction currently in use. Oil extraction has traditionally targeted the more easily accessible reserves but there are other stocks in sand and shale that are plentiful if technologically more difficult to acquire. However, as the Deepwater Horizon oil spill of 2010 showed, the premature use of new technologies in pursuit of new stocks has had a significant environmental cost. Although the long-term sustainability of energy may require investment and a shift to renewable energy sources, in some cases this conflicts with human aspects of environmental security. For instance, the growing use of biofuels could diversify energy sources and reduce dangerous emissions of greenhouse gases. However, the production of biomass crops for fuel has reduced the availability of agricultural land for food production. Thus, Oxfam (2012) estimates that, between 2000 and 2010, land acquired by foreign investors was the equivalent of that required to feed 1 billion people, a similar number to those that suffer from chronic malnutrition. Instead of growing food, people have been forcibly evicted from their land and two-thirds of such land acquisitions have been used to grow export crops, mainly those like palm oil and sugar cane that can be used as biofuels.

Food and water

While the fuels for power generation, cars and homes are increasingly securitized, the fuels for human bodies (food and water) are usually not. Food is a neglected human right. Article 25 of the 1948 Universal Declaration of Human Rights claimed that:

> Everyone has the right to a standard of living adequate for the health and well-being of himself and of his family, including food, clothing, housing and medical care and necessary social services, and the right to security in the event of unemployment, sickness, disability, widowhood, old age or other lack of livelihood in circumstances beyond his control.

With around 900 million people experiencing chronic hunger and malnutrition being related to at least a third of child deaths worldwide, food resources are a critically important human security issue (World Health Organization, 2012). The UNDP (1994: 27) defines food security as physical access to food, which means there must be enough food and people can access it. In general, food prices declined from the 1960s, with a spike in the 1970s caused by the oil crisis (Godfray et al., 2010). However, since 2002, prices have risen substantially, with a peak in 2008 that slowed longer term trends in the reduction of global hunger and forced many people to reduce their calorific intake and change to cheap, less nutritious foods (FAO/WFP/IFAD, 2011, 2012). While advances in fertiliser technology have made food crops far more abundant than Malthus could have predicted, there are now some concerns that peaks in phosphorus availability may be approaching in the next few decades that might undercut food production (Cordell et al., 2009).

Much like energy security, food security relates to the security and resilience of supply as well as the ability of those in need to pay for it. Food crises arise from natural and human-made political causes. Earthquakes, floods and hurricanes may create short-term crises, and drought may contribute to famine crises, although famine is generally thought of as a phenomenon produced by poor policy making and conflict. Environmental changes, such as the degradation of agricultural land and fish stocks, are important factors in local and regional food security (Ericksen, 2008a). These are not just natural phenomena, however, since the evidence suggests that civil wars produce a substantial decline in fish catches, 13 times more than a weather phenomenon like El Niño (Hendrix and Glaser, 2011). Further, it is not just the amount but the quality and safety of food that affects malnutrition. In many cases, the safety of food is compromised through contamination and high levels of pesticide residues that play a major role in cases of diarrhoea, cholera and other diseases (Maxwell and Slater, 2003).

Food insecurity is about access to food, not only overall levels of availability. It is therefore a distributional issue and relates to complex developments such as urbanization and wider political economic systems that determine how people can access food by converting financial, political and other assets into food (Sen, 1981; Dreze and Sen, 1989). Indeed, viewing access to food as a human right requires not only that the food is provided in the short term but that economic and political systems are created to ensure that people are empowered to realize that right (Kent, 2005). For some, adopting a view akin to the deep ecological perspective, food security and accessibility are part of a system in which it is better to explore integrated systems rather than distinct social and ecological systems: food security and insecurity encountered as resilience, vulnerability and adaptability are neither social (nor political) nor ecological but profoundly socio-ecological (Young et al., 2006; Ericksen, 2008a, 2008b). Indeed, conceptualizing the human security dimensions of environmental security in this way links climate change and human insecurity in a complex system of vulnerability, in which 'the more people are dependent on climate sensitive forms of natural capital, and the less they rely on economic or social forms of capital, the more at risk they are from climate change' (Barnett and Adger, 2007: 641). Clearly, food security and insecurity are related to wider environmental security concerns of climate change, resource depletion and the incidence of civil wars (as both cause and effect). Climate factors affect food production and water quality that in turn produce hundreds of thousands of extra deaths each year, with up to 17 per cent of malnutrition-related deaths being attributable to climate change factors (World Health Organization, 2013).

Water security raises human and national security issues – worldwide, 14% of people lack access to clean water and 41% to basic sanitation (Pogge, 2008: 103). The 2007 Intergovernmental Panel on Climate Change report highlighted that the distribution of water across the planet's surface is changing, with severe storms in some places, longer heat waves and droughts in others, ongoing rises in sea levels and aggressive flooding. This is predicted to have strong effects on human security, with an expectation that by 2020 some African countries will see reduced crop yields from rain-fed agriculture of up to 50%, freshwater supplies across Asia will decline and increase morbidity and mortality from diarrhoeal disease, and there will be significant water security problems in parts of Australia and New Zealand. Further, the security of water supplies is a central aspect of critical infrastructure protection in the USA and Europe, which highlights terrorist threats and wider pollution and disruption of supplies. Water security therefore connects climate and human security in important ways. While water security is also distributional, it is not distributed by a market with uneven power relations but partly by nature – rivers cross many states, and the quantity and quality of water access in one country is affected by development projects, agriculture, and military and political factors upstream. Here, the domestic and micro-politics of local water supplies and economic development within one state may affect the human and national security of another. Homer-Dixon (1994) argues that it is the most likely renewable resource to produce conflict, since it is so fundamental to survival and because upstream actions by one state (such as dams or pollution) will have negative effects on those downstream. Further, adaptation to other resource issues is harder for water, which still relies on territorial access rather than global markets (Gleick, 1991; Kahl, 2006). Nevertheless, there is some evidence that levels of economic development interact with water resources, such that poor and developed countries have a lower risk of conflict over water since the first have limited demand and the second have reached a point where they can invest in technologies that reduce the need for water consumption for economic activity (Gleditsch et al., 2006).

The prospect of water supplies contributing to the logics and limits of regional stability and security is seen as particularly important in the Middle East, where water resources have been a source of conflict for five millennia. For instance, one of the reasons Syria gave sanctuary to the PKK (a terrorist organization in Turkey) was due to conflicting sovereignty claims with Turkey over the use of waters from the Euphrates and Tigris rivers. The negotiated end of support for the PKK, however, was facilitated by a 1987 deal to release water supplies to Syria. Later, the Euphrates river and the Sea of Galilee became central to negotiations between Israel and Syria in the Arab–Israeli peace process (Williams, 2001; Altunisik and Tür, 2006). However, the logics of water politics are not inherently conflictual and the interdependencies of water may promote cooperation rather than conflict (Gleick, 1993; Yoffe and Wolf, 1999). Water supply also contributes to the limits of human security, since water availability and purity affect food production, drought or flooding may produce displacement and refugee flows, and limited water supplies set stark limits on economic development and poverty reduction.

Conclusion

The dominant way in which environmental issues have been securitized is their incorporation into existing strategic security rationales premised on a concern with violent conflict and the interests of powerful states. The prospects for population change and environmentally induced resource scarcity to generate conflict are the subject of much debate. The ongoing risk-based securitization of climate change posits a different logic of security to environmental issues that relies on taming and managing risk and anticipated future (and present) harms. While there is no overarching climate security regime, environmental issues of different types have been subject to varying degrees of political attention. The security of food and water supplies is clearly a matter of life and death for many poor populations. The security of energy supplies is a matter of the security of the environment that exists in tension with the security of ways of life and modes of consumption. Exploring these side by side shows that the security of life for some and of ways of life for others can often conflict. Whether or not this conflict can be resolved by cornucopian hopes for market and technology-based adaptation is debatable. By understanding environmental security as a national security issue related to Malthusian fears of restive poor populations or statist concerns of energy supplies, security studies has done a disservice to the complexity and values of environmental security. Alternative views drawing on green theory, deep ecology and other critical approaches to understanding security emphasize that the security of the environment and the security of people are deeply entwined, and that a fundamentally different ontology is required to tackle environmental insecurity. It is, in part, the combination of this unfamiliar ontology that conflicts with traditional geopolitical divisions and the continued presence of uncertainties about the nature of nature that militate against wider securitization. This, however, may not be undesirable.

Chapter 14

Conclusion

What are we to make of understanding security? Security has no settled or universally accepted meaning. This book has not been a search for one, but has sought to explore the ways in which many different securities are understood and practised. It began with three main claims:

(1) Security is about life and death, ways of life and the prevention, delay or manner of death.
(2) Security is a powerful word, operative as a noun/condition, an adjective/value, and a verb/practice or type of politics.
(3) Security is comprehensible only through the specific relationships in which it is entangled with other things.

Likewise, understanding is both a condition (of ontological security: the knowledge that one's knowledge is sufficiently reliable to enable predictable living in the world) and a verb: a process of cognition, interaction, thought, reflection, evidence gathering, valuing, asserting, arguing, agreeing, dismissing, ignoring, interpreting and misinterpreting. Together, these establish the logics and limits of security.

Logics and limits

Diverse logics and limits are claimed to shape security. Realism is dominated by the logics of power, self-help and anarchic structure, and liberalism by a logic of progress through reason via institutions and democracy. Critical approaches assert varying logics, such as the logic of appropriateness in relation to norms and expectations, the logic of exceptionalism in securitization theory, the logic of practicality, the dynamics of discourse, or the potential paths towards security as emancipation. These play out in various ways in the issues covered in this book, but they are derivative logics that assert a deeper set of logics and limits.

Insecurity, threat, vulnerability and risk

Security is about living in a dangerous world. The predominant logic of security is one of response: it always sits in juxtaposition and opposition to some claimed insecurity. Security, then, comprises reaction against action, or response against anticipated harm. There are two pervasive ways of understanding insecurities – threats and risks. Threat is a rationalistic construct of interactions between intentional actors, it pertains to a calculus of intentions + capabilities of others. In responsive logic, it pertains to interests + capabilities, which are construed as vulnerabilities and strategies. Strategic action against threat tends to seek to intervene in the cost–benefit calculations of a potential enemy by making threatening actions either too costly or unlikely to succeed, as in deterrence, compellence and coercion, or unnecessary through reassurance. Thus, it is about changing the mind of another actor. Risk is different. It is largely, but not exclusively, probabilistic: its primary calculation is probability x impact, which may be negative or positive. This calculation is often found in security issues that do not relate to the actions of other states or people but to wider depersonalized phenomena. The logic of response to risk is largely managerial, although this may take many forms, from a prudential and precautionary logic in which uncertainty is acted on as if it were certain, to a pre-emptive logic that aims to prevent what is feared perhaps through the use of violence. Both logics of response seek to remake the anticipated world by intervening in some way that is rational and has a degree of predictability. In both, security is predicated on some form of control, although in risk, it is the control of future harms that is emphasized more.

Both threats and risks also have an understanding of vulnerability. Nuclear deterrence supported by rationalist assumptions functioned through threat and ensuring vulnerability rather than eradicating it. Precautionary logics of risk seek to minimize vulnerability and compensate for what remains through resilience conceived as adaptive capacities. Security practices in some areas tend to speak of reducing vulnerabilities rather than combating threats. Security becomes not the ability to deter or compel an identifiable opponent but to manage risks and build greater resilience and adaptability into the fabric of daily life, so that terrorist attacks, natural disasters and so on have minimum negative effects.

The responsive logic of security against insecurity separates the two and then articulates two major sets of relationships. First, the nature of response is determined by the nature of insecurity, such that power is met with power, violence with violence, regional problems with regional solutions, global problems with global solutions, or the recent claim that since transnational threats of terror and crime are organized as networks, 'it takes networks to fight networks' (Arquilla and Rondfeldt, 1996: 81). Second, this separation enables varying logics of relationships to be asserted, such that competitive logics of behaviour derive from the externalization of threats in international affairs, or that threats and responses are mutually constitutive, such that it is not just that we respond to threats from outside, but that our fears and responses contribute to the actions and intentions of others. This is not a legitimation, it is a sensibility, an understanding of 'counter-fear' (Booth and Wheeler, 2008). The logics and limits of these relationships and notions of risk and its management are understood in relation to deeper conditions – those of uncertainty.

Uncertainty

Security is often understood as a quest for certainty (Dillon, 1996). For most understandings, the limits of certainty in practical security knowledge produce the logics of security. In the concept of the security dilemma, the scarcity of security in international affairs is conditioned by the limits of certainty that can be achieved about the intentions and capabilities of other states. Failing to trust the information provided by others states, since words are cheap, states may look to assess others' military capabilities. However, these are often ambiguous and the same military preparations and technologies may be part of an impending attack or a peaceful intention. As noted by Booth and Wheeler (2008), this condition of uncertainty gives rise to three interpretations:

- *fatalism* that asserts a deterministic world in which states want but never achieve 100 per cent certainty and respond to this impossibility with power
- *mitigator* perspectives that view the conditions of uncertainty as variable, making peace and stability strong in some situations, but weak in others
- *transcender* views for which the effects of uncertainty can be escaped through enhanced social relations such as in security communities (see Chapters 5 and 6).

While a base level of uncertainty is seen as pervasive, atop this may exist various forms of information and communication. In every view but fatalism, these specific relationships make a difference to the limits of security; for example, communication viewed as mere 'signalling' is impoverished and unreliable, whereas enduring relationships of multichannel communication may enable reliable expectations, even trust, to construct security communities.

In some forms of security, uncertainty is met with a quest for certainty through information. If states lack trust in each other's words, they may place their trust in the information and analysis of their own (or allies) intelligence agencies. Domestically and internationally, the expansion of surveillance powers, from CCTV to monitoring and preventing money laundering and terrorist finance, embodies a desire for more and more information. We trade insurance premiums for protection against the unpredictability of the future through actuarial calculations that produce some predictive certainty and resilience – we insure to ensure our ways of life. In other areas, the uncertainty is accepted and limits the horizons and forms of politics; for example, uncertainty about what future technologies may bring is seen as limiting the practice of arms control and disarmament to incremental, short-term measures rather than measures addressing the asymmetries of power or ensuring more peaceful order. In both, the central premise of security is control through certainty. However, the demand for certainty can never be met, it is more like an addiction than a quest – searching for this goal always leads to a desire for more. Dillon (1996: 32) claims that 'just as certainty is never certain of itself, (inter)national security never succeeds in securing itself. For each consists in exactly the same demand, which redoubles with any act that might satisfy it.'

Yet most understandings of security seek to produce certainty about their own assumptions. They seek an ontological security that their knowledge of security is reliable and sufficient to enable strategic action. In rationalist theories, certainties of the regular patterns of security interactions, behaviours and their outcomes (such as power balancing, or the democratic peace) rely on assertions of the rationality of security actors. Even some critical schools simply seek different security in regularities. The proposition that securitization entails a move into a exceptional, urgent and potentially violent politics rests on assuming a distinction between security and normal politics; Booth's CSS accepts the existential condition of uncertainty, but is anchored by the assumption that more emancipatory forms of security can be identified and strengthened. While poststructuralists seek to reveal alternative political imaginations, in which certainty, control and security are not so easily drawn together or their damaging effects revealed, this hope remains alien to much security theorizing.

Rationality and rationalization

Rationalization means two things: subjecting to control by reason largely by removing the 'irrational', and, more simply, making sense of something. Both are central to understanding security. The rationalization of violence, in the first sense, has been central to understanding security since the mythical (if sometimes successful) post-Westphalian rationalization of violence by the state, which sought to exclude religion and ideas and render violence an instrumental tool of decisions about material factors undertaken on the basis of cost–benefit analysis. The rationalization of violence instantiated the now familiar distinction of the logics and limits of security in the hierarchical pacified inside of the state (characterized by law and order enabling significant security) and insecurity and war in the anarchic outside (characterized by self-help, competition and scarce security). Internationally, too, the dominant Clausewitzean concepts of war emphasize the subordination of violence to reason as inherent in all real wars. Extending this, some liberals now claim an obsolescence of war in toto, building on the inherent irrationality and thus impossibility of nuclear war posited by deterrence theorists of the Cold War.

Much security politics still seeks the rationalization of violence in international and domestic affairs. Many forms of international cooperation (regimes, alliances or security communities) or democratization in the democratic peace seek to pacify or at least stabilize interstate relations. Practices of domestic and international policing and surveillance seek to detect and punish deviance in the protection of law and order. Contemporary forms of arms control prohibit weapons deemed inherently abhorrent and indiscriminate (biological and chemical weapons, anti-personnel landmines, cluster munitions). Evolving practices of warfare emphasize discrimination, precision and the protection of (our) soldiers. Indeed, more broadly, the Clausewitzean dream of the subordination of violence to reason is now pursued not just through states' cost–benefit calculations on a case-by-case basis but also through the large body of international humanitarian law that limits the conduct of war, the treatment of civilians and prisoners and so on. This is based, in part, on older traditions of just war theorizing that posed the questions of right intentions, prospects of success, the use of proportionate means, and legitimate authorization. These questions and criteria are now formative of the major contours of debate on intervention in civil wars and crimes against humanity. These practices have prompted some rearticulation of sovereignty away from a right to nonintervention towards a shared Responsibility to Protect, combining the demands of interstate stability with human security, thereby indicating that the rationalization of violence remains a predominant concern of security.

Rationalization in the second sense, of making comprehensible, has tended to rely on assuming rationality – that states are rational calculating actors. Here, pure rationality is seldom asserted, but a rationality that is 'bounded', limited by imperfect information, conflicting goals, bureaucratic politics, or simply limited time to decide. This indicates that the conditions only ever exist for somewhat imperfect rationality. The centre of rationalist thought remains an assumption of the primacy of cost–benefit calculations on the basis of relatively universal reason and interests.

Several decades of constructivist and critical thought have brought this into question by criticizing the rationalization (limiting and exclusion) that this operated through. First, rationalist and rationalized foundations of understanding have previously excluded cultural or psychological variations. Culture is now widely seen as important in states' decision making. Even classical realists agree, and draw attention to the differences in 'strategic cultures' between Cold War adversaries and others. Culture, however, is still often viewed as an intervening variable that complicates but does not fundamentally alter the equation of security with a strategic cost–benefit calculus. Second, the realist rationalization of violence as an instrument of self-interest in anarchy distanced ethics from politics, and arguably limited the scope and potential for politics. Thus, Ashley (1984: 228) criticized neorealism for being so reductionist and deterministic in its explanations that it 'deprives political interaction of those practical capacities which make social learning and creative change possible', thus producing a 'rationalization of global politics'. Too much rationalization, then, can produce a denial of the political nature of security and insecurity by reducing it to materialist rationalization devoid of ethics or choice.

The assumed rationality of security enables the denigration of anything deemed 'irrational'. Most notably, in the contemporary period, assertions of new religiously motivated terror and suicide terrorism, perhaps enabled by access to weapons of mass destruction, contrast the rational violence of states and earlier secular terrorists with a new irrational, undeterrable, incomprehensible terror. This rhetoric is often far from reality, but can serve to legitimate coercive measures against a foe that cannot be rational and therefore cannot be reasoned with. The exclusion of the irrational from the rational, however, is not a novel invention for contemporary global terror. Rather, the assertion of reason against unreason has diminished the understanding of security to a cost–benefit calculus devoid of other human experience. Thus, there is a distinction between reason and emotion, such that the terms generally used to refer to subjective and emotional issues are sometimes rendered mere metaphors for underlying rationality – greed for power or fear of the unknown are deemed rational and explicable on a material basis. Fear is deemed inevitable and trust deemed naive. In other ways, emotion is the source of threat to security due to its supposed absence of rationality; hatred, for example, is deemed a feature of religious terrorists and the mad, bad leaders of rogue states. They are dangerous because they cannot be reasoned with on the basis of manipulation of costs and benefits (such as through deterrence). Our (rational) security is therefore particularly undermined by their (irrational) hatred. Rationalism means that somehow our own emotions, true fears, desires and hatreds are absent or subjugated to reason, much as Clausewitz said the passions of the people and the unpredictability of war were by the state. Other emotions that emerge in human relationships are entirely absent from security: love, affection and friendliness do not feature in interstate security even though they are central to individual ontological security.

Towards hybridity

While logics of response, conditions of uncertainty, and rationalism and rationalization operate by exclusion and distinction – inside-outside, subject-object, material-ideational, politics-ethics, public-private, rational-irrational – many aspects of contemporary security may indicate a need to move beyond such binaries to a fuller exploration of hybridities. This means accepting a messy world, rather than analysing it by reducing it to a limited set of variables and debating their relative importance. This may be ontologically threatening to the field of security studies, but many security practices are ahead of theorists in this regard. Perhaps it is too much to ask of the field to produce ordered thought. When it did, it legitimated many undesirable things and left out the insecurity of billions of people. Certainly, there is something to be said of disorderly fragmented understanding when faced with a fragmented world that is ordered only through some exercise of power – be that military, economic, conceptual or ideological.

Location

In much debate, the question, What is security? has been implicitly supplanted by, Where is security? This can no longer be understood solely in universal terms of states in anarchy. Rather, specific relations and geographical spaces alter the logics and limits of security. From attempts to build a global collective or even a common security, to collective defence through alliances, cooperative issue-based regimes and pluralistic security communities, the various formations of security instantiate different logics that combine conflict and cooperation in ways determined by specific histories and interactions. Whether these are additional to underlying patterns or supplant one socially constructed system with another is hotly debated. However, the regionalization of security shows that the material (and especially territorial) and ideational foundations of political communities and security relations are in flux and thus cannot be seen as eternally given.

Contemporary practices show a dispersal of security. Border controls have become diffused from ports and airports to networks of off-shore bordering. Surveillance practices have become dispersed and together with critical infrastructure protection mean that security/insecurity is now encountered in our finances, transportation, energy supply and many aspects of daily life. National security has become entangled in neoliberal state-building, and the security of our ways of life now links to transnational, regional and global distributions of natural resources. When security becomes dispersed, however, it is important to hold open the possibility that it changes in the process. It does not necessarily mean that security comes to dominate and subject all interactions to a logic of fear and protection, but that the dispersal of security may be rearticulating and changing older distinctions on which understandings are based. In other words, security is not just transposed into other areas, but translated and adapted in the process. This remains underexplored.

Security is shifting from the fixities of territorial relations towards tackling moving targets. Flows of various types are securitized, from terrorists (and their ideologies), to migrants, weapons, drugs and diseases. While disrupting the domestic-international distinction, the dominant view of such threats is a thin one: flows of migrants, drugs, weapons and terrorist attacks cut across the boundaries of political community but are not themselves formative of different political communities. Yet exploring the agency of migrants and the variations in citizenship they have, or the differently territorialized (rather than deterritorialized) organization of crime and terrorism in networks implies that a thicker view of these transversalities is needed. That these threats have been discursively located in a reconfigured map of order and anarchy corresponding to strong and weak states demonstrates the resilience and adaptation of the traditional map of security and its relations to the state. However, new spatialities of security are emerging and are undertheorized, which might reconfigure this further.

It is important to note that the spatialities of security are made by human interactions, particularly through war. The familiar territorialization of political community and the inside-outside were made and are being remade through war making as state making; transnational crime, the mutual vulnerabilities of human and state security, the insecurities of the poor, and the environmental dimensions of security are made by histories of violence and consumption. Even cyberspace has military origins, with the internet arising from the ARPANET project of the US Department of Defense in the 1960s (Castells, 2001).

Cyberspace is a new spatiality of security that has not been explored in depth in this book since understandings of security have only begun to engage with it. Cyberspace has been securitized as the discourse around the internet has shifted from one of a 'global village' to one of a 'virtual battle-space' (Manjikian, 2010). Cyber-threats are, however, articulated in familiar terms: crime and terrorism, and espionage and warfare by states. Central to all these are notions of cyber-attack – the virtualization of weaponry no longer reliant on ballistic force but the weapons of code and transmission attacking the functioning of communication and control networks. In the popular imagination, cyberspace, comprising the virtual space of information flows, is a relatively boundless global system. However, territorial political divisions are relevant in the formation and security of cyberspace (Herrera, 2007). Some states are 'filterers' of the internet, blocking websites, blogs and discussion forums related to opposition movements, human rights, minority groups and so on, such as China, Myanmar, Iran, Syria and others (Deibert and Rohozinski, 2010). States also have access to more information about their citizens and those of other countries than previously, with as yet undetermined implications. What is different about cyberspace, however, is that it engages different notions of community, rights and values. If security is about acquired values and the distribution of responsibility to other authorities, then cyber-security becomes unclear. How are rights and their protection articulated among the internet's participants? How might this affect security? Who is responsibilized for protection? All are open questions that security studies has yet to fully engage with, even as powerful states invest in their solution.

Ontological hybridity

What is security made of? Most understandings of security operate on the basis of a distinction between the material and the ideational. The early development of realism posited competition for material resources or something inherent in human nature as the foundation of competitive logics of security. This was articulated against the idealism of early liberal thought. Materialism has been closely related to rationalization: from the Westphalian rationalization of violence on a material basis to Waltz's invitation to theorize by abstracting everything but material power capabilities. While neoliberalism accepted much of the materialism of realism, the development of critical approaches to security has re-emphasized the ideational: the role of norms, values and identities, of ideas and expectations and subjectivities produced in interaction with others. This theoretical contest over what matters more (matter or ideas) lies behind the different logics of security thought (consequences, appropriateness, arguing and so on). But do we really encounter security in this way? Do our lives and ways of life easily divide into the material and ideational aspects? No, both are encountered at once. Perhaps, rather than an ontology of choices between these, security should be understood as the range of specific practices and situations that entangle the material and ideational.

Many contemporary security issues do this. For example, while mainstream security politics and theory view the environment as a set of resources awaiting exploitation, critical views articulate a radical ecology in which human life and ways of life are entangled with the natural and the technological. While this radically different ontology has perhaps limited its uptake in security politics, other areas of security practice have a similar ontological premise. Homeland security relates increasingly to the human-made rather than natural environment, but the view is more ecological in the sense that it views critical infrastructure and cyberspace as part of the fabric of daily life. So dominant views of environmental security and homeland security articulate fundamentally different ontologies. Yet ontology is not issue specific. How is it that such dissonant philosophical claims can coexist? Perhaps the answer is as mundane as the fact that both ontological claims serve to legitimate and protect particular Western ways of life and consumption.

Academic understandings of security are only beginning to explore the implications of breaking down the traditional ontological distinctions between ideas and matter, the social, natural and technological. There is much wider social and political theory that does this by exploring how 'objects' are active in constituting complex relations (Latour, 2005; Bennett, 2010; Braun and Whatmore, 2010; Coole and Frost, 2010). This type of approach has recently been used to discuss some issues, such as the practices of arms control (Pouliot, 2010; Bourne, 2012), or critical infrastructure and urban security (Coward, 2009a, 2012; Aradau, 2010; Lundborg and Vaughan-Williams, 2011; Adey and Anderson, 2012). However, these complex ontologies may also help readdress the various ways that technology is understood in relation to security. In interstate relations, the uncertainties of technology are viewed negatively as limiting the scope for long-term cooperation in military affairs. In environmental security, these same uncertainties about future technologies are sometimes viewed optimistically as the space in which human innovation can solve the seemingly intractable issues of energy and food security, as markets and technologies combine in modernist cornucopian hopes for the mastery of nature by technology. Technologies also enable the diffusion of security logics throughout society, as practices of surveillance, border control and cyber-security produce a responsibilization of civil society and the private sector. That these are among the defining security issues of the day may give fertile ground for exploring the implications of hybrid ontologies.

Hybrid security and the state

Security has traditionally been associated with the state. Even moves to value human security have increasingly converged in the reinstating of the state as a responsible and effective sovereign. Contemporary categorizations of a spectrum of states – from strong to weak, failing to failed – reorient theorizing of the state, power and security away from an assumption of states as singular, unitary rational actors towards a practical security logic that seeks to produce them. Whether the state is viewed as a coercively powerful protection racket or the outgrowth of a social contract in which security is provided in exchange for certain rights and duties, security lies at the heart of the state. Here, security may be conceived narrowly as physical protection against the violence of others, or more widely as the rule of law and the securing of liberty and particular ways of life. The understanding of insecurity as risk and security as its management, and the associated dispersal of security practices in complex spatialities in many places is rearticulating the state. This is most prominent in the role of the private sector, from the rise of private military companies to the domestic use of private security firms and the responsibilization of private companies for critical infrastructure protection, or private citizens for surveillance and alertness. This is no simple privatization, but the rearticulation of the public-private divide in more complex ways. From supplies of energy and food, to the material infrastructures of daily life or the security of information and communication, the state is articulating itself as a provider of security as a public good in a new way. The state remains a provider of security but does so not only as a Hobbesian leviathan but also as an enabler, investor, adviser and partner to the private sector and society.

How well constructed is security?

Perhaps the time is ripe for new questions about security. The heated debate on what should count as a security issue and who or what should be secured has largely subsided without clear resolution. Certainly, security encompasses a wider range of issues than it once did, and notions of human security, regional security and even global or world security are now well-established organizing ideas for some strands of understanding. Much attention has focused now on *how* security issues are made (on securitization through speech acts and practices). However, while the debate is less heated, understanding security is encountering even deeper questions. If security is becoming hybridized in its location, what it is made of, and how the state's role is understood, then the questions that arise are no longer: What is security? What are its inherent logics and limits? And how is it made? Instead, the questions now are: Where is security? What is it made of? And how are its relationships articulated and distributed? The central question for the future, then, may be one that has been implied by the foregoing understandings of security, but seldom addressed explicitly. So, it is not a matter of whether or not security is constructed, but a question of how well it is constructed.

Further Reading

Introduction: What is Security?

An excellent starting point for engaging the meaning of security is Wolfers, '"National security" as an ambiguous symbol' (1952). Recent contestation of the meaning and functioning of security can be approached through the issues raised in Chapter 1 in combination with Baldwin's 'The concept of security' (1997) and Smith's 'The contested concept of security' (2005). A view that seeks to explore the value of security by exposing its particular theoretical roots and possible alternatives can be found in Der Derian's excellent essay 'The value of security: Hobbes, Marx, Nietzsche, and Baudrillard' (1995) and Huysmans' 'Security! What do you mean? From concept to thick signifier' (1998). For a more advanced and in-depth interrogation, see Dillon, *Politics of Security: Towards a Political Philosophy of Continental Thought* (1996).

1 Understanding and Theorizing Security

The changing approach to understanding security can be explored in Buzan and Hansen's *The Evolution of International Security Studies* (2009). A traditionalist response to this can be found in Miller, 'The hegemonic illusion? Traditional security studies in context' (2010). The early steps to broadening the scope of security are most easily grasped by reading Ullman's 'Redefining security' (1983) and Buzan's *People, States and Fear* (1991), in which the sectors of security were first outlined. A defence of the traditional military focus of the field of security studies can be found in Walt, 'The renaissance of security studies' (1991).

The deeper issues of ontology and epistemology and the deepening of security in this regard are discussed throughout the book, but this chapter can be augmented by reading Zalewski's 'All these theories yet the bodies keep piling up: theories, theorists, theorising' (1996) and much of the book in which this is to be found: Smith, Booth and Zalewski (eds) *International Theory: Positivism and Beyond* (1996). Wider engagement with such issues in IR that are relevant to theorizing security can be found in Hollis and Smith's *Explaining and Understanding International Relations* (1990). The importance of levels of analysis and explanation can be explored in Waltz's *Man, the State and War* (1959). The debate over agency and structure is complex and permeates much security theorizing but can be explored further in Wight's 'They shoot dead horses don't they? Locating agency in the agent-structure problematique' (1999) and his book, *Agents, Structures and International Relations: Politics as Ontology* (2006), along with Doty's 'Aporia: a critical exploration of the agent-structure problematique in international relations theory' (1997).

2 Traditional Rationalist Approaches to Security

One of the best and most accessible books about realism is Donnelly's *Realism and International Relations* (2000). However, there is no substitute for reading realists in their own words. For those interested in the prehistory of realism, Machiavelli's short *The Prince* (1985) is available in numerous versions. Classical realism can be engaged through one of many editions of Morgenthau's *Politics Among Nations* (1948), as well as Carr's *The Twenty Years' Crisis, 1919–1939: An Introduction to the Study of International Relations* (1946). Structural realism should be understood by reading Waltz's *Theory of International Politics* (1979) and his 'Structural realism after the cold war' (2000), and Mearsheimer's *The Tragedy of Great Power Politics* (2001). An excellent collection of discussions about realism from its critics can be found in Booth (ed.) *Realism and World Politics* (2011). However, the classic treatments of the debates between neorealism and liberalism remain Baldwin (ed.) *Neorealism and Neoliberalism: The Contemporary Debate* (1983) and Keohane (ed.) *Neorealism and its Critics* (1986). The balance of power and its evolution can be explored through Sheehan, *Balance of Power: History and Theory* (1996), Little, *The Balance of Power in International Relations: Metaphors, Myths and Models* (2007) and Paul, Wirtz and Fortmann (eds) *Balance of Power: Theory and Practice in the 21st Century* (2004).

On liberalism, Doyle's 'Kant, liberal legacies and foreign policy' (1983) and his 'Liberalism and world politics' (1986) are important starting points, as are Keohane and Nye, *Power and Interdependence: World Politics in Transition* (1977) and Keohane and Martin, 'The promise of institutionalist theory' (1995). A somewhat different and wider view of liberalism that emphasizes the importance of preferences as well as power is provided by Moravcsik, 'Taking preferences seriously: the liberal theory of international politics' (1997). On the democratic peace, read Russett, *Grasping the Democratic Peace: Principles for a Post-Cold War World* (1993) and the realist reply to liberal explanations provided by Layne, 'Kant or can't: the myth of the democratic peace' (1994).

3 Critical Approaches and New Frameworks

A good textbook handling the range of critical approaches to security studies is Peoples and Vaughan-Williams, *Critical Security Studies: An Introduction* (2010). Understanding the origins of critical approaches requires engagement with its initially broad formulation in Booth (ed.) *Critical Security Studies and World Politics* (1995) and the more diverse range of views in Krause and Williams (eds) *Critical Security Studies: Concepts and Cases* (1995). The maturing of critical approaches can be addressed by reading the collection of essays demonstrating the diversity and rigour of research methods used by critical scholars in Salter and Mutlu (eds) *Research Methods in Critical Security Studies: An Introduction* (2013).

Those interested in securitization should read the initial framework developed in Buzan, Waever and de Wilde, *Security: A New Framework for Analy-*

sis (1998) and the edited collection highlighting recent developments in Balzaq (ed.) *Securitization Theory: How Security Problems Emerge and Dissolve* (2011). While poststructuralism and practice theories resist easy summary, a good place to start is Campbell's *Writing Security: United States Foreign Policy and the Politics of Identity* (1998) and 'Why fight?: Humanitarianism, principles, and post-structuralism' (1998). For the Paris School, Bigo's numerous works should be consulted, particularly Bigo and Tsoukala, 'Understanding (in)security' (2008). On recent practice theories, there is Adler and Pouliot (eds) *International Practices* (2011). A strong overview of feminist thought in security is Sjoberg's *Gender and International Security: Feminist Perspectives* (2010). To understand the Welsh School of critical security studies, reading Booth's *Theory of World Security* (2007) should be accompanied by earlier works, including Booth, 'Security and emancipation' (1991) and Wyn Jones, *Security, Strategy, and Critical Theory* (1999).

4 The Sovereign State and Internal Security

To gain a deeper understanding of the meaning and evolution of sovereignty, Krasner's *Sovereignty: Organized Hypocrisy* (1999) and Biersteker and Weber (eds) *State Sovereignty as Social Construct* (1996) are essential reading. The history of state formation is much disputed, but a good starting point is Tilly's classic essay, 'War making and state making as organised crime' (1985). While historical sociology, like that of Tilly and others, has made only infrequent appearances in security studies and wider IR, Hobson's *The State and International Relations* (2000) is an important corrective. How the territorial sovereign state has shaped understanding in politics and security is discussed in a critical vein in the concept of the 'territorial trap' in Agnew and Corbridge, *Mastering Space: Hegemony, Territory and International Political Economy* (1995). The mutually constitutive relations of states, communities and security are discussed in depth in Weldes (ed.) *Cultures of Insecurity: States, Communities, and the Production of Danger* (1999). Transformations of the state and sovereignty are discussed in Axtmann, 'The state of the state: the model of the modern state and its contemporary transformation' (2004). They are also seen in diverse internal security practices from policing, which can be explored in Reiner, *The Politics of the Police* (2010) and Neocleus, *The Fabrication of Social Order: A Critical Theory of Police Power* (2000). Practices of surveillance are best explored through the separate field of surveillance studies, the most important of which is Lyon, *Surveillance Society: Monitoring Everyday Life* (2001), and the contemporary security perspective on the changing social contract this implies can be found in Chesterman, 'Privacy and surveillance in the age of terror' (2010). The changing formations of public and private security are addressed in Abrahamsen and Williams, *Security Beyond the State: Private Security in International Politics* (2011), and the changing meaning of protection is analysed in Bigo, 'Protection: security, territory and population' (2006) and the blurring of the inside-outside distinction in his 'The Möbius ribbon of internal and external security(ies)' (2001). Contemporary practices of homeland security and critical infrastructure protection can be better understood by reading Dunn Cavelty and Kristensen (eds) *Securing 'the Homeland': Critical Infrastructure, Risk and (In)security* (2008), Coward, 'Network-centric violence, critical infrastructure and the urbanization of security' (2009) and Aradau, 'Security that matters: critical infrastructure and the objects of protection' (2010).

5 Acting under Uncertainty: The Security Dilemma, Strategy and Risk

The first statement of the 'security dilemma' should be read in Herz, 'Idealist internationalism and the security dilemma' (1950), and Butterfield, *History and Human Relations* (1951). Jervis revitalized the concept in *Perception and Misperception in International Politics* (1976) and 'Cooperation under the security dilemma' (1978). By far the most comprehensive treatment and set of critical reflections on the security dilemma and the underlying condition of uncertainty is Booth and Wheeler's *The Security Dilemma: Fear, Cooperation and Trust in World Politics* (2008), which highlights three major logics. Issues of risk are newer but still relate to conditions of uncertainty, and a good starting point is Petersen, 'Risk analysis: A field within security studies?' (2012). Critical engagement with risk can be found in Aradau, Lobo-Guerrero and van Munster, 'Security, technologies of risk, and the political' (2008) and the remainder of the special issue of *Security Dialogue* it introduces.

6 Global and Regional Security Formations

A liberal view of security institutions is developed in Haftendorn, Wallander and Keohane, *Imperfect Unions: Security Institutions over Time and Space* (1999). A realist argument against them is stated in Mearsheimer, 'The false promise of international institutions (1994/95). Specific types of security formations are the subject of interlinked but separate literatures. On alliances, Walt's *The Origins of Alliances* (1987) and Snyder's *Alliance Politics* (1997) are the most prominent realist texts. On regimes, a diverse literature is effectively handled in Haggard and Simmons, 'Theories of international regimes' (1987) and Hasenclever, Mayer and Rittberger, *Theories of International Regimes* (1997). Security communities should be understood by reading Deutsch's initial formulation, *Political Community in the North Atlantic Area* (1957) and Adler and Barnett's further development and application of the concept in their edited volume, *Security Communities* (1998). The importance of regional dimensions to security and security interdependencies is discussed in the contending views and empirical studies found in Lake and Morgan (eds) *Regional Orders: Building Security a New World* (1997) and Buzan and Waever, *Regions and Powers: The Structure of International Security* (2003).

7 War and Killing

Von Clausewitz is a good starting point for understanding war. His *On War* (2008) is reproduced and accompanied by some excellent essays. Recent reflections on his importance can be found in Strachan and Herberg-Rothe (eds) *Clausewitz in the Twenty-first Century* (2007). Realist understandings of war are expressed with sophistication in Gray's *War, Peace and International Relations: An Introduction to Strategic History* (2012), while systematic realist accounts of the causes of war are found in Levy and Thompson's *Causes of War* (2010) and van Evera's *Causes of War: Power and the Roots of Conflict* (1999). The transformations of war can be explored through van Creveld, *The Transformation of War* (1991) and a seminal discussion of the 'new' wars in Kaldor, *New and Old Wars: Organized Violence in a Global Era* (1999). The development of war is discussed from a more sociologically informed perspective in Shaw's *War and Genocide: Organized Killing in Modern Society* (2003) and his earlier work *Dialectics of War: An Essay in the Social Theory of Total War and Peace* (1988). Spectator sport war is discussed in McInnes, *Spectator Sport War: The West and Contemporary Conflict* (2002), and Der Derian's account of the virtualization of war in *Virtuous War: Mapping the Military-Industrial-Media-Entertainment Network*, 2nd edn (2009) is well worth reading for a broadly poststructuralist perspective.

8 Arms Trade, Arms Control and Disarmament

Discussion of the importance of arms for international security is analysed in Buzan and Herring, *The Arms Dynamic in World Politics* (1998). One of the most thorough histories of the arms trade and its relations to security is Krause's *Arms and the State: Patterns of Military Production and Trade* (1992). The rise of proliferation as an international security issue is analysed by Mutimer, *The Weapons State: Proliferation and the Framing of Security* (2000). The polarized debate on proliferation between Waltz and Sagan has been replayed several times, as in their *The Spread of Nuclear Weapons: A Debate Renewed* (2002). A wider range of perspectives on proliferation can be found in Potter and Mukhatzhanova (eds) *Forecasting Nuclear Proliferation in the 21st Century*, vol. 1: *The Role of Theory* (2010). Diverse opinions and in-depth discussions of arms control and disarmament can be found in Larsen and Wirtz (eds) *Arms Control and Cooperative Security* (2009), Gray's *House of Cards: Why Arms Control Must Fail* (1992) and Croft's *Strategies of Arms Control: A History and Typology* (1996). A collection of discussions on contemporary arms control issues, largely from a range of critical perspectives, is edited by Cooper and Mutimer in a special issue of *Contemporary Security Policy*, introduced by their essay 'Arms control for the 21st century: controlling the means of violence' (2011).

9 Human Security

Perhaps the best entry point to how security scholars understand human security is the series of short comments on the concept in the journal *Security Dialogue* 35(3) (2004). An excellent conceptual unpacking of human security is Newman, 'Human security and constructivism' (2001). Longer treatments of the concept from its supporters can be found in Nef, *Human Security and Mutual Vulnerability: The Global Political Economy of Development and Underdevelopment*, 2nd edn (1999), Hampson, Daudelin, Hay et al., *Mad-*

ness in the Multitude: Human Security and World Disorder (2002) and Tadjbakhsh and Chenoy, *Human Security: Concepts and Implications* (2007). Critical perspectives are collected in Chandler and Hynek (eds) *Critical Perspectives on Human Security: Rethinking Emancipation and Power in International Relations* (2011), as well as in discussions, such as Christie's 'Critical voices and human security: To endure, to engage or to critique?' (2010). Discussion of the links between human and state security are pervasive in the debates, but given focus in Liotta's 'Boomerang effect: the convergence of national and human security' (2002), while in-depth analysis of the practical history of human security can be found in Macfarlane and Khong's *Human Security and the UN: A Critical History* (2006) and Martin and Owen's 'The second generation of human security: lessons from the UN and EU experience' (2010).

10 Weak States and Intervention

For initial discussion of the problem of state weakness and state collapse, Zartman's *Collapsed States: The Disintegration and Restoration of Legitimate Authority* (1995) is a good introduction, followed by more recent mainstream discussions by Rotberg, including *State Failure and State Weakness in a Time of Terror* (2003) and his edited collection *When States Fail: Causes and Consequences* (2004). Critiques of the association of weak states with transnational threats can be found in Patrick, 'Weak states and global threats: Fact or fiction?' (2006) and Bøås and Jennings, '"Failed states" and "state failure": Threats or opportunities?' (2007). The practices of conflict intervention raise issues of sovereignty and order addressed by pluralist and solidarist perspectives, for which see Jackson, *The Global Covenant: Human Conduct in a World of States* (2000) and Wheeler, *Saving Strangers: Humanitarian Intervention in International Society* (2000). Contemporary practices of conflict intervention have implications for state sovereignty as a responsibility to protect, on which Bellamy's *Responsibility to Protect* (2009) is helpful. Some good overviews of the issues and successes and failures of intervention include Seybolt, *Humanitarian Military Intervention: The Conditions for Success and Failure* (2007) and Holzgrefe and Keohane (eds) *Humanitarian Intervention: Ethical, Legal and Political Dilemmas* (2003).

11 Terrorism and Counterterrorism

A vast literature exists on terrorism. Traditional mainstream approaches are found in Wilkinson's *Terrorism vs Democracy: The Liberal State Response* (2011) and Hoffman's *Inside Terrorism* (2006). Recent critical approaches are explored in Jackson, Jarvis, Gunning and Breen-Smyth, *Terrorism: A Critical Introduction* (2011). Discussion of state terrorism is best approached via critical scholarship such as Blakeley's *State Terrorism and Neoliberalism: The North in the South* (2009), while a seminal but limited engagement with state sponsorship of terror is Byman's *Deadly Connections: States that Sponsor Terrorism* (2005). Arguments that there is a 'new terrorism' are articulated by

Laqueur, *The New Terrorism: Fanaticism and the Arms of Mass Destruction* (1999) and – on motivations – Cronin, 'Behind the curve: globalization and international terrorism' (2002/03), whose *How Terrorism Ends: Understanding the Decline and Demise of Terrorist* (2009) offers an array of insights into counterterrorism.

12 Migration, Crime and Borders

On migration, nuanced critical engagement can be found in Guild, *Security and Migration in the 21st Century* (2009), Huysmans, *The Politics of Insecurity: Fear, Migration and Asylum in the EU* (2006), Squire (ed.) *The Contested Politics of Mobility: Borderzones and Irregularity* (2011) and van Munster, *Securitizing Immigration: The Politics of Risk in the EU* (2009). Early discussions of transnational crime as a security issue can be found in Berdal and Serrano (eds) *Transnational Organised Crime and International Security: Business as Usual?* (2002) and Edwards and Gill (eds) *Transnational Organised Crime: Perspectives on Global Security* (2003). Friman's (ed.) *Crime and the Global Political Economy* (2009) gives an excellent discussion of key issues, as do Galeotti, *Global Crime Today: The Changing Face of Organised Crime* (2005) and van Schendel and Abraham (eds) *Illicit Flows and Criminal Things: States, Borders and the Other Side of Globalization* (2005). The growth of transnational policing is well analysed from critical perspectives in Sheptycki (ed.) *Issues in Transnational Policing* (2000) and Beare (ed.) *Critical Reflections on Transnational Organized Crime, Money Laundering, and Corruption* (2005). Changes in border security and the wider practices of bordering are thoroughly discussed in Albert, Jacobson and Lapid (eds) *Identities, Borders, Orders: Rethinking International Relations Theory* (2001), the work of Andreas, including 'Redrawing the line: borders and security in the twenty-first century' (2003) and *Border Games: Policing the US-Mexico Divide*, 2nd edn (2009), and Vaughan-Williams, *Border Politics: The Limits of Sovereign Power* (2009).

13 Environmental, Energy and Resource Security

On resource conflict, Klare's pessimistic view can be found in *Resource Wars: The New Landscape of Global Conflict* (2002), and the major neo-Malthusian view in Homer-Dixon's 'Environmental scarcities and violent conflict: evidence from cases' (1994). Placing this in debate with 'cornucopian' views is done in Gleditsch, 'Environmental conflict: neomalthusians vs. cornucopians' (2003). Arguments against the securitization of environmental issues are most effectively expressed in Deudney, 'The case against linking environmental degradation and national security' (1990). The most thorough treatments of environmental security from a critical perspective are from McDonald, *Security, the Environment and Emancipation: Contestation Over Environmental Change* (2012) and particularly Dalby's excellent, far-reaching discussions in *Environmental Security* (2002) and *Security and Environmental Change* (2008).

Bibliography

9-11 Commission (2004) *Final Report of the National Commission on Terrorist Attacks upon the United States* (Washington DC: 9-11 Commission).

Aas, K.F. (2007) 'Analysing a world in motion: global flows meet "criminology of the other"', *Theoretical Criminology* 11(2) 283–303.

Abraham, I. and van Schendel, W. (2005) 'Introduction: the making of illicitness', in Abraham, I. and van Schendel, W. (eds) *Illicit Flows and Criminal Things: States, Borders, and the Other Side of Globalization* (Bloomington: Indiana University Press).

Abrahamsen, R. (2005) 'Blair's Africa: the politics of securitization and fear,' *Alternatives* 30(1) 50–80.

Abrahamsen, R. and Williams, M.C. (2011) *Security Beyond the State: Private Security in International Politics* (Cambridge: CUP).

Acharya, A. (2006) 'Securitization in Asia: functional and normative implications,' in Caballero-Anthony, M., Emmers, R. and Acharya, A. (eds) *Non-Traditional Security in Asia: Dilemmas in Securitisation* (London: Ashgate).

Adamson, F. (2006) 'Crossing borders: international migration and national security,' *International Security* 31(1) 165–99.

Adey, P. (2004) 'Secured and sorted mobilities: examples from the airport,' *Surveillance and Society* 1(4) 500–19.

Adey, P. (2009) 'Facing airport security: affect, biopolitics, and the preemptive securitisation of the mobile body,' *Environment and Planning D: Society and Space* 27(2) 274–95.

Adey, P. and Anderson, B. (2012) 'Anticipating emergencies: technologies of preparedness and the matter of security,' *Security Dialogue* 43(2) 99–117.

Adler, E. (1997) 'Imagined (security) communities: cognitive regions in international relations,' *Millennium* 26(2) 249–77.

Adler, E. (2008) 'The spread of security communities: communities of practice, self-restraint, and NATO's post-cold war transformation,' *European Journal of International Relations* 14(2) 195–230.

Adler, E. and Barnett, M. (1998a) 'A framework for the study of security communities,' in Adler, E. and Barnett, M. (eds) *Security Communities* (Cambridge: CUP).

Adler, E. and Barnett, M. (1998b) 'Security communities in theoretical perspective,' in Adler, E. and Barnett, M. (eds) *Security Communities* (Cambridge: CUP).

Adler, E. and Haas, P.M. (1992) 'Epistemic communities, world order, and the creation of a reflective research program,' *International Organization* 46(1) 367–90.

Adler, E. and Pouliot, V. (eds) (2011) *International Practices* (Cambridge: CUP).

Agnew, J. and Corbridge, S. (1995) *Mastering Space: Hegemony, Territory and International Political Economy* (London: Routledge).

Åhäll, L. (2012) 'The writing of heroines: motherhood and female agency in political violence,' *Security Dialogue* 43(4) 287–303.

Alagappa, M. (1997) 'Regional institutions, the UN and international security: a framework for analysis,' *Third World Quarterly* 18(3) 421–42.

Albert, M. and Buzan, B. (2011) 'Securitization, sectors and functional differentiation,' *Security Dialogue* 42(4/5) 413–25.

Albrecht, P. and Kyed, H.M. (2011) 'Introduction: non-state and customary actors in development programs', in Albrecht, P., Kyed, H.M., Isser, D. and Harper, E. (eds) *Perspectives on Involving Non-state and Customary Actors in Justice and Security Reform* (Rome: International Development Law Organization).

Alden, E. and Roberts, B. (2011) 'Are U.S. borders secure? Why we don't know, and how to find out,' *Foreign Affairs* 90(4) 19–26.

Alker, H. and Biersteker, T. (2011) 'The powers and pathologies of networks: insights from the political cybernetics of Karl W. Deutsch and Norbert Wiener,' *European Journal of International Relations* 17(2) 351–78.

Allison, G. (1971) *Essence of Decision: Explaining the Cuban Missile Crisis* (Boston: Little, Brown).

Allison, G. (2006) *Nuclear Terrorism: The Risks and Consequences of the Ultimate Disaster* (London: Constable & Robinson).

Allison, R. (2004) 'Regionalism, regional structures and security management in Central Asia,' *International Affairs* 80(3) 463–83.

Allison, R. (2008) 'Russia resurgent? Moscow's campaign to "coerce Georgia to peace",' *International Affairs* 84(6) 1145–71.

Al-Sumait, F., Lingle, C. and Domke, D. (2009) 'Terrorism's cause and cure: the rhetorical regime of democracy in the US and UK,' *Critical Studies on Terrorism* 2(1) 7–25.

Altmann, J. (2006) *Military Nanotechnology: Potential Applications and Preventive Arms Control* (Abingdon: Routledge).

Altunisik, M.B. and Tür, Ö. (2006) 'From distant neighbours to partners? Changing Syrian-Turkish relations,' *Security Dialogue* 37(2) 229–48.

Amoore, L. (2006) 'Biometric borders: governing mobilities in the war on terror,' *Political Geography* 25(3) 336–51.

Amoore, L. (2009) 'Algorithmic war: everyday geographies of the war on terror,' *Antipode* 41(1) 49–69.

Amoore, L. and de Goede, M. (2005) 'Governance, risk and dataveillance in the war on terror,' *Crime, Law and Social Change* 43(2/3) 149–73.

Amoore, L. and de Goede, M. (eds) (2008) *Risk and the War on Terror* (Abingdon: Routledge).

Anderson, B. (1991) *Imagined Communities: Reflections on the Origins and Spread of Nationalism* (London: Verso).

Andreas, P. (1998) 'Smuggling wars: law enforcement and law evasion in a changing world,' *Transnational Organized Crime* 4(2) 75–90.

Andreas, P. (1999) 'When policies collide: market reform, market prohibition, and the narcotization of the Mexican economy,' in Friman H.R. and Andreas, P. (eds) *The Illicit Global Economy and State Power* (Lanham: Rowman & Littlefield).

Andreas, P. (2002) 'Transnational crime and economic globalization,' in Berdal, M. and Serrano, M. (eds) *Transnational Organised Crime & International Security: Business as Usual?* (Boulder: Lynne Rienner).

Andreas, P. (2003) 'Redrawing the line: borders and security in the twenty-first century,' *International Security* 28(2) 78–111.

Andreas, P. (2008) *Blue Helmets and Black Markets: The Business of Survival in the Siege of Sarajevo* (Ithaca: Cornell University Press).

Andreas, P. (2009) *Border Games: Policing the US–Mexico Divide*, 2nd edn (Ithaca: Cornell University Press).

Andreas, P. and Greenhill, K.M. (2010a) 'Introduction: the politics of numbers,' in Andreas, P. and Greenhill, K.M. (eds) *Sex, Drugs and Body Counts: The Politics of Numbers in Global Crime and Conflict* (Ithaca: Cornell University Press).

Andreas, P. and Greenhill, K.M. (eds) (2010b) *Sex, Drugs and Body Counts: The Politics of Numbers in Global Crime and Conflict* (Ithaca: Cornell University Press).

Andreas, P. and Nadelmann, E. (2006) *Policing the Globe: Criminalization and Crime Control in International Relations* (Oxford: OUP).

Andreas, P. and Price, R. (2001) 'From war fighting to crime fighting: transforming the American national security state,' *International Studies Review* 3(3) 31–52.

Andreas, P. and Wallman, J. (2009) 'Illicit markets and violence: What is the relationship?,' *Crime, Law and Social Change* 52(3) 225–9.

Aning, E.K. (2010) 'Security, the war on terror, and official development assistance,' *Critical Studies on Terrorism* 3(1) 7–26.

Annan, K. (1999) *Report of the Secretary General on the Work of the Organization*, UN Document A/54/1 (New York: UN).

Aradau, C. (2004) 'Security and the democratic scene: desecuritization and emancipation,' *Journal of International Relations and Development* 7(4) 388–413.

Aradau, C. (2006) 'Limits of security, limits of politics? A response,' *Journal of International Relations and Development* 9(1) 81–90.

Aradau, C. (2008) *Rethinking Trafficking in Women: Politics out of Security* (Basingstoke: Palgrave Macmillan).

Aradau, C. (2010) 'Security that matters: critical infrastructure and the objects of protection,' *Security Dialogue* 41(5) 491–514.

Aradau, C. and van Munster, R. (2007) 'Governing terrorism through risk: taking precautions, (un) knowing the future,' *European Journal of International Relations* 13(1) 89–115.

Aradau, C. and van Munster, R. (2012) 'The securitization of catastrophic events: trauma, enactment, and preparedness exercises,' *Alternatives* 37(3) 227–39.

Aradau, C., Huysmans, J. and Squire, V. (2010) 'Acts of European citizenship: a political sociology of mobility,' *Journal of Common Market Studies* 48(4) 945–65.

Aradau, C., Lobo-Guerrero, L. and van Munster, R. (2008) 'Security, technologies of risk, and the political: guest editors' introduction,' *Security Dialogue* 39(2/3) 147–54.

Arkin, W. (2001) 'Operation Allied Force: the most precise application of air power in history,' in Bacevich, A.J. and Cohen, E.A. (eds) *War over Kosovo: Politics and Strategy in a Global Age* (New York: Columbia University Press).

Arquilla, J. and Ronfeldt, D.F. (1996) *The Advent of Netwar* (Santa Monica: RAND).

Arquilla, J. and Ronfeldt, D.F. (eds) (2001) *Networks and Netwars: The Future of Terror, Crime, and Militancy* (Santa Monica: RAND).

Ashley, R.K. (1984) 'The poverty of neorealism', *International Organization* 38(2) 225–86.

Ashley, R.K. (1988) 'Untying the sovereign state: a double reading of the anarchy problematique,' *Millennium* 17(2) 227–62.

Atack, I. (2005) *The Ethics of Peace and War* (Edinburgh: Edinburgh University Press).

Atia, M. (2007) 'In whose interest? Financial surveillance and the circuits of exception in the war on terror,' *Environment and Planning D: Society and Space* 25(3) 447–75.

Atran, S. (2006) 'The moral logic and growth of suicide terrorism,' *Washington Quarterly* 29(2) 127–47.

Austin, J.L. (1962) *How To Do Things With Words* (Oxford: Clarendon Press).

Avant, D. (2005) *The Market for Force: The Consequences of Privatizing Security* (Cambridge: CUP).

Avci, G. (1999) 'Immigrant categories: The many sides of one coin?', *European Journal of Migration and Law* 1(2) 199–213.

Axelrod, R. and Keohane, R.O. (1985) 'Achieving cooperation under anarchy: strategies and institutions,' *World Politics* 38(1) 226–64.

Axtmann, R. (2004) 'The state of the state: the model of the modern state and its contemporary transformation,' *International Political Science Review* 25(3) 259–79.

Axworthy, L. (1997) 'Canada and human security: the need for leadership', *International Journal* 52(2) 183–96.

Ayoob, M. (1986) 'Regional security and the third world,' in Ayoob, M. (ed.) *Regional Security and the Third World* (Beckenham: Croom Helm).

Ayoob, M. (2002) 'Humanitarian intervention and state sovereignty,' *International Journal of Human Rights* 6(1) 81–102.

Baaz, M.E. and Stern, M. (2009) 'Why do soldiers rape? Masculinity, violence, and sexuality in the armed forces in the Congo (DRC),' *International Studies Quarterly* 53(2) 495–518.

Baldwin, D.A. (1997) 'The concept of security', *Review of International Studies* 23(1) 5–26.

Balibar, E. (1998) 'The borders of Europe,' trans, J. Swenson, in Cheah, P. and Robbins, B. (eds) *Cosmopolitics: Thinking and Feeling Beyond the Nation* (Minneapolis: University of Minnesota Press).

Ballentine, K. and Sherman, J. (eds) (2003) *The Political Economy of Armed Conflict: Beyond Greed and Grievance* (Boulder: Lynne Rienner).

Balzacq, T. (2005) 'The three faces of securitization: political agency, audience and context,' *European Journal of International Relations* 11(2) 171–201.

Balzacq, T. (ed.) (2011) *Securitization Theory: How Security Problems Emerge and Dissolve* (London: Routledge).

Barkawi, T. (1998) 'Strategy as a vocation: Weber, Morgenthau and modern strategic studies,' *Review of International Studies* 24(2) 159–84.

Barkawi, T. (2006) *Globalization and War* (Oxford: Rowman & Littlefield).

Barnett, J. (2001) *The Meaning of Environmental Security: Ecological Politics and Policy in the New Security Era* (London: Zed Books).

Barnett, J. and Adger, N. (2007) 'Climate change, human security and violent conflict,' *Political Geography* 26(6) 639–55.

Barnett, J.P. (2010) 'Environmental security,' in Burgess, J.P. (ed) *The Routledge Handbook of the New Security Studies* (Abingdon: Routledge).

Barnett, M. (2002) *Eyewitness to a Genocide: The United Nations and Rwanda* (Ithaca: Cornell University Press).

Barnett, M. (2006) 'Building a republican peace: stabilizing states after war,' *International Security* 30(4) 87–112.

Barnett, M. and Solingen, E. (2007) '"Designed to fail or failure of design?" The origins and legacy of the Arab League', in Acharya, A. and Johnston, A.I. (eds) *Crafting Cooperation: Regional International Institutions in Comparative Perspective* (Cambridge: CUP).

Bassford, C. (2007) 'The primacy of policy and the "trinity" in Clausewitz's mature thought,' in Strachan, H. and Herberg-Rothe, A. (eds) *Clausewitz in the Twenty-First Century* (Oxford: OUP).

Baudrillard, J. (1995) *The Gulf War Did Not Take Place* (Bloomington: Indiana University Press).

Bauman, Z. (1998) *Globalization: The Human Consequences* (Cambridge: Polity).

Bauman, Z. (2001) 'Wars of the globalization era,' *European Journal of Social Theory* 4(1): 11–28.

Bauman, Z. (2000) *Liquid Modernity* (London: Polity).

Beck, U. (1992) *Risk Society: Towards a New Modernity* (London: Sage).

Beck, U. (1999) *World Risk Society* (Cambridge: Polity).

Behringer, R.M. (2005) 'Middle power leadership on the human security agenda,' *Cooperation and Conflict* 40(3) 305–42.

Bellamy, A.J. (2003) 'Humanitarian intervention and the three traditions,' *Global Society* 17(1) 3–20.

Bellamy, A.J. (2004) *Security Communities and their Neighbours: Regional Fortresses or Global Integrators?* (Basingstoke: Palgrave Macmillan).

Bellamy, A.J. (2008) 'Conflict prevention and the responsibility to protect,' *Global Governance* 14(4) 135–56.

Bellamy, A.J. and Williams, P.D. (2005) 'Who's keeping the peace? Regionalization and contemporary peace operations' *International Security* 29(4) 157–95.

Belloni, R. (2001) 'Civil society and peacebuilding in Bosnia and Herzegovina,' *Journal of Peace Research* 38(2) 163–80.

Bennett, J. (2010) *Vibrant Matter: A Political Ecology of Things* (London: Duke University Press).

Berdal, M. and Malone, D.M. (eds) (2000) *Greed and Grievance: Economic Agendas in Civil Wars* (London: Lynne Rienner).

Berdal, M. and Serrano, M. (eds) (2002) *Transnational Organised Crime & International Security: Business as Usual?* (Boulder: Lynne Rienner).

Berdal, M. and Ucko, D.H. (2009) 'Introduction,' in Berdal, M. and Ucko, D.H. (eds) *Reintegrating Armed Groups After Conflict: Politics, Violence and Transition* (London: Routledge).

Bergen, P. (2013) 'Al Qaeda's track record with chemical weapons,' CNN, 7 May, available at http://edition.cnn.com/2013/05/06/opinion/bergen-chemical-weapons-syria.

Bergen, P. and Tiedemann, K. (2010) *The Year of the Drone: An Analysis of U.S. Drone Strikes in Pakistan, 2004–2010* (Washington DC: New America Foundation).

Berger, M.T. (2007) 'States of nature and the nature of states: the fate of nations, the collapse of states and the future of the world,' *Third World Quarterly* 28(6) 1203–14.

Bergesen, A.J. and Lizardo, O. (2004) 'International terrorism and the world-system,' *Sociological Theory* 22(1) 38–52.

Bernabéu, I. (2007) 'Laying the foundations of democracy? Reconsidering security sector reform under UN auspices in Kosovo,' *Security Dialogue* 38(1) 71–92.

Betts, R.K. (1992) 'Systems for peace or causes of war? Collective security, arms control, and the new Europe,' *International Security* 17(1) 5–43.

Betts, R.K. (2007) *Enemies of Intelligence: Knowledge and Power in American National Security* (New York: Columbia University Press).

Beyer, A.C. (2010) *Counterterrorism and International Power Relations: The EU, ASEAN and Hegemonic Global Governance* (London: I.B. Tauris).

Bialasiewicz, L., Campbell, D., Elden, S. et al. (2007) 'Performing security: the imaginative geographies of current US strategy,' *Political Geography* 26(4) 405–22.

Bieler, A. and Morton, A.D. (2001) 'The Gordian knot of agency-structure in international relations,' *European Journal of International Relations* 7(1) 5–35.

Biersteker, T.J. (2003) 'The rebordering of North America? Implications for conceptualizing borders after September 11,' in Andreas, P. and Biersteker, T.J. (eds) *The Rebordering of North America: Integration and Exclusion in a New Security Context* (London: Routledge).

Biersteker, T.J. and Weber, C. (eds) (1996) *State Sovereignty as Social Construct* (Cambridge: CUP).

Bigo, D. (2001a) 'The Möbius ribbon of internal and external security(ies),' in Albert, M., Jacobson, D. and Lapid, Y. (eds) *Identities, Borders, Orders: Rethinking International Relations Theory* (Minneapolis: University of Minnesota Press).

Bigo, D. (2001b) 'Migration and security,' in Guiraudon, V. and Joppke, C. (eds) *Controlling a New Migration World* (London: Routledge).

Bigo, D. (2002) 'Security and immigration: towards a critique of the governmentality of unease,' *Alternatives* 27(1) 63–92.

Bigo, D. (2006) 'Protection: security, territory and population,' in Huysmans, J., Dobson, A. and Prokhovnik, R. (eds) *The Politics of Protection: Sites of Insecurity and Political Agency* (London: Routledge).

Bigo, D. (2011) 'Pierre Bourdieu and international relations: power of practices, practices of power,' *International Political Sociology* 5(3) 225–58.

Bigo, D. and Tsoukala, A. (2008) 'Understanding (in)security,' in Bigo, D. and Tsoukala, A. (eds) *Terror, Insecurity and Liberty: Illiberal practices of Liberal Regimes after 9/11* (Abingdon: Routledge).

Bigo, D., Carrera, S., Guild, E. and Walker, R.J. (2007) 'The changing landscape of European liberty and security: mid-term report on the results of the CHALLENGE project,' Research Paper No. 4 (Brussels: CEPS).

Bilgin, P. (2004) 'Whose Middle East? Geopolitical inventions and practices of security', *International Relations* 18(1) 17–33.

Bilgin, P. (2010) 'The "Western-centrism" of security studies: "blind spot" or constitutive practice?', *Security Dialogue* 41(6) 615–22.

Bilgin, P. and Morton A.D. (2002) 'Historicising representations of "failed states": Beyond the Cold War annexation of the social sciences?,' *Third World Quarterly* 23(1) 55–80.

Bitzinger, R.A. (ed.) (2009) *The Modern Defense Industry: Political, Economic, and Technological Issues* (Santa Barbara: Praeger).

Bjola, C. and Kronprobst, M. (2007) 'Security communities and the habitus of restraint: Germany and the United States on Iraq,' *Review of International Studies* 33(2) 285–305.

Blakeley, R. (2007) 'Bringing the state back into terrorism studies,' *European Political Science* 6(3) 228–53.

Blakeley, R. (2009) *State Terrorism and Neoliberalism: The North in the South* (Abingdon: Routledge).

Blanchard, E.M. (2003) 'Gender, international relations, and the development of feminist security theory,' *Signs: Journal of Women in Culture and Society* 28(4) 1289–312.

Bloom, M. (2004) 'Palestinian suicide bombing: public support, market share, and outbidding,' *Political Science Quarterly* 199(1) 61–88.

Bloom, M. (2011) *Bombshell: Women and Terrorism* (Philadelphia: University of Pennsylvania Press).

Blumi, I. (2010) 'Illicit trade and the emergence of Albania and Yemen,' in Zartman, I.W. (ed.) *Understanding Life in the Borderlands: Boundaries in Depth and Motion* (Athens: University of Georgia Press).

Bøås, M. and Jennings, K.M. (2005) 'Insecurity and development: the rhetoric of the "failed state",' *European Journal of Development Research* 17(3) 385–95.

Bøås, M. and Jennings, K.M. (2007) '"Failed states" and "state failure": Threats or opportunities?,' *Globalizations* 4(4) 475–85.

Boettcher, W.A. (2004) 'Military intervention decisions regarding humanitarian crises: framing induced risk behavior,' *Journal of Conflict Resolution* 48(3) 331–55.

Bohr, A. (2004) 'Regionalism in Central Asia: new geopolitics, old regional order,' *International Affairs* 80(3) 485–502.

Booth, K. (1991) 'Security and emancipation,' *Review of International Studies* 17(4) 313–26.

Booth, K. (1994) 'Strategy,' in Groom, A.J. and Light, M. (eds) *Contemporary International Relations: A Guide to Theory* (London: Pinter).

Booth, K. (1997) 'Security and self: reflections of a fallen realist,' in Krause, K. and Williams, M.C. (eds) *Critical Security Studies: Concepts and Cases* (London: UCL Press).

Booth, K. (2005a) 'Critical explorations,' in Booth, K. (ed.) *Critical Security Studies and World Politics* (Boulder: Lynne Rienner).

Booth, K. (2005b) 'Beyond critical security studies,' in Booth, K. (ed.) *Critical Security Studies and World Politics* (Boulder: Lynne Rienner).

Booth, K. (2007) *Theory of World Security* (Cambridge: CUP).

Booth, K. and Vale, P. (1997) 'Critical security studies and regional insecurity: the case of Southern Africa,' in Krause, K. and Williams, M.C. (eds) *Critical Security Studies: Concepts and Cases* (London: UCL Press).

Booth, K. and Wheeler, N. (2008) *The Security Dilemma: Fear, Cooperation, and Trust in World Politics* (Basingstoke: Palgrave Macmillan).

Bosold, D. (2011) 'Development of the human security field: a critical examination,' in Chandler, D. and Hynek, N. (eds) *Critical Perspectives on Human Security: Rethinking Emancipation and Power in International Relations* (Abingdon: Routledge).

Boureston, J. and Russell, J.A. (2009) 'Illicit nuclear procurement networks and nuclear proliferation: challenges for intelligence, detection, and interdiction,' *STAIR* 4(2) 24–50.

Bourke, J. (1999) *An Intimate History of Killing: Face-to-face Killing in Twentieth-century Warfare* (London: Granta).

Bourne, M. (2007) *Arming Conflict: The Proliferation of Small Arms* (Basingstoke: Palgrave Macmillan).

Bourne, M. (2011a) 'Netwar geopolitics: security, failed states and illicit flows,' *British Journal of Politics and International Relations* 13(4) 490–513.

Bourne, M. (2011b) 'Controlling the shadow trade,' *Contemporary Security Policy* 32(1) 215–40.

Bourne, M. (2012) 'Guns don't kill people, cyborgs do: a Latourian provocation for transformatory arms control and disarmament,' *Global Change, Peace and Security* 24(1) 141–63.

Bourne, M. and Greene, O. (2012) 'Governance and control of SALW after armed conflicts,' in Greene, O. and Marsh, N. (eds) *Small Arms, Crime and Conflict: Global Governance and the Threat of Armed Violence* (London: Routledge).

Boyd, D. and Scouras, J. (2010) 'The dark matter of terrorism', *Studies in Conflict & Terrorism* 33(12) 1124–39.

Brafman Kittner, C. (2007) 'The role of safe havens in Islamist terrorism,' *Terrorism and Political Violence*, 19(3) 307–29.

Brahimi, L. (2000) *Report of the Panel on United Nations Peace Operations* (New York: UN).

Brauch, H.G. (2011) 'Concepts of security threats, challenges, vulnerabilities and risks,' in Brauch, H.G., Spring, U.O., Mesjasz, C. et al. (eds) *Coping with Global Environmental Change, Disasters and Security: Threats, Challenges, Vulnerabilities and Risks* (Heidelberg: Springer).

Braun, B. and Whatmore, S.J. (eds) (2010) *Political Matter: Technoscience, Democracy, and Public Life* (Minneapolis: University of Minnesota Press).

Breen Smyth, M., Gunning, J., Jackson, R. et al. (2008) 'Critical terrorism studies: an introduction,' *Critical Studies on Terrorism* 1(1) 1–4.

Brodie, B. (1978) 'The development of nuclear strategy,' *International Security* 2(4) 65–83.

Brodie, B. (2008) 'A guide to the reading of *On War*,' in von Clausewitz, C. *On War*, ed. and trans. M. Howard and P. Paret (Princeton: Princeton University Press).

Brown, C. (2012) 'The "practice turn", phronesies and classical realism: towards a phronetic international political theory?,' *Millennium* 40(3) 439–56.

Brown, M.E. and Rosecrance, R.N. (eds) (1999) *The Costs of Conflict: Prevention and Cure in the Global Arena* (Lanham: Rowman & Littlefield).

Brzezinski, Z. (2003/04) 'Hegemonic quicksand,' *The National Interest*, 74 5–16.

Buckle P., Mars, G. and Smale, R.S. (2000) 'New approaches to assessing vulnerability and resilience', *Australian Journal of Emergency Management* 1 8–14.

Buckley, J. (1999) *Air Power in the Age of Total War* (London: Taylor & Francis).

Bueger, C. (2011) 'Drops in the bucket? A review of onshore responses to Somali piracy,' *WMU Journal of Maritime Affairs* 11(1) 15–31.

Bueger, C., Stockbruegger, J. and Werthes, S. (2011) 'Pirates, fishermen and peacebuilding: options for counter-piracy strategy in Somalia,' *Contemporary Security Policy* 32(2) 356–81.

Bueno de Mesquita, B. (1981) *The War Trap* (New Haven: Yale University Press).

Bueno de Mesquita, B. (1985) 'The war trap revisited: a revised expected utility model,' *American Political Science Review* 79(1) 156–77.

Bull, H. (1959) 'Disarmament and the international system,' *Australian Journal of Politics & History* 5(1) 41–50.

Bull, H. (1961) *The Control of the Arms Race: Disarmament and Arms Control in the Missile Age* (New York: Praeger).

Bull, H. (1976) 'Arms control and world order,' *International Security* 1(1) 3–16.

Bull, M. (2008) *Governing the Heroin Trade: From Treaties to Treatment* (Aldershot: Ashgate).

Bunker, R.J. (2007) 'Weapons of mass disruption and terrorism,' *Terrorism and Political Violence* 12(1) 37–46.

Bunn, M. (2006) 'A mathematical model of the risk of nuclear terrorism,' *Annals of the American Academy of Political and Social Science* 607 103–20.

Bunn, M. and Wier, A. (2006) 'Terrorist nuclear weapons construction: How difficult?,' *Annals of the American Academy of Political and Social Science* 607 133–49.

Bures, O. (2006) 'Regional peacekeeping operations: Complementing or undermining the United Nations Security Council?,' *Global Change, Peace and Security* 18(2) 83–99.

Burgess, J.P. (2009) 'There is no European security, only European securities,' *Cooperation and Conflict* 44(3) 309–28.

Burke, A. (2002) 'Aporias of security,' *Alternatives* 27(1) 1–27.

Burke, J. (2004) 'Al Qaeda,' *Foreign Policy* 142 18–26.

Busby, J.W. (2008) 'Who cares about the weather?: Climate change and U.S. national security,' *Security Studies* 17(3) 468–504.

Butler, J. (1990) *Gender Trouble: Feminism and the Subversion of Identity* (Abingdon: Routledge).

Butterfield, H. (1951) *History and Human Relations* (London: Collins).

Buzan, B. (1987) *Introduction to Strategic Studies* (London: Macmillan).

Buzan, B. (1991) *People, States and Fear: An Agenda for International Security Studies in the post-Cold War Era*, 2nd edn (London: Longman).

Buzan, B. (2004) 'A reductionist, idealistic notion that adds little analytical value,' *Security Dialogue* 35(3) 369–70.

Buzan, B. and Hansen, L. (2009) *The Evolution of International Security Studies* (Cambridge: CUP).

Buzan, B. and Herring, E. (1998) *The Arms Dynamic in World Politics* (London: Lynne Rienner).

Buzan, B. and Waever, O. (2003) *Regions and Powers: The Structure of International Security* (Cambridge: CUP).

Buzan, B., Little, R. and Jones, R. (1993) *The Logic of Anarchy: Neorealism to Structural Realism* (New York: Columbia University Press).

Buzan, B., Waever, O. and de Wilde, J. (1998) *Security: A New Framework for Analysis* (Boulder: Lynne Rienner).

Byman, D.L. (2005) *Deadly Connections: States that Sponsor Terrorism* (Cambridge: CUP).

Byman, D.L. (2008) 'The changing nature of state sponsorship of terrorism,' *Saban Center Analysis Paper* 16.

Cabinet Office (2008) *The National Security Strategy of the United Kingdom*, cm 7291 (Norwich: TSO).

Caldwell, S. (2009) *Supply Chain Security* (Washington DC: GAO).

Calvocoressi, P., Wint, G. and Pritchard, J. (1990) *Total War: The Causes and Courses of the Second World War* (New York: Pantheon Books).

Campbell, C. and Laherrere, J. (1998) 'The end of cheap oil?,' *Scientific American* 278(3) 78–84.

Campbell, D. (1998a) *Writing Security: United States Foreign Policy and the Politics of Identity*, rev. edn (Manchester: Manchester University Press).

Campbell, D. (1998b) *National Deconstruction: Violence, Identity, and Justice in Bosnia* (Minneapolis: University of Minnesota Press).

Campbell, D. (1998c) 'Why fight?: Humanitarianism, principles, and post-structuralism,' *Millennium* 27(3) 497–521.

Carnegie Endowment for International Peace (2009) *The Global Proliferation Status Map*, www.carnegieendowment.org/2009/02/26/global-proliferation-status-map/ss7.

Carpenter, R.C. (2006) 'Recognizing gender-based violence against civilian men and boys in conflict situation,' *Security Dialogue* 37(1) 83–103.

Carr, E.H. (1946) *The Twenty Years' Crisis, 1919–1939: An Introduction to the Study of International Relations*, 2nd edn (New York: St Martin's Press).

Carr, E.H. and Cox, M. (2001) *The Twenty Years' Crisis, 1919–1939: An Introduction to the Study of International Relations*, with new introduction by Michael Cox (Basingstoke: Palgrave – now Palgrave Macmillan).

Carter, A.B., Deutch, J. and Zelikow, P. (1998) 'Catastrophic terrorism,' *Foreign Affairs* 77(6) 80–94.

Cashman, G. and Robinson, L.C. (2007) *An Introduction to the Causes of War: Patterns of Interstate Conflict from World War 1 to Iraq* (Lanham: Rowman & Littlefield).

Castells, M. (1996) *The Information Age: Economy, Society and Culture*. vol. I: *The Rise of the Network Society* (Oxford: Blackwell).

Castells, M. (1998) *The Information Age: Economy, Society and Culture*. vol. III: *End of Millennium* (Oxford: Blackwell).

Castells, M. (2001) *The Internet Galaxy: Reflections on the Internet, Business and Society* (Oxford: OUP).

Cawthra, G. and Luckham, R. (eds) (2003a) *Governing Insecurity: Democratic Control of Military and Security Establishments in Transitional Democracies* (London: Zed Books).

Cawthra, G. and Luckham, R. (2003b) 'Democratic control and the security sector: the scope for transformation and its limits,' in Cawthra, G. and Luckham, R. (eds) *Governing Insecurity: Democratic Control of Military and Security Establishments in Transitional Democracies* (London: Zed Books).

Center on International Cooperation (2012) *Annual Review of Global Peace Operations 2012: Briefing Paper*, www.cic.nyu.edu/peacekeeping/docs/gpo_2012.pdf.

Cerny, P. (1998) 'Neomedievalism, civil war and the new security dilemma: globalization as durable disorder,' *Civil Wars* 1(1) 36–64.

Ceyhan, A. (2008) 'Technologization of security: management of uncertainty and risk in the age of biometrics,' *Surveillance and Society* 5(2) 102–23.

Chalfin, B. (2006) 'Global customs regimes and the traffic in sovereignty: enlarging the anthropology of the state,' *Current Anthropology* 47(2) 243–76.

Chalk, P. (2008) *The Maritime Dimension of International Security: Terrorism, Piracy, and Challenges for the United States* (Santa Monica: RAND).

Chalmers, M. (2007) 'Spending to save? The cost-effectiveness of conflict prevention,' *Defence and Peace Economics* 18(1) 1–23.

Chambliss, W.J. (1989) 'State-organized crime: the American Society of Criminology, 1988 Presidential Address,' *Criminology* 27(2) 183–208.

Chandler, D. (2004) 'The responsibility to protect? Imposing the liberal peace,' *International Peacekeeping* 11(1) 59–81.

Chandler, D. (2006) *Empire in Denial: The Politics of Statebuilding* (London: Pluto Press).

Chandler, D. (2008) 'Human security: the dog that didn't bark,' *Security Dialogue* 39(4) 427–38.

Chandler, D. (2010) 'Risk and the biopolitics of global insecurity,' *Conflict, Security and Development* 10(2) 287–97.

Chandler, D. (2012) ''Resilience and human security: the post-interventionist paradigm,' *Security Dialogue* 43(3) 213–29.

Chesterman, S. (2001) *Just War or Just Peace? Humanitarian Intervention and International Law* (Oxford: OUP).

Chesterman, S. (2010) 'Privacy and surveillance in the age of terror,' *Survival* 52(5) 31–46.

Chikering, R. and Förster, S. (eds) (2000) *Great War, Total War: Combat and Mobilization on the Western Front, 1914–1918* (Cambridge: CUP).

Christensen, T. (2002) 'The contemporary security dilemma: deterring a Taiwan conflict,' *Washington Quarterly* 25(4) 7–21.

Christie, R. (2010) 'Critical voices and human security: To endure, to engage or to critique?,' *Security Dialogue* 41(2) 169–90.

CHS (Commission on Human Security) (2003) *Human Security Now* (New York: CHS).

Chyba, C.F. and Greninger, A.L. (2004) 'Biotechnology and bioterrorism: an unprecedented world,' *Survival* 46(2) 143–62.

Ciuta, F. (2010) 'Conceptual notes on energy security: Total or banal security?,' *Security Dialogue* 41(2) 123–44.

Clark, I. (1999) *Globalization and International Relations Theory* (Oxford: OUP).

Claude, I. (1962) *Power and International Relations* (New York: Random House).

Clunan, A.L. and Trinkunas, H.A. (eds) (2010) *Ungoverned Spaces: Alternatives to State Authority in an Era of Softened Sovereignty* (Stanford: Stanford University Press).

CNET (1997) 'Net founders face java future', *CNET News*, 2 April, at http://news.cnet.com/Net-founders-face-Java-future/2100-1001_3-278526.html.

Coady, C.A.J. (2002) 'The ethics of armed humanitarian intervention,' *Peaceworks*, 45 24–5.

Coady, C.A.J. (2004) 'Terrorism and innocence,' *Journal of Ethics* 8(1) 37–58.

Coaffee, J. (2006) 'From counter-terrorism to resilience,' *European Legacy* 11(4) 389–403.

Coaffee, J. and Murakami Wood, D. (2006) 'Security is coming home: rethinking scale and constructing resilience in the global urban response to terrorist risk,' *International Relations* 20(4) 503–17.

Cockayne, J. and Lupel, A. (2009) 'Introduction: rethinking the relationship between peace operations and organized crime', *International Peacekeeping* 16(1) 4–19.

Cockayne, J. and Lupel, A. (2011) *Peace Operations and Organized Crime: Enemies or Allies?* (London: Routledge).

Cohen, E.A. (2001) 'Kosovo and the new American way of war,' in Bacevich, A.J. and Cohen, E.A. (eds) *War over Kosovo: Politics and Strategy in a Global Age* (New York: Columbia University Press).

Cohen, G., Joutz, F. and Lougani, P. (2011) *Measuring Energy Security: Trends in the Diversification of Oil and Natural Gas Supplies* (Washington DC: IMF).

Cohn, C. (1987) 'Sex and death in the rational world of defense intellectuals,' *Signs* 12(4) 687–718.

Coker, C. (2004) *The Future of War: The Re-Enchantment of War in the Twenty-First Century* (Oxford: Blackwell).

Coker, C. (2009) *War in an Age of Risk* (London: Polity).

Colletta, N.J. and Muggah, R. (2009) 'Rethinking post-war security promotion,' *Journal of Security Sector Management* 7(1) 1–25.

Collier, P. (2010) 'The political economy of natural resources,' *Social Research* 77(4) 1105–32.

Collier, P. and Hoeffler, A. (2005) 'Resource rents, governance, and conflict,' *Journal of Conflict Resolution* 49(4) 625–33.

Collier, S.J. and Lakoff, A. (2008) 'Distributed preparedness: space, security and citizenship in the United States,' in Cowen, D. and Gilbert, E. (eds) *War, Citizenship, Territory* (New York: Routledge).

Collins, A. (1997) *The Security Dilemma and the End of the Cold War* (Basingstoke: Macmillan – now Palgrave Macmillan).

Collins, A. (2004) 'State-induced security dilemma: maintaining the tragedy,' *Cooperation and Conflict* 39(1) 27–44.

Collins, S.D. (2004) 'Dissuading state support of terrorism: Strikes or sanctions? (An analysis of dissuasion measures employed against Libya),' *Studies in Conflict and Terrorism* 27(1) 1–18.

Comfort, L.K. (2005) 'Risk, security and disaster management,' *Annual Review of Political Science* 8 335–56.

Conteh-Morgan, E. (2005) 'Peacebuilding and human security: a constructivist perspective,' *International Journal of Peace Studies* 10(1) 69–86.

Coole, D. and Frost, S. (eds) (2010) *New Materialisms: Ontology, Agency, and Politics* (Durham: Duke University Press).

Cooper, N. (2005) 'Picking out the pieces of the liberal peaces: representations of conflict economies and the implications for policy,' *Security Dialogue* 36(4) 463–78.

Cooper, N. (2006) 'Putting disarmament back in the frame,' *Review of International Studies* 32(2) 353–76.

Cooper, N. and Mutimer, D. (2011) 'Introduction: arms control for the 21st century: controlling the means of violence', *Contemporary Security Policy* 32(1) 3–19.

Cooper, N. and Pugh, M. (2002) 'Security-sector transformation in post-conflict societies,' Conflict, Security & Development Group, Working Papers, 5.

Cooper, R. (2003) *The Breaking of Nations* (London: Atlantic Books).

Copeland, D.C. (1996) 'Neorealism and the myth of bipolar stability: toward a new dynamic realist theory of major war,' *Security Studies* 5 29–89.

Cordell, D., Drangert, J.O. and White, S. (2009) 'The story of phosphorus: global food security and food for thought,' *Global Environmental Change* 19(2) 292–305.

Coronil, F. (1997) *The Magical State: Nature, Money, and Modernity in Venezuela* (Chicago: University of Chicago Press).

Coward, M. (2009a) 'Network-centric violence, critical infrastructure and the urbanization of security,' *Security Dialogue* 40(4/5) 399–418.

Coward, M. (2009b) *Urbicide: The Politics of Urban Destruction* (Abingdon: Routledge).

Coward, M. (2012) 'Between us in the city: materiality, subjectivity and community in the era of global urbanization,' *Environment and Planning D: Society and Space* 30(3) 468–81.

Cowen, D. and Gilbert, E. (eds) (2008) *War, Citizenship, Territory* (London: Routledge).

Cox, R.W. (1981) 'Social forces, states, and world orders: beyond international relations theory,' *Millennium* 10(2) 126–55.

Cox, R.W. (1999) 'Civil society at the turn of the millennium: prospects for an alternative world order,' *Review of International Studies* 25 (1) 3–28.

Cragin, K. and Chalk, P. (2003) *Terrorism and Development: Using Social and Economic Development to Inhibit a Resurgence of Terrorism* (Santa Monica: RAND).

Cramer, C. (2002) 'Homo economicus goes to war: methodological individualism, rational choice and the political economy of war,' *World Development* 30(11) 1845–64.

Crenshaw, M. (1981) 'The causes of terrorism,' *Comparative Politics* 13(4) 397–9.

Crenshaw, M. (1991) 'How terrorism declines,' *Terrorism and Political Violence* 3(1) 69–87.

Crenshaw, M. (2007) 'Explaining suicide terrorism: a review essay,' *Security Studies* 16(1) 133–62.

Cresswell, T. (2011) 'Mobilities 1: catching up,' *Progress in Human Geography* 35(4) 550–8.

Croft, S. (1996) *Strategies of Arms Control: A History and Typology* (Manchester: Manchester University Press).

Cronin, A.K. (2002/03) 'Behind the curve: globalization and international terrorism,' *International Security* 27(3) 30–58.

Cronin, A.K. (2008) *Ending Terrorism: Lessons for Defeating al-Qaeda* (London: Routledge).

Cronin, A.K. (2009) *How Terrorism Ends: Understanding the Decline and Demise of Terrorist Campaigns* (Princeton: Princeton University Press).

Crosston, M. (2009) 'Neoconservative democratization in theory and practice: Developing democrats or raising radical Islamists?,' *International Politics* 46(2/3) 298–326.

Dabelko, G.D. (2009) 'Planning for climate change: the security community's precautionary principle,' *Climatic Change* 96(1/2) 13–21.

Dalby, S. (2002) *Environmental Security* (Minneapolis: University of Minnesota Press).

Dalby, S. (2008) *Security and Environmental Change* (London: Polity).

Davis, D.E. (2009) 'Non-state armed actors, new imagined communities, and shifting patterns of sovereignty and insecurity in the modern world,' *Contemporary Security Policy* 30(2) 221–45.

Debrix, F. (1999) *Re-Envisioning Peacekeeping: The United Nations and the Mobilization of Ideology* (Minneapolis: University of Minnesota Press).

De Carvalho, B., Leira, H. and Hobson, J.M. (2011) 'The big bangs of IR: the myths that your teachers still tell you about 1648 and 1919,' *Millennium* 39(3) 735–58.

De Genova, N. (2007) 'The production of culprits: from deportability to detainability in the aftermath of "homeland security",' *Citizenship Studies* 11(5) 421–48.

Deger, S. and Smith, R. (1983) 'Military expenditure and growth in less developed countries,' *Journal of Conflict Resolution* 27(2) 335–53.

De Goede, M. (2003) 'Hawala discourses and the war on terrorist finance,' *Environment and Planning D: Society and Space* 21 513–32.

De Goede, M. (2008) 'The politics of preemption and the war on terror in Europe,' *European Journal of International Relations* 14(1) 161–85.

De Goede, M. and Randalls, S. (2009) 'Precaution, pre-emption: arts and technologies of the actionable future,' *Environment and Planning D: Society and Space* 27 859–78.

Deibert, R.J. and Rohozinski, R. (2010) 'Risking security: policies and paradoxes of cyberspace security,' *International Political Sociology* 4(1) 15–32.

De Larrinaga, M. and Doucet, M.G. (2008) 'Sovereign power and the biopolitics of human security,' *Security Dialogue* 39(5) 517–37.

Den Boer, M. (2002) 'Law-enforcement cooperation and transnational organized crime in Europe, in Berdal, M. and Serrano, M. (eds) *Transnational Organized Crime and International Security: Business as Usual?* (Boulder: Lynne Rienner).

Deng, F., Kimaro, S., Lyons, T., et al. (1996) *Sovereignty as Responsibility: Conflict Management in Africa* (Washington DC: Brookings Institution Press).

Der Derian, J. (2001) *Virtuous War: Mapping the Military-Industrial-Media-Entertainment Network* (Boulder: Westview).

Der Derian, J. (1995) 'The value of security: Hobbes, Marx, Nietzsche, and Baudrillard,' in Lipschutz, R. (ed.) *On Security* (New York: Columbia University Press).

Der Derian, J. (2009) *Virtuous War: Mapping The Military-Industrial-Media-Entertainment Network*, 2nd edn (New York: Routledge).

De Soysa, I. (2000) 'The resource curse: Are civil wars driven by rapacity or paucity?,' in Berdal, M.R. and Malone, D.M. (eds) *Greed and Grievance: Economic Agendas in Civil Wars* (Boulder: Lynne Rienner).

De Soysa, I. (2002) 'Ecoviolence: Shrinking pie, or honey pot?,' *Global Environmental Politics* 2(4) 1–34.

Detraz, N.A. (2010) 'The genders of environmental security,' in Sjoberg, L. (ed.) *Gender and International Security: Feminist Perspectives* (Abingdon: Routledge).

Deudney, D.H. (1990) 'The case against linking environmental degradation and national security,' *Millennium* 19(3) 461–76.

Deudney, D.H. (1999) 'Environmental security: a critique,' in Deudney, D.H. and Matthew, R.A. (eds) *Contested Grounds: Security and Conflict in the New Environmental Politics* (Albany: State University of New York Press).

Deutsch, K.W. (1957) *Political Community in the North Atlantic Area* (Princeton: Princeton University Press).

Deutsch, K.W. (1966) *The Nerves of Government* (New York: Free Press).

Dillon, M. (1996) *Politics of Security: Towards a Political Philosophy of Continental Thought* (London: Routledge).

Dillon, M. (2005) 'Global security in the 21st century: circulation, complexity and contingency,' Chatham House Briefing Paper 05/02.

Dillon, M. (2008) 'Underwriting security,' *Security Dialogue* 39(2/3) 309–32.

Dillon, M. and Lobo-Guerrero, L. (2008) 'Biopolitics of security in the 21st century: an introduction,' *Review of International Studies* 34(2) 265–92.

Dillon, M. and Neal, A. (eds) (2008) *Foucault on Politics, Security and War* (Basingstoke: Palgrave Macmillan).

Dillon, M. and Reid, J. (2009) *The Liberal Way of War: Killing to Make Life Live* (London: Routledge).

Dishman, C. (2005) 'The leaderless nexus: when crime and terrorism converge,' *Studies in Conflict and Terrorism* 28(3) 237–52.

Dolnik, A. (2007) *Understanding Terrorist Innovation: Technology, Tactics and Global Trends* (Abingdon: Routledge).

Donnelly, J. (1986) 'International human rights: a regime analysis,' *International Organization* 40(3) 599–642.

Donnelly, J. (2000) *Realism and International Relations* (Cambridge: CUP).

Doty, R.L. (1997) 'Aporia: a critical exploration of the agent-structure problematique in international relations theory,' *European Journal of International Relations* 3(3) 365–92.

Doty, R.L. (2007) 'States of exception on the Mexico–US border: security, "decisions", and civilian border patrols,' *International Political Sociology* 1(2) 113–27.

Downs, E.S. (2004) 'The Chinese energy security debate,' *China Quarterly* 177 21–41.

Downs, G.W. (1994) 'Beyond the debate on collective security,' in Downs, G.W. (ed.) *Collective Security Beyond the Cold War* (Michigan: University of Michigan Press).

Downs, G.W., Rocke, D.M. and Siverson, R.M. (1985) 'Arms races and cooperation,' *World Politics* 38(1) 118–46.

Doyle, M. and Sambanis, N. (2000) 'International peacebuilding: a theoretical and quantitative analysis,' *American Political Science Review* 94(4) 778–801.

Doyle, M.W. (1983) 'Kant, liberal legacies and foreign policy', *Philosophy and Public Affairs* 12(3) 205–35, 12(4) 323–53.

Doyle, M.W. (1986) 'Liberalism and world politics', *American Political Science Review* 80(4) 1151–69.

Dreze, J. and Sen, A.K. (1989) *Hunger and Public Action* (Oxford: Clarendon Press).

Duffield, J. (1994) 'Explaining the long peace in Europe: the contributions of regional security regimes,' *Review of International Studies* 20(4) 369–88.

Duffield, M. (2001) *Global Governance and the New Wars: The Merging of Development and Security* (London: Zed Books).

Duffield, M. (2007) *Development, Security and Unending War: Governing the World of Peoples* (London: Polity).

Duffield, M. (2010) 'The liberal way of development and the development-security impasse: exploring the global life-chance divide,' *Security Dialogue* 41(1) 53–76.

Dunn Cavelty, M. (2007) 'Cyber-terror: looming threat or phantom menace? The framing of the US cyber-threat debate,' *Journal of Information Technology and Politics* 4(1) 19–36.

Dunn Cavelty, M. and Kristensen, K.S. (2008) 'Introduction: securing "the homeland": critical infrastructure, risk and insecurity,' in Dunn Cavelty, M. and Kristensen, K.S. (eds) *Securing 'the Homeland': Critical Infrastructure, Risk and (In)security* (New York: Routledge).

Dunne, T. and Wheeler, N.J. (2011) '"We the people": contending discourses of security in human rights theory and practice,' in Chandler, D. and Hynek, N. (eds) *Critical Perspectives on Human Security: Rethinking Emancipation and Power in International Relations* (London: Routledge).

Duyvesteyn, I. (2004) 'How new is the new terrorism?,' *Studies in Conflict and Terrorism* 27(5) 439–54.

Dzinesa, G.A. (2007) 'Postconflict disarmament, demobilization, and reintegration of former combatants in Southern Africa,' *International Studies Perspectives* 8(1) 73–89.

Eadie, P. (2007) 'Poverty, security and the Janus-faced state,' *British Journal of Politics and International Relations* 9(4) 636–53.

Ebo, A. (2007) 'The role of security sector reform in sustainable development: donor policy trends and challenges,' *Conflict, Security & Development* 7(1) 27–60.

Edkins, J. (2003) 'Humanitarianism, humanity, human,' *Journal of Human Rights* 2(2) 253–8.

Edwards, A. and Ferstman, C. (eds) (2009) *Human Security and Non-citizens: Law, Policy and International Affairs* (Cambridge: CUP).

Edwards, A. and Gill, P. (eds) (2003) *Transnational Organised Crime: Perspectives on Global Security* (London: Routledge).

Eilstrup-Sangiovanni, M. and Jones, C. (2008) 'Assessing the dangers of illicit networks: why al-Qaida may be less threatening than many think,' *International Security* 33(2) 7–44.

Eisner, M. (2003) 'Long term historical trends in violent crime,' *Crime and Justice: A Review of Research* 30 83–142.

Eisner, M. (2008) 'Modernity strikes back? A historical perspective on the latest increase in interpersonal violence (1960–1990), *International Journal of Conflict and Violence* 2(2) 288–316.

Elden, S. (2007) 'Terror and territory', *Antipode* 39(5) 821–45.

Enders, W. and Sandler, T. (1999) 'Transnational terrorism in the post-cold war era,' *International Studies Quarterly* 43(1) 145–67.

Englebert, P. and Tull, D.M. (2008) 'Postconflict reconstruction in Africa: flawed ideas about failed states,' *International Security* 32(4) 106–39.

English, R. (2009) *Terrorism: How to Respond* (Oxford: OUP).

Enloe, C. (1989) *Bananas, Beaches, and Bases: Making Feminist Sense of International Politics* (Berkeley: University of California Press).

Enloe, C. (2010) *Nimo's War, Emma's War: Making Feminist Sense of the Iraq War* (Berkeley: University of California Press).

Ericksen, P.J. (2008a) 'What is the vulnerability of a food system to global environmental change,' *Ecology and Society* 13(2) 14–32.

Ericksen, P.J. (2008b) 'Conceptualizing food systems for global environmental change research,' *Global Environmental Change* 18(1) 234–45.

Ericson, R.V. (2007) *Crime in an Insecure World* (Cambridge: Polity).

Ericson, R.V. and Haggerty, K. (1997) *Policing the Risk Society* (Oxford: Clarendon Press).

Eriksson, J. (1999) 'Observers or advocates? On the political role of security analysts,' *Cooperation and Conflict* 34(3) 311–30.

EU (2012) *The EU Strategy towards the Eradication of Trafficking in Human Beings 2012–2016.*

European Commission (2006) *Supply Chain Security: EU Customs' Role in the Fight Against Terrorism,* http://ec.europa.eu/taxation_customs/resources/documents/common/publications/info_docs/customs/customs_security_en.pdf.

Ewald, F. (2002) 'The return of Descartes's malicious demon: an outline of a philosophy of precaution,' in Baker, T. and Simon, J. (eds) *Embracing Risk* (Chicago: Chicago University Press).

Ewan, P. (2007) 'Deepening the human security debate: beyond the politics of conceptual clarification,' *Politics* 27(3) 182–9.

Eyerman, J. (1998) 'Terrorism and democratic states: soft targets or accessible systems,' *International Interactions* 24(2) 151–70.

Falk, R. (2004) *The Declining World Order: America's Imperial Geopolitics* (London: Routledge).

FAO/WFP/IFAD (2011) *The State of Food Insecurity in the World 2011* (Rome: FAO).

FAO/WFP/IFAD (2012) *The State of Food Insecurity in the World 2012* (Rome: FAO).

Farrell, T. (2007) 'The limits of security governance: technology, law, and war,' in Rappert, B. (ed.) *Technology and Security: Governing Threats in the New Millennium* (Basingstoke: Palgrave Macmillan).

Farwell, J.P. and Rohozinski, R. (2011) 'Stuxnet and the future of cyber war,' *Survival* 53(1) 23–40.

Fawcett, L. (2003) 'The evolving architecture of regionalization', in Pugh, M. and Sidhu, W.P. (eds) *The United Nations and Regional Security: Europe and Beyond* (Boulder: Lynne Rienner).

Fawcett, L. (2004) 'Exploring regional domains: a comparative history of regionalism,' *International Affairs* 80(3) 429–46.

Fawn, R. (2009) '"Regions" and their study: Wherefrom, what for and whereto?,' *Review of International Studies* 35(S1) 5–34.

Fearon, J.D. (1994) 'Domestic political audiences and the escalation of international disputes,' *American Political Science Review* 88(3) 577–92.

Felbab-Brown, V. (2005) 'Afghanistan: when counternarcotics undermines counterterrorism', *Washington Quarterly* 28(4) 55–72.

Ferguson, C.D. and Potter, W.C. with Sands, A. et al. (2005) *The Four Faces of Nuclear Terrorism* (Abingdon: Routledge).

Fierke, K. (1998) *Changing Games, Changing Strategies: Critical Investigations in Security* (Manchester: Manchester University Press).

Fierke, K. (2005) *Diplomatic Interventions: Conflict and Change in a Globalizing World* (Basingstoke: Palgrave Macmillan).

Findlay, M. (2000) *The Globalisation of Crime* (Cambridge: CUP).

Finnemore, M. (2003) *The Purpose of Intervention: Changing Beliefs about the Use of Force* (Ithaca: Cornell University Press).

Fiorentini, G. and Peltzman, S. (1997) *The Economics of Organised Crime* (Cambridge: CUP).

Fitzpatrick, M. (2007) *Nuclear Black Markets: Pakistan, A.Q. Khan and the Rise of Proliferation Networks – A Net Assessment* (London: IISS).

Floyd, R. (2010) *Security and the Environment: Securitisation Theory and US Environmental Policy* (Cambridge: CUP).

Floyd, R. (2011) 'Can securitization theory be used in normative analysis? Towards a just securitization theory,' *Security Dialogue* 42(4/5) 427–39.

Flynn, S. (2002) 'America the vulnerable,' *Foreign Affairs* 81(1) 60–74.

Flynn, S. (2008) 'America the resilient: defying terrorism and mitigating natural disasters,' *Foreign Affairs* 87(2) 2–8.

Fortna, V. (2004) *Peace Time: Cease-Fire Agreements and the Durability of Peace* (Princeton: Princeton University Press).

Fortna, V. (2008) *Does Peacekeeping Work? Shaping Belligerents' Choices after Civil War* (Princeton: Princeton University Press).

Foucault, M. (2004) *Society Must be Defended: Lectures at the Collège de France, 1975–76* (London: Penguin).

Foucault, M. (2007) *Security, Territory, Population; Michel Foucault: Lectures at the Collège de France: 1977–78* (Basingstoke: Palgrave Macmillan).

Frazier, D. and Stewart-Ingersoll, R. (2010) 'Regional powers and security: a framework for understanding order within regional security complexes,' *European Journal of International Relations* 16(4) 731–53.

Freedman, L. (2003) *The Evolution of Nuclear Strategy*, 3rd edn (Basingstoke: Palgrave Macmillan).

Friedberg, A.L. (1988) *The Weary Titan: Britain and the Experience of Relative Decline: 1895–1905* (Princeton: Princeton University Press).

Friman, H.R. (2009a) 'Crime and globalization,' in Friman, H.R. (ed.) *Crime and the Global Political Economy* (Boulder: Lynne Rienner).

Friman, H.R. (2009b) 'Drug markets and the selective use of violence,' *Crime, Law and Social Change*, 52(3) 285–95.

Friman, H.R. (2009c) 'Externalising the costs of prohibition,' in Friman, H.R. (ed.) *Crime and the Global Political Economy* (Boulder: Lynne Rienner).

Friman, H.R. and Andreas, P. (1999) 'International relations and the illicit global economy,' in Friman, H.R. and Andreas, P. (eds) *The Illicit Global Economy and State Power* (Lanham: Rowman & Littlefield).

Frost, R.M. (2005) *Nuclear Terrorism after 9/11* (London: IISS).

Fuhrmann, M. (2009) 'Spreading temptation: proliferation and peaceful nuclear cooperation agreements,' *International Security* 34(1) 7–41.

Fukuyama, F. (1992) *The End of History and the Last Man* (New York: Avon).

Fukuyama, F. (2004) *State-building: Governance and World Order in the 21st Century* (Ithaca: Cornell University Press).

Fund for Peace (2012) *The Failed States Index 2012*, www.foreignpolicy.com/failed_states_index_2012_interactive.

Gaddis, J.L. (1987) *The Long Peace: Inquiries into the History of the Cold War* (Oxford: OUP).

Galeotti, M. (ed.) (2005) *Global Crime Today: The Changing Face of Organised Crime* (London: Routledge).

Gallant, T.W. (1999) 'Brigandage, piracy, capitalism, and state-formation: transnational crime from a historical world-systems perspective,' in Heyman, J. (ed.) *States and Illegal Practices* (Oxford: Berg).

Galtung, J. (1969) 'Violence, peace and peace research,' *Journal of Peace Research* 6(3) 167–91.

Gambetta, D. (ed.) (2005) *Making Sense of Suicide Missions* (Oxford: OUP).

Garland, D. (2001) *The Culture of Control: Crime and Social Order in Contemporary Society* (Oxford: OUP).

Gates, S. and Reich, S. (eds) (2009) *Child Soldiers in the Age of Fractured States* (Pittsburgh: University of Pittsburgh Press).

Geneva Declaration (2008) *Global Burden of Armed Violence* (Geneva: Geneva Declaration).

Geneva Declaration (2011) *Global Burden of Armed Violence 2011: Lethal Encounters* (Cambridge: CUP).

George, A.L. (2004) 'Coercive diplomacy,' in Art, R.J. and Waltz, K.N. (eds) *The Use of Force: Military Power and International Politics*, 6th edn (Oxford: Rowman & Littlefield).

Ghani, A. and Lockhart, C. (2008) *Fixing Failed States: A Framework for Rebuilding a Fractured World* (Oxford: OUP).

Giddens, A. (1985) *The Nation-State and Violence* (Cambridge: Polity).

Giddens, A. (1991) *Modernity and Self-Identity: Self and Society in the Late Modern Age* (Stanford: Stanford University Press).

Giddens, A. (2002) *Runaway World: How Globalisation is Reshaping Our Lives* (London: Profile Books).

Gilpin, R. (1981) *War and Change in World Politics* (Cambridge: CUP).

Glaser, C. (1994/95) 'Realists as optimists: cooperation as self-help', *International Security* 19(3) 50–90.

Glaser, C. (1997) 'The security dilemma revisited,' *World Politics* 50(1) 171–201.

Gleditsch, N.P. (2003) 'Environmental conflict: neomalthusians vs. cornucopians' in Brauch, H.G., Liotta, P.H., Marquina, A. et al. (eds) *Security and the Environment in the Mediterra-*

nean: Conceptualising Security and Environmental Conflicts (Berlin: Springer).

Gleditsch, N.P., Furlong, K., Hegre, H. et al. (2006) 'Conflicts over shared rivers: Resource scarcity or fuzzy boundaries?,' *Political Geography* 25(4) 361–82.

Gleick, P.H. (1991) 'Environment and security: the clear connections,' *Bulletin of the Atomic Scientists* 47(3) 17–21.

Gleick, P.H. (1993) 'Water and conflict: fresh water resources and international security,' *International Security* 18(1) 79–112.

Glenny, M. (2008) *McMafia: Crime Without Frontiers* (London: Bodley Head).

Godfray, H.C., Beddington, J.R., Crute, I.R. et al. (2010) 'Food security: the challenge of feeding 9 billion people,' *Science*, 327(5967) 812–18.

Goertz, G. and Diehl, P. (1992) *Territorial Changes and International Conflict* (London: Routledge).

Goh, G. (2003) 'The "ASEAN Way": non-intervention and ASEAN's role in conflict management,' *Stanford Journal of East Asian Affairs* 3(1) 113–18.

Goldblat, J. (2002) *Arms Control: The New Guide to Negotiations and Agreements* (London: Sage).

Goodhand, J. (2008) 'Corrupting or consolidating the peace? The drugs economy and post-conflict peacebuilding in Afghanistan,' *International Peacekeeping* 15(3) 405–23.

Goodman, R. (2006) 'Humanitarian intervention and pretexts for war', *American Journal of International Law* 100 107–41.

Gootenberg, P. (2005) 'Talking like a state: drugs, borders and the language of control,' in van Schendel, W. and Abraham, I. (eds) *Illicit Flows and Criminal Things: States, Borders and the Other Side of Globalization* (Bloomington: Indiana University Press).

Gootenberg, P. (2008) *Andean Cocaine: The Making of a Global Drug* (Chapel Hill: University of North Carolina Press).

Gootenberg, P. (2009) 'Talking about the flow: drugs, borders, and the discourse of drug control,' *Cultural Critique* 71 13–46.

Goulding, M. (1993) 'The evolution of United Nations peacekeeping,' *International Affairs* 69(3) 451–64.

Graham, B., Talent, J., Allison, G. et al. (2008) *World At Risk: The Report of the Commission on the Prevention of Weapons of Mass Destruction Proliferation and Terrorism* (New York: Vintage Books).

Graham, S. (2010) 'Disruption by design: urban infrastructure and political violence,' in Graham, S. (ed.) *Disrupted Cities: When Infrastructure Fails* (London: Routledge).

Grainger, A. (2007) 'Supply chain security: adding to a complex operational and institutional environment,' *World Customs Journal* 1(2) 17–29.

Gray, C. (1986) *National Security and National Style* (Lanham: Hamilton Press).

Gray, C. (1992) *House of Cards: Why Arms Control Must Fail* (Ithaca: Cornell University Press).

Gray, C. (1999) 'Clausewitz rules OK? The future is the past – with GPS,' *Review of International Studies* 25(5) 161–82.

Gray, C. (2012) *War, Peace and International Relations: An Introduction to Strategic History*, 2nd edn (London: Routledge).

Gray, C. and Payne, K. (1980) 'Victory is possible,' *Foreign Policy* 39 14–27.

Grayson, K. (2008) 'Human security as power/knowledge: the biopolitics of a definitional debate,' *Cambridge Review of International Affairs* 21(3) 383–401.

Green, P. (1966) *Deadly Logic* (Columbus: Ohio State University Press).

Greenhill, K.M. (2010) 'Counting the cost: the politics of numbers in armed conflict,' in Andreas, P. and Greenhill, K.M. (eds) *Sex, Drugs, and Body Counts: The Politics of Numbers in Global Crime and Conflict* (Ithaca: Cornell University Press).

Gregory, D. (2011) 'From a view to a kill: drones and late modern war,' *Theory, Culture and Society* 28(7/8) 188–215.

Griset, P.L. and Mahan, S. (2003) *Terrorism in Perspective* (London: Sage).

Guelke, A. (1998) *The Age of Terrorism and the International Political System* (London: I.B. Tauris).

Guelke, A. (2008) *The New Age of Terrorism and the International Political System* (London: I.B. Tauris).

Guild, E. (2009) *Security and Migration in the 21st Century* (Cambridge: Polity).

Gunaratna, R. (2002) *Inside Al Qaeda* (New York: Columbia University Press).

Gunning, J. (2007) 'A case for critical terrorism studies?', *Government and Opposition* 42(3) 363–93.

Gupta, S., de Mello, L. and Sharan, R. (2001) 'Corruption and military spending,' *European Journal of Political Economy* 17(4) 749–77.

Gurr, N. and Cole. B. (2000) *The New Face of Terrorism: Threats from Weapons of Mass Destruction* (London: I.B. Tauris).

Guzzini, S. (2011) 'Securitization as a causal mechanism,' *Security Dialogue* 42(4/5) 329–41.

Haas, E. (1953) 'The balance of power: prescription, concept or propaganda,' *World Politics* 5(4) 442–77.

Haas, E. (1958) *The Uniting of Europe* (Stanford: Stanford University Press).

Haas, E. (1982) 'Words can hurt you: or, who said what to whom about regimes,' *International Organization* 36(2) 207–43.

Haas, P. (1989) 'Do regimes matter? Epistemic communities and Mediterranean pollution control,' *International Organization* 43(3) 377–403.

Haddad, E. (2008) *The Refugee in International Society: Between Sovereigns* (Cambridge: CUP).

Haftendorn, H. (1991) 'The security puzzle: theory-building and discipline-building in international security', *International Studies Quarterly* 35(1) 3–17.

Haggard, S. and Simmons, B.A. (1987) 'Theories of international regimes,' *International Organization* 41(3) 491–517.

Hagmann, J. and Cavelty, M.D. (2012) 'National risk registers: security scientism and the propagation of permanent insecurity,' *Security Dialogue* 43(1) 79–96.

Hagmann, T. and Hoehne, M.V. (2009) Failures of the state failure debate: evidence from the Somali territories,' *Journal of International Development* 21(1) 42–57.

Hall, R.B. and Biersteker, T. (eds) (2002) *The Emergence of Private Authority in Global Governance* (Cambridge: CUP).

Halperin, M. (1961) 'Nuclear weapons and limited war,' *Journal of Conflict Resolution* 5(2) 146–66.

Halperin, M. (1963) *Limited War in the Nuclear Age* (New York: Wiley).

Hampson, F.O. (2004) 'A concept in need of a global policy response', *Security Dialogue* 35(3) 349–50.

Hampson, F.O. and Daudelin, J. (2002) *Madness in the Multitude: Human Security and World Disorder* (Oxford: OUP).

Hampson, F.O. and Mendeloff, D. (2007) 'Intervention and the nation-building debate,' in Crocker, C.A., Hampson, F.O. and Aall, P.R. (eds) *Leashing the Dogs of War: Conflict Management in a Divided World* (Washington DC: United States Institute of Peace).

Handrahan, L. (2004) 'Conflict, gender, ethnicity and post-conflict reconstruction,' *Security Dialogue* 35(4) 429–45.

Hänggi, H. (2006) 'Approaching peacebuilding from a security governance perspective,' in Bryden, A. and Hänggi, H. (eds) *Security Governance in Post-Conflict Peacebuilding* (Geneva: DCAF).

Hansen, L. (2000) 'The little mermaid's silent security dilemma and the absence of gender in the Copenhagen School,' *Millennium* 29(2) 285–306.

Hansen, L. (2001) 'Gender, nation, rape: Bosnia and the construction of security,' *International Feminist Journal of Politics* 3(1) 55–75.

Hansen, L. and Nissenbaum, H. (2009) 'Digital disaster, cyber security, and the Copenhagen School,' *International Studies Quarterly* 53(4) 1155–75.

Hansen, S.J. (2012) 'The dynamics of Somali piracy,' *Studies in Conflict and Terrorism* 35(7/8) 523–30.

Harbom, L., Högbladh, S. and Wallensteen, P. (2006) 'Armed conflict and peace agreements', *Journal of Peace Research* 43(5) 617–31.

Hardt, M. and Negri, A. (2000) *Empire* (Cambridge: Harvard University Press).

Hasenclever, A., Mayer, P. and Rittberger, V. (1997) *Theories of International Regimes* (Cambridge: CUP).

Heathershaw, J. (2008) 'Unpacking the liberal peace: the dividing and merging of peacebuilding discourses,' *Millennium* 36(3) 597–621.

Held, D. (1995) *Democracy and the Global Order: From the Modern State to Cosmopolitan Governance* (Cambridge: Polity).

Hendrix, C.S. and Glaser, S.M. (2011) 'Civil conflict and world fisheries: 1952–2004,' *Journal of Peace Research* 48(4) 481–95.

Hensel, P.R. (2012) 'Territory; geography, contentious issues, and world politics,' in Vasquez, J.A. (ed.) *What Do We Know About War?*, 2nd edn (Lanham: Rowman & Littlefield).

Herbst, J. (2004) 'Let them fail: state failure in theory and practice: implications for policy,' in Rotberg, R.I. (ed.) *When States Fail: Causes and Consequences* (Princeton: Princeton University Press).

Herrera, G.L. (2007) 'Cyberspace and sovereignty: thoughts on physical space and digital space,' in Dunn Cavelty, M., Mauer, V. and Krishna-Hensel, S.F. (eds) *Power and Security in the Information Age: Investigating the Role of the State in Cyberspace* (Aldershot: Ashgate).

Herz, J. (1950) 'Idealist internationalism and the security dilemma,' *World Politics* 2(2) 157–80.

Herz, J. (1951) *Political Realism and Political Idealism: A Study in Theories and Realities* (Chicago: University of Chicago Press).

Herz, J. (1966) *International Relations in the Atomic Age* (New York: Columbia University Press).

Herz, J. (1981) 'Political realism revisited,' *International Studies Quarterly* 25(2) 182–97.

Hettne, B. (1999) 'Globalization and the new regionalism: the second great transformation,' in Björn, I.A. and Sunkel, O. (eds) *Globalism and the New Regionalism* (New York: Macmillan).

Heupel, M. (2007) 'Adapting to transnational terrorism: the UN Security Council's evolving approach to terrorism,' *Security Dialogue* 38(4) 477–99.

Heyman, D. (2002) *Lessons from the Anthrax Attacks: Implications for U.S. Bioterrorism Preparedness* (Washington DC: Center for Strategic and International Studies).

Higgott, R.A. and Nossal, K.R. (1998) 'Australia and the search for a security community in the 1990s,' in Adler, E. and Barnett, M. (eds) *Security Communities* (Cambridge: CUP).

Himes, J. (2011) 'A new approach to piracy,' *Proceedings* 137(10) 50–5.

Hobbes, T. (1993) *Leviathan*, reproduced in Williams, H., Wright, M. and Evans, A. (eds) *A Reader in International Relations and Political Theory* (Buckingham: Open University Press).

Hobbs, D. (1998) 'Going down the glocal: the local context of organised crime,' *Howard Journal* 37(4) 407–22.

Hobsbawm, E. (1981) *Bandits*, rev. edn (New York: Pantheon Books).

Hobson, J.A. (2000) *The State and International Relations* (Cambridge: CUP).

Hoffman, B. (1993) *Holy Terror: The Implications of Terrorism Motivated by a Religious Imperative* (Santa Monica: RAND).

Hoffman, B. (1995) '"Holy terror": the implications of terrorism motivated by a religious imperative,' *Studies in Conflict and Terrorism* 18(4) 271–84.

Hoffman, B. (2006) *Inside Terrorism* (New York: Columbia University Press).

Hoffman, B. (2008) 'Myths of grass-roots terrorism: why Osama bin Laden still matters,' *Foreign Affairs* 87(3) 133–8.

Hollis, M. (1996) 'The last post?,' in Smith, S., Booth, K. and Zalewski, M. (eds) *International Theory: Positivism and Beyond* (Cambridge: CUP).

Hollis, M. and Smith, S. (1990) *Explaining and Understanding International Relations* (Oxford: Clarendon Press).

Holmes, S. (2005) 'Al-Qaeda, September 11, 2001,' in Gambetta, D. (ed.) *Making Sense of Suicide Missions* (Oxford: OUP).

Holtom, P. (2010) 'Nothing to report: the lost promise of the UN Register of Conventional Arms,' *Contemporary Security Policy* 31(1) 61–87.

Holtom, P., Bromley, M., Wezeman, P.D. and Wezeman, S.T. (2011) *SIPRI Fact Sheet: Trends in International Arms Transfers, 2010* (Stockholm: SIPRI).

Holtom, P., Bromley, M., Wezeman, P.D. and Wezeman, S.T. (2012) *SIPRI Fact Sheet: Trends in International Arms Transfers, 2011* (Stockholm: SIPRI).

Holtom, P., Bromley, M., Wezeman, P.D. and Wezeman, S.T. (2013) *SIPRI Fact Sheet: Trends in International Arms Transfers, 2012* (Stockholm: SIPRI).

Holzgrefe, J.L. (2003) 'The humanitarian intervention debate,' in Holzgrefe, J.L. and Keohane, R.O. (eds) *Humanitarian Intervention: Ethical, Legal and Political Dilemmas* (Cambridge: CUP).

Homer-Dixon, T. (1991) 'On the threshold: environmental change as causes of acute conflict,' *International Security* 16(2) 76–116.

Homer-Dixon, T. (1994) 'Environmental scarcities and violent conflict: evidence from cases,' *International Security* 19(1) 5–40.

Homer-Dixon, T. (2002) 'The rise of complex terrorism,' *Foreign Policy* 128 52–62.

Honig, J.W. (2007) 'Clausewitz's *On War*: problems of text and translation,' in Strachan, H. and Herberg-Rothe, A. (eds) *Clausewitz in the Twenty-first Century* (Oxford: OUP).

Hoogensen, G. and Stuvøy, K. (2006) 'Gender, resistance and human security,' *Security Dialogue* 37(2) 207–28.

House of Commons Select Committee on Foreign Affairs (2000) *Foreign Affairs: Fourth Report* (London: TSO).

Howard, M. (2002) *Clausewitz: A Very Short Introduction* (Oxford: OUP).

Howard, M. (2008) 'The influence of Clausewitz,' in Clausewitz, C. *On War*, ed. and trans. M. Howard and P. Paret (Princeton: Princeton University Press).

Howard, T. (2010) 'Failed states and the spread of terrorism in sub-Saharan Africa,' *Studies in Conflict and Terrorism* 33(11) 960–88.

Hudson, H. (2005) 'Doing security as though humans matter: a feminist perspective on gender and the politics of human security,' *Security Dialogue* 36(2) 155–74.

Human Security Centre (2005) *Human Security Report 2005: War and Peace in the 21st Century* (Oxford: OUP).

Humphreys, M. (2005) 'Natural resources and armed conflict: issues and options,' in Ballentine, K. and Nitzschke, H. (eds) *Profiting from Peace: Managing the Resource Dimensions of Civil War* (Boulder: Lynne Rienner).

Hurrell, A. (1995) 'Explaining regionalism in world politics,' *Review of International Studies* 21(4) 331–58.

Hurrell, A. (2007) 'One world? Many worlds? The place of regions in the study of international society,' *International Affairs* 83(1) 127–46.

Hutchinson, S. and O'Malley, P. (2007) 'A crime-terror nexus? Thinking on some of the links between terrorism and criminality,' *Studies in Conflict and Terrorism* 30(12) 1095–107.

Huth, P.K. and Alee, T.L. (2003) *The Democratic Peace and Territorial Conflict in the Twentieth Century* (Cambridge: CUP).

Huysmans, J. (1998) 'Security! What do you mean? From concept to thick signifier,' *European Journal of International Relations* 4(4) 479–506.

Huysmans, J. (2000) 'The EU and the securitization of migration,' *Journal of Common Market Studies* 38(5) 751–77.

Huysmans, J. (2006) *The Politics of Insecurity: Fear, Migration and Asylum in the EU* (London: Routledge).

Huysmans, J. (2011) 'What's in an act? On security speech acts and little security nothings,' *Security Dialogue* 42(4/5) 371–83.

Huysmans, J. and Squire, V. (2009) 'Migration and security,' in Mauer, V. and Dunn Cavelty, M. (eds) *The Routledge Handbook of Security Studies* (London: Routledge).

Hymans, J. (2006) *The Psychology of Nuclear Proliferation: Identity, Emotions and Foreign Policy* (Cambridge: CUP).

ICISS (International Commission on Intervention and State Sovereignty) (2001) *The Responsibility to Protect* (Ottawa: ICISS).

Ignatieff, M. (2001) *Virtual War: Kosovo and Beyond* (London: Vintage).

Ilardi, G.J. (2004) 'Redefining the issues: the future of terrorism research and the search for empathy,' in Silke, A. (ed.) *Research on Terrorism: Trends, Achievements & Failures* (London: Frank Cass).

Intergovernmental Panel on Climate Change (2007) *Climate Change 2007: Synthesis Report* (Valencia: IPCC).

International Crisis Group (2008) *Russia vs Georgia: The Fallout* (Brussels: ICG).

International Institute for Strategic Studies (2012) *The Military Balance 2012* (London: IISS).

International Labour Organization (2012) *Global Estimate of Forced Labour: Executive Summary* (Geneva: ILO).

International Narcotics Control Board (2007) *2006: Precursors and Chemicals Frequently used in the Illicit Manufacture of Narcotic Drugs and Psychotropic Substances* (Vienna: INCB).

International Organization for Migration (2008) *World Migration Report 2008: Managing Labour Mobility in the Evolving Global Economy* (Geneva: IOM).

Isin, E.F. and Rygiel, K. (2007) 'Abject spaces: frontiers, zones, camps,' in Dauphinee, E. and Masters, C. (eds) *Logics of Biopower and the War on Terror* (Basingstoke: Palgrave Macmillan).

Ivanova, K. and Sandler, T. (2006) 'CBRN incidents: political regimes, perpetrators, and targets,' *Terrorism and Political Violence* 18(3) 423–48.

Jabri, V. (2006) 'War, security and the liberal state,' *Security Dialogue* 37(1) 47–64.

Jackson, B. (2006) 'Groups, networks, or movements: a command-and-control-driven approach to classifying terrorist organizations and its application to Al Qaeda,' *Studies in Conflict and Terrorism* 29(3) 241–62.

Jackson, R. (2000) *The Global Covenant: Human Conduct in a World of States* (Oxford: OUP).

Jackson, R. (2005) *Writing the War on Terrorism: Language, Politics and Counter-terrorism* (Manchester: Manchester University Press).

Jackson, R. (2007) 'Research for counterterrorism: terrorism studies and the reproduction of state hegemony', paper presented at the annual meeting of the International Studies Association 48th Annual Convention, Hilton Chicago, 28 February.

Jackson, R. (2008) 'The ghosts of state terror: knowledge, politics and terrorism studies,' *Critical Studies on Terrorism* 1(3) 377–92.

Jackson, R., Breen-Smyth, M. and Gunning, J. (eds) (2009a) *Critical Terrorism Studies: A New Research Agenda* (Abingdon: Routledge).

Jackson, R., Murphy, E. and Poynting, S. (eds) (2009b) *Contemporary State Terrorism: Theory and Practice* (Abingdon: Routledge).

Jackson, R., Jarvis, L., Gunning, J. and Breen-Smyth, M. (2011) *Terrorism: A Critical Introduction* (Basingstoke: Palgrave Macmillan).

Jackson, R.H. (1990) *Quasi-states: Sovereignty, International Relations and the Third World* (Cambridge: CUP).

Jacoby, T. (2007) 'Hegemony, modernisation and post-war reconstruction,' *Global Society* 21(4) 521–37.

Jenkins, B. (1975) 'International terrorism: a new mode of conflict,' in Carlton, D. and Schaerf, C. (eds) *International Terrorism and World Security* (London: Croom Helm).

Jenkins, B. (1999) 'Foreword,' in Lesser, I., Hoffman, B. Arquila, J. et al. (eds) *Countering the New Terrorism* (Santa Monica: RAND).

Jensen, R.B. (2008) 'Nineteenth century anarchist terrorism: How comparable to the terrorism of al-Qaeda?,' *Terrorism and Political Violence* 20(4) 589–96.

Jervis, R. (1976) *Perception and Misperception in International Politics* (Princeton: Princeton University Press).

Jervis, R. (1978) 'Cooperation under the security dilemma,' *World Politics* 30(2) 167–214.

Jervis, R. (1979) 'Deterrence theory revisited,' *World Politics* 31(2) 289–324.

Jervis, R. (1982) 'Security regimes,' *International Organization* 32(3) 357–78.

Jervis, R. (1982/83) 'Deterrence and perception,' *International Security* 7(3) 3–30.

Jervis, R. (1991) 'The future of world politics: Will it resemble the past?,' *International Security* 16(3) 39–73.

Jervis, R. (2001) 'Was the cold war a security dilemma?', *Journal of Cold War Studies* 3(1) 36–60.

Job, B.L. (ed.) (1992) *The Insecurity Dilemma: National Security of Third World States* (Boulder: Lynne Rienner).

Joffé, G. (2008) 'The European Union, democracy and counter-terrorism in the Maghreb,' *Journal of Common Market Studies* 46(1) 147–71.

Jojarth, C. (2009) *Crime, War, and Global Trafficking: Designing International Cooperation* (Cambridge: CUP).

Jones, B.G. (2008) 'The global political economy of social crisis: towards a critique of the "failed state" ideology,' *Review of International Political Economy* 15(2) 180–205.

Jones, D.M. and Smith. M.L. (2009) 'We're all terrorists now: Critical – or hypocritical – studies "on" terrorism?', *Studies in Conflict and Terrorism* 32(4) 292–302.

Jones, S.G. and Libicki, M.C. (2008) *How Terrorist Groups End: Lessons for Countering Al Qaeda* (Santa Monica: RAND).

Jurgensmeyer, M. (2000) *Terror in the Mind of God: The Global Rise of Religious Violence* (Berkeley: University of California Press).

Kahl, C.H. (2006) *States, Scarcity and Civil Strife in the Developing World* (Princeton: Princeton University Press).

Kahler, M. and Walter, B.F. (eds) (2006) *Territoriality and Conflict in an Era of Globalization* (Cambridge: CUP).

Kahn, H. (1960) 'The arms race and some of its hazards,' *Daedalus* 89(4) 744–80.

Kahn, H. (1962) *Thinking About the Unthinkable* (New York: Horizon Press).

Kaldor, M. (1982) *The Baroque Arsenal* (London: Andre Deutsch).

Kaldor, M. (1999) *New and Old Wars: Organized Violence in a Global Era* (Stanford: Stanford University Press).

Kaldor, M. (2007) *Human Security: Reflections on Globalization and Intervention* (Cambridge: Polity).

Kant, I. (2005) *Perpetual Peace* (New York: Cosimo).

Kaplan, R. (1994) 'The coming anarchy: how scarcity, crime, overpopulation, tribalism, and disease are rapidly destroying the social fabric of our planet,' *Atlantic Monthly* 273(2) 44–76.

Karl, D.J. (1996/97) 'Proliferation pessimism and emerging nuclear powers,' *International Security* 21(3) 87–119.

Katzenstein, P. (ed.) (1996) *The Culture of National Security* (New York: Columbia University Press).

Katzenstein, P. (2005) *A World of Regions. Asia and Europe in the American Imperium* (Ithaca: Cornell University Press).

Kaufmann, C. (1996) 'Possible and impossible solutions to ethnic civil wars,' *International Security* 20(4) 136–75.

Kaunert, C., Léonard, S. and MacKenie, A. (2012) 'The social construction of an EU interest in counter-terrorism: US influence and internal struggles in the cases of PNR and SWIFT,' *European Security* 21(4) 474–96.

Kavalski, E. (2008) 'The complexity of global security governance: an analytical overview,' *Global Society* 22(4) 423–42.

Kay, S. (2004) 'NATO, the Kosovo war and neoliberal theory,' *Contemporary Security Policy* 25(2) 252–79.

Keane, R. (2006) 'EU foreign policy motivation: a mix of human security and realist elements,' in Maclean, S.J., Black, D.R. and Shaw, T.M. (eds) *A Decade of Human Security: Global Governance and New Multilateralisms* (Farnham: Ashgate).

Keegan, J. (1993) *A History of Warfare* (London: Hutchinson).

Keen, D. (1998) *Adelphi Paper 320: The Economic Functions of Violence in Civil Wars* (London: IISS).

Keen, D. (2001) 'The political economy of war,' in Stewart, F. and Fitzgerald, V. (eds) *War and Underdevelopment*, vol. 1: *The Economic and Social Consequences of Conflict* (Oxford: OUP).

Keller, E.J. and Rothchild, D. (eds) (1996) *African in the New International Order: Rethinking State Sovereignty and Regional Security* (Boulder: Lynne Rienner).

Kellman, B. (2007) *Bioviolence: Preventing Biological Terror and Crime* (Cambridge: CUP).

Kelmendi, A. (1999) *Statement before the Senate Subcommittee on Immigration of the Committee on the Judiciary*, 14 April, www.loc.gov/law/find/hearings/pdf/00068691710.pdf.

Kelsen, H. (1948) 'Collective security and collective self-defense under the Charter of the United Nations,' *American Journal of International Law* 42 783–96.

Kenney, M. (2007a) *From Pablo to Osama: Trafficking and Terrorist Networks, Government Bureaucracies, and Competitive Adaptation* (Pennsylvania: Pennsylvania State University Press).

Kenney, M. (2007b) 'The architecture of drug trafficking: network forms of organisation in the Colombian cocaine trade,' *Global Crime* 8(3) 233–59.

Kent, G. (2005) *Freedom from Want: The Human Right to Adequate Food* (Washington DC: Georgetown University Press).

Keohane, D. (ed.) (2008a) 'Towards a European defence market,' *Chaillot Papers* 113.

Keohane, D. (2008b) 'The absent friend: EU foreign policy and counter-terrorism,' *Journal of Common Market Studies* 46(1) 125–46.

Keohane, R.O. (1984) *After Hegemony: Cooperation and Discord in the World Political Economy* (Princeton: Princeton University Press).

Keohane, R.O. (1986) 'Theory of world politics: structural realism and beyond,' in Keohane, R.O. (ed.) *Neorealism and its Critics* (New York: Columbia University Press).

Keohane, R.O. (1988) 'International institutions: two approaches,' *International Studies Quarterly* 32(4) 379–96.

Keohane, R.O. (1993) 'Institutional theory and the realist challenge after the cold war,' in Baldwin, D.A. (ed.) *Neorealism and Neoliberalism: The Contemporary Debate* (New York: Columbia University Press).

Keohane, R.O. and Martin, L.L. (1995) 'The promise of institutionalist theory,' *International Security* 20(1) 39–51.

Keohane, R.O. and Nye, J. (1977) *Power and Interdependence: World Politics in Transition* (Boston: Little, Brown).

Keohane, R.O. and Victor, D.G. (2011) 'The regime complex for climate change,' *Perspectives on Politics* 9(1) 7–23.

King, C. (2008) 'The five-day war: managing Moscow after the Georgia crisis,' *Foreign Affairs* 87(6) 2–11.

King, G. and Murray, C. (2002) 'Rethinking human security,' *Political Science Quarterly* 116(4) 585–610.

Kinsey, C. (2006) *Corporate Soldiers and International Security: The Rise of Private Military Companies* (Abingdon: Routledge).

Kissinger, H.A. (1960) 'Limited war: Conventional or nuclear? A reappraisal,' *Daedalus* 89(4) 800–17.

Klare, M.T. (2001) 'The new geography of conflict', *Foreign Affairs* 80(3) 49–61.

Klare, M.T. (2002) *Resource Wars: The New Landscape of Global Conflict* (New York: Henry Holt).

Klare, M.T. (2008) *Rising Powers Shrinking Planet: The New Geopolitics of Energy* (New York: Metropolitan Books).

Klare, M.T. and Volman, D. (2006) 'America, China and the scramble for Africa's oil,' *Review of African Political Economy* 33(108) 297–309.

Klein, B.S. (1994) *Strategic Studies and World Order: The Global Politics of Deterrence* (Cambridge: CUP).

Knight, M. (2009) 'Security sector reform, democracy, and the social contract: from implicit to explicit,' *Journal of Security Sector Management* 7(1) 1–20.

Knight, M. and Özerdam, A. (2004) 'Guns, camps, and cash: disarmament, demobilization and reinsertion of former combatants in transitions from war to peace,' *Journal of Peace Research* 41(4) 499–516.

Knopf, J.W. (2009) 'Three items in one: deterrence as concept, research program and political issue,' in Paul, T.V., Morgan, P.M. and Wirtz, J.J. (eds) *Complex Deterrence: Strategy in the Global Age* (Chicago: University of Chicago Press).

Kolodziej, E.A. (1999) 'Security studies for the next millennium: Quo vadis?,' *Contemporary Security Policy* 20(3) 18–38.

Krahmann, E. (2003) 'Conceptualizing security governance,' *Cooperation and Conflict* 38(1) 5–26.

Krahmann, E. (2008) 'Security: Collective good or commodity?,' *European Journal of International Relations* 14(3) 379–404.

Krain, M. (2005) 'International intervention and the severity of genocides and politicides,' *International Studies Quarterly* 49(2) 363–87.

Krasner, S.D. (1982a) 'Structural causes and regime consequences: regimes as intervening variables,' *International Organization* 36(2) 185–205.

Krasner, S.D. (1982b) 'Regimes and the limits of realism: regimes as autonomous variables,' *International Organization* 36(2) 497–510.

Krasner, S.D. (1999) *Sovereignty: Organized Hypocrisy* (Princeton: Princeton University Press).

Krasner, S.D. and Pascual, C. (2005) 'Addressing state failure,' *Foreign Affairs* 84(4) 153–63.

Kratochwil, F. (1989) *Rules, Norms and Decisions* (Cambridge: CUP).

Krause, K. (1992) *Arms and the State: Patterns of Military Production and Trade* (Cambridge: CUP).

Krause, K. (2004) 'The key to a powerful agenda, if properly delimited,' *Security Dialogue* 33(3) 367–8.

Krause, K. (2008) 'Building the agenda of human security: policy and practice within the Human Security Network,' *International Social Science Journal* 59(S1) 65–79.

Krause, K. and Latham, A. (1998) 'Constructing non-proliferation and arms control: the norms of western practice,' *Contemporary Security Policy* 19(1) 23–54.

Krause, K. and Williams, M.C. (eds) (1997) *Critical Security Studies: Concepts and Cases* (London: UCL Press).

Kreuger, A. (2007) *What Makes a Terrorist: Economics and the Roots of Terrorism* (Princeton: Princeton University Press).

Kreutz, J. (2010) 'How and when armed conflicts end: introducing the UCDP Conflict Termination dataset,' *Journal of Peace Research* 47(2) 243–50.

Kristensen, K.S. (2008) '"The absolute protection of our citizens": critical infrastructure protection and the practice of security,' in Dunn Cavelty, M. and Kristensen, K.S. (eds) *Securing 'the Homeland': Critical Infrastructure, Risk and (In)security* (New York: Routledge).

Kroenig, M. (2010) *Exporting the Bomb: Technology Transfer and the Spread of Nuclear Weapons* (Ithaca: Cornell University Press).

Kubicek, P. (2009) 'The Commonwealth of Independent States: An example of failed regionalism?,' *Review of International Studies* 35(S1) 237–56.

Kupchan, C.A. and Kupchan, C.A. (1991) 'Concerts, collective security, and the future of Europe,' *International Security* 16(1) 114–61.

Kuperman, A. (2000) 'Rwanda in retrospect,' *Foreign Affairs* 79(1) 94–118.

Kuperman, A. (2004) 'Humanitarian hazard: revisiting doctrines of intervention,' *Harvard International Review* 26(1) 64–8.

Kuperman, A. (2008) 'The moral hazard of humanitarian intervention: lessons from the Balkans,' *International Studies Quarterly* 52(1) 49–80.

Kurki, M. and Wight, C. (2007) 'International relations and social science,' in Dunne, T., Kurki, M. and Smith, S. (eds) *International Relations Theories: Discipline and Diversity* (Oxford: OUP).

Kydd, A.H. (2005) *Trust and Mistrust in International Relations* (Princeton: Princeton University Press).

LaCasse, C. and Plourde, A. (1995) 'On the renewal of concern for the security of oil supply,' *Energy Journal* 16(2) 1–23.

Lacina, B., Gleditsch, N.P. and Russett, B. (2006) 'The declining risk of death in battle,' *International Studies Quarterly* 50(3) 673–80.

Lake, D.A. (2009) 'Regional hierarchy: authority and local international order,' *Review of International Studies* 35(1) 35–58.

Lake, D.A. and Morgan, P.M. (eds) (1997) *Regional Orders: Building Security a New World* (University Park: Penn State University Press).

Lang, A.F. (2009) 'Conflicting rules: global constitutionalism and the Kosovo intervention,' *Journal of Intervention and Statebuilding* 3(2) 185–204.

Lapid, Y. (1989) 'The third debate: on the prospects of international theory in a post-positivist era,' *International Studies Quarterly* 33(3) 235–54.

Laqueur, W. (1996) 'Post-modern terrorism,' *Foreign Affairs* 75(5) 24–36.

Laqueur, W. (1999) *The New Terrorism: Fanaticism and the Arms of Mass Destruction* (Oxford: OUP).

Larsen, J. and Wirtz, J. (eds) (2009) *Arms Control and Cooperative Security* (Boulder: Lynne Rienner).

Larson, R.H. (1980) 'B.H. Liddell Hart apostle of limited war,' *Military Affairs* 44(2) 70–4.

Lash, S. and Urry, J. (1994) *Economies of Signs and Space* (London: Sage).

Latour, B. (2005) *Reassembling the Social: An Introduction to Actor-Network Theory* (Oxford: OUP).

Layne, C. (1994) 'Kant or can't: the myth of the democratic peace,' *International Security* 19(2) 5–49.

Layne, C. (2000) 'US hegemony and the perpetuation of NATO,' *Journal of Strategic Studies* 23(3) 59–91.

Layne, C. (2006) *The Peace of Illusions: American Grand Strategy from 1940 to the Present* (Ithaca: Cornell University Press).

Le Billon, P. (2001) 'The political ecology of war: natural resources and armed conflicts,' *Political Geography* 20(5) 561–84.

Lebow, R.N and Stein, J.G. (1989) 'Rational deterrence theory: I think, therefore I deter,' *World Politics* 41(2) 208–24.

Lebow, R.N. and Stein, J.G. (1995) 'Deterrence and the cold war,' *Political Science Quarterly* 110(2) 157–81.

Lee, R. (2006) 'Nuclear smuggling, rogue states and terrorists,' *China and Eurasia Forum Quarterly* 4(2) 25–32.

Lemanski, C. (2012) 'Everyday human (in)security: rescaling for the southern city,' *Security Dialogue* 43(1) 61–78.

Lemke, D. (2002) *Regions of War and Peace* (Cambridge: CUP).

Lemkin, R. (1944) *Axis Rule in Occupied Europe: Laws of Occupation – Analysis of Government – Proposals for Redress* (Washington DC: Carnegie Endowment for International Peace).

Lesser, I.O., Hoffman, B., Arquila, J. et al. (eds) (1999) *Countering the New Terrorism* (Santa Monica: RAND).

Levi, M.A. (2007) *On Nuclear Terrorism* (Cambridge: Harvard University Press).

Levi, M.A. (2008) *Deterring State Sponsorship of Nuclear Terrorism* (New York: Council on Foreign Relations Press).

Levi, M.A. and Kelly, H.C. (2002) 'Weapons of mass disruption,' *Scientific American* November 77–81.

Levy, J.S. (1987) 'Declining power and the preventive motivation for war,' *World Politics* 40(1) 82–107.

Levy, J.S. (1988) 'Domestic politics and war,' *Journal of Interdisciplinary History* 18(4) 653–73.

Levy, J.S. and Thompson, W.R. (2010) *Causes of War* (Oxford: Wiley-Blackwell).

Lewis, J. (2004) 'Cyber terror: missing in action,' in Clarke, D. (ed.) *Technology and Terrorism* (Piscataway: Transaction).

Lewis, T.G. (2006) *Critical Infrastructure Protection in Homeland Security: Defending a Networked Nation* (Hoboken: John Wiley & Sons).

Liang, X. (2011) 'Proposed U.S. arms sales reach new heights,' *Arms Control Today* 41(2).

Licklider, R. (1995) 'The consequences of negotiated settlements in civil wars, 1945–1993,' *American Political Science Review* 89(3) 681–90.

Lieber, K.A. (2007) 'The new history of World War I and what it means for international relations,' *International Security* 32(2) 155–91.

Linklater, A. (1998) *The Transformation of Political Community* (London: Polity).

Liotta, P.H. (2002a) 'Boomerang effect: the convergence of national and human security,' *Security Dialogue* 33(4) 473–88.

Liotta, P.H. (2002b) 'Converging interests and agendas: the boomerang returns,' *Security Dialogue* 33(4) 495–8.

Litfin, K.T. (1999) 'Constructing environmental security and ecological interdependence,' *Global Governance* 5(3) 359–77.

Little, R. (2007) *The Balance of Power in International Relations: Metaphors, Myths and Models* (Cambridge: CUP).

Loader, I. and Walker, N. (2007) *Civilizing Security* (Cambridge: CUP).

Lobasz, J.K. (2009) 'Beyond border security: feminist approaches to human trafficking,' *Security Studies* 18(2) 319–44.

Lobo-Guerrero, L. (2008) '"Pirates", stewards, and the securitization of global circulation,' *International Political Sociology* 2(3) 219–35.

Lobo-Guerrero, L. (2010) *Insuring Security: Biopolitics, Security and Risk* (Abingdon: Routledge).

Lomborg, B. (2001) 'Resource constraints or abundance?,' in Diehl, P.F. and Gleditsch, N.P. (eds) *Environmental Conflict* (Boulder: Westview Press).

Lonergan, S.C. (ed.) (1997) *Environmental Change, Adaptation, and Security* (Dordrecht: Kluwer).

Longman, T. (1998) 'Rwanda: chaos from above,' in Villalón, L.A. and Huxtable, P.A. (eds) *The African State at a Critical Juncture: Between Disintegration and Reconfiguration* (Boulder: Lynne Rienner).

Lott, A.D. (2004) *Creating Insecurity: Realism, Constructivism and US Security Policy* (Aldershot: Ashgate).

Löwenheim, O. (2007) *Predators and Parasites: Persistent Agents of Transnational Harm and Great Power Authority* (Michigan: University of Michigan Press).

Luard, E. (1988) *The Blunted Sword: The Erosion of Military Power in Modern World Politics* (London: I.B. Tauris).

Luard, E. (1992) *Basic Texts in International Relations* (Basingstoke: Macmillan – now Palgrave Macmillan).

Lundborg, T. and Vaughan-Williams, N. (2011) 'Resilience, critical infrastructure, and molecular security: the excess of "life" in biopolitics,' *International Political Sociology* 5(4) 367–83.

Luttwak, E.N. (1999) 'Give war a chance,' *Foreign Affairs* 78(4) 36–44.

Lutz, J.M. and Lutz, B.J. (2008) *Global Terrorism*, 2nd edn (London: Routledge).

Lynn-Jones, S.M. (1995) 'Offense-defense theory and its critics,' *Security Studies* 4(4) 660–91.

Lynn-Jones, S.M. (1998) 'Why the United States should spread democracy,' Centre for Science and International Affairs Discussion Paper 98-07.

Lyon, D. (2001) *Surveillance Society: Monitoring Everyday Life* (Buckingham: Open University Press).

Mabee, B. (2003) 'Security studies and the "security state": security provision in historical context,' *International Relations* 17(2) 135–51.

Mabee, B. (2009) *The Globalization of Security* (Basingstoke: Palgrave Macmillan).

McCoy, A. (2003) *The Politics of Heroin: CIA Complicity in the Global Drug Trade, Afghanistan, Southeast Asia, Central America, Colombia* (Chicago: Lawrence Hill).

McDonald, M. (2002) 'Human security and the construction of security', *Global Society* 16(3) 277–95.

McDonald, M. (2009) 'Emancipation and critical terrorism studies,' in Jackson, R., Breen-Smyth, M. and Gunning, J. (eds) *Critical Terrorism Studies: A New Research Agenda* (London: Routledge).

McDonald, M. (2012) *Security, the Environment and Emancipation: Contestation over Environmental Change* (London: Routledge).

Macfarlane, S.N. (1997) 'On the front lines in the near abroad: the CIS and the OSCE in Georgia's civil wars,' *Third World Quarterly* 18(3) 509–26.

Macfarlane, S.N. (2004) 'The United States and regionalism in Central Asia,' *International Affairs* 80(3) 447–61.

Macfarlane, S.N. and Khong, Y.F. (2006) *Human Security and the UN: A Critical History* (Bloomington: Indiana University Press).

MacGinty, R. (2006) *No War, No Peace: Rethinking Peace and Conflict* (Basingstoke: Palgrave Macmillan).

MacGinty, R. (2008) 'Indigenous peace-making versus the liberal peace,' *Cooperation and Conflict* 43(2) 139–63.

MacGinty, R. (2010) 'Hybrid peace: the interaction between top-down and bottom-up peace,' *Security Dialogue* 41(4) 391–412.

McGrew, A.G. (2002) 'Liberal internationalism: between realism and cosmopolitanism,' in Held, D. and McGrew, A.G. (eds) *Governing Globalization: Power, Authority and Global Governance* (London: Polity).

Machiavelli, N. (1532/1985) *The Prince*, 2nd edn, trans. and with an Introduction by H.C. Mansfield (Chicago: University of Chicago Press).

McInnes, C. (1999) 'Spectator sport warfare,' *Contemporary Security Policy* 20(3) 142–65.

McInnes, C. (2002) *Spectator Sport War: The West and Contemporary Conflict* (Boulder: Lynne Rienner).

McInnes, C. (2003) 'A different kind of war? September 11 and the United States Afghan War,' *Review of International Studies* 29(2) 165–84.

Mack, A. (2004) 'A signifier of shared values,' *Security Dialogue* 33(3) 366–7.

Mackay, A., Sedra, M. and Burt, G. (2011) 'Security sector reform (SSR) in insecure environments: learning from Afghanistan,' *Journal of Security Sector Management* 8(3) 1–20.

MacKenzie, M. (2009) 'Securitization and desecuritization: female soldiers and the reconstruction of women in post-conflict Sierra Leone', *Security Studies* 18(2) 241–61.

McKeown, R. (2009) 'Norm regress: US revisionism and the slow death of the torture norm,' *International Relations* 23(1) 5–25.

McNevin, A. (2006) 'Political belonging in a neoliberal era: the struggle of the sans-papiers,' *Citizenship Studies* 10(2) 135–51.

McSherry, J.P. (2005) *Predatory States: Operation Condor and Covert War in Latin America* (Plymouth: Rowman & Littlefield).

McSweeney, B. (1996) 'Identity and security: Buzan and the Copenhagen School,' *Review of International Studies* 22(1) 81–94.

Mair, S. (2008) 'A new approach: the need to focus on failing states,' *Harvard International Review* 29(4) 52–5.

Makarenko, T. (2004) 'The crime-terror continuum: tracing the interplay between transnational organised crime and terrorism,' *Global Crime* 6(1) 129–45.

Malesevic, S. (2010) *The Sociology of War and Violence* (Cambridge: CUP).

Maley, W. (2002) 'Twelve theses on the impact of humanitarian intervention,' *Security Dialogue* 33(3) 265–78.

Mamdani, M. (2002) 'Good Muslim, bad Muslim: a political perspective on culture and terrorism,' *American Anthropologist* 104(3) 766–75.

Mandel, R. (1999) *Deadly Transfers and the Global Playground: Transnational Security Threats in a Disorderly World* (Westport: Praeger).

Mandel, R. (2010) *Dark Logic: Transnational Criminal Tactics and Global Security* (Stanford: Stanford University Press).

Manjikian, M.M. (2010) 'From global village to virtual battlespace: the colonizing of the internet and the extension of realpolitik,' *International Studies Quarterly* 54(2) 381–401.

Mann, M. (1987) 'The roots and contradictions of modern militarism,' *New Left Review* 162 35–50.

Mann, M. (1993) *The Sources of Social Power*, vol. 2, *the Rise of Classes and Nation States 1760–1914* (Cambridge: CUP).

Mansfield, E.D. and Snyder, J. (1995) 'Democratization and war,' *Foreign Affairs* 74(3) 79–97.

March, J.G. and Olsen, J.P. (1998) 'The institutional dynamics of international political orders,' *International Organization* 52(4) 943–69.

Markusen, A. (1999) 'The rise of world weapons,' *Foreign Policy* 114 40–51.

Martin, M. and Owen, T. (2010) 'The second generation of human security: lessons from the UN and EU experience,' *International Affairs* 86(1) 211–24.

Marx, K. (2001) *The Eighteenth Brumaire of Louis Bonaparte* (London: Electric Book).

Massumi, B. (2007) 'Potential politics and the primacy of preemption,' *Theory and Event* 10(2).

Masters, D. (2008) 'The origin of terrorist threats: Religious, separatist, or something else?,' *Terrorism and Political Violence* 20(3) 396–414.

Matthew, R.A. (1999) 'Introduction: mapping contested ground,' in Deudney, D.H. and Matthew, R.A. (eds) *Contested Grounds: Security and Conflict in the New Environmental Politics* (Albany: State University of New York Press).

Matthew, R.A. and Shambaugh, G.E. (1998) 'Sex, drugs, and heavy metal: transnational threats and national vulnerabilities,' *Security Dialogue* 29(2) 163–75.

Mau, S., Brabandt, H., Laube, L. and Roos, C. (2012) *Liberal States and the Freedom of Movement: Selective Borders, Unequal Mobility* (Basingstoke: Palgrave Macmillan).

Maxwell, S. and Slater, R. (2003) 'Food policy old and new,' ODI Briefing Paper, www.odi.org.uk/sites/odi.org.uk/files/odi-assets/publications-opinion-files/1862.pdf.

Mayer, M. (2012) 'Chaotic climate change and security,' *International Political Sociology* 6(2) 165–85.

Mearsheimer, J.J. (1983) *Conventional Deterrence* (Ithaca: Cornell University Press).

Mearsheimer, J.J. (1994/95) 'The false promise of international institutions,' *International Security* 19(3) 5–49.

Mearsheimer, J.J. (2001) *The Tragedy of Great Power Politics* (New York: W.W. Norton).

Mearsheimer, J.J. (2006) 'Conversations in international relations: interview with John J. Mearsheimer (Part I),' *International Relations* 20(1) 105–23.

Mearsheimer, J.J. and van Evera, S. (1995) 'When peace means war,' *The New Republic* 213(25) 16–21.

Menjivar, C. and Rodriguez, N. (eds) (2005) *When States Kill: Latin America, the U.S., and Technologies of Terror* (Austin: University of Texas Press).

Menkhaus, K. (2006) 'Governance without government in Somalia: spoilers, state building, and the politics of coping,' *International Security* 31(3) 74–106.

Menkhaus, K. and Shapiro, J.N. (2010) 'Non-state actors and failed states: lessons from Al Qa'ida's experiences in the Horn of Africa,' in Clunan, A.L. and Trinkunas, H.A. (eds) *Ungoverned Spaces: Alternatives to State Authority in an Era of Softened Sovereignty* (Stanford: Stanford University Press).

Merchant, C. (1992) *Radical Ecology: The Search for a Livable World* (New York: Routledge).

Merchant, C. (1996) *Earthcare: Women and the Environment* (New York: Routledge).

Merchant, C. (2004) *Reinventing Eden: The Fate of Nature in Western Culture* (New York: Routledge).

Methmann, C. and Rothe, D. (2012) 'Politics for the day after tomorrow: the logic of apocalypse in global climate politics,' *Security Dialogue* 43(4) 323–44.

Miller, S.E. (2010) 'The hegemonic illusion? Traditional strategic studies in context', *Security Dialogue* 41(6) 639–48.

Milliken, J. and Krause, K. (2002) 'State failure, state collapse, and state reconstruction: concepts, lessons and strategies,' *Development and Change* 33(5) 753–74.

Moltz, J.C. (2011) *The Politics of Space Security: Strategic Restraint and the Pursuit of National Interests*, 2nd edn (Stanford: Stanford University Press).

Monkkonen, E.H. (2002) *Crime, Justice, History* (Columbus: Ohio State University Press).

Montgomery, E.B. (2006) 'Breaking out of the security dilemma: realism, reassurance and the problem of uncertainty,' *International Security* 31(2) 151–85.

Moravcsik, A. (1997) 'Taking preferences seriously: the liberal theory of international politics,' *International Organization* 51(4) 513–53.

Morgan, P.M. (1985) 'Saving face for the sake of deterrence,' in Jervis, R., Lebow, R.N. and Stein, J.G. (eds) *Psychology and Deterrence* (Baltimore: Johns Hopkins University Press).

Morgan, P.M. (1992) 'Safeguarding security studies,' *Arms Control* 13(3) 464–79.

Morgan, P.M. (1997) 'Regional security complexes and regional orders,' in Lake, D.A. and Morgan, P.M. (eds) *Regional Orders: Building Security a New World* (University Park: Penn State University Press).

Morgan, P.M. (2003) *Deterrence Now* (Cambridge: CUP).

Morgenthau, H.J. (1946) *Scientific Man vs Power Politics* (Chicago: University of Chicago Press).

Morgenthau, H.J. (1948) *Politics Among Nations: The Struggle for Power and Peace* (New York: Alfred A. Knopf).

Morgenthau, H.J. (1952) 'Another "great debate": the national interest of the United States,' *American Political Science Review* 46(4) 961–88.

Morgenthau, H.J. (1962) *Politics in the Twentieth Century*, vol. I: *The Decline of Democratic Politics* (Chicago: University of Chicago Press).

Morgenthau, H.J. (1972) *Politics Among Nations: The Struggle for Power and Peace*, 5th edn (New York: Alfred A. Knopf).

Morgenthau, H.J. (2006) *Politics Among Nations: The Struggle for Power and Peace*, 7th edn, rev. K.W. Thompson and W.D. Clinton (New York: McGraw-Hill).

Morgenthau, H.J. and Lang, A.F. (eds) (2004) *Political Theory and International Affairs: Hans J. Morgenthau on Aristotle's the Politics* (Westport: Greenwood).

Morris, J. and McCoubrey, H. (1999) 'Regional peacekeeping in the post-Cold War era,' *International Peacekeeping* 6(2) 129–51.

Morselli, C. (2005) *Contacts, Opportunities, and Criminal Enterprise* (Toronto: University of Toronto Press).

Morton, A.D. (2005) 'The "failed state" of international relations,' *New Political Economy* 10(3) 371–9.

Morton, A.D. and Bilgin, P. (2002) 'Historicizing representations of "failed states": beyond the cold war annexation of the social Sciences,' *Third World Quarterly* 23(1) 55–80.

Moul, W. (2003) 'Power parity, preponderance, and war between great powers, 1816–1989,' *Journal of Conflict Resolution* 47(4) 468–89.

Mowatt-Larssen, R. (2010) *Al Qaeda Weapons of Mass Destruction Threat: Hype or Reality?* (Cambridge: Belfer Center for Science and International Affairs).

Mueller, J. (1988) 'The essential irrelevance of nuclear weapons: stability in the postwar world,' *International Security* 13(2) 55–79.

Mueller, J. (1989) *Retreat from Doomsday: The Obsolescence of Major War* (New York: Basic Books).

Mueller, J. (2004) *The Remnants of War* (Ithaca: Cornell University Press).

Mueller, J. (2006) 'Is there still a terrorist threat?: The myth of the omnipresent enemy,' *Foreign Affairs* 85(5) 2–8.

Muggah, R. (2009) 'Introduction: the emperor's clothes?,' in Muggah, R. (ed.) *Security and Post-Conflict Reconstruction: Dealing with Fighters in the Aftermath of War* (London: Routledge).

Muggah, R. and Krause, K. (2006) 'A true measure of success? The discourse and practice of human security in Haiti,' in Maclean, S.J., Black, D.R. and Shaw, T.M. (eds) *A Decade of Human Security: Global Governance and New Multilateralisms* (Farnham: Ashgate).

Muggah, R. and Krause, K. (2009) 'Closing the gap between peace operations and post-conflict insecurity: towards a violence reduction agenda,' *International Peacekeeping* 16(1) 136–50.

Muller, B.J. (2010) *Security, Risk and the Biometric State: Governing Borders and Bodies* (Abingdon: Routledge).

Müller, H. and Schmidt, A. (2010) The little known story of deproliferation: why states give up nuclear weapons activities, in Potter, W.C. and Mukhatzhanova, G. (eds) *Forecasting Nuclear Proliferation in the 21st Century*, vol. 1: *The Role of Theory* (Stanford: Stanford University Press).

Mulligan, S. (2010) 'Energy, environment and security: critical links in a post-peak world,' *Global Environmental Politics* 10(4) 79–100.

Murphy, A.B. (1996) 'The sovereign state system as political-territorial ideal: historical and contemporary considerations,' in Biersteker, T.J. and Weber, C. (eds) *State Sovereignty as Social Construct* (Cambridge: CUP).

Murphy, M.N. (2011) *Somalia: The New Barbary? Piracy and Islam in the Horn of Africa* (New York: Columbia University Press).

Musah, A.F. and Fayemi, K. (eds) (2000) *Mercenaries: An African Security Dilemma* (London: Pluto Press).

Mutimer, D. (2000) *The Weapons State: Proliferation and the Framing of Security* (Boulder: Lynne Rienner).

Myers, N. (1987) 'Population, environment, and conflict,' *Environmental Conservation* 14(1) 15–22.

Myers, N. (1993) *Ultimate Security: The Environmental Basis of Political Stability* (New York: W.W. Norton).

Nabulsi, K. (2005) *Traditions of War: Occupation, Resistance, and the Law* (Oxford: OUP).

Nadelmann, E. (1990) 'Global prohibition regimes: the evolution of norms in international society,' *International Organization* 44(4) 479–526.

Naim, M. (2003) 'The five wars of globalization,' *Foreign Policy* 134 28–37.

Naim, M. (2005) *Illicit: How Smugglers, Traffickers and Copycats are Hijacking the Global Economy* (London: William Heinemann).

Narine, S. (1998) 'ASEAN and the management of regional security,' *Pacific Affairs* 71(2) 195–214.

Nash, K. (2009) 'Between citizenship and human rights,' *Sociology* 43(6) 1067–83.

Nathan, L. and Toft, M.D. (2011) 'Civil war settlements and the prospects for peace,' *International Security* 36(1) 202–10.

National Intelligence Council (2008) *Global Trends 2025: A Transformed World* (Washington DC: NIC).

NATO (2009a) 'Piracy, ports and failed states: organised crime's frontlines,' *NATO Review*, 5, www.nato.int/docu/review/2009/Organized_Crime/EN/index.htm.

NATO (2009b) 'Organised crime and terrorist groups: comrades or chameleons,' *NATO Review*, 5, www.nato.int/docu/review/2009/Organized_Crime/Terrorism_Relation_OrganizedCrime/EN/index.htm.

Naylor, R.T. (2004) *Wages of Crime: Black Markets, Illegal Finance, and the Underworld Economy*, rev. edn (Ithaca: Cornell University Press).

Naylor, R.T. (2009) 'Violence and illegal economic activity: a deconstruction,' *Crime, Law and Social Change* 52(3) 231–42.

Nef, J. (1999) *Human Security and Mutual Vulnerability: The Global Political Economy of Development and Underdevelopment*, 2nd edn (Ottawa: IDRC).

Neff, S.C. (2005) *War and the Law of Nations: A General History* (Cambridge: CUP).

Neibuhr, R. (1932) *Moral Man and Immoral Society: A Study in Ethics and Politics* (New York: Charles Scribner's Sons).

Neocleous, M. (2000) *The Fabrication of Social Order: A Critical Theory of Police Power* (London: Pluto Press).

Neocleous, M. (2008) *Critique of Security* (Edinburgh: Edinburgh University Press).

Neufeld, M. (2004) 'Pitfalls of emancipation and discourses of security: reflections on Canada's "security with a human face",' *International Relations* 18(1) 109–23.

Neumann, P.R. (2009) *Old and New Terrorism* (Cambridge: Polity).

New America Foundation (2013) 'The drone war in Pakistan,' at http://natsec.newamerica.net/drones/pakistan/analysis.

Newman, E. (2001) 'Human security and constructivism,' *International Studies Perspectives* 2(3) 239–51.

Newman, E. (2006) 'Exploring the "root causes" of terrorism,' *Studies in Conflict and Terrorism* 29(8) 749–72.

Newman, E. (2007) 'Weak states, state failure, and terrorism,' *Terrorism and Political Violence* 19(4) 463–88.

Newman, E. (2009) 'Failed states and international order: constructing a post-Westphalian world,' *Contemporary Security Policy* 30(3) 421–43.

Newman, E. (2010) 'Critical human security studies,' *Review of International Studies* 36(1) 77–94.

Newman, E. and van Selm, J. (eds) (2003) *Refugees and Forced Displacement: International Security, Human Vulnerability, and the State* (Tokyo: United Nations University Press).

Ngoma, N. (2006) 'Disarmament, demobilisation and reintegration: a conceptual discourse,' in Chileshe, G. (ed.) *Civil-Military Relations in Zambia: A Review of Zambia's Contemporary CMR History and Challenges of Disarmament, Demobilisation and Reintegration* (Cape Town: Institute for Security Studies).

Nicholson, M. (1989) *Formal Theories in International Relations* (Cambridge: CUP).

Nicholson, M. (1992) *Rationality and the Analysis of International Conflict* (Cambridge: CUP).

Nicholson, M. (1996) 'The continued significance of positivism?,' in Smith, S., Booth, K. and Zalewski, M. (eds) *International Theory: Positivism and Beyond* (Cambridge: CUP).

Niemann, M. (2007) 'War making and state making in Central Africa,' *Africa Today* 53(3) 21–39.

Nissenbaum, H. (2005) 'Where computer security meets national security,' *Ethics and Information Technology* 7(2) 61–73.

Norris, P., Kern, M. and Just, M. (eds) (2003) *Framing Terrorism: The News Media, the Government and the Public* (London: Routledge).

Nye, J.S. (1968) *International Regionalism* (Boston: Little, Brown).

Nye, J.S. (1987) 'Nuclear learning and U.S.–Soviet security regimes,' *International Organization* 41(3) 371–402.

Nye, J.S. and Lynn-Jones, S.M (1988) 'International security studies: a report of a conference on the state of the field,' *International Security* 12(4) 5–27.

Nyers, P. (2003) 'Abject cosmopolitanism: the politics of protection in the anti-deportation movement,' *Third World Quarterly* 24(6) 1069–93.

Nyers, P. (2006) 'Taking rights, mediating wrongs: disagreements over the political agency of non-status refugees,' in Huysmans, J., Dobson, A. and Prokhovnik, R. (eds) *The Politics of Protection: Sites of Insecurity and Political Agency* (London: Routledge).

O'Manique, C. (2006) 'The "securitisation" of HIV/AIDS in sub-Saharan Africa: a critical feminist lens,' in Maclean, S.J., Black, D.R. and Shaw, T.M. (eds) *A Decade of Human Security: Global Governance and New Multilateralisms* (Farnham: Ashgate).

O'Neill, R. (2008) 'Hedley Bull and arms control,' in Bell, C. and Thatcher, M. (eds) *Remembering Hedley* (Canberra: ANU Press).

OECD (Organisation for Economic Cooperation and Development) (2005) *Security System Reform and Governance* (Paris: OECD).

OECD (2007) *OECD DAC Handbook on Security System Reform (SSR)* (Paris: OECD DAC).

Oels, A. (2013) 'Rendering climate change governable by risk: from probability to contingency,' *Geoforum* 45 17–29.

Onuf, N. (1989) *World of Our Making* (Columbia: University of South Carolina Press).

Osgood, C.E. (1962) *An Alternative to War or Surrender* (Urbana: University of Illinois Press).

Osgood, R.E. (1957) *Limited War: The Challenge to American Strategy* (Chicago: University of Chicago Press).

Osiander, A. (2001) 'Sovereignty, international relations, and the Westphalian myth', *International Organization* 55(2) 251–87.

O'Sullivan, M.L. (2003) *Shrewd Sanctions: Statecraft and State Sponsors of Terrorism* (Washington DC: Brookings Institution Press).

Ó Tuathail, G. (1999) 'De-territorialised threats and global dangers: geopolitics and risk society,' in Newman, D. (ed.) *Boundaries, Territory and Postmodernity* (London: Frank Cass).

Ó Tuathail, G. and Dalby, S. (eds) (1998) *Rethinking Geopolitics* (London: Routledge).

Ó Tuathail, G., Dalby, S. and Routledge, P. (eds) (2006) *The Geopolitics Reader*, 2nd edn (Abingdon: Routledge).

Overbeek, H. (2000) 'Transnational historical materialism: theories of transnational class formation and world order,' in Palan, R. (ed.) *Global Political Economy: Contemporary Theories* (London: Routledge).

Owen, N.A., Inderwildi, O.R. and King, D.A. (2010) 'The status of conventional world oil reserves: Hype or cause for concern?,' *Energy Policy* 38(8) 4743–9.

Owen, T. (2004) 'Human security – conflict, critique and consensus: colloquium remarks and a proposal for a threshold-based definition,' *Security Dialogue* 35(3) 373–87.

Owen, T. (2008) 'The critique that doesn't bite: a response to David Chandler's "Human security: the dog that didn't bark",' *Security Dialogue* 39(4) 445–53.

Owens, P. (2004) 'Xenophilia, gender and sentimental humanitarianism,' *Alternatives* 29 285–304.

Owens, P. (2008) 'Distinctions, distinctions: "Public" and "private" force?,' *International Affairs* 84(5) 977–90.

Oxfam (2012) *Our Land, Our Lives: Time Out on the Global Land Rush* (Oxford: Oxfam).

Packer, J. (2006) 'Becoming bombs: mobilizing mobility in the war of terror,' *Cultural Studies* 20(4) 378–99.

Palme, O. (1982) *Common Security: A Program for Disarmament* (New York: Palme Commission).

Paoli, L. (2002) 'The paradoxes of organized crime,' *Crime, Law and Social Change* 37(1) 51–97.

Paoli, L. (2003) 'The "invisible hand of the market": the illegal drugs trade in Germany, Italy and Russia,' in van Duyne, P., von Lampe, K. and Newell, J.L. (eds) *Criminal Finances and Organising Crime in Europe* (Nijmegen: Wolf).

Paoli, L. and Fijnaut, C. (2004) 'Introduction to Part I: the history of the concept,' in Fijnaut, C. and Paoli, L. (eds) *Organised Crime in Europe: Concepts, Patterns and Control Policies in the European Union and Beyond* (Dordrecht: Springer).

Paoli, L., Greenfield, V.A. and Reuter, P. (2009) *The World Heroin Market: Can Supply be Cut?* (Oxford: OUP).

Pape, R. (1996) *Bombing to Win: Air Power and Coercion in War* (Ithaca: Cornell University Press).

Pape, R. (2003) 'The strategic logic of suicide terrorism,' *American Political Science Review* 97(3) 343–61.

Pape, R. (2012) 'When duty calls: a pragmatic standard of humanitarian intervention,' *International Security* 37(1) 41–80.

Paret, P. (2008) 'The genesis of *On War*,' in von Clausewitz, C. *On War*, ed. and trans. M. Howard and P. Paret (Princeton: Princeton University Press).

Paris, R. (2001) 'Human security: Paradigm shift or hot air?,' *International Security* 26(2) 87–102.

Paris, R. (2002) 'International peacebuilding and the "mission civilisatrice",' *Review of International Studies* 28(4): 637–56.

Paris, R. (2010) 'Saving liberal peacebuilding,' *Review of International Studies* 36(2) 337–65.

Paris, R. and Sisk, T.D. (eds) (2009) *The Dilemmas of Statebuilding: Confronting the Contradictions of Postwar Peace Operations* (London: Routledge).

Parport, J. and Zalewski, M. (eds) (1998) *The 'Man' in Question in International Relations* (Boulder: Westview Press).

Paskal, C. (2010) 'The vulnerability of energy infrastructure to environmental change,' *China and Eurasia Forum Quarterly* 8(2) 149–63.

Passas, N. (2001) 'Globalization and transnational crime: effects of criminogenic asymmetries,' in Williams, P. and Vlassis, D. (eds) *Combating Transnational Crime: Concepts, Activities and Responses* (London: Frank Cass).

Passas, N. (2002) 'Cross-border crime and the interface between legal and illegal actors,' in van Duyne, P., von Lamp, K. and Passas, N. (eds) *Upperworld and Underworld in Cross-Border Crime* (Nijmegen: Wolf).

Passas, N. (2006) 'Fighting terror with error: the counter-productive regulation of informal value transfers,' *Crime, Law and Social Change* 45(4/5) 315–36.

Patomaki, H. (2002) *After International Relations: Critical Realism and the (re)Construction of World Politics* (London: Routledge).

Patomaki, H. and Wight, C. (2000) 'After postpositivism? The promises of critical realism,' *International Studies Quarterly* 44(2) 213–37.

Patrick, S. (2006) 'Weak states and global threats: Fact or fiction?,' *Washington Quarterly* 29(2) 27–53.

Patrick, S. and Brown, K. (2007) *Greater than the Sum of its Parts? Assessing 'Whole of Government' Approaches to Fragile States* (New York: International Peace Academy).

Pattison, J. (2011) 'Legitimacy and humanitarian intervention: Who should intervene?,' *International Journal of Human Rights* 12(3) 395–413.

Patton, P. (1995) 'Introduction', in Baudrillard, J. *The Gulf War Did Not Take Place* (Bloomington: Indiana University Press).

Paul, T.V. (2004) 'Introduction: the enduring axioms of balance of power theory and their contemporary relevance,' in Paul, T.V., Wirtz, J.J. and Fortmann, M. (eds) *Balance of Power: Theory and Practice in the 21st Century* (Stanford: Stanford University Press).

Peet, J. (1992) *Energy and the Ecological Economics of Sustainability* (Washington DC: Island Press).

Peluso, N.L. and Watts, M.J. (2001) 'Violent environments,' in Peluso, N.L. and Watts, M.J. (eds) *Violent Environments* (Ithaca: Cornell University Press).

Peoples, C. (2008) 'Assuming the inevitable? Overcoming the inevitability of outer space weaponization and conflict,' *Contemporary Security Policy* 29(3) 502–20.

Peoples, C. (2010) *Justifying Ballistic Missile Defence: Technology, Security and Culture* (Cambridge: CUP).

Peoples, C. (2011) 'Security after emancipation? Critical theory, violence and resistance,' *Review of International Studies*, 37(3) 1113–35.

Peoples, C. and Vaughan-Williams, N. (2010) *Critical Security Studies: An Introduction* (Abingdon: Routledge).

Perlo-Freeman, S., Sköns, E., Solmirano, C. and Wilandh, H. (2013) *Trends in World Military Expenditure, 2012* (Stockholm: SIPRI).

Perry, W.J. (2001) 'Preparing for the next attack,' *Foreign Affairs* 80(6) 31–47.

Peters, S. (2004) 'Coercive western energy security strategies: "resource wars" as a new threat to global security,' *Geo-Politics* 9(1) 187–212.

Petersen, K.L. (2012) 'Risk analysis: A field within security studies?,' *European Journal of International Relations* 18(4) 693–717.

Petersen, K.L. and Tjalve, V.S. (2013) '(Neo) republican security governance? US homeland security and the politics of "shared responsibility",' *International Political Sociology* 7(1) 1–18.

Petersen, V.S. (ed.) (1992) *Gendered States: Feminist (re)Visions of International Relations* (Boulder: Lynne Rienner).

Piazza, J.A. (2006) 'Rooted in poverty? Terrorism, poor economic development, and social cleavages,' *Terrorism and Political Violence* 18(1) 159–77.

Piazza, J.A. (2007) 'Draining the swamp: democracy promotion, state failure, and terrorism in 19 Middle Eastern countries,' *Studies in Conflict and Terrorism* 30(6) 521–39.

Piazza, J.A. (2008) 'Incubators of terror: Do failed and failing states promote transnational terrorism?,' *International Studies Quarterly* 52(3) 469–88.

Picarelli, J.T. (2006) 'The turbulent nexus of transnational organised crime and terrorism: a theory of malevolent international relations,' *Global Crime* 7(1) 1–24.

Pick, D. (1993) *War Machine: The Rationalisation of Slaughter in the Modern Age* (New Haven: Yale University Press).

Pierson, C. (2004) *The Modern State*, 2nd edn (London: Routledge).

Pillar, P.R. (2003) *Terrorism and US Foreign Policy* (Washington DC: Brookings Institution Press).

Pillar, P.R. (2004) 'Counterterrorism after Al Qaeda,' *Washington Quarterly* 27(3) 101–13.

Pirages, D. and DeGeest, T.M. (2004) *Ecological Security: An Evolutionary Perspective on Globalization* (Oxford: Rowman & Littlefield).

Pluta, A.M. and Zimmerman, P.D. (2006) 'Nuclear terrorism: a disheartening dissent,' *Survival* 48(2) 55–69.

Pogge, T. (2008) *World Poverty and Human Rights*, 2nd edn (Cambridge: Polity).

Poku, N.K. and Graham, D. (eds) (2000) *Migration, Globalisation and Human Security* (London: Routledge).

Posen, B. (1993) 'The security dilemma and ethnic conflict,' *Survival* 3(1) 27–47.

Posen, B. (2003) 'The sources of military doctrine,' in Art, R.J. and Waltz, K. (eds) *The Use of Force: Military Power and International Politics*, 6th edn (Lanham: Rowman & Littlefield).

Pouligny, B. (2005) 'Civil society and post-conflict peacebuilding: ambiguities of international programmes aimed at building "new" societies,' *Security Dialogue* 36(4) 495–510.

Pouliot, V. (2008) 'The logic of practicality: a theory of practice of security communities,' *International Organization* 62(2) 257–88.

Pouliot, V. (2010) *International Security in Practice: The Politics of NATO–Russia Diplomacy* (Cambridge: CUP).

President's Commission on Critical Infrastructure Protection (1997) *Critical Foundations: Protecting America's Infrastructures* (Washington DC: PCCIP).

Price, B.C. (2012) 'Targeting top terrorists: how leadership decapitation contributes to counterterrorism,' *International Security* 36(4) 9–46.

Price, R.M. (1997) *The Chemical Weapons Taboo* (Ithaca: Cornell University Press).

Prins, G. (1993) 'Putting environmental security in context,' in Prins, G. (ed.) *Threats Without Enemies: Facing Environmental Insecurity* (London: Earthscan).

Prins, G. (1998) 'The four-stroke cycle in security studies,' *International Affairs* 74(4) 781–808.

Proedrou, F. (2007) 'The EU–Russia energy approach under the prism of interdependence,' *European Security* 16(3/4) 329–55.

Pugh, M. and Sidhu, W.P. (eds) (2003) *The United Nations & Regional Security: Europe and Beyond* (Boulder: Lynne Rienner).

Pugh, M., Cooper, N. with Goodhand, J. (2004) *War Economies in a Regional Context: Challenges of Transformation* (Boulder: Lynne Rienner).

Quillen, C. (2002) 'A historical analysis of mass casualty bombers,' *Studies in Conflict and Terrorism* 25(2) 279–92.

Quinn, A. and Cox, M. (2007) 'For better, for worse: how America's foreign policy became wedded to liberal universalism,' *Global Society* 21(4) 499–519.

Qureshi, A. (2010) ''War on terror': the African front,' *Critical Studies on Terrorism* 3(1) 49–61.

Ralph, J. (1999) 'Security dilemmas and the end of the cold war,' *Review of International Studies* 25(4) 721–5.

Ralph, J. (2001) *Beyond the Security Dilemma: Ending America's Cold War* (Basingstoke: Ashgate).

Ramakrishna, K. and Tan, A. (2002) 'The new terrorism: diagnosis and prescriptions,' in Tan, A. and Ramakrishna, K. (eds) *The New Terrorism: Anatomy, Trends and Counter-Strategies* (Singapore: Eastern Universities Press).

Ranstorp, M. (1994) 'Hizbullah's command leadership: its structures, decision-making and relationship with Iranian clergy and institutions,' *Terrorism and Political Violence* 6(3) 303–39.

Rapin, A.J. (2009) 'Does terrorism create terror?,' *Critical Studies on Terrorism* 2(2) 165–79.

Rapoport, A. (1964) *Strategy and Conscience* (New York: Schocken).

Rapoport, D.C. (1984) 'Fear and trembling: terrorism in three religious traditions,' *American Political Science Review* 78(3) 658–77.

Rapoport, D.C. (1999) 'Terrorism and weapons of the apocalypse,' *National Security Studies Quarterly* 5(1) 49–67.

Rasmussen, M.V. (2006) *The Risk Society at War: Terror, Technology and Strategy in the Twenty First Century* (Cambridge: CUP).

Ray, J.L. (1995) *Democracy and International Conflict: An Evaluation of the Democratic Peace Proposition* (Columbia: University of South Carolina Press).

Rees, W. (2006) *Transatlantic Counter-terrorism Cooperation: The New Imperative* (Abingdon: Routledge).

Rees, W. and Aldrich, R. (2005) 'Contending cultures of counterterrorism: Transatlantic divergence or convergence?,' *International Affairs* 81(5) 905–23.

Reid, J. (2003) 'Deleuze's war machine: nomadism against the state,' *Millennium* 32(1) 57–85.

Reiner, R. (2010) *The Politics of the Police*, 4th edn (Oxford: OUP).

Reno, W. (1999) *Warlord Politics and African States* (London: Lynne Rienner).

Reuter, P. (1983) *Disorganized Crime: The Economics of the Visible Hand* (Cambridge: MIT Press).

Reuveny, R. (2007) 'Climate change-induced migration and violent conflict,' *Political Geography* 26(6) 6556–673.

Rice, C. (2005) 'The promise of the democratic peace: why promoting freedom is the only realistic path to security,' *Washington Post*, 1 December, B07.

Richmond, O.P. (2007) *The Transformation of Peace* (Basingstoke: Palgrave Macmillan).

Richmond, O.P. and Franks, J. (2007) 'Liberal hubris? Virtual peace in Cambodia,' *Security Dialogue* 38(1) 27–48.

Richmond, O.P. and Franks, J. (2009) 'The impact of orthodox terrorism discourses on the liberal peace: Internalisation, resistance, or hybridisation?,' *Critical Studies on Terrorism* 2(2) 201–18.

Richmond, O.P. and Tellidis, I. (2012) 'The complex relationship between peacebuilding and terrorism approaches: towards post-terrorism and a post-liberal peace?,' *Terrorism and Political Violence* 24(1) 120–43.

Risse, T. (2000) '"Let's argue!": Communicative action in world politics,' *International Organization* 54(1) 1–39.

Risse-Kappen, T. (ed.) (1995) *Bringing Transnational Relations Back In: Non-State Actors, Domestic Structures and International Institutions* (Cambridge: CUP).

Rizer, K. (2001) 'Bombing dual-use targets: legal, ethical and doctrinal perspectives', *Air and Space Power Journal*, www.airpower.maxwell.af.mil/airchronicles/cc/Rizer.html.

Roberts, D. (2008) 'The intellectual perils of broad human security: deepening the critique of international relations,' *Politics* 28(2) 124–27.

Robertson, L.R. (2003) *The Dream of Civilized Warfare: World War 1 Flying Aces and the American Imagination* (Minneapolis: University of Minnesota Press).

Roe, P. (2000) 'Former Yugoslavia: The security dilemma that never was?,' *European Journal of International Relations* 6(3) 373–93.

Roe, P. (2005) *Ethnic Violence and the Societal Security Dilemma* (London: Routledge).

Roe, P. (2012) 'Is securitization a "negative" concept? Revisiting the normative debate over normal versus extraordinary politics,' *Security Dialogue* 43(3) 249–66.

Rose, G. (1998) 'Neoclassical realism and theories of foreign policy,' *World Politics* 51(1) 144–72.

Rose, N. (2000) 'Government and control,' *British Journal of Criminology* 40(2) 321–39.

Rose, N. (2001) 'The politics of life itself,' *Theory, Culture & Society* 18(6) 1–30.

Rosecrance, R. (1986) *The Rise of the Trading State: Commerce and Conquest in the Modern World* (New York: Basic Books).

Rosenau, J. (1980) *The Study of Global Interdependence: Essays on the Transnationalisation of World Affairs* (New York: Nichols).

Ross, M. (2003) 'The natural resource curse: how wealth can make you poor,' in Bannon, I. and Collier, P. (eds) *Natural Resources and Violent Conflict: Options and Actions* (Washington DC: World Bank).

Rotberg, R.I. (2002) 'Failed states in a world of terror,' *Foreign Affairs* 81(4) 127–40.

Rotberg, R.I. (2003) 'Failed states, collapsed states, weak states: causes and indicators,' in Rotberg, R.I. (ed.) *State Failure and State Weakness in a Time of Terror* (Washington DC: Brookings Institution Press).

Rotberg, R.I. (2004) 'The failure and collapse of nation-states: breakdown, prevention, and repair,' in Rotberg, R.I. (ed.) *When States Fail: Causes and Consequences* (Princeton: Princeton University Press).

Rothschild, E. (1995) 'What is security?', *Daedalus* 124(3) 53–98.

Rudolph, C. (2003) 'Security and the political economy of international migration,' *American Political Science Review* 97(4) 603–20.

Ruff, J. (2001) *Violence in Early Modern Europe 1500–1800* (Cambridge: CUP).

Ruggie, J.G. (1982) 'International regimes, transactions, and change: embedded liberalism in the postwar economic order,' *International Organization* 36(2) 379–415.

Ruggie, J.G. (1993) 'Territoriality and beyond: problematizing modernity in international relations', *International Organization* 46(1) 139–74.

Ruggiero, V. (2003) 'Global markets and crime,' in Beare, M.E. (ed.) *Critical Reflections on Transnational Organized Crime, Money Laundering, and Corruption* (Toronto: University of Toronto Press).

Rummel, R.J. (1998) *Statistics of Democide: Genocide and Mass Murder since 1900* (London: Transaction).

Russell, J.A. (2006) 'Peering into the abyss: non-state actors and the 2016 proliferation environment,' *Nonproliferation Review* 13(3) 645–57.

Russett, B. (1993) *Grasping the Democratic Peace: Principles for a Post-Cold War World* (Princeton: Princeton University Press).

Ruzicka, J. and Wheeler, N. (2010) 'The puzzle of trusting relationships in the Nuclear Non-Proliferation Treaty,' *International Affairs* 86(1) 69–85.

Sagan, S. and Waltz, K. (2003) *The Spread of Nuclear Weapons: A Debate Renewed* (New York: W.W. Norton).

Sageman, M. (2004) *Understanding Terror Networks* (Philadelphia: University of Pennsylvania Press).

Sageman, M. (2006) 'Islam and Al Qaeda,' in Pedahzur, A. (ed.) *Root Causes of Suicide Terrorism: The Globalization of Martyrdom* (London: Routledge).

Sageman, M. (2008) *Leaderless Jihad: Terror Networks in the Twenty-First Century* (Philadelphia: University of Pennsylvania Press).

Salehyan, I. (2008) 'From climate change to conflict? No consensus yet,' *Journal of Peace Research* 45(3) 315–26.

Salter, M. (2004) 'Passports, mobility, and security: How smart can the border be?,' *International Studies Perspectives* 5(1) 71–91.

Salter, M. (ed.) (2008a) *Politics at the Airport* (Minneapolis: University of Minnesota Press).

Salter, M. (2008b) 'Imagining numbers: risk, quantification, and aviation security,' *Security Dialogue* 39(2/3) 243–66.

Salter, M. and Mutlu, C.E. (eds) (2013) *Research Methods in Critical Security Studies* (London: Routledge).

Sambanis, N. (2000) 'Partition as a solution to ethnic war: an empirical critique of the theoretical literature,' *World Politics* 52(4) 437–83.

Sandler, T. (1995) 'On the relationship between democracy and terrorism,' *Terrorism and Political Violence* 7(4) 1–9.

Sandler, T. and Enders, W. (2004) 'An economic perspective on transnational terrorism,' *European Journal of Political Economy* 20(2) 301–16.

Scarry, E. (1985) *The Body in Pain: The Making and Unmaking of the World* (Oxford: OUP).

Schelling, T. (1966) *Arms and Influence* (New Haven: Yale University Press).

Schelling, T. and Halerpin, M. (1961) *Strategy and Arms Control* (New York: Twentieth Century Fund).

Scheuerman, W.E. (2007) 'Was Morgenthau a realist? Revisiting scientific man vs power politics,' *Constellations* 14(4) 506–30.

Schmid, A. (2004) 'Terrorism: the definitional problem', *Case Western Reserve Journal of International Law* 36(2/3) 375–420.

Schmid, A.P. and Jongman, A.J. (2005) *Political Terrorism: A New Guide to Actors, Authors, Concepts, Data Bases, Theories, & Literature* (New York: Transaction).

Schmidt, B.C. (2004) 'Realism as tragedy,' *Review of International Studies* 30(3) 427–41.

Schmidt, B.C. (2007) 'Realist conceptions of power,' in Berenskoetter, F. and Williams, M.J. (eds) *Power in World Politics* (Abingdon: Routledge).

Schmitt, C. (1996) *The Concept of the Political* (Chicago: University of Chicago Press).

Schroeder, U.C. and Friesendorf, C. (2009) 'State-building and organized crime: implementing the international law enforcement agenda,' *Journal of International Relations and Development* 12(2) 137–67.

Schweller, R. (1994) 'Bandwagoning for profit: bringing the revisionist state back in,' *International Security* 19(1) 72–107.

Schweller, R. (1996) 'Neorealism's status-quo bias: What security dilemma?,' *Security Studies* 5(3) 90–121.

Scott, P.D. and Marshall, J. (1998) *Cocaine Politics: Drugs, Armies and the CIA in Central America* (Berkeley: University of California Press).

Sen, A.K. (1981) *Poverty and Famines: An Essay on Entitlement and Deprivation* (Oxford: OUP).

Senese, P.D. and Vasquez, J.A. (2008) *The Steps to War: An Empirical Study* (Princeton: Princeton University Press).

Serrano, M. (2002) 'Transnational organized crime and international security: Business as usual?,' in Berdal, M. and Serrano, M. (eds) *Transnational Organized Crime and International Security: Business as Usual?* (Boulder: Lynne Rienner).

Seybolt, T. (2007) *Humanitarian Military Intervention: The Conditions for Success and Failure* (Stockholm: SIPRI).

Shah, N. (2010) 'Security must be defended – or, the survival of security,' *Security Dialogue* 41(6) 631–8.

Shaw, M. (2003) *War and Genocide: Organized Killing in Modern Society* (Cambridge: Polity).

Shaw, M. (2005) *The New Western Way of War: Risk-Transfer War and its Crisis in Iraq* (Cambridge: Polity).

Shea, J. (1999) *Morning Briefing by NATO Spokesman Jamie Shea*, 8 May, www.nato.int/kosovo/press/b990508a.htm.

Shea, J. and Marani, G. (1999) *NATO Press Conference 15 April 1999*, www.nato.int/kosovo/press/p990415a.htm.

Shearer, D. (1998) *Private Armies and Military Intervention* (Oxford: OUP).

Sheehan, M. (1996) *Balance of Power: History and Theory* (London: Routledge).

Sheehan, M. (2007) *The International Politics of Space* (Abingdon: Routledge).

Sheehan, M. (2010) 'The evolution of modern warfare,' in Baylis, J., Wirtz, J. and Gray, C. (eds) *Strategy in the Contemporary World*, 3rd edn (Oxford: OUP).

Sheller, M. and Urry, J. (2003) 'Mobile transformations of "public" and "private" life,' *Theory, Culture & Society* 20(3) 107–25.

Sheller, M. and Urry, J. (2006) 'The new mobilities paradigm,' *Environment and Planning A* 38(2) 207–26.

Shelley, L.I. (1999) 'Transnational organized crime: the new authoritarianism,' in Friman H.R. and Andreas, P. (eds) *The Illicit Global Economy and State Power* (Lanham: Rowman & Littlefield).

Shelley, L.I. (2005) 'Unravelling the new criminal nexus,' *Georgetown Journal of International Affairs* 6(1) 5–13.

Shelley, L.I. (2006) 'Trafficking in nuclear materials: criminals and terrorists,' *Global Crime* 7(3/4) 544–60.

Shepherd, L. (2008a) *Gender, Violence, and Security: Discourse as Practice* (London: Zed Books).

Shepherd, L. (2008b) 'Power and authority in the production of United Nations Security Council Resolution 1325,' *International Studies Quarterly* 52(2) 383–404.

Sheptycki, J. (ed.) (2000) *Issues in Transnational Policing* (London: Routledge).

Sheptycki, J. (2005) 'Against transnational organized crime,' in Beare, M. (ed.) *Critical Reflections on Transnational Organized Crime, Money Laundering, and Corruption* (Toronto: University of Toronto Press).

Sheptycki, J. (2007) 'Criminology and the transnational condition: a contribution to international political sociology,' *International Political Sociology* 1(4) 391–406.

Shittecatte, C. (2006) 'Toward a more inclusive global governance and enhanced human security,' in Maclean, S.J., Black, D.R. and Shaw, T.M. (eds) *A Decade of Human Security: Global Governance and New Multilateralisms* (Farnham: Ashgate).

Simmons, M.R. (2005) *Twilight in the Desert* (New York: John Wiley).

Simon, J. (2007) *Governing Through Crime: How the War on Crime Transformed American Democracy* (Oxford: OUP).

Simon, J.L. (1996) *The Ultimate Resource 2* (Princeton: Princeton University Press).

Singer, J.D. (1961) 'The level-of-analysis problem in international relations,' *World Politics* 14(1) 77–92.

Singer, J.D. (1972) 'The "Correlates of War" Project: interim report and rationale,' *World Politics* 24(2) 243–70.

Singer, P.W. (2006) *Children At War* (Berkeley: University of California Press).

Singer, P.W. (2007) *Corporate Warriors: The Rise of the Privatized Military Industry* (Ithaca: Cornell University Press).

Singh, R. (2011) 'Coping with water- and wastewater-related risks in megacity Delhi,' in Brauch, H.G., Spring, U.O, Mesjasz, C. et al. (eds) *Coping with Environmental Change, Disasters and Security Threats, Challenges, Vulnerabilities and Risks* (Heidelberg: Springer).

SIPRI (2013a) *SIPRI Military Expenditure Database*, www.sipri.org/research/armaments/milex/milex_database.

SIPRI (2013b) *SIPRI Arms Transfers Database*, www.sipri.org/databases/armstransfers.

SIPRI (2013c) *The Financial Value of the Global Arms Trade*, www.sipri.org/research/armaments/transfers/measuring/financial_values.

Sjoberg, L. (2009) 'Introduction to security studies: feminist contributions,' *Security Studies* 18(2) 183–213.

Slater, J. and Nardin, T. (1986) 'Nonintervention and human rights,' *Journal of Politics* 48(1) 86–96.

Smith, E.M. and Weiss, T.G. (1997) 'UN task-sharing: Towards or away from global governance?,' *Third World Quarterly* 18(3) 595–619.

Smith, R.P. (1980) 'Military expenditure and investment in OECD countries, 1954–1973,' *Journal of Comparative Economics* 4(1) 19–32.

Smith, S. (1996) 'Positivism and beyond,' in Smith, S., Booth, K. and Zalewski, M. (eds) *International Theory: Positivism and Beyond* (Cambridge: CUP).

Smith, S. (2004) 'Singing our world into existence: international relations theory and September 11,' *International Studies Quarterly* 48(3) 499–515.

Smith, S. (2005) 'The contested concept of security' in Booth, K. (ed.) *Critical Security Studies and World Politics* (Boulder: Lynne Rienner).

Smith, S. and Benjamin, D. (2000) 'America and the new terrorism,' *Survival* 42(1) 59–75.

Smith-Windsor, B.A. (2002) 'Terrorism, individual security, and the role of the military: a reply to Liotta,' *Security Dialogue* 33(4) 489–94.

Snidal, D. (1991) 'Relative gains and the pattern of international cooperation,' *American Political Science Review* 85(3) 701–26.

Snyder, G. (1984) 'The security dilemma in alliance politics,' *World Politics* 36(4) 461–95.

Snyder, G. (1996) 'Process variables in neo-realist theory,' *Security Studies* 5(3) 167–92.

Snyder, G. (1997) *Alliance Politics* (Ithaca: Cornell University Press).

Snyder, G. (2002) 'Mearsheimer's world: offensive realism and the struggle for security,' *International Security* 27(1) 149–73.

Snyder, J. (1977) *The Soviet Strategic Culture: Implications for Limited Nuclear Operations* (Santa Monica: RAND).

Snyder, J. (1984) *The Ideology of the Offensive: Military Decision Making and the Disasters of 1914* (Ithaca: Cornell University Press).

Snyder, J. and Lieber, K. (2008) 'Correspondence: defensive realism and the "new" history of World War I,' *International Security* 33(1) 174–94.

Söderbaum, F. and Shaw, T.M. (eds) (2003) *Theories of New Regionalism* (Basingstoke: Palgrave Macmillan).

Soguk, N. (1999) *States and Strangers: Refugees and Displacements of Statecraft* (Minneapolis: University of Minnesota Press).

Soja, E. (1971) *The Political Organisation of Space* (Washington DC: Association of American Geographers).

Solingen, E. (2007) *Nuclear Logics: Contrasting Paths in East Asia and the Middle East* (Princeton: Princeton University Press).

Sørensen, G. (2011) '"Big and important things" in IR: structural realism and the neglect of changes in statehood,' in Booth, K. (ed.) *Realism and World Politics* (London: Routledge).

Spear, J. (2006) 'From political economies of war to political economies of peace: the contribution of DDR after wars of predation,' *Contemporary Security Policy* 27(1) 168–89.

Spiegel, S.J. and Le Billon, P. (2009) 'China's weapons trade: from ships of shame to the ethics of global resistance,' *International Affairs* 85(2) 323–46.

Spillius, A. (2010) 'Nuclear terrorism is gravest threat to global security, Barak Obama warns,' *The Telegraph*, 12 April, www.telegraph.co.uk/news/worldnews/northamerica/usa/7580210/Nuclear-terrorism-is-gravest-threat-to-global-security-Barack-Obama-warns.html.

Sprinzak, E. (2000) 'Rational fanatics,' *Foreign Policy* 120 66–73.

Squire, V. (2009) *The Exclusionary Politics of Asylum* (Basingstoke: Palgrave Macmillan).

Squire, V. (2011) 'The contested politics of mobility: politicizing mobility, mobilizing politics,' in Squire, V. (ed.) *The Contested Politics of Mobility: Borderzones and Irregularity* (London: Routledge).

Stavrianakis, A. (2010) *Taking Aim at the Arms Trade: NGOs, Global Civil Society and the World Military Order* (London: Zed Books).

Steans, J. (2009) *Gender and International Relations* (Oxford: Polity).

Steenkamp, C. (2011) 'In the shadows of war and peace: making sense of violence after peace accords,' *Conflict, Security & Development* 11(3) 357–83.

Stein, A.A. (1982) 'Coordination and collaboration: regimes in an anarchic world,' *International Organization* 36(2) 299–324.

Stein, J.G. (1985) 'Detection and defection: security "regimes" and the management of international conflict,' *International Journal* 40(4) 599–627.

Stein, J.G. (1991) 'Reassurance in international conflict management,' *Political Science Quarterly* 106(3) 431–51.

Sterling, C. (1994) *Crime Without Frontiers: The Worldwide Expansion of Organised Crime and the Pax Mafiosa* (London: Little, Brown).

Stern, J. (1999) *The Ultimate Terrorists* (Cambridge: Harvard University Press).

Stewart, F. (ed.) (2008) *Horizontal Inequalities and Conflict: Understanding Group Violence in Multiethnic Societies* (Basingstoke: Palgrave Macmillan).

Stokes, D. (2005) *America's Other War: Terrorising Colombia* (London: Zed Books).

Strachan, H. and Herberg-Rothe, A. (2007) 'Introduction,' in Strachan, H. and Herberg-Rothe, A. (eds) *Clausewitz in the Twenty-First Century* (Oxford: OUP).

Strange, S. (1996) *The Retreat of the State: The Diffusion of Power in the World Economy* (Cambridge: CUP).

Study Group of Europe's Security Capabilities (2004) *A Human Security Doctrine for Europe: The Barcelona Report of the Study Group on Europe's Security Capabilities*, http://eprints.lse.ac.uk/40209/1/A_human_security_doctrine_for_Europe%28author%29.pdf.

Suchman, M.C. and Eyre, D. (1992) 'Military procurement as rational myth: notes on the social construction of weapons proliferation,' *Sociological Forum* 7(1) 137–61.

Suhrke, A. (1999) 'Human security and the interests of states,' *Security Dialogue* 30(3) 265–76.

Suskind, R. (2007) *The One Percent Doctrine: Deep Inside America's Pursuit of its Enemies since 9/11* (New York: Simon & Schuster).

Sylvester, C. (1994) *Feminist Theory and International Relations in a Postmodern Era* (Cambridge: CUP).

Sylvester, C. (2012) 'War experiences/war practices/war theory,' *Millennium* 40(3) 480–503.

Tadjbakhsh, S. and Chenoy, A.M. (2007) *Human Security: Concepts and Implications* (London: Routledge).

Tagliacozzo, E. (2010) 'Violent undertows: smuggling as dissent in nineteenth-century Southeast Asia,' in Colas, A. and Mabee, B. (eds) *Mercenaries, Pirates, Bandits and Empires: Private Violence in Historical Context* (London: Hurst).

Tang, S. and Montgomery, E.B. (2007) 'Uncertainty and reassurance in international politics,' *International Security* 32(1) 193–200.

Tannenwald, N. (2007) *The Nuclear Taboo: The United States and the Non-use of Nuclear Weapons Since 1945* (Cambridge: CUP).

Taylor, A.J.P. (1964) *The Origins of the Second World War* (Harmondsworth: Penguin).

Testas, A. (2004) 'Determinants of terrorism in the Muslim world: an empirical cross-sectional analysis,' *Terrorism and Political Violence* 16(2) 253–73.

Tezcür, G.M. (2010) When democratization radicalizes: the Kurdish nationalist movement in Turkey,' *Journal of Peace Research* 47(6) 775–89.

Thachuk, K.L. (ed.) (2007) *Transnational Threats: Smuggling and Trafficking in Arms, Drugs, and Human Life* (Westport: Praeger).

Thakur, R. (2004) 'Iraq and the responsibility to protect,' *Behind the Headlines* 62(1) 1–16.

Themnér, L. and Wallensteen, P. (2011) 'Armed conflict, 1946–2010,' *Journal of Peace Research* 48(4) 525–36.

Thomas, C. (2000) *Global Governance, Development and Human Security: The Challenge of Poverty and Inequality* (London: Pluto Press).

Thomas, C. (2004) 'A bridge between the interconnected challenges confronting the world,' *Security Dialogue* 35(3) 353–4.

Thomas, N. and Tow, W.T. (2002) 'The utility of human security: sovereignty and humanitarian intervention,' *Security Dialogue* 33(2) 177–92.

Thomson, J.E. (1994) *Mercenaries, Pirates and Sovereigns: State-building and Extra-territorial Violence in Early Modern Europe* (Princeton: Princeton University Press).

Tickner, J.A. (1992) *Gender in International Relations: Feminist Perspectives on Achieving Global Security* (New York: Columbia University Press).

Tilly, C. (1975) 'Reflections on the history of European state making,' in Tilly, C. (ed.) *The Formation of Nation States in Western Europe* (Princeton: Princeton University Press).

Tilly, C. (1985) 'War making and state making as organised crime,' in Evans, P., Rueschemeyer, D. and Skocpol, T. (eds) *Bringing the State Back In* (Cambridge: CUP).

Tilly, C. (2003) *The Politics of Collective Violence* (Cambridge: CUP).

Tilly, C. (2004) 'Terror, terrorism, terrorists,' *Sociological Theory* 22(1): 5–13.

Toft, M.D. (2010) 'Ending civil wars: A case for rebel victory?,' *International Security* 34(4): 7–36.

Toros, H. (2008) '"We don't negotiate with terrorists!": Legitimacy and complexity in terrorist conflicts,' *Security Dialogue* 39(4) 407–26.

Toros, H. and Gunning, J. (2009) 'Exploring a critical theory approach to terrorism studies,' in Jackson, R., Breen-Smyth, M. and Gunning, J. (eds) *Critical Terrorism Studies: A New Research Agenda* (London: Routledge)

Toulmin, S.E. (1990) *Cosmopolis: The Hidden Agenda of Modernity* (Chicago: University of Chicago Press).

Trachtenberg, M. (1991) *History and Strategy* (Princeton: Princeton University Press).

Trombetta, J. (2008) 'Environmental security and climate change: analysing the discourse,' *Cambridge Review of International Affairs* 21(4) 585–602.

Tuchman Mathews, J. (1989) 'Redefining security,' *Foreign Affairs* 68(2) 162–77.

Tucker, D. (2001) 'What's new about the new terrorism and how dangerous is it?,' *Terrorism and Political Violence* 13(3) 1–14.

Tuman, J. (2003) *Communicating Terror: The Rhetorical Dimensions of Terrorism* (London: Sage).

Ullman, R. (1983) 'Redefining security,' *International Security* 8(1) 129–53.

UN (1992) *An Agenda for Peace: Preventive Diplomacy, Peacemaking and Peacekeeping* (New York: UN).

UN (2004) *A More Secure World: Our Shared Responsibility*, Report of the Secretary-General's High-level Panel on Threats, Challenges and Change, www.un.org/secureworld/report2.pdf.

UN (2005a) *In Larger Freedom: Towards Security, Development and Human Right for All* (New York: UN).

UN (2005b) *2005 World Summit Outcome* (New York: UN).

UNDP (UN Development Programme) (1994) *Human Development Report 1994* (New York: UN).

UNDPKO (UN Department of Peacekeeping Operations) (2012a) 'Surge in uniformed UN peacekeeping personnel from 1991-present,' www.un.org/en/peacekeeping/documents/chart.pdf.

UNDPKO (2012b) 'Fatalities,' www.un.org/en/peacekeeping/resources/statistics/fatalities.shtml.

UNDPKO (2012c) 'Ranking of military and police contributions to UN operations', www.un.org/en/peacekeeping/contributors/2012/Nov12_2.pdf.

UNDPKO (2012d) 'Financing peacekeeping,' www.un.org/en/peacekeeping/operations/financing.shtml.

UN General Assembly (UNGA) (1965) Resolution 2131: *Declaration on the Inadmissibility of Intervention in the Domestic Affairs of States and the Protection of Their Independence and Sovereignty*, www.un-documents.net/a20r2131.htm.

UNGA (1970) *Declaration on Principles of International Law Concerning Friendly Relations* (New York: UN).

UNGA (2010) *Our Challenges Are Shared; So, too, Is Our Commitment to Enhance Freedom from Fear, Freedom from Want, Freedom to Live in Dignity*', says Secretary-General, GA/10942, www.un.org/News/Press/docs/2010/ga10942.doc.htm.

UN GIFT (2012) *Human Trafficking: The Facts*, www.unglobalcompact.org/docs/issues_doc/labour/Forced_labour/HUMAN_TRAFFICKING_-_THE_FACTS_-_final.pdf.

UNODC (UN Office on Drugs and Crime) (2010a) *The Globalization of Crime: A Transnational Organized Crime Threat Assessment* (Vienna: UNODC).

UNODC (2010b) *Afghanistan Opium Survey 2010: Summary Findings* (Vienna: UNODC).

UNODC (2013) *World Drug Report 2012* (New York: UNODC).

UN Security Council (1992) *Note by the President of the Security Council*, UN Document S/23500 (New York: UN).

Urry, J. (2000) *Sociology beyond Societies: Mobilities of the Twenty-first Century* (London: Routledge).

Urry, J. (2007) *Mobilities* (Cambridge: Polity).

US Department of Homeland Security (2002) *The Department of Homeland Security*, www.dhs.gov/xlibrary/assets/book.pdf.

US Department of Homeland Security (2007) *The National Strategy for Homeland Security* (Washington DC: DHS).

US Energy Information Administration (2013) *AEO2013 Early Release Overview* (Washington DC: US Department of Energy).
US Government (2002) *The National Security Strategy of the United States of America* (Washington DC: US Government).
US Government (2011) *National Strategy for Counterterrorism* (Washington DC: US Government).
US Government Accountability Office (2006) *Critical Infrastructure Protection* (Washington DC: GAO).
Uvin, P. (2004) 'A field of overlaps and interactions', *Security Dialogue* 35(3) 352–3.
Valentino, B.A. (2011) 'The true costs of humanitarian intervention: the hard truth about a noble notion,' *Foreign Affairs* 90(6) 60–73.
Van Creveld, M. (1991) *The Transformation of War* (New York: Free Press).
Van de Voort, M., O'Brien, K., Rahman, A. and Valeri, L. (2003) *'Seacurity': Improving the Security of the Global Sea-Container Shipping System* (Santa Monica: RAND).
Van Evera, S. (1999) *Causes of War: Power and the Roots of Conflict* (Ithaca: Cornell University Press).
Van Munster, R. (2009) *Securitizing Immigration: The Politics of Risk in the EU* (Basingstoke: Palgrave Macmillan).
Van Schendel, W. (2005) 'Spaces of engagement: how borderlands, illicit flows and territorial states interlock,' in Abraham, I. and van Schendel, W. (eds) *Illicit Flows and Criminal Things: States, Borders, and the Other Side of Globalization* (Bloomington: Indiana University Press).
Vasquez, J.A. (1987) 'The steps to war: toward a scientific explanation of correlates of war findings,' *World Politics* 40(1) 108–45.
Vasquez, J.A. (1997) 'The realist paradigm and degenerative versus progressive research programs: an appraisal of neotraditional research on Waltz's balancing proposition,' *American Political Science Review* 91(4) 899–912.
Vasquez, J.A. (2012) 'What do we know about war?,' in Vasquez, J.A. (ed.) *What Do We Know About War?*, 2nd edn (Lanham: Rowman & Littlefield).
Vaughan-Williams, N. (2009a) *Border Politics: The Limits of Sovereign Power* (Edinburgh: Edinburgh University Press).
Vaughan-Williams, N. (2009b) 'The generalised biopolitical border? Re-conceptualising the limits of sovereign power', *Review of International Studies* 35(4) 729–49.
Vega, J.F. (2007) 'War as "art": aesthetics and politics in Clausewitz's social thinking', in Strachan, H. and Herberg-Rothe, A. (eds) *Clausewitz in the Twenty-First Century* (Oxford: OUP).
Villalón, L.A. and Huxtable, P.A. (eds) (1998) *The African State at a Critical Juncture: Between Disintegration and Reconfiguration* (Boulder: Lynne Rienner).
Vlcek, W. (2007) 'Surveillance to combat terrorist financing in Europe: Whose liberty, whose security?,' *European Security* 16(1) 99–119.
Voelkner, N. (2011) 'Managing pathogenic circulation: human security and the migrant health assemblage in Thailand,' *Security Dialogue* 42(3) 239–59.
Voeten, E. (2005) 'The political origins of the UN Security Council's ability to legitimize the use of force,' *International Organization* 59(3) 527–57.
Von Clausewitz, C. (2008) *On War*, ed. and trans. M. Howard and P. Paret (Princeton: Princeton University Press).
Von Lampe, K. (2006) 'The interdisciplinary dimensions of the study of organized crime,' *Trends in Organized Crime* 9(3) 77–5.
Von Lampe, K. and Johansen, P.O (2004) 'Organized crime and trust: on the conceptualization and empirical relevance of trust in the context of criminal networks,' *Global Crime* 6(2) 159–84.
Waever, O. (1995) 'Securitization and desecuritization,' in Lipschutz, R.D. (ed.) *On Security* (New York: Columbia University Press).
Waever, O. (1996) 'The rise and fall of the inter-paradigm debate,' in Smith, S., Booth, K. and Zalewski, M. (eds) *International Theory: Positivism and Beyond* (Cambridge: CUP).
Waever, O. (1998) 'Insecurity, security, asecurity in the West European non-war community,' in Adler, E. and Barnett, M. (eds) *Security Communities* (Cambridge: CUP).
Waever, O. (1999) 'Securitizing sectors? Reply to Eriksson,' *Cooperation and Conflict* 34(3) 334–40.
Waever, O. (2004) 'Aberystwyth, Paris, Copenhagen: new "schools" in security theory and their origins between core and periphery,' paper presented at the annual meeting of the International Studies Association, Montreal, 17–20 March.
Walker, J. and Cooper, M. (2011) 'Genealogies of resilience: from systems ecology to the political economy of crisis adaptation,' *Security Dialogue* 42(2) 143–60.
Walker, R.B.J. (1993) *Inside/Outside: International Relations as Political Theory* (Cambridge: CUP).
Walker, R.B.J. (1995) 'International relations and the concept of the political,' in Booth, K. and Smith, S. (eds) *International Relations Theory Today* (Cambridge: Polity).
Walker, R.B.J. (2003) 'Polis, cosmopolis, politics,' *Alternatives* 28(2) 267–86.
Walker, R.B.J. (2006) 'On the protection of nature and the nature of protection,' in Huysmans, J., Dobson, A. and Prokhovnik, R. (eds) *The Politics of Protection: Sites of Insecurity and Political Agency* (London: Routledge).
Walker, W. (2007) 'Nuclear enlightenment and counter-enlightenment,' *International Affairs* 83(3) 431–53.

Wallander, C.A. (2000) 'Institutional assets and adaptability: NATO after the cold war,' *International Organization* 54(4) 705–35.

Wallander, C.A. and Keohane, R.O. (1999) 'Risk, threat, and security institutions,' in Haftendorn, H., Keohane, R.O. and Wallander, C.A. (eds) *Imperfect Unions: Security Institutions over Time and Space* (Oxford: OUP).

Wallander, C.A., Haftendorn, H. and Keohane, R.O. (1999) 'Introduction,' in Haftendorn, H., Keohane, R.O. and Wallander, C.A. (eds) *Imperfect Unions: Security Institutions over Time and Space* (Oxford: OUP).

Wallensteen, P. and Johansen, P. (2004) 'Security Council decisions in perspective,' in Malone, D. (ed.) *The UN Security Council: From the Cold War to the 21st Century* (Boulder: Lynne Rienner).

Walt, S.M. (1987) *The Origins of Alliances* (Ithaca: Cornell University Press).

Walt, S.M. (1991) 'The renaissance of security studies', *International Studies Quarterly* 35(2) 211–39.

Walt, S.M. (1997) 'Why alliances endure or collapse,' *Survival* 39(1) 156–79.

Walt, S.M. (1999) 'Rigor or rigor mortis? Rational choice and security studies,' *International Security* 23(4) 5–48.

Walters, W. (2002a) 'Deportation, expulsion, and the international police of aliens,' *Citizenship Studies* 6(3) 265–92.

Walters, W. (2002b) 'Mapping Schengenland: denaturalising the border,' *Environment and Planning D: Society and Space* 20(5) 564–80.

Waltz, K.N. (1959) *Man, The State, and War: A Theoretical Analysis* (New York: Columbia University Press).

Waltz, K.N. (1979) *Theory of International Politics* (New York: McGraw-Hill).

Waltz, K.N. (1996) 'International politics is not foreign policy,' *Security Studies* 6(1) 54–7.

Waltz, K.N. (2000) 'Structural realism after the cold war,' *International Security* 25(1) 5–41.

Walzer, M. (2006) *Just and Unjust Wars: A Moral Argument with Historical Illustrations*, 4th edn (New York: Basic Books).

Ward, C.A. (2003) 'Building capacity to combat international terrorism: the role of the United Nations Security Council,' *Journal of Conflict and Security Law* 8(2) 289–305.

Webber, M. (2009) 'The Kosovo war: a recapitulation,' *International Affairs* 85(3) 447–59.

Weber, M. (1919/1991) 'Politics as vocation,' in Gerth, H.H. and Wright Mills, C. (eds) *From Max Weber: Essays in Sociology* (Abingdon: Routledge).

Weimann, G. (2006) *Terror on the Internet: The New Arena, the New Challenges* (Washington DC: United States Institute of Peace).

Weinberg, L.B. and Eubank, W.L. (1998) 'Terrorism and democracy: what recent events disclose,' *Terrorism and Political Violence* 10(1) 108–18.

Weinberg, L.B., Pedahzur, A. and Hirsch-Hoefler, S. (2004) 'The challenges of conceptualizing terrorism,' *Terrorism and Political Violence* 16(4) 777–94.

Weiss, T.G. (2003) 'The illusion of UN Security Council reform,' *Washington Quarterly* 26(4) 147–61.

Weiss, T.G. (2004) 'The sunset of humanitarian intervention? The responsibility to protect in a unipolar era,' *Security Dialogue* 35(2) 135–53.

Weldes, J., Laffey, M., Gusterson, H. and Duvall, R. (eds) (1999) *Cultures of Insecurity: States, Communities, and the Production of Danger* (Minneapolis: University of Minnesota Press).

Wendt, A. (1992) 'Anarchy is what states make of it: the social construction of power politics,' *International Organization* 46(2) 391–425.

Wendt, A. (1995) 'Constructing international politics,' *International Security* 20(1) 71–81.

Wendt, A. (1999) *Social Theory of International Politics* (Cambridge: CUP).

Wendt, A. and Barnett, M. (1993) 'Dependent state formation and third world militarization,' *Review of International Studies* 19(4) 321–47.

Wheeler, N. (2000) *Saving Strangers: Humanitarian Intervention in International Society* (Oxford: OUP).

Wheelis, M. and Dando, M. (2000) 'New technology and future developments in biological weapons,' *Disarmament Forum* 4 43–50.

Whitman, J. (2005) 'Humanitarian intervention in an era of pre-emptive self-defence,' *Security Dialogue* 36(3) 259–74.

Whitman, J. (2007) 'Global governance and twenty-first century technology,' in Rappert, B. (ed.) *Technology and Security: Governing Threats in the New Millennium* (Basingstoke: Palgrave Macmillan).

World Health Organization (2012) *Children: Reducing Mortality*, fact sheet No 178, www.who.int/mediacentre/factsheets/fs178/en/.

World Health Organization (2013) *Quantifying Environmental Health Impacts*, www.who.int/quantifying_ehimpacts/global/globclimate/en/index.html.

Wibben, A.T. (2008) 'Human security: toward an opening,' *Security Dialogue* 39(4) 455–62.

Wight, C. (1999) 'They shoot dead horses don't they? Locating agency in the agent-structure problematique,' *European Journal of International Relations* 5(1) 109–42.

Wight, C. (2006) *Agents, Structures and International Relations: Politics as Ontology* (Cambridge: CUP).

Wight, M. (1978) *Power Politics* (New York: Holmes & Meier).

Wilkinson, C. (2007) 'The Copenhagen School on tour in Kyrgyzstan: Is securitization theory useable outside Europe?,' *Security Dialogue* 38(1) 5–25.

Wilkinson, P. (1974) *Political Terrorism* (London: Macmillan).

Wilkinson, P. (1981) 'Can a state be "terrorist"?,' *International Affairs* 57(3) 467–72.

Wilkinson, P. (2011) *Terrorism vs Democracy: The Liberal State Response*, 3rd edn (Abingdon: Routledge).

Williams, B.G. (2010) 'The CIA's covert predator drone war in Pakistan, 2004–2010: the history of an assassination campaign,' *Studies in Conflict and Terrorism* 33(10) 871–92.

Williams, M.C. (1998) 'Identity and the politics of security,' *European Journal of International Relations* 4(2) 204–25.

Williams, M.C. (2003) 'Words, images, enemies: securitization and international politics,' *International Studies Quarterly* 47(4) 511–31.

Williams, M.C. (2007) *Culture and Security: Symbolic Power and the Politics of International Security* (Abingdon: Routledge).

Williams, M.C. (2011) 'Securitization and the liberalism of fear,' *Security Dialogue* 42(4/5) 453–63.

Williams, M.C. and Neumann, I.B. (2000) 'From alliance to security community: NATO, Russia, and the power of identity,' *Millennium* 29(2) 357–87.

Williams, P. (2001) 'Turkey's H_2O diplomacy in the Middle East,' *Security Dialogue* 32(1) 27–40.

Williams, P. (2002a) 'Transnational organized crime and the state,' in Bruce-Hall, R. and Biersteker, T.J. (eds) *The Emergence of Private Authority in Global Governance* (Cambridge: CUP).

Williams, P. (2002b) 'Cooperation among criminal organizations,' in Berdal, M. and Serrano, M. (eds) *Transnational Organized Crime and International Security: Business as Usual?* (Boulder: Lynne Rienner).

Williams, P. (2009) 'Illicit markets, weak states and violence: Iraq and Mexico,' *Crime, Law and Social Change* 52(3) 323–36.

Willis, H.H. and Ortiz, D. (2004) *Evaluating the Security of the Global Containerized Supply Chain* (Santa Monica: RAND).

Wilson, C. (2008) *Botnets, Cybercrime, and Cyberterrorism: Vulnerabilities and Policy Issues for Congress* (Washington DC: Congressional Research Service).

Windsor, J.L. (2003) 'Promoting democratization can combat terrorism,' *Washington Quarterly* 26(3) 43–58.

Wohlforth, W.C. (1994/95) 'Realism and the end of the cold war,' *International Security* 19(3) 91–129.

Wolfers, A. (1952) '"National security" as an ambiguous symbol,' *Political Science Quarterly* 67(4) 481–502.

Wood, J. and Dupont, B. (eds) (2006) *Democracy, Society and the Governance of Security* (Cambridge: CUP).

Woodiwiss, M. (2003a) 'Transnational organized crime: the strange career of an American concept,' in Beare, M. (ed) *Critical Reflections on Transnational Organized Crime, Money Laundering, and Corruption* (Toronto: University of Toronto Press).

Woodiwiss, M. (2003b) *Organized Crime and American Power* (Toronto: University of Toronto Press).

Woodiwiss, M. (2005) *Gangster Capitalism: The United States and the Global Rise of Organised Crime* (London: Constable & Robinson).

Wright, T. (2007) *State Terrorism in Latin America: Chile, Argentina, and International Human Rights* (Lanham: Rowman & Littlefield).

Wyn Jones, R. (1999) *Security, Strategy, and Critical Theory* (Boulder: Lynne Rienner).

Yoffe, S.B. and Wolf, A.T. (1999) 'Water, conflict and cooperation: geographical perspectives, *Cambridge Review of International Affairs* 12(2) 19–213.

Young, O.R. (1982) 'Regime dynamics: the rise and fall of international regimes,' *International Organization* 36(2) 277–97.

Young, O.R., Berkhout, G., Gallopin, M. et al. (2006) 'The globalization of socio-ecological systems: an agenda for scientific research,' *Global Environmental Change* 16(3) 304–16.

Zagare, F.C. (1987) *The Dynamics of Deterrence* (Chicago: University of Chicago Press).

Zagare, F.C. and Kilgour, D.M. (2000) *Perfect Deterrence* (Cambridge: CUP).

Zagart, A.B. (2009) *Spying Blind: The CIA, the FBI, and the Origins of 9/11* (Princeton: Princeton University Press).

Zaitseva, L. (2002) 'Illicit trafficking in the southern tier and Turkey since 1999: A shift from Europe?,' *The Nonproliferation Review* 9(3) 168–82.

Zaitseva, L. and Hand, K. (2003) 'Nuclear smuggling chains: suppliers, intermediaries, and end-users,' *American Behavioural Scientist* 46(6) 822–44.

Zalewski, M. (1996) '"All these theories yet the bodies keep piling up": theories, theorists, theorising,' in Smith, S., Booth, K. and Zalewski, M. (eds) *International Theory: Positivism and Beyond* (Cambridge: CUP).

Zartman, I.W. (ed.) (1997) *Governance as Conflict Management: Politics and Violence in West Africa* (Washington DC: Brookings Institution Press).

Zartman, I.W. (2005) *Cowardly Lions: Missed Opportunities to Prevent Deadly Conflict and State Collapse* (Boulder: Lynne Rienner).

Zartman, I.W. (2010) *Understanding Life in the Borderlands: Boundaries in Depth and Motion* (Athens: University of Georgia Press).

Zehfuss, M. (2012) 'Contemporary western war and the idea of humanity,' *Environment and Planning D: Society and Space* 30(5) 861–76.

Zieck, M. (1997) *UNHCR and Voluntary Repatriation: A Legal Analysis* (The Hague: Kluwer).

Zulaika, J. and Douglass, W.A. (1996) *Terror and Taboo: The Follies, Fables, and Faces of Terrorism* (New York: Routledge).

Zuriek, E. and Salter, M. (eds) (2005) *Global Surveillance and Policing: Borders, Security, Identity* (London: Routledge).

Index

Printed in Great Britain
by Amazon